Frommer's 96

Los Angeles

by Dan Levine

with Special Coverage by Stephanie Avnet

SO-CEX-888

Macmillan • USA

ABOUT THE AUTHOR

Dan Levine is an incessant traveler with a degree in history from New York University. In addition to authoring *Frommer's Los Angeles,* he has contributed to *Frommer's Europe from $50 a Day* and coauthored *Frommer's California* and *Frommer's Walking Tours: London.* When not traveling, Dan lives and writes in Santa Barbara.

A native of Los Angeles and an avid traveler, antique hound, and pop history enthusiast, **Stephanie Avnet** is also a contributor to *Frommer's California* and *Frommer's Hawaii from $60 a Day.*

MACMILLAN TRAVEL

A Simon & Schuster Macmillan Company
1633 Broadway
New York, NY 10019

ISBN 0-02-860864-X
ISSN 0899-3238

Editor: Cheryl Farr
Map Editor: Douglas Stallings
Production Editor: Trudy Brown
Design by Michele Laseau
Digital cartography by John Decamillis and Ortelius Design

SPECIAL SALES

Bulk purchases (10+ copies) of Frommer's Travel Guides are available to corporations at special discounts. The Special Sales Department can produce custom editions to be used as premiums and/or for sales promotions to suit individual needs. Existing editions can be produced with custom cover imprints such as corporate logos. For more information write to: Special Sales, Simon & Schuster, 8th floor, 1633 Broadway, New York, NY 10019.

Manufactured in the United States of America

Contents

List of Maps

INVITATION TO THE READER

In researching this book, we discovered many wonderful places—hotels, restaurants, shops, and more. We're sure you'll find others. Please tell us about them, so we can share the information with your fellow travelers in upcoming editions. If you were disappointed with a recommendation, we'd love to know that, too. Please write to:

Frommer's Los Angeles '96
Macmillan Travel
1633 Broadway
New York, NY 10019

AN ADDITIONAL NOTE

Please be advised that travel information is subject to change at any time—and this is especially true of prices. We therefore suggest that you write or call ahead for confirmation when making your travel plans. The authors, editors, and publisher cannot be held responsible for the experiences of readers while traveling. Your safety is important to us, however, so we encourage you to stay alert and be aware of your surroundings. Keep a close eye on cameras, purses, and wallets, all favorite targets of thieves and pickpockets.

WHAT THE SYMBOLS MEAN

✪ Frommer's Favorites

Hotels, restaurants, attractions, and entertainment you should not miss.

⑤ Super-Special Values

Hotels and restaurants that offer great value for your money.

The following abbreviations are used for credit cards:

AE	American Express	EU	Eurocard
CB	Carte Blanche	JCB	Japan Credit Bank
DC	Diners Club	MC	MasterCard
DISC	Discover	V	Visa
ER	enRoute		

Postcards from L.A.: Introducing the City of Angels

Los Angeles is not a humble city. Like a celebrity who chooses a front table at Spago, L.A. is a star that just loves to be noticed. With every red sports car, $100-million-dollar movie, and self-congratulatory awards show, the city—and the industry inextricably intertwined with it—appears to cry out for the attention, if not the adoration, of the entire world. It doesn't even matter if the attention is kind; being in the spotlight is what matters. It's all part of the fantasy.

It's become cliché to refer to Los Angeles—and its alter ego, Hollywood, more the city's state of mind than a neighborhood within it—as a place where the lines between fantasy and reality are routinely obscured. But the profusion of platinum bottle-blondes with infeasibly buoyant breasts is just one of a million reasons why it's hard to deny such a stereotype. The media has enthusiastically perpetuated this duplicity by painting the city as larger than life, with broad strokes that leave a lot to the imagination. The city has come to be perceived the world over as a self-centered, bacchanalian, live-for-today kind of place; it's an image that is heightened by the threat of earthquakes, firestorms, floods, and mud slides. If the inevitable Big One will soon drop the entire city into the sea, why not have fun, take kamikaze risks, push yourself to the extreme, wield your power while you can?

Having survived a long, leisurely pioneering infancy, and an uncouth adolescence characterized by intensive exploitation, Los Angeles has now blossomed into one of the world's major cultural centers. The movies, TV, and music that issues forth from here is seen, heard, and felt throughout the world; the pop products of the city's efforts govern who we are and how we spend our time and how we think more than we would ever like to admit. The city is America's—and often the world's—tastemaker, its cultural barometer. When it comes to what's hot and what's not, Angelenos can confidently say that they heard—or started—the buzz here first. But it's also the Zsa Zsa Gabor of world power centers, the flamboyant, nouveau-riche peer that New York and Paris and Tokyo—and we, the onlookers—can't deny, but refuse to wholly acknowledge, either.

People here still believe. The sun comes out every day and smacks them in the face and they march off gamely to face insurmountable odds. Los Angeles may be the most renewable city in the world.
> —Tom Shales, *Washington Post*

The relentless drive for new experiences is an important part of L.A.'s collective psyche, but it's far from the whole reality. And it's not all swimming pools and movie stars. The majority of residents in this suburban city live their workaday tract-home lives just like the rest of us. Most natives aren't part of the entertainment industry, and few residents at all are the Beautiful People we identify with the city. Nevertheless, Angelenos like to believe that their reality is a little off-kilter, just a little bigger and brighter and more influential than that of their peers in Dayton or Dallas or Des Moines or Denver.

L.A. is a cosmopolitan city in the true sense of the word—it's a cornucopia of lifestyles and cultures and a sometimes uneasy mix of races that is at once both thrilling and uncomfortable. It's not an easy place to master. The sprawling city has no cultural center, and its layout is difficult to grasp. Cars keep residents insulated from each other; everything, it seems, is equipped with big locks, strong gates, and piercingly loud alarms.

Despite all appearances, however, L.A. is a very welcoming place. Unlike many other cities, where difficult reservations and velvet ropes are really meant to exclude, in Los Angeles these obstacles are only meant to give the appearance of exclusivity. This is the nation's carnival, where everyone's out of place and everybody belongs, where you can be so unfashionable that you're hip, so cold you're the hottest thing in town.

The best way to approach this colossal Technicolor world is with a critical conscience and tongue firmly in cheek. Recognize its influence, and humor its self-importance. Keep in mind your media-made preconceptions, then discover L.A. for what it is: glitzy, grimy, glittery, powerful—the world capital of pop culture.

1 Frommer's Favorite L.A. Experiences

- **Tour Warner Brothers Studios:** Get a real-life glimpse behind the scenes. Let the hordes have Universal.
- **Visit the Entrance Court at Mann's Chinese Theatre:** Compare your shoe size to the footprints of Ginger Rogers or Cary Grant—and your nose to Jimmy Durante's.
- **Watch a TV Taping:** Watch one of your favorite TV sitcoms being taped, or try for your own 15 minutes of fame by auditioning for a game show.
- **Go to Spago:** Still a thrill—and a world-class dining experience—after all these years.

- **Go to the Getty:** Learn how to spot a fake, ponder Van Gogh's *Irises,* then stroll around the gardens high above the Pacific at Malibu's Getty Museum.
- **Pay Your Respects at the Cemetery of the Stars:** Visit Humphrey Bogart, Clark Gable, Karen Carpenter, and all their friends at Forest Lawn.
- **Relive *Rebel Without a Cause:*** For a view of the city—and a film memory—without compare, head to Griffith Observatory.
- **Go Gidget:** Watch a vollyball tournament in Manhattan Beach, weightlifters doing their thing at Venice Beach, or a bikini contest in Marina del Rey.
- **Visit the Happiest Place on Earth:** Disneyland. Go on a weekday to avoid the crowds.
- **Spend a Day Downtown:** See the city from the observation deck atop City Hall, stop in for a snack at the bustling Grand Central Market, stroll along Hispanic L.A.'s colorful and historic Olvera Street, then have an authentic Asian lunch in Chinatown.
- **Take a Grave Line Tour:** Tour the places where Hollywood's rich and famous, from Marilyn Monroe to Divine, met their untimely demises—in a hearse, of course.
- **Shop:** Spend an afternoon shopping for diamonds on Rodeo or rhinestones on Melrose.
- **Stroll Wilshire Boulevard's Museum Mile:** Natural history meets pop culture meets modern art with the La Brea Tar Pits, the Museum of Miniatures, the Petersen Automobile Museum, and the L.A. County Museum of Art.
- **Visit Venice's Ocean Front Walk:** Rollerblade, or just stroll, taking in the human carnival swirling around you.
- **Ride a Historic Carousel:** Take a turn, then play an old-fashioned game of skeeball at the Santa Monica Pier.
- **Take a Gondola Getaway:** Smooch with your sweetie in a gondola on the canals of Long Beach's Naples Island.
- **Experience the Best of Malibu:** Sunbathe at Zuma Beach, rent a surfboard and hit the waves at Surfrider, or just watch the sun set from Paradise Cove.
- **Have a Rock-and-Roll Evening at the Roxy or Whiskey-A-Go-Go on the Fabled Sunset Strip:** Follow it with a 2am breakfast at Ben Frank's Canter's.
- **See a Show at McCabe's:** Spend a memorable evening snacking on cookies and cider while enjoying live acoustic music with a hundred of your closest friends at McCabe's Guitar Shop.
- **Take a Gourmet Picnic to the Pops at the Hollywood Bowl:** What better way to spend an L.A. evening than under the stars with a bottle of wine and a big band?
- **Cruise Mulholland Drive:** See how the other half lives, then pull over to see the lights of the city twinkle below.

2 Los Angeles Yesterday and Today

Dateline

- 1781 Los Angeles is founded.
- 1821 Spain grants independence to Mexico and, thus, to California.
- 1846 The so-called Bear Flag Republic is proclaimed; the U.S. flag is raised in Yerba Buena (San Francisco) and Los Angeles.
- 1850 California becomes the 31st state.
- 1875 The Santa Fe Railroad reaches Los Angeles.
- 1881 The *Los Angeles Times* begins publication.
- 1892 Oil is discovered in downtown Los Angeles, at what is now the intersection of 2nd Street and Glendale Boulevard.
- 1900 The population of California approaches 1.5 million; Los Angeles has more than 102,000 residents.
- 1902 The first movie house,

continues

They say the only other place on the planet with weather this perfect is Greece. That perfect climate—blue skies and warm temperatures from New Year's to Christmas, and almost every day in between—coupled with cheap land prices, drew filmmakers from the unpredictable East to the diverse L.A. basin. Sprawled between sea and mountains, the area encompassed treeless deserts, bountiful forests, sandy beaches, and high rocky peaks—what more could enterprising movie-makers ask for?

The city was founded by the Spanish on the site of a Native American village in 1781, but it wasn't until after the first film studio was established, in 1911, that Los Angeles really took off. Within five years, movies like D.W. Griffith's *Birth of a Nation* were being produced by the hundreds. By World War I the Hollywood studio system was firmly entrenched, with the young trio of Charles Chaplin, Douglas Fairbanks, and "America's Sweetheart," Mary Pickford, at its fore.

When the box office boomed in the 1920s and 1930s, so did the population of Los Angeles. Easterners—including the dust-bowl refugees depicted in John Steinbeck's *The Grapes of Wrath*—came to the burgeoning urban paradise in droves in order to find their fortunes. The world-famous Hollywood sign, erected in 1923, was built as an advertisement for just one of many fledgling real estate developments that began to crop up on the "outskirts" of the city. Los Angeles, and Hollywood, was all that much more alluring during the Great Depression; the city flourished as Americans ached for an escape from their less-than-inspiring reality, one provided by Hollywood's cinematic fantasies. With each glamorous, idyllic portrayal of California, Los Angeles's popularity—and population—grew.

This was the Golden Age of Hollywood, a era that gave rise to some of movie's most enduring stars, America's own brand of royalty: bad girl Bette Davis, romantic leading man Cary Grant, blond bombshell Jean Harlow, everyman James Stewart, pint-sized Shirley Temple, and more, including screen legends Humphrey Bogart, Clark Gable, James Cagney, Marlene Dietrich, Carole

Lombard, Gary Cooper, Katharine Hepburn, and Spencer Tracy. The thirties were capped by the release of an astounding number of screen gems, including two of its most enduring classics, *Gone With The Wind* and *The Wizard of Oz.*

The opening of the Arroyo Seco Parkway in 1940, linking Hollywood and Pasadena with the first of what would be a network of freeways, ushered in a new era for the city. From that time on, car culture flourished in Los Angeles; it became perhaps the city's most distinctive feature (for more on this subject, see "From Horseless Carriages to Hot Rods: L.A.'s Love Affair with the Automobile," below). America's automobile companies successfully conspired to undermine Los Angeles's public transportation system by halting the trolley service that once plied downtown, and advocating the construction of auto-friendly roads. The growth of the freeways led to the development of L.A.'s suburban sprawl, turning Los Angeles into a city without a single geographical focus. The suburbs became firmly entrenched in the L.A. landscape during World War II, when shipyards and munitions factories, as well as aerospace giants McDonnell Douglas, Lockheed, Rockwell, and General Dynamics, opened their doors in Southern California.

After the war, the threat of television put the movie industry into a tailspin. But instead of being destroyed by the "tube," Hollywood was strengthened when that industry made its home here as well. Soon afterward, in the fifties and sixties, the avant-garde discovered Los Angeles as well; the city became popular with artists, beats, and hippies, many of whom settled in Venice.

In 1965, rising racial tensions coupled with intense summer heat set off major race riots in the Watts section of Los Angeles. In 1968, Robert F. Kennedy was fatally shot at Los Angeles's Ambassador Hotel after winning the California Democratic Party presidential primary. As the city entered the 1970s, it appeared to some that the dream factory was becoming a nightmare.

Impressions

If you tilt the whole country sideways, Los Angeles is the place where everything loose will fall.
—Frank Lloyd Wright

the Electric Theatre, opens on Main Street.

- **1909** Santa Monica Pier is erected to accommodate cargo and passenger ships.
- **1911** Hollywood's first film studio is established.
- **1912** More than 16 motion-picture companies are operating out of Hollywood; the first U.S. gas station opens at the corner of Grand Avenue and Washington Street.
- **1913** Cecil B. DeMille directs the film industry's first full-length feature, *The Squaw Man,* in a barn near Selma and Vine Streets.
- **1920** Douglas Fairbanks builds the mansion known as "Pickfair" in the foothills of Beverly Hills for his young bride, America's sweetheart, Mary Pickford.
- **1922** The Hollywood Bowl opens.
- **1923** The Hollywood sign is erected to

continues

advertise a real estate development.

- **1927** The first "talkie" is released, *The Jazz Singer*, with Al Jolson.
- **1928** Los Angeles's first airport, Mines Field (on the current site of LAX) opens, with only a single dirt strip as a runway.
- **1929** The Academy of Motion Picture Arts and Sciences bestows its first Oscar.
- **1940** L.A.'s first freeway, the Arroyo Seco Parkway, opens, connecting Hollywood and Pasadena.
- **1945** The world's largest toy manufacturer, Mattel, maker of Barbie, is founded in Hawthorne.
- **1947** The first TV station west of the Mississippi, KTLA, begins broadcasting; the Rams football team comes to Los Angeles from Cleveland, Ohio; the Hollywood Freeway opens, linking L.A. with the San Fernando Valley.

continues

Perhaps in response to the increasingly violent society, the 1970s gave rise to a number of exotic religions and cults that found eager adherents in Southern California. The spiritual "New Age" born in the "Me" decade found life into the 1980s, in the face of a population growing beyond manageable limits, an increasingly polluted environment, and escalating social ills. At the same time, California became very rich. Real estate values soared, banks and businesses prospered, and the entertainment industry boomed.

In the 1990s Angelenos are on the leading edge of American pop culture. But they've discovered, as the world shakes its collective head and wags its unified finger, that that isn't always all it's cracked up to be. The nation's economic, social, and environmental problems have become their own, have even become amplified in the larger-than-life arena. The spotlight was turned on the city in 1991, when four white police officers were videotaped beating African-American motorist Rodney King. The officers' shocking acquittal in the spring of 1992 sparked three days of rioting and looting. The very public trial of accused parent-slayers Lyle and Erik Menendez, the investigation of child abuse allegations against the self-proclaimed "King of Pop," Michael Jackson, and the lengthy murder trial of a certain famous football legend (who shall here remain nameless) has drawn the city even more criticism. The fires, rioting, mud slides, and the major earthquake that barraged Los Angeles in the last few years emphasized the city's fragility and forced its citizens to take notice of their urban reality.

Out of the ashes, however, some good is coming. A new consciousness is rising among ever-resilient Angelenos. Residents of neighboring suburbs have been brought together by their shared adversity. I'm not trying to lead you to believe that all is harmony and bliss, but the city's residents—rich and poor, famous and unknown, young and old, black and white and every color in between—have begun to realize that the city they all call home is one and the same. The city has fought the adversity of the past few years by coming together to clean up and shape up, particularly after the riots and the earthquake. It's this kind of resilience that will keep Los Angeles going against any odds, whether they be natural disaster, O. J., or anything else the future might hold.

3   Wolfgang Puck and the Birth of California Cuisine

Southern California's own unique cuisine, now known the world over as California Cuisine, can be traced back to 1979, when 25-year-old chef Michael McCarty opened Michael's in Santa Monica. McCarty's combination of French technique with local ingredients is de rigeur today, but was a radical departure from the traditional Parisian cookery that was then the standard on the L.A. dining scene.

Since Michael's opened its doors, California-style cuisine has evolved, integrating techniques and ingredients from the international cultures so prevalent in cosmopolitan Los Angeles, with particular emphasis on Japanese and Mexican cookery. In true L.A. style, preparations are light and health conscious; they're often accompanied by some variation on salsa, from the traditional Mexican-style garnish to nouveau mango chutney.

No one has been a more successful in the genre than Wolfgang Puck, a German émigré who made his mark serving wood-fired individual pizzas topped with a galaxy of untraditional ingredients like duck sausage, shiitake mushrooms, leeks, artichokes, and other California-grown ingredients. After the triumph of his still-popular über-restaurant, Spago, Puck duplicated his success with Chinois on Main, a Franco-Chinese eatery taking what McCarty did a step further, and Malibu's Granita, which puts Puck's unique California twist on seafood.

Despite Michael McCarty's undisputed title as the father of California Cuisine, it has been Puck who has brought the nouvelle cuisine not only into its creative own, but beyond the city's limits and into restaurant kitchens across the nation and around the world. He has been its shameless marketer, making appearances everywhere, from the finest European kitchens to the stage of *Late Night with David Letterman*. With his line of frozen foods and the opening of the first of what is sure to be many moderately priced Wolfgang Puck Cafes, L.A.'s superchef has fired up his ovens for the masses, bringing California Cuisine into America's malls—and freezers—across the country.

You'll feel Puck's influence throughout your visit to Los Angeles. In the last ten years or so, he

- **1950** L.A.'s population is almost 2 million.
- **1955** Disneyland opens.
- **1956** Capitol Records Tower, the nation's first circular office building, opens for business. The architectural stacked-records concept is the brainchild of Capitol recording stars Nat King Cole and Johnny Mercer.
- **1961** Hollywood's Walk of Fame is started by the Hollywood Chamber of Commerce.
- **1962** California overtakes New York as the nation's most populous state; Dodger Stadium opens on land purchased by owner Walter O'Malley.
- **1965** Rioting in the Watts section of the city leaves 34 dead and over 1,000 injured.
- **1968** Robert F. Kennedy is fatally shot at the Ambassador Hotel after winning California's Democratic Party presidential primary.

continues

- **1980** L.A.'s population is nearly 3 million.
- **1984** Los Angeles hosts the Summer Olympic Games.
- **1990** MetroRail's Blue Line opens with service between Long Beach and downtown Los Angeles; First Interstate Tower, designed by I.M. Pei, opens for business; it's the tallest building west of Chicago's Sears Tower.
- **1992** In the Los Angeles race riots, resulting from the acquittal of the officers involved in the Rodney King beating, more than 40 are dead, hundreds injured.
- **1993** Firestorms sweep through the Los Angeles area.
- **1994** An earthquake measuring 6.8 on the Richter scale shakes the city; Los Angeles hosts the World Cup soccer finals and closing ceremonies.
- **1995** O.J. Simpson found not guilty of the murders of Nicole Brown Simpson and Ron Goldman.

has managed to be the dining scene's most defining influence; he's been to L.A.'s—one might even say to the world's—kitchens what the Beatles were to pop music. Even more directly, rarely in the kitchen himself, the jet-setting superchef has had an uncanny knack for hiring kitchen help as smart and creative as him-self; Spago alumni have gone on to open top restaurants around the city, among them Campanile, Eclipse, and Carrots.

While you're in Los Angeles, be sure to splurge on at least one meal at one of the top restaurants featuring the city's own home-grown—and now world-famous—cuisine. See Chapter 6, "Dining," for all the details, and remember to make your reservations well in advance, particularly if you opt for one of the star-studded heavyweights (such as Spago itself). Enjoy!

4   From Horseless Carriages to Hot Rods: L.A.'s Love Affair with the Automobile

by Stephanie Avnet

The Southern California lifestyle is so closely tied to the automobile that it has given rise to a whole subculture of the car. Since its introduction to the infant city it would grow up with, the automobile has become a pop phenomenon all its own, inextricably intertwined with the personality of Los Angeles—and the identities of its residents. What's more, although the first "horseless carriages" emerged from the Midwest, it has been Hollywood's influence that has defined the entire nation's passion for the car.

During the early 1920s, movie comedians Laurel and Hardy and the Keystone Cops began to blend their brand of physical humor with the popular Ford Model T. And a visionary coach builder named Harley Earl was busy in his shop on South Main Street, building special vehicles for the movies—the *Ben Hur* racing chariots—and designing flamboyant custom automobiles for the wealthy movie stars of the day. Earl would later be recruited by General Motors, bringing along with him from Hollywood to Detroit an obsession with style over substance that would culminate in the legendary tailfins of the '50s.

As movie director Cecil B. DeMille once said, both cars and movies captured Americans' love of motion and speed. Car culture as it was depicted in motion pictures continued to set the pace for the country. In *Rebel Without A Cause*, James Dean's troubled teenager and his hot-rodding buddies assert their independence through their jalopies (in several memorable confrontations filmed on the roads around the Griffith Observatory in the Hollywood Hills). As authorities cracked down on dangerous street racing, locally based *Hot Rod Magazine* helped spawn the movement to create legal drag strips, and the sport of professional drag racing was born. The art of auto body customizing also came into being here, pioneered by George Barris, the "King of Kustomizers."

The world watched Southern California's physical landscape change to acccomodate the four-wheeled resident. In postwar suburban tracts the garage, which had traditionally been a separate shed, grew attached to the house and became the family's main entrance. The Arroyo Seco Parkway (now the Pasadena Freeway) opened in 1940, its curvaceous lanes modeled after the landscaped parkways of the New York City metropolitan area, each turn placed to open up a series of scenic vistas for the driver. (Later L.A. freeways, reflecting a greater concern with speed, were modeled after the straight, efficient autobahns of Europe.)

Meanwhile, businesses in town built signs in an attempt to catch the eye of the driving customer; as the cars got faster, the signs got larger and brighter. A look at the gargantuan billboards on the Sunset Strip shows where *that* trend ended up. Another scourge of the modern landscape, the mini-mall, actually started innocently enough in 1927 with the first "supermarket." The term was coined by Hattem's (at the corner of Western Avenue and 43rd Street), where several grocers lined up side by side, set back from the street to provide plentiful parking and one-stop convenience for their customers.

The 1930s saw the emergence of Streamline Moderne design throughout Los Angeles, and the car's lifeline, the gas station, was no exception to this style. The awnings of 1920s-era stations, which had vanished in most parts of the country, remained in fashion in the Southwest in order to protect motorists from sun and heat; when interpreted by thirties designers, the Moderne canopy became a distinct local variation. Following World War II, L.A. saw the first "Gas-a-teria," ancestor of today's ubiquitous self-serve station.

But perhaps the most enduring feature to arise from the phenomenon of the automobile is the drive-up, drive-in, and drive-through business. In the mid-1920s someone thought to punch through their outer wall in order to serve the motoring customer. By the next decade, Los Angeles boasted the world's largest collection of establishments that you could patronize from the privacy and comfort of your car. There were drive-up bank teller windows (now replaced by ATMs), drive-thru

Impressions

If [Los Angeles] is hell, why is it so popular?
—Bryce Nelson, *The New York Times*

florists and dry cleaners, drive-thru dairies (Alta Dena still maintains several in the Southland), and drive-up restaurants. These weren't the impersonal fast-food joints of today, but real restaurants (like the popular Dolores Drive-In chain) with cheerful carhops bringing your freshly made order to you on a window tray. (Bob's Big Boy Restaurant in Toluca Lake invites patrons with vintage autos to cruise over and enjoy nostalgic carhop service on Friday and Saturday nights.)

Perhaps the most popular of these drive-in landmarks are the movie theaters. Los Angeles had the second one in the whole country (at the corner of Pico and Westwood Boulevards); the city still boasts at least a dozen that screen first-run films, among them the Winnetka in Chatsworth, the Hi-Way 39 in Westminster, and the Foothill in Azusa. At the drive-in theater, you were able to enjoy the picture—along with all those great snack-bar treats—without sacrificing any of the comforts of home. Long established as a teenage make-out haven, one theater gained popularity in a more spiritual way when Reverend Robert Schuller began to deliver Sunday morning sermons to a comfortably parked audience at the Orange County Drive-In. His slogan: "Come as you are, in the family car."

The trend to view the car as an extension of the home persists today, with the marketing of telephones, fax machines, electric shavers, vacuum cleaners, and more, all car sized and capable of plugging into the dashboard cigarette lighter socket and functioning inside your car. What more could the auto-loving Angeleno ask for?

For more Southern California automobile lore, visit the Petersen Automotive Museum at 6060 Wilshire Boulevard, Los Angeles (☎ 213/930-2277); see Chapter 7 for details.

Planning a Trip to Los Angeles

In the pages that follow, we've compiled everything you need to know to handle the practical details of planning your trip in advance—airlines, weather, a calendar of events, and more.

1 Visitor Information & Money

VISITOR INFORMATION

For information on the city, contact the Los Angeles Convention and Visitors Bureau (633 W. 5th St., Suite 600, Los Angeles, CA 90071; ☎ 213/624-7300). In addition, almost every municipality and economic district in the city has a dedicated tourist bureau or chamber of commerce that will be more than happy to send you information on their particular parcel; see "Orientation" in Chapter 4 for a complete list.

MONEY

You never have to carry a lot of cash in Los Angeles. Automated teller machines (ATMs) are located at virtually every bank in the city, and credit cards are accepted by the vast majority of L.A.'s hotels, restaurants, attractions, shops, and nightspots.

The ubiquitous Bank of America accepts Plus, Star, and Interlink cards, while First Interstate Bank is on-line with the Cirrus system. Both banks have dozens of branches all around the city. For the location of the nearest ATM, call **800/424-7787** for the Cirrus network or **800/843-7587** for the Plus system. Most ATMs will make cash advances against MasterCard and Visa. American Express cardholders can write a personal check, guaranteed against the card, for up to $1,000 in cash at an American Express office (see "Fast Facts: Los Angeles" in Chapter 4 for locations).

U.S.-dollar traveler's checks are also widely accepted for goods and services, and can be exchanged for cash at banks and check-issuing offices.

What Things Cost in Los Angeles	U.S. $
Taxi from the airport to downtown	30.00
Bus fare to any destination within the city	1.35
Double room at the Beverly Hills Hotel (very expensive)	250.00
Double room at the Radisson-Huntley Hotel (expensive)	145.00
Double room at the Kawada Hotel (inexpensive)	80.00
Lunch for one at Cafe Pinot (moderate)	14.00
Lunch for one at Roscoe's House of Chicken (inexpensive)	7.00
Dinner for one, without wine, at Morton's (expensive)	45.00
Dinner for one, without wine, at Cha Cha Cha (moderate)	30.00
Dinner for one, without wine, at the Source (inexpensive)	12.00
Glass of beer	3.00
Coca-Cola	1.25
Cup of coffee	1.25
Admission to the J. Paul Getty Museum	Free
Movie ticket	7.50
Theater ticket	25.00

2 When to Go

Tourism peaks during summer—coastal hotels fill to capacity, restaurant reservations can be hard to come by, and top attractions are packed to the gills with visitors and locals who are off from work or school. Summer can be stiflingly hot and smoggy in the inland valleys, but the beach communities almost always remain comfortable.

Moderate temperatures, fewer crowds, and sometimes lower hotel rates make travel to L.A. most pleasurable during the winter. The city is particularly delightful from early autumn to late spring, when the skies are less smoggy. Winter is L.A.'s rainy season, but don't let that deter you. Despite some well-publicized recent storms, rain is still the exception rather than the rule. Los Angeles is a perfect winter destination; even in January, daytime temperature readings regularly reach into the 60s and higher—sometimes even into the 80s.

It's possible to sunbathe throughout the year, but only die-hard enthusiasts and wet-suited surfers venture into the ocean in winter. The water is warmest in summer and fall, but even then the Pacific is too chilly for many. As you can see below, Los Angeles remains relatively temperate year-round.

Los Angeles's Average Temperatures

	Jan	Feb	Mar	Apr	May	Jun	Jul	Aug	Sept	Oct	Nov	Dec
Avg. High (°F)	65	66	67	69	72	75	81	81	81	77	73	69
Avg. Low (°F)	46	48	49	52	54	57	60	60	59	55	51	49

L.A. AREA CALENDAR OF EVENTS

January

- ✪ **Tournament of Roses,** Pasadena. A spectacular parade down Colorado Boulevard, with lavish floats, music, and extraordinary equestrian entries, followed by the Rose Bowl Game. Call **818/449-4100** for details, or just stay home and watch it on TV (you'll have a better view). January 1.

- **Oshogatsu,** Los Angeles. Participate in traditional Japanese ceremonies and enjoy foods and crafts at this New Year's celebration at the Japanese American Cultural and Community Center in Little Tokyo. Call **213/628-2725.** First weekend in January.

- **Martin Luther King Parade,** Long Beach. This annual parade down Alameda and 7th Streets ends with a festival in Martin Luther King Park. For more information, contact the Council of Special Events (☎ **310/570-6816**). Third Monday in January.

- **Native American Film Festival.** Cinematic works by or about Native Americans express their visions, diversity, and ideas. Call **213/221-2164** for schedule and details. Mid-January.

February

- **Chinese New Year,** Los Angeles. Colorful dragon dancers parade through the streets of downtown's Chinatown. Chinese opera and other events are scheduled. For this year's schedule, contact the Chinese Chamber of Commerce (977 N. Broadway, Room E, Los Angeles, CA 90012; ☎ **213/617-0396**). Early February.

- **Mardi Gras,** West Hollywood. The festivities—including live jazz and lots of food—take place along Santa Monica Boulevard, from Doheny Drive to La Brea Avenue, and along the alley behind Santa Monica Boulevard. Contact the West Hollywood Chamber of Commerce (☎ **800/368-6020**) for details. Late February.

March

- **Los Angeles Marathon.** This 26.2-mile run through the streets of Los Angeles attracts thousands of participants. The run starts in downtown Los Angeles. Call **310/444-5544** for registration or spectator information. Early March.

- ✪ **American Indian Festival and Market,** Los Angeles Natural History Museum. A showcase of Native American arts and culture; the fun includes traditional dances, storytelling, and arts and crafts, as well as a chance to sample Native American foods. Admission to the museum includes festival tickets. For further details, call **213/744-3314.** Late March.

April

- **Renaissance Pleasure Fair,** San Bernardino. This annual event is one of America's largest Renaissance festivals. Set in the relatively remote Glen Ellen Regional Park, it's a re-created Elizabethan marketplace with costumed performers and living history displays. The fair provides an entire day's activities, shows and festivities, food and crafts. You're encouraged to come in period costume. For ticket information, call **800/523-2473.** Weekends from April through June.

- **Toyota Grand Prix,** Long Beach. An exciting weekend of Indy-class auto racing and entertainment in and around downtown Long Beach draws world-class drivers from the Unites States and Europe. Contact the Grand Prix Association (3000 Pacific Ave., Long Beach, CA 90806; ☎ **310/436-9953** or 800/752-9524) for information. Mid-April.

May

✪ **Cinco de Mayo,** Los Angeles. A week-long celebration of one of Mexico's most jubilant holidays takes place throughout the city. There's a carnival-like atmosphere with large crowds, live music, dances, and food. The main festivities are held at El Pueblo de Los Angeles State Historic Park, downtown; call **213/628-1274** for information. Other events are held around the city. The week surrounding May 5.

- **Redondo Beach Wine Festival.** This is the largest outdoor wine-tasting event in Southern California. For exact dates and this year's locations, contact the Redondo Beach Chamber of Commerce (200 N. Pacific Coast Hwy., Redondo Beach, CA 90277; ☎ **310/376-6912**). Early May.

- **Venice Art Walk,** Venice Beach. An annual weekend event that gives visitors a chance to take docent-guided tours, visit five artist's studios, and take a Sunday self-guided art walk through the private studios and homes of more than 50 emerging and well-known artists. Call **310/392-8630, ext. 342,** for details. Mid-May.

- **National Orange Show,** San Bernardino. This 11-day county fair includes various stadium events, celebrity entertainment, livestock shows, and carnival rides. Call **909/888-6788.** Mid-May.

- **Long Beach Lesbian & Gay Pride Parade and Festival,** Shoreline Park, Long Beach. There's more than 100 decorated floats, health-awareness booths, live rock and country music, dancing, and food. Call **310/987-9191.** One Sunday in late May.

June

- **Playboy Jazz Festival,** Los Angeles. Bill Cosby is the traditional master of ceremonies, presiding over top artists at the Hollywood Bowl. Call **310/246-4000.** Mid-June.

- **Annual Grand National Irish Fair and Music Festival,** Griffith Park, Los Angeles. Gaelic music and dance ring in this traditional event; you might even see a leprechaun, if you're lucky. Phone **213/395-8322** for dates and details. Mid-June.

- **Cajun & Zydeco Festival.** The spirit of New Orleans comes alive in Southern California during this weekend of celebration. There's Cajun and Creole food, contemporary Cajun and Zydeco music, dancing, dance lessons, and a children's Mardi Gras parade. Call **310/427-3713** for this year's location and information. Mid-June.

- **Mariachi USA Festival,** Los Angeles. A two-day family-oriented celebration of Mexican culture and tradition at the Hollywood Bowl, where festival-goers pack their picnic baskets and enjoy music, ballet folkloric, and related performances by special guests. Call **310/451-5044.** Late June.

July

○ **Fourth of July Celebration,** Pasadena. Southern California's most spectacular display of fireworks follows an evening of live entertainment at the Rose Bowl. Call **818/577-3100.** July 4.

- **Fireworks Display at the Marina,** Marina del Rey. Burton Chase Park is a favorite place to ooh and aah at the traditional Fourth of July fireworks. Arrive in the afternoon to get the best parking and viewing sites. July 4.

○ **Hollywood Bowl Summer Festival,** Los Angeles. Summer season at the Hollywood Bowl brings the world's best sounds of jazz, pop, and classical music to a beautiful open-air setting. The season includes an annual Fourth of July concert. The season runs from July through mid-September; phone the box office (☎ **213/850-2000**) for information and this year's schedule.

○ **Summer Festival & Pageant of the Masters,** Laguna Beach. A fantastic performance-art production in which live actors re-create the paintings of the Old Masters. Ticket prices range from $10 to $40. Call **714/497-6582** or 800/487-FEST. Early June through late August.

- **International Surf Festival,** Torrance and Hermosa, Manhattan, and Redondo beaches. Four beachside cities collaborate in the oldest international surf festival in California. Competitions include surfing, boogie boarding, sand-castle building, and other beach-related categories. Contact the International Surf Festival Committee (☎ **310/376-6911**) for information. End of July.

August

- **Long Beach International Sea Festival.** An annual event with recreational activities, all focusing on the sand and surf, for the whole family. Call **310/570-3100**. Early August.

- **Nisei Week Japanese Festival,** Los Angeles. This week-long celebration of Japanese culture and heritage is held in the Japanese American Cultural and Community Center Plaza in Little Tokyo. Festivities include parades, food, music, arts, and crafts. Call **213/687-7193.** Mid-August.

- **African Marketplace and Cultural Fair.** African arts, crafts, food, and music are featured at this cultural-awareness event. Call **213/734-1164.** Held weekends from the second week of August through Labor Day at Rancho La Cienega Park, 5001 Rodeo Road; to get there, take I-10 to the La Brea Ave. exit.

- **Long Beach Sea Festival.** This festival is dedicated to a variety of water-related events, including a sailboat regatta and jet ski and swimming competitions. For information and schedule, contact the Long Beach Department of Parks and Recreation (2760 Studebaker Rd., Long Beach, CA 90804; ☎ 310/421-9431). Last two weeks of August.

September

- **Rods 'N Rock-N-Roll Show,** the Queen's Marketplace, *Queen Mary* Seaport, Long Beach. This festival has pre-1970 hot rods on display, as well as exhibit booths and live rock music. Call **310/ 435-3511.** Early September.

- **Los Angeles County Fair,** Pomona. Horse racing, arts, agricultural displays, celebrity entertainment, and carnival rides are among the attractions of the largest county fair in the world. Held at the Los Angeles County Fair and Exposition Center; call **909/623-3111** for information. Late September.

- **Long Beach Blues Festival.** An annual outdoor festival featuring top names in blues music. Call **310/985-5566.** Usually in late September.

- **Watts Towers Day of the Drum Festival,** Los Angeles. This event celebrates the historic role of drums and drummers throughout the world. All kinds of performances are held, from Afro-Cuban folkloricos to East Indian tabla players. Call **213/847-4646.** Late September.

- **Catalina Island Jazz Trax Festival.** More than 10 contemporary jazz greats travel to the island to play at the legendary Casino Ballroom. The festival takes place over two consecutive three-day weekends. Call **619/458-9586** or 800/866-TRAX for more information. Late September or early October.

October

- **Annual Bob Hope Celebrity Golf Tournament,** Riverside. Bob Hope is the honorary chairman of this annual tournament. For ticket and other information, contact the Riverside Convention and Visitors Bureau (3443 Orange St., Riverside, CA 92501; ☎ **909/ 787-7950;** fax 909/787-4940)

- **Whale Festival,** Long Beach. Join in building a life-size whale from sand, and enjoy a family sand sculpture contest, food, crafts, children's activities, entertainment, booths on sea life and issues, and a watermelon feast. Call **310/548-7562.** Late October.

November

- **Catalina Island Triathalon.** This is one of the top 100 triathalons in the world. Participants run on unpaved roads, swim in the cleanest bay on the West Coast, and bike on challenging trails. There's also a "kid's tri." Call **818/597-1383.** Early November.

- **Bandfest,** Los Angeles. Bands participating in the Hollywood Christmas Parade compete in various categories in a battle of the marching bands. Call **213/469-8311.** Late November.

- **Doo Dah Parade,** Pasadena. An outrageous spoof of the Rose Parade, featuring participants such as the Briefcase Brigade and a kazoo-playing marching band. Call **818/796-2591.** Saturday after Thanksgiving.
- **Hollywood Christmas Parade.** This spectacular star-studded parade marches down Hollywood Boulevard just after Thanksgiving. For information, phone **213/469-2337.**

December

- **Parade of a Thousand Lights,** Long Beach. Decorated boats parade along the harbor at Shoreline Village. Call **310/435-4093.** Early December.

3 Insurance & Safety Concerns

INSURANCE

Many travelers are covered by their hometown health insurance policies in the event of an accident or sudden illness while away on vacation. Make sure that your Health Maintenance Organization (HMO) or insurance carrier can provide services for you while you're in California. If there's any doubt, a health insurance policy that specifically covers your trip is advisable.

You can also protect yourself with insurance against lost or damaged baggage and trip-cancellation or interruption costs. These coverages are often combined into a single comprehensive plan, sold through travel agents, credit- and charge-card companies, and automobile and other clubs.

Most travel agents can sell low-cost health, loss, and trip-cancellation insurance to their vacationing clients. Compare these rates and services with those offered by local banks as well as by your personal insurance carrier.

PERSONAL SAFETY

Los Angeles suffers from one of the highest crime rates in the nation, but visitors are rarely victims; only a tiny percentage of the city's tens of millions of annual visitors are targets of crime. Still, there are precautions everyone should take.

Know where you're going in advance. It may feel very unsettling to stray into East and South-Central Los Angeles unknowingly. Don't let your car advertise that you're a visitor. Place maps, travel brochures, this guidebook, and other valuables out of sight—in the glove compartment or trunk. When parking for the night, ask yourself if you've left anything in your car that could be of any value whatsoever—then remove it.

Homelessness is a big problem in Los Angeles. Panhandlers are especially prevalent in Santa Monica, Venice, and downtown. Most homeless people are harmless; however, some are chronic law violators who may infringe on the rights of others. A combination of respect and caution is suggested.

EARTHQUAKES

In the rare event of an earthquake, you should know about a few simple precautions that every California schoolkid is taught:

If you're in a tall building, don't run outside; instead, move away from windows and toward the center of the building. Crouch under a desk or table, or stand in a doorway or against a wall. If you're in bed, get under the bed or stand in the doorway, or crouch under a sturdy piece of furniture. When exiting the building, use stairwells, *not* elevators.

If you're in your car, pull over to the side of the road and stop, but wait until you're away from bridges or overpasses and telephone or power poles and lines. Stay in your car.

If you're out walking, stay outside and away from trees, power lines, and buildings. If you're in an area with tall buildings, stand in a doorway.

4 Tips for Special Travelers

FOR TRAVELERS WITH DISABILITIES

All of Los Angeles's public museums and tourist attractions are fitted with wheelchair ramps to accommodate physically challenged visitors, and most hotels offer special accommodations and services for wheelchair-bound and other disabled guests. These include large bathrooms, ramps, and telecommunication devices for the deaf. The **California Travel Industry Association** (2500 Wilshire Blvd., Suite 603, Los Angeles, CA 90057; ☎ **213/384-3178**) provides information and referrals to specially equipped sights and hotels around the city and state. California issues special license plates to physically disabled drivers and honors plates issued by other states. You'll find specially marked "handicapped" parking spots wherever you go.

The **Los Angeles County Commission on Disabilities** (383 Hall of Administration, 500 W. Temple St., Los Angeles, CA 90012; ☎ **213/974-1053** or TDD 213/974-1707) publishes a free brochure listing services and facilities offered by the city's private- and public-sector agencies. Call or write for a copy.

FOR GAY & LESBIAN TRAVELERS

Gay- and lesbian-oriented business and services are concentrated in West Hollywood. There are many gay-oriented publications with information and up-to-date listings, including *The Advocate,* a biweekly national magazine; *Frontiers,* a Southern California–based biweekly; and *Nightlife,* a local weekly with comprehensive listings of entertainment places, complete with maps. These and other periodicals are available at most newsstands citywide.

A Different Light (8853 Santa Monica Blvd., West Hollywood; ☎ **310/854-6601**) is Los Angeles's best gay bookshop; it's one of the largest of its kind on the West Coast. **Sisterhood Bookstore** (1351 Westwood Blvd., West Los Angeles; ☎ **310/477-7300**) is one of the best sources for lesbian-oriented books, magazines, and newspapers.

See Chapter 10 for listings of clubs and bars that cater primarily to gays and lesbians.

FOR SENIORS

In California, "senior citizen" usually means anyone 65 or older. Seniors regularly receive discounts at museums and attractions; when available, these discounts are listed in the following chapters under their appropriate headings. Ask for discounts everywhere—at hotels, movie theaters, museums, restaurants, and attractions—you may be surprised how often you'll be offered reduced rates. When making airline reservations, ask about a senior discount, but find out if there's a cheaper promotional fare before committing yourself.

FOR STUDENTS

A high school or college ID often entitles you to discounts at attractions (particularly at museums), and sometimes to reduced rates at restaurants, shops, and nightspots. Keep your ID with you, and always inquire.

5 Getting There

ARRIVING BY PLANE

All major U.S. carriers serve Los Angeles International Airport (LAX). Domestic airlines flying in and out of LAX include Alaska Airlines (☎ 800/426-0333), America West (☎ 800/235-9292), American Airlines (☎ 800/433-7300), Delta Air Lines (☎ 800/221-1212), Northwest Airlines (☎ 800/225-2525), Southwest Airlines (☎ 800/435-9792), TWA (☎ 800/221-2000), United Airlines (☎ 800/241-6522), and USAir (☎ 800/428-4322).

The five biggest domestic airlines—American, Delta, Northwest, TWA, and United—have all considerably raised their domestic fares in the past two years, but occasional "sales" and competition from smaller carriers still makes Los Angeles one of the cheapest cities to reach from almost any other major American city. Across the board, the cheapest seats are currently being offered by no-frills Southwest Airlines, but their service and schedules are much more limited than the big five. The lowest airfares from New York usually fluctuate between $400 and $500, and between $300 and $400 from Chicago; sometimes you can do a little better, especially by calling the airlines directly.

Several smaller carriers are known for the excellent and comprehensive service they provide up and down the California coast. America West (☎ 800/235-9292), American Eagle (☎ 800/433-7300), Skywest (☎ 800/453-9417), United Express (☎ 800/241-6522), and USAir Express (☎ 800/428-4322) are some of the biggest carriers offering regular service between California cities. The lowest round-trip fare between San Francisco and L.A. is about $198—on occasion, it's even less.

You might be able to get a great deal on airfare by calling a consolidator, such as **Travac** (989 Ave. of the Americas, New York, NY 10018; ☎ 212/563-3303 or 800/TRAV-800) and Unitravel

(1177 N. Warson Rd., P.O. Box 12485, St. Louis, MO 63132; ☎ 314/569-0900 or 800/325-2222).

LOS ANGELES AREA AIRPORTS

There are five airports in the Los Angeles area. Most visitors fly into **Los Angeles International Airport** (☎ 310/646-5252). Better known as LAX, this behemoth airport is situated oceanside, between Santa Monica and Manhattan Beach. Despite its size, LAX is a convenient place to land, located within minutes of all the city's beach communities, and not more than a half-hour from downtown, Hollywood, or the Westside. Despite its size, the eight-terminal airport has a rather straightforward, easy-to-understand design. Free blue, green, and white Airline Connections shuttle buses (☎ 310/646-2911) connect the terminals at LAX and stop in front of each ticket building. Special handicapped-accessible minibuses are also available. Travelers Aid of Los Angeles (☎ 310/646-2270) operates booths in each terminal.

One of the area's smaller airports might be more convenient for you, landing you closer to your destination and allowing you to avoid the traffic and bustle of LAX. **Burbank-Glendale-Pasadena Airport** (2627 N. Hollywood Way, Burbank; ☎ 818/840-8840) is the best place to land if you're locating in Hollywood or the valleys. The small airport has especially good links to Las Vegas and other southwestern cities. **Long Beach Municipal Airport** (4100 Donald Douglas Dr., Long Beach; ☎ 310/421-8293), south of LAX, is the best place to land if you are visiting Long Beach or northern Orange County and want to avoid L.A. entirely. **Orange County/John Wayne Airport** (19051 Airport Way N., Anaheim; ☎ 714/252-5200) is closest to Disneyland, Knott's Berry Farm, and other Orange County attractions. **Ontario International Airport** (Terminal Way, Ontario; ☎ 909/988-2700) is the least popular airport for tourists. Primarily a commuter airport, Ontario is popular with business people heading to San Bernardino, Riverside, and other inland communities.

TRANSPORTATION FROM (AND TO) LAX

BY CAR All the major car-rental firms operate off-site branches that are reached via shuttle from the terminals. See "Getting Around" in Chapter 4 for a list of major rental companies.

BY TAXI Taxis line up outside each terminal, and rides are metered. Expect to pay about $25 to Hollywood and downtown, $22 to Beverly Hills, $20 to Santa Monica, and $45 to Pasadena. These prices include a $2.50 service charge for rides originating at LAX.

BY RAIL The city's new Metro Green Line connects LAX with Norwalk, an eastern L.A. city where few visitors want to go. At it's midsection, though, the Green Line is intersected by the Blue Line, a light-rail service that operates between downtown and Long Beach. By transferring from the Green to the Blue Line, visitors arriving at LAX can now travel from the airport to Downtown or Long Beach by train. The service operates from 6am to 9pm; fares had not been set by press time. Call the Los Angeles County Metropolitan Transit Authority (MTA) at 213/626-4455 or 800/252-7433 for information.

BY SHUTTLE   Many city hotels provide free shuttles for their guests; ask about transportation when you make reservations. **Super Shuttle** (☎ 310/782-6600), a private ride-sharing service, offers regularly scheduled minivans from LAX to any location in the city. The set fare can range from about $10 to $50, depending on your destination. When traveling to the airport for your trip home, reserve your shuttle at least one day in advance.

BY PUBLIC BUS   The city's MTA buses also go between LAX and many parts of the city. Phone MTA Airport Information (☎ 213/626-4455 or 800/252-7433) for the schedules and fares.

Leaving LAX by Car

To reach Santa Monica and other northern beach communities, exit the airport, turn left onto Sepulveda Boulevard, then follow the signs to Calif. 1 (Pacific Coast Highway) north.

To reach Huntington, Newport, and other southern beach communities, turn right onto Sepulveda Boulevard, then follow the signs to Calif. 1 (the Pacific Coast Highway) south.

To reach Beverly Hills or Hollywood, exit the airport via Century Boulevard, then take I-405 north to Santa Monica Boulevard.

To reach downtown, exit the airport via Century Boulevard, then take I-405 north to I-10 east.

To reach Pasadena, exit the airport, turn right onto Sepulveda Boulevard south, then take I-105 east to I-110 north.

A SHORTCUT TO LAX   One of the city's busiest interchanges is from the Santa Monica Freeway (I-10) to the San Diego Freeway (I-405) on the way to Los Angeles International Airport. Therefore, when heading to LAX for your flight home, the scenic route may prove to be the fastest. From the Santa Monica Freeway (I-10) westbound, exit south to La Brea Avenue. Go right on Stocker Street, then left on La Cienega Boulevard. Veer right on La Tijera Boulevard and left on Airport Boulevard, then follow the signs.

ARRIVING BY CAR

California is well connected to the rest of the United States by several major highways. Among them are Interstate 5, which enters the state from the north; Interstate 10, which originates in Jacksonville, Florida, and terminates in Los Angeles; and U.S. 101, which follows the western seaboard from Los Angeles north to the Oregon state line. If you're planning to take smaller roads, call the California Highway Patrol (☎ 213/953-7383) to check road conditions before heading out.

If you're driving in from the north, you have two choices: the quick route, along I-5 through the middle of the state, or the scenic route along the coast.

Heading south along I-5, you'll pass a small town called Grapevine. This marks the start of the mountain pass known as the Grapevine. Once you've reached the southern end of the mountain pass, you'll be in the San Fernando Valley, and you've arrived in Los Angeles County. To reach the beach communities and L.A.'s Westside take I-405 south; to get to Hollywood, take Calif. 170 south to U.S. 101 south (this route is called the Hollywood Freeway the entire way); the I-5 will take you through downtown and into Orange County.

If you're taking the scenic coastal route in from the north, take U.S. 101 to I-405, I-5, or stay on U.S. 101, following the instructions as listed above to your final destination.

If you're approaching from the east, you'll be coming in on I-10. For Orange County, take Calif. 57 south. I-10 continues through downtown and terminates at the beach. If you're heading to the Westside, take the I-405 north. To get to the beaches, take Calif. 1 (PCH) north or south, depending on your destination.

From the south, head north on I-5. At the southern end of Orange County, I-405 splits off to the west; take this road to the Westside and beach communities. Stay on I-5 to reach downtown.

Here are some handy driving times if you're on one of those see-the-U.S.A. car trips: From Phoenix, it's about six hours (okay, seven, if you drive the speed limit) to Los Angeles on I-10. Las Vegas is 265 miles northeast of Los Angeles (about a 4- or 5-hour drive). San Francisco is 390 miles north of Los Angeles, and San Diego is 115 miles south.

Before you set out on a big car trip, you might want to join the **American Automobile Association (AAA)** (☎ 800/336-4357), which has hundreds of offices nationwide. Members receive excellent maps (they'll even help you plan an exact itinerary) and emergency road service.

ROAD MAPS   California's freeway signs frequently indicate direction by naming a town rather than a point on the compass. If you've never heard of Canoga Park you might be in trouble, unless you have a map. The best state road guide is the comprehensive Thomas Bros. *California Road Atlas,* a 300-plus-page book of maps with schematics of towns and cities statewide. It costs $20, but is a good investment if you plan to do a lot of exploring. Smaller, accordion-style maps are handy for the state as a whole or for individual cities and regions. These foldout maps usually cost $2 to $3 and are available at gas stations, pharmacies, supermarkets, and tourist-oriented shops everywhere.

ARRIVING BY TRAIN

Amtrak (☎ 800/USA-RAIL) connects Los Angeles with about 500 American cities. Trains bound for Southern California leave daily from New York and pass through Chicago and Denver. The journey takes about 3^1/$_2$ days, and seats fill up quickly. As of this writing, the lowest round-trip fare was $339 from New York and $269 from Chicago. These heavily restricted tickets are good for 45 days and allow up to three stops along the way.

The *Sunset Limited* is Amtrak's regularly scheduled transcontinental service, originating in Florida and making 52 stops along the way as it passes through Alabama, Mississippi, Louisiana, Texas, New Mexico, and Arizona before arriving in Los Angeles. The train, which runs three times weekly, features reclining seats, a sightseeing car with large windows, and a full-service dining car. Round-trip coach fares begin at $259; sleeping accommodations are available for an extra charge.

Amtrak also runs trains up and down the California coast, connecting Los Angeles with San Francisco and all points in between. A one-way ticket can often be had for as little as $50. The coastal journey, aboard Amtrak's *Coast Starlight*, is a fantastically beautiful trip that runs from Seattle to Oakland; crosses Salinas, the artichoke capital of the world; climbs San Luis Obispo's bucolic hills; drops into Santa Barbara; then runs down the Malibu coast into Los Angeles. You can then continue on to San Diego if you like. It's a popular journey—make reservations well in advance.

Call Amtrak for a brochure outlining routes and prices for the entire system. Ask about special family plans, tours, and other money-saving promotions the rail carrier may be offering.

The L.A. terminus is Union Station (800 N. Alameda; ☎ **213/ 624-0171**), on downtown's northern edge. Completed in 1939, the station was the last of America's great train depots—a unique blend of Spanish Revival and Streamline Moderne architecture that still functions as a modern-day transport center (see "Architectural Highlights," in Chapter 7, for more details). From the station, you can take one of the many taxis that line up outside the station, or board the Metro Blue Line to Long Beach.

ARRIVING BY BUS

Bus travel is an inexpensive and often flexible option. **Greyhound/ Trailways** (☎ **800/231-2222**) can get you here from anywhere, and offers several money-saving multiday passes. Round-trip fares vary depending on your point of origin, but few, if any, ever exceed $200. The main Los Angeles bus station is downtown at 1716 E. 7th Street, east of Alameda (☎ **213/262-1514**). For additional area terminal locations and local fare and schedule information, phone **213/262-1514**.

PACKAGE TOURS

Operators offering escorted tours in Southern California include Caravan (401 N. Michigan Ave., Chicago, IL 60611; ☎ 312/321-9800 or 800/227-2826); Collette Tours (162 Middle St., Pawtucket, RI 02860; ☎ 401/728-3805 or 800/832-4656); Gadabout Tours (700 E. Tahquitz Way, Palm Springs, CA 92262; ☎ 619/325-5556 or 800/ 952-5068); and Globus (5301 South Federal Circle, Littleton, CO 80123; ☎ 303/797-2800 or 800/221-0090).

Independent fly/drive packages (no escorted tour groups, just a bulk rate on your airfare, hotel, and possibly your rental car) are offered by American Airlines Fly AAway Vacations (☎ 800/634-5555), Delta Dream Vacations (☎ 800/872-7786), TWA Getaway Vacations (☎ 800/438-2929), and United Airlines' Vacation Planning Center (☎ 800/328-6877).

3

For Foreign Visitors

American fads and fashions have spread across other parts of the world to such a degree that the United States may seem like familiar territory before your arrival. But there are still many peculiarities and uniquely American situations any foreign visitor will encounter and may find confusing or perplexing. This chapter will provide some specifics about getting to the United States as economically and effortlessly as possible, plus some helpful information about how things are done in California—from receiving mail to making a local or long-distance telephone call.

1 Preparing for Your Trip

ENTRY REQUIREMENTS

DOCUMENT REGULATIONS   Canadian nationals need only proof of Canadian residence to visit the United States. Citizens of the United Kingdom and Japan need only a current passport. Citizens of other countries, including Australia and New Zealand, usually need two documents: a valid passport with an expiration date at least six months later than the scheduled end of their visit to the United States and a tourist visa available at no charge from a U.S. embassy or consulate.

To get a tourist or business visa to enter the United States, contact the nearest American embassy or consulate in your country; if there is none, you will have to apply in person in a country where there is a U.S. embassy or consulate. Present your passport, a passport-size photo of yourself, and an application, available through the embassy or consulate, completed by you. You may be asked to provide information about how you plan to finance your trip or show a letter of invitation from a friend with whom you plan to stay. Those applying for a business visa may be asked to show evidence that they will not receive a salary in the United States. Be sure to check the length of stay on your visa; usually it is six months. If you want to stay longer, you may file for an extension with the Immigration and Naturalization Service once you are in the country. If permission to stay is granted, a new visa is not required unless you leave the United States and want to reenter.

MEDICAL REQUIREMENTS   No inoculations are needed to enter the United States unless you are coming from, or have stopped over in, areas known to be suffering from epidemics, particularly cholera or yellow fever.

If you have a disease requiring treatment with medications containing narcotics or drugs requiring a syringe, carry a valid signed generic prescription from your physician to allay any suspicions that you are smuggling drugs. The prescription brands you are accustomed to buying in your country may not be available in the United States.

CUSTOMS REQUIREMENTS   Every adult visitor may bring in, free of duty: 1 liter of wine or hard liquor; 200 cigarettes or 100 cigars (but no cigars from Cuba) or 3 pounds of smoking tobacco; and $100 worth of gifts. These exemptions are offered to travelers who spend at least 72 hours in the United States and who have not claimed them within the preceding 6 months. It is altogether forbidden to bring foodstuffs (particularly cheese, fruit, cooked meats, and canned goods) and plants (vegetables, seeds, tropical plants, and so on) into the country. Foreign tourists may bring in or take out up to $10,000 in U.S. or foreign currency with no formalities; larger sums must be declared to Customs on entering or leaving.

INSURANCE

Unlike most other countries, the United States does not have a national health system. Because the cost of medical care is extremely high, we strongly advise all travelers to secure health coverage before setting out on their trip. You may want to take out a comprehensive travel policy that covers (for a relatively low premium) sickness or injury costs (medical, surgical, and hospital); loss or theft of your baggage; trip-cancellation costs; guarantee of bail in case you are arrested; costs of accident, repatriation, or death. Such packages (for example, "Europe Assistance" in Europe) are sold by automobile clubs at attractive rates, as well as by insurance companies and travel agencies and at some airports.

MONEY

The U.S. monetary system has a decimal base: One American **dollar** ($1) = 100 **cents** (100¢). Dollar **bills** commonly come in $1 (a buck), $5, $10, $20, $50, and $100 denominations (the last two are not welcome when paying for small purchases, and are usually not accepted in taxis or at subway ticket booths). There are six coin denominations: 1¢ (one cent, or "penny"); 5¢ (five cents, or "nickel"); 10¢ (ten cents, or "dime"); 25¢ (twenty-five cents, or "quarter"); 50¢ (fifty cents, or "half dollar"); and the $1 pieces (both the older, large silver dollar and the newer, small Susan B. Anthony coin).

Traveler's checks in U.S. dollars are accepted at most hotels, motels, restaurants, and large stores. Sometimes picture identification is required. American Express, Thomas Cook, and Barclay's Bank traveler's checks are readily accepted in the United States.

Credit cards are the method of payment most widely used: Visa (BarclayCard in Britain), MasterCard (EuroCard in Europe, Access in Britain, Diamond in Japan), American Express, Discover, Diners Club, enRoute, JCB, and Carte Blanche, in descending order of acceptance.

You can save yourself trouble by using "plastic" rather than cash or traveler's checks in 95% of all hotels, motels, restaurants, and retail stores. A credit card can also serve as a deposit for renting a car, as proof of identity, or as a "cash card," enabling you to draw money from automated teller machines (ATMs) that accept them.

If you plan to travel for several weeks or more in the United States, you may want to deposit enough money into your credit-card account to cover anticipated expenses and avoid finance charges in your absence. This also reduces the likelihood of your receiving an unwelcome big bill on your return.

You can telegraph (wire) money, or have it telegraphed to you very quickly using the **Western Union** system (☎ **800/325-6000**).

SAFETY

While tourist areas are generally safe, crime is on the increase everywhere, and U.S. urban areas tend to be less safe than those in Europe or Japan. Visitors should always stay alert. This is particularly true of large U.S. cities. It is wise to ask the city's or area's tourist office if you're in doubt about which neighborhoods are safe.

Remember also that hotels are open to the public, and in a large hotel, security may not be able to screen everyone entering. Always lock your room door—don't assume that once inside your hotel you are automatically safe and no longer need be aware of your surroundings.

DRIVING   Safety while driving is particularly important. Question your rental agency about personal safety, or ask for a brochure of traveler safety tips when you pick up your car. Obtain written directions, or a map with the route marked in red, from the agency showing how to get to your destination. And, if possible, arrive and depart during daylight hours.

Recently more and more crime has involved cars and drivers. If you drive off a highway into a doubtful neighborhood, leave the area as quickly as possible. If you have an accident, even on the highway, stay in your car with the doors locked until you assess the situation or until the police arrive. If you are bumped from behind on the street or are involved in a minor accident with no injuries and the situation appears to be suspicious, motion to the other driver to follow you. Never get out of your car in such situations.

If you see someone on the road who indicates a need for help, do not stop. Take note of the location, drive on to a well-lighted area, and telephone the police by dialing 911. Park in well-lighted, well-traveled areas if possible.

Always keep your car doors locked, whether attended or unattended. Never leave any packages or valuables in sight. If someone attempts to rob you or steal your car, do not try to resist the thief/carjacker—report the incident to the police department immediately.

2 Getting to the U.S.

Travelers from overseas can take advantage of **APEX (advance purchase excursion) fares** offered by all the major U.S. and European carriers. Aside from these, attractive values are offered by Virgin Atlantic from London to Los Angeles.

A number of U.S. airlines offer service from Europe to the United States. If they do not have direct flights from Europe to Los Angeles, they can book you straight through on a connecting flight. You can make reservations by calling the following numbers in London: **American** (☎ 0181/572-5555), **Continental** (☎ 4412/9377-6464), **Delta** (☎ 0800/414-767), and **United** (☎ 0181/990-9900).

And, of course, many international carriers serve LAX. Helpful numbers include **Virgin Atlantic** (☎ 0293/747-747 in London), **British Airways** (☎ 0345/222-111 in London), and **Aer Lingus** (☎ 01/844-4747 in Dublin or 061/415-556 in Shannon). **Qantas** (☎ 008/177-767 in Australia) has flights from Sydney to Los Angeles; you can also take United from Australia to Los Angeles. **Air New Zealand** (☎ 0800/737-000 in Auckland or 64-3/379-5200 in Christchurch) also offers service to LAX. Canadian travelers might book flights on **Air Canada** (in Canada ☎ 800/268-7240 or 800/361-8620), which offers direct service from Toronto, Montreal, Calgary, and Vancouver to Los Angeles.

The visitor arriving by air, no matter what the port of entry, should cultivate patience and resignation before setting foot on U.S. soil. Getting through immigration control may take as long as two hours on some days, especially summer weekends, so have your guidebook or something else to read handy. Add the time it takes to clear customs and you will see you should make a very generous allowance for delay in planning connections between international and domestic flight—figure on two to three hours at least.

In contrast, for the traveler arriving by car or rail from Canada, the border-crossing formalities have been streamlined to the vanishing point. And for the traveler by air from Canada, Bermuda, and some places in the Caribbean, you can sometimes go through Customs and Immigration at the point of departure, which is much quicker.

3 Getting Around the U.S.

On their trans-Atlantic or trans-Pacific flights, some large U.S. airlines offer special discount tickets for any of their U.S. destinations (American Airline's Visit USA program and Delta's Discover America program, for example). The tickets or coupons are not on sale in the United States and must be purchased before you leave your point of departure. This system is the best, easiest, and fastest way to see the United States at low cost. You should obtain information well in advance from your travel agent or the office of the airline concerned, since the conditions attached to these discount tickets can be changed without advance notice.

International visitors can also buy a **USA Railpass,** good for 15 or 30 days of unlimited travel on Amtrak. The pass is available through many foreign travel agents. Prices in 1995 for a 15-day pass are $229 off peak, $340 peak; a 30-day pass costs $339 off peak, $425 peak (off peak is August 31 to June 15). (With a foreign passport, you can also buy passes at some Amtrak offices in the United States, including locations in San Francisco, Los Angeles, Chicago, New York, Miami, Boston, and Washington, D.C.) Reservations are generally required and should be made for each part of your trip as early as possible.

Visitors should also be aware of the limitations of long-distance rail travel in the United States. With a few notable exceptions (for instance, the Northeast Corridor line between Boston and Washington, D.C.), service is rarely up to European standards: Delays are common, routes are limited and often infrequently served, and fares are rarely significantly lower than discount airfares. Thus, cross-country train travel should be approached with caution.

The cheapest way to travel the United States is by bus. Greyhound/Trailways, the sole nationwide bus line, offers an **Ameripass** for unlimited travel for 7 days (for $359), 15 days (for $459), and 30 days (for $559). Bus travel in the United States can be both slow and uncomfortable, so this option is not for everyone. In addition, bus stations are often located in undesirable neighborhoods.

FAST FACTS: For the Foreign Traveler

Automobile Organizations   Auto clubs will supply maps, suggested routes, guidebooks, accident and bail-bond insurance, and emergency road service. The major auto club in the United States, with 955 offices nationwide, is the American Automobile Association (AAA). Members of some foreign auto clubs have reciprocal arrangements with the AAA and enjoy its services at no charge. If you belong to an auto club, inquire about AAA reciprocity before you leave. The AAA can provide you with an International Driving Permit validating your foreign license, although drivers with valid licenses from most home countries don't really need this permit. You may be able to join the AAA even if you are not a member of a reciprocal club. To inquire, call 619/233-1000 or 800/222-4357. In addition, some automobile rental agencies now provide these services, so you should inquire about their availability when you rent your car.

Business Hours   Offices are usually open weekdays from 9am to 5pm. Banks are open weekdays from 9am to 3pm or later and sometimes Saturday morning. Shops, especially department stores and those in shopping complexes, tend to stay open late—until about 9pm weekdays and until 6pm weekends. Shops are usually open six days a week, sometimes Sundays as well.

Climate   See "When to Go" in Chapter 2.

Currency   See "Preparing for Your Trip" earlier in this chapter.

Currency Exchange   The "foreign-exchange bureaus" so common in Europe are rare in the United States. They're at major international airports, and there are a few in most major cities, but they're nonexistent in medium-size cities and small towns. Try to avoid having to change foreign money, or traveler's checks denominated other than in U.S. dollars, at small-town banks, or even at branches in a big city; in fact leave any currency other than U.S. dollars at home (except the cash you need for the taxi or bus ride home when you return to your own country); otherwise, your own currency may prove more nuisance to you than it's worth.

Drinking Laws   The legal age to drink alcohol is 21.

Electric Current   The United States uses 110–120 volts, 60 cycles, compared to 220–240 volts, 50 cycles, as in most of Europe. Besides a 100-volt converter, small appliances of non-American manufacture, such as hairdryers or shavers, will require a plug adapter, with two flat, parallel pins. The easiest solution to the power struggle is to purchase dual voltage appliances that operate on both 110 and 220 volts, and then all that is required is a U.S. adapter plug.

Embassies/Consulates   All embassies are located in Washington, D.C. Listed here are the West Coast consulates of the major English-speaking countries. The Australian Consulate is located at 611 N. Larchmont, Los Angeles, CA 90004 (☎ **213/469-4300**). The Canadian Consulate is at 300 South Grand Ave., Suite 1000, Los Angeles, CA 90071 (☎ **213/346-2700**). The Irish Consulate is located at 655 Montgomery St., Suite 930, San Francisco, CA 94111 (☎ **415/392-4214**). The New Zealand Consulate is at 12400 Wilshire Blvd., Los Angeles, CA 90025 (☎ **310/207-1605**). Contact the U.K. Consulate at 11766 Wilshire Blvd., Suite 400, Los Angeles, CA 90025 (☎ **310/477-3322**).

Emergencies   Call **911** for fire, police, and ambulance. If you encounter such traveler's problems as sickness, accident, or lost or stolen baggage, call the Traveler's Aid Society (☎ 310/646-5252), an organization that specializes in helping distressed travelers. U.S. hospitals have emergency rooms, with a special entrance where you will be admitted for quick attention.

Gasoline (Petrol)   One U.S. gallon equals 3.75 liters, while 1.2 U.S. gallons equals 1 imperial gallon. A gallon of unleaded gas (short for gasoline), which most rental cars accept, costs about $1.30 if you fill your own tank (it's called "self-serve"); about 10¢ more if the station attendant does it (called "full-service"). Most gas stations in Los Angeles are strictly self-serve stations.

Holidays   On the following national legal holidays, banks, government offices, post offices, and many stores, restaurants, and museums are closed: January 1 (New Year's Day), third Monday in January (Martin Luther King, Jr., Day), third Monday in February (Presidents' Day), last Monday in May (Memorial Day), July 4 (Independence Day), first Monday in September (Labor Day), second Monday in October (Columbus Day), November 11 (Veterans Day/Armistice Day), last Thursday in November (Thanksgiving Day), and December 25 (Christmas Day). The Tuesday following the first Monday in November is Election Day.

Legal Aid If you are stopped for a minor infraction (for example, of the highway code, such as speeding), never attempt to pay the fine directly to a police officer; you may be arrested on the much more serious charge of attempted bribery. Pay fines by mail, or directly into the hands of the clerk of the court. If accused of a more serious offense, it is best to say and do nothing before consulting a lawyer. Under U.S. law, an arrested person is allowed one telephone call to a party of his or her choice. Call your embassy or consulate.

Mail You may receive mail c/o General Delivery at the main post office of the city or region where you expect to be. The addressee must pick it up in person, and must produce proof of identity (driver's license, credit card, passport, and so on).

Mailboxes are blue with a red-and-white logo, and carry the inscription "U.S. Mail." Within the United States, it costs 20¢ to mail a standard-size postcard and 32¢ to send an oversize postcard (larger than $6 \times 4^1/_4$ inches, or 15.4×10.8 centimeters). Letters that weigh up to 1 ounce (that's about five 11×8-inch, or 28.2×20.5-centimeter, pages) cost 32¢ plus 23¢ for each additional ounce. A postcard to Mexico costs 35¢, a $^1/_2$-ounce letter 40¢; a postcard to Canada costs 40¢, a 1-ounce letter 52¢. A postcard to Europe, Australia, New Zealand, the Far East, South America, and elsewhere costs 50¢, while a $^1/_2$-ounce letter is 60¢, and a 1-ounce letter is $1.

Medical Emergencies See "Emergencies," above.

Taxes In the United States there is no VAT (value-added-tax) or other indirect tax at a national level. There is a $10 Customs tax, payable on entry to the United States, and a $6 departure tax. Sales tax is levied on goods and services by state and local governments, however, and is not included in the price tags you'll see on merchandise. These taxes are not refundable. In Los Angeles, the sales tax is 8.25%.

Telephone and Fax Pay phones can be found on street corners, as well as in bars, restaurants, public buildings, and stores and at service stations. Some accept 20¢, most are 25¢. If the telephone accepts 20¢, you may also use a quarter (25¢), but you will not receive change.

In the past few years, many American companies have installed "voice-mail" systems, so be prepared to deal with a machine instead of a receptionist if calling a business number. Listen carefully to the instructions (you'll probably be asked to dial 1, 2, or 3 or wait for an operator to pick up); if you can't understand, sometimes dialing 0 (zero, not the letter O) will put you in touch with an operator within the company. It's frustrating even for locals!

For long-distance or international calls, it's most economical to charge the call to a telephone charge card or a credit card; or you can use a lot of change. The pay phone will instruct you how much to deposit and when to deposit it into the slot on the top of the telephone box.

For long-distance calls in the United States, dial 1 followed by the area code and number you want. For direct overseas calls, first dial 011, followed by the country code (Australia, 61; Republic of Ireland, 353; New Zealand, 64; United Kingdom, 44; and so on), and then by the city code (for example, 71 or 81 for London, 21 for Birmingham, 1 for Dublin) and the number of the person you wish to call.

Before calling from a hotel room, always ask the hotel phone operator if there are any telephone surcharges. There almost always are, and they often are as much as 75¢ or $1, even for a local call. These charges are best avoided by using a public phone, calling collect, or using a telephone charge card.

For reversed-charge or collect calls and for person-to-person calls, dial 0 (zero) followed by the area code and number you want; an operator will then come on the line, and you should specify that you are calling collect, or person-to-person, or both. If your operator-assisted call is international, immediately ask to speak with an overseas operator.

For local directory assistance ("Information"), dial 411; for long-distance information dial 1, then the appropriate area code and 555-1212.

Most hotels have fax machines available for their customers, and there is usually a charge to send or receive a facsimile. You will also see signs for public faxes in the windows of small shops.

Telephone Directory   The local phone company provides two kinds of telephone directories. The general directory, called the "white pages," lists personal residences and businesses separately, in alphabetical order. The first few pages are devoted to community-service numbers, including a guide to long-distance and international calling, complete with country codes and area codes.

The second directory, the "yellow pages," lists all local services, businesses, and industries by type, with an index at the back. The listings cover not only such obvious items as automobile repairs by make of car, or drugstores (pharmacies), often by geographical location, but also restaurants by type of cuisine and geographical location, bookstores by special subject and/or language, places of worship by religious denomination, and other information that a visitor might otherwise not readily find. The yellow pages also include city plans or detailed area maps, often showing postal ZIP codes and public transportation.

Time   California is on Pacific time, which is three hours earlier than on the U.S. East Coast. For instance, when it is noon in Los Angeles, it is 3pm in New York and Miami; 2pm in Chicago, in the central part of the country; and 1pm in Denver, Colorado, in the midwestern part of the country. California, like most of the rest of the United States, observes daylight saving time during the summer; in late spring, clocks are moved ahead one hour and then are turned back again in the fall. This results in lovely long summer evenings, when the sun sets as late as 8:30 or 9pm.

Tipping   Some rules of thumb: bartenders, 10 to 15%; bellhops, at least 50¢ per bag, or $2 to $3 for a lot of luggage; cab drivers, 10% of the fare; cafeterias and fast-food restaurants, no tip; chambermaids, $1 per day; checkroom attendants, $1 per garment; theater ushers, no tip; gas-station attendants, no tip; hairdressers and barbers, 15 to 20%; waiters and waitresses, 15 to 20% of the check; valet parking attendants, $1.

THE AMERICAN SYSTEM OF MEASUREMENTS

Length

1 inch (in.)	=	2.54cm			
1 foot (ft.)	=	12in.	=	30.48cm	=	.305m
1 yard	=	3ft.			=	.915m
1 mile (mi.)	=	5,280ft.	=	1.609km	

To convert miles to kilometers, multiply the number of miles by 1.61 (for example, 50 miles × 1.61 = 80.5km). Note that this conversion can be used to convert speeds from miles per hour (m.p.h.) to kilometers per hour (km/h).

To convert kilometers to miles, multiply the number of kilometers by .62 (for example, 25km ×.62 = 15.5 miles). Note that this same conversion can be used to convert speeds from kilometers per hour to miles per hour.

Capacity

1 fluid ounce (fl. oz.)			=	.03 liter		
1 pint	=	16 fl. oz.	=	.47 liter		
1 quart	=	2 pints	=	.94 liter		
1 gallon (gal.)	=	4 quarts	=	3.79 liter	=	.83 Imperial gal.

To convert U.S. gallons to liters, multiply the number of gallons by 3.79 (for example, 12gal. × 3.79 = 45.48 liters).

To convert U.S. gallons to Imperial gallons, multiply the number of U.S. gallons by .83 (for example, 12 U.S. gal. × .83 = 9.96 Imperial gal.).

To convert liters to U.S. gallons, multiply the number of liters by .26 (for example, 50 liters × .26 = 13 U.S. gal.).

To convert Imperial gallons to U.S. gallons, multiply the number of Imperial gallons by 1.2 (for example, 8 Imperial gal. × 1.2 = 9.6 U.S. gal.).

Weight

1 ounce (oz.)			=	28.35 grams		
1 pound (lb.)	=	16oz.	=	453.6 grams	=	.45 kilograms
1 ton	=	2,000lb.	=	907 kilograms	=	.91 metric ton

To convert pounds to kilograms, multiply the number of pounds by .45 (for example, 90lb. × .45 = 40.5kg).

To convert kilograms to pounds, multiply the number of kilograms by 2.2 (for example, 75kg × 2.2 = 165lb.).

Area

1 acre		=	.41 hectare		
1 square mile (sq. mi.) =	640 acres	=	2.59 hectares	=	2.6km^2

To convert acres to hectares, multiply the number of acres by .41 (for example, 40 acres × .41 = 16.4ha).

To convert square miles to square kilometers, multiply the number of square miles by 2.6 (for example, 80 sq. mi. × 2.6 = 208km^2).

To convert hectares to acres, multiply the number of hectares by 2.47 (for example, 20ha ×2.47 = 49.4 acres).

To convert square kilometers to square miles, multiply the number of square kilometers by .39 (for example, 150km^2 × .39 = 58.5 sq. mi.).

Temperature

To convert degrees Fahrenheit to degrees Celsius, subtract 32 from °F, multiply by 5, then divide by 9 (for example, 85°F − 32 × 5/9 = 29.4°C).

To convert degrees Celsius to degrees Fahrenheit, multiply °C by 9, divide by 5, and add 32 (example, 20°C × 9/5 + 32 = 68°F).

4

Getting to Know Los Angeles

The freeways crisscrossing the Los Angeles metropolitan area are your lifelines to the sights, but it will take you a little time to master their maze. Even locals sometimes have trouble making their way around this sprawling city. This chapter will familiarize you with the setup of the city and will start you on the road to negotiating it like a native.

1 Orientation

VISITOR INFORMATION CENTERS

The **Los Angeles Convention and Visitors Bureau** (633 W. 5th St., Suite 600, Los Angeles, CA 90071; ☎ **213/624-7300**) is the city's main source for information. Write for a free visitors' kit. The bureau staffs a Visitors Information Center at 685 S. Figueroa Street, between Wilshire Boulevard and 7th Street, which is open Monday through Friday from 8am to 5pm and Saturday from 8:30am to 5pm.

Many Los Angeles-area communities also have their own information centers:

Visitor Information Center Hollywood (Janes House, 6541 Hollywood Blvd., Hollywood, CA 90028; ☎ **213/689-8822**); open Monday through Saturday from 9am to 5pm.

Beverly Hills Visitors Bureau (239 S. Beverly Dr., Beverly Hills, CA 90212; ☎ **310/271-8174** or 800/345-2210; fax 310/858-8032); open Monday through Friday from 9am to 5pm.

Hollywood Arts Council (P.O. Box 931056, Dept. 1995, Hollywood, CA 90093; ☎ **213/462-2355**) distributes the magazine *Discover Hollywood* for a $2 postage and handling fee. It contains listings and schedules for the area's many theaters, galleries, music venues, and comedy clubs.

Long Beach Area Convention & Visitors Bureau (One World Trade Center, Suite 300, Long Beach, CA 90831; ☎ **310/436-3645** or 800/4LB-STAY; fax 310/435-5653); open Monday through Friday from 8:30am to 5pm.

Marina del Rey Chamber of Commerce/Visitor and Convention Bureau (☎ **310/821-0555**) has walk-in hours Monday through Friday from 9am to 5pm at 4371 Glencoe Ave., B-14, Marina del Rey, CA 90292. For information by mail, write 13428 Maxella Ave., Box 441, Marina del Rey, CA 90292. A 24-hour updated bulletin board listing local restaurant, lodging, shopping, boating, and relocation information is available by calling the InfoCenter System at 800/919-0555.

Pasadena Convention and Visitors Bureau (171 S. Los Robles Ave., Pasadena, CA 91101; ☎ **818/795-9311;** fax 818/795-9656); open Monday through Friday from 8am to 5pm, and Saturday from 10am to 4pm. The Bureau also has an information hotline (☎ **818/ 795-9311**), which operates when the office is closed for the holidays.

Redondo Beach Chamber of Commerce (200 N. Pacific Coast Highway, Redondo Beach, CA 90277; ☎ **310/376-6911**); open Monday through Friday from 8:30am to 5pm.

Santa Monica Convention and Visitors Bureau (2219 Main St., Santa Monica, CA 90405; ☎ **310/393-7593**). **The Santa Monica Visitors Bureau Palisades Park** is located near the Santa Monica Pier, at 1400 Ocean Avenue (between Santa Monica Blvd. and Broadway), and is open daily from 10am to 5pm.

West Hollywood Convention and Visitors Bureau (8687 Melrose Ave., M-26, West Hollywood, CA 90096; ☎ **310/289-2525** or 800/ 368-6020; fax 310/289-2529); open Monday through Friday from 8am to 6pm.

OTHER INFORMATION SOURCES

Local tourist boards are terrific for uncritical information regarding attractions and special events, but they often fail to keep a figurative finger on the pulse of what's really happening, especially with regard to food, culture, and nightlife. Several city-oriented newspapers and magazines offer up-to-date info on current happenings. *L.A. Weekly,* a free weekly listings magazine, is packed with information on current events around town. It's available from sidewalk newsracks and in many stores and restaurants around the city. The *Los Angeles Times* "Calendar" section of the Sunday paper is an excellent guide to the world of entertainment in and around L.A., and includes listings of what's doing and where to do it. *Los Angeles Magazine* and the even trendier upstart *Buzz* are city-based monthlies full of news, information, and previews of L.A.'s art, music, and food scenes. Both are available at newsstands around town.

CITY LAYOUT

Los Angeles is not a single compact city, but a sprawling suburbia comprising dozens of disparate communities. Most of the city's communities are located on the flatlands of a huge basin, between mountains and ocean. Even if you've never visited L.A. before, you'll recognize the names of many of these areas, such as Hollywood, Beverly Hills, Santa Monica, and Malibu. Ocean breezes push the city's infamous smog inland, toward dozens of less well known residential communities, and through mountain passes into the suburban sprawl of the San Fernando and San Gabriel valleys.

Downtown Los Angeles—which isn't where most tourists will establish themselves—is situated in the center of the basin, about 12 miles east of the Pacific Ocean. Most visitors will spend the bulk of their time either on the coast, or on the city's Westside (see "Neighborhoods in Brief," below, for complete details on all of the city's sectors).

The Freeway System

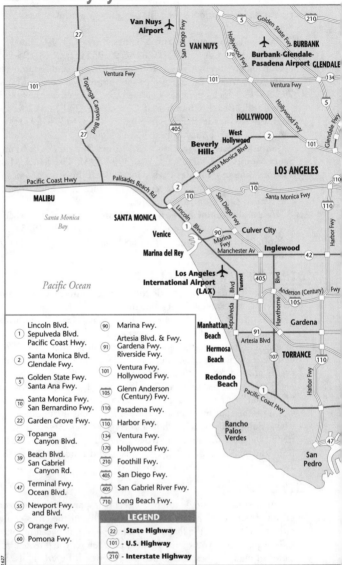

Lincoln Blvd.
(1) Sepulveda Blvd.
Pacific Coast Hwy.

(2) Santa Monica Blvd.
Glendale Fwy.

(5) Golden State Fwy.
Santa Ana Fwy.

(10) Santa Monica Fwy.
San Bernardino Fwy.

(22) Garden Grove Fwy.

(27) Topanga
Canyon Blvd.

(39) Beach Blvd.
San Gabriel
Canyon Rd.

(47) Terminal Fwy.
Ocean Blvd.

(55) Newport Fwy.
and Blvd.

(57) Orange Fwy.

(60) Pomona Fwy.

(90) Marina Fwy.

(91) Artesia Blvd. & Fwy.
Gardena Fwy.
Riverside Fwy.

(101) Ventura Fwy.
Hollywood Fwy.

(105) Glenn Anderson
(Century) Fwy.

(110) Pasadena Fwy.

(110) Harbor Fwy.

(134) Ventura Fwy.

(170) Hollywood Fwy.

(210) Foothill Fwy.

(405) San Diego Fwy.

(605) San Gabriel River Fwy.

(710) Long Beach Fwy.

LEGEND

(22) - State Highway

(101) - U.S. Highway

(210) - Interstate Highway

MAIN ARTERIES & STREETS

Nothing has had a greater effect on the growth and development of Los Angeles than the extensive freeway system that connects the city's patchwork of communities.

U.S. 101, called the Ventura Freeway in the San Fernando Valley and the Hollywood Freeway in the city, runs across L.A. in a roughly

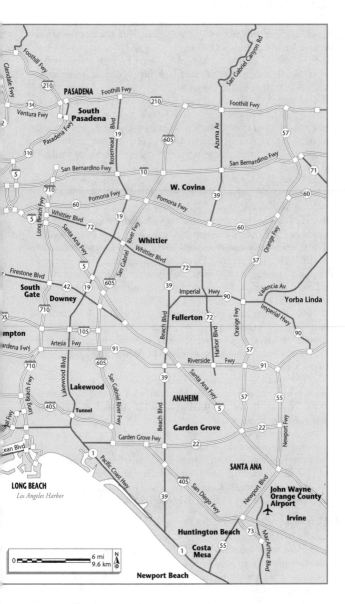

northwest-southeast direction, from the San Fernando Valley to the center of downtown.

Calif. 134 continues as the Ventura Freeway after U.S. 101 turns east/southeast into the city and becomes the Hollywood Freeway. This branch of the Ventura Freeway continues directly east, through the valley towns of Burbank and Glendale, to **I-210** (the Foothill

Freeway), which will take you through Pasadena and out toward the eastern edge of Los Angeles County.

I-5, otherwise known as the Golden State Freeway north of I-10, and the Santa Ana Freeway south of I-10, bisects downtown on its way from San Francisco to San Diego.

I-10, labeled the Santa Monica Freeway west of I-5 and the San Bernardino Freeway east of I-5, is the city's major east-west freeway, connecting the San Gabriel Valley with downtown and Santa Monica.

I-405, also known as the San Diego Freeway, runs north-south through L.A's Westside, connecting the San Fernando Valley with LAX and the southern beach areas.

Calif. 90, the Marina Freeway, is a tiny east-west stretch connecting I-405 to Calif. 1 (known as Lincoln Boulevard in this neck of the woods) in Marina del Rey.

I-105, Los Angeles's newest freeway—called the Glenn Anderson Freeway or the Century Freeway—extends from LAX east to I-605.

I-110, commonly known as the Harbor Freeway, starts in Pasadena as **Calif. 110** (the Pasadena Freeway); it turns into the interstate in downtown Los Angeles and runs directly south, where it dead ends in San Pedro. The section that is now the Pasadena Freeway is Los Angeles's historic first freeway, known as the Arroyo Seco when it opened in 1940.

I-710, a.k.a. the Long Beach Freeway, runs in a north-south direction through East Los Angeles and dead ends at Long Beach.

I-605, the San Gabriel River Freeway, runs roughly parallel to the I-710 further east, through the cities of Hawthorne and Lynwood and into the San Gabriel Valley.

Calif. 1—called Highway 1, Pacific Coast Highway, or simply PCH—is really a highway (more like a surface thruway) rather than a freeway. It skirts the ocean, linking all of L.A.'s beach communities, from Malibu to Long Beach.

The freeways are complemented by a complex web of surface streets. From north to south, the major east-west thoroughfares connecting downtown to the beaches are Sunset Boulevard, Santa Monica Boulevard, Wilshire Boulevard, and Olympic, Pico, and Venice boulevards. The section of Sunset Boulevard that runs between Crescent Heights Boulevard and Doheny Drive is the famed Sunset Strip.

STREET MAPS

Because Los Angeles is so spread out, a good map of the area is essential. Foldout maps are available at gas stations, hotels, bookshops, and tourist-oriented shops around the city. If you're going to be in Los Angeles for a week or more, or plan on doing some extensive touring, you might want to invest in the all-inclusive *Thomas Guide*, a comprehensive book of city maps that depicts every single road in the city. The ring-bound edition is sold in most area bookstores and costs about $15. Abridged versions cost about $5, and are often available at many of the outlets listed above.

NEIGHBORHOODS IN BRIEF

Los Angeles is a very confusing city, with fluid neighborhood lines and equally elastic labels. We have found that the best way to grasp the city is to break it into five regions—**Downtown, Hollywood, Westside, The Beaches,** and **The Valleys**—each of which encompasses a more-or-less distinctive patchwork of city neighborhoods and independently incorporated communities.

DOWNTOWN

Los Angeles was founded by the Spaniards in 1781 near what is now downtown's Olvera Street. Roughly bounded by the concrete moats that are the U.S. 101, I-110, I-10, and I-5 freeways, L.A.'s downtown is home to a tight cluster of high-rise offices, a historic district, and the neighborhoods of Koreatown, Chinatown, and Little Tokyo. For our purposes, the neighborhoods of Silverlake and Los Feliz, Exposition Park, and East and South-Central Los Angeles all fall under the downtown umbrella.

Once the automobile craze reached its height in the 1920s, the suburbs were opened for development and downtown fell into serious disrepair. But the construction of skyscrapers—facilitated by earthquake-proof technology—has transformed downtown Los Angeles into the business center of the city. Despite the relatively recent construction of cultural centers—the Music Center, the Museum of Contemporary Art, and the Wells Fargo Museum are all here—and a few smart restaurants, downtown is not the hub it would be in most cities. As far as tourists—and many residents—are concerned, downtown is definitely not the city's epicenter; the Westside, Hollywood, and the beaches are all more popular.

El Pueblo de Los Angeles Historic District, a 44-acre ode to the city's early years, is worth a visit on your way to Los Angeles City Hall and the *Los Angeles Times* buildings. Neither **Chinatown** nor **Little Tokyo** is on the scale of its San Francisco equivalents and, quite honestly, neither is especially worth going out of your way for. Of downtown's three major ethnic areas, **Koreatown,** located west of U.S. 101 and centering around Western and Vermont avenues, is the most colorful.

Silverlake, a residential neighborhood located just north of downtown, and the adjacent **Los Feliz,** just to the west, are arty areas containing mobile taco vendors, theaters, graffiti, and art galleries—all in equally plentiful proportions.

Exposition Park, just south and west of downtown, is home to the Los Angeles Memorial Coliseum and the L.A. Sports Arena. The park also contains the Los Angeles County Museum of Natural History, the Museum of Afro-American History and Culture, and the California State Museum of Science and Industry. The University of Southern California is next door.

East and South-Central L.A., just east and south of downtown, are home to the city's large, infamous barrios. It was here, at Florence and Normandie avenues, where the 1992 L.A. Riots were centered, and where a news station's reporter, hovering above in a helicopter, videotaped Reginald Denny being pulled from the cab of his truck and beaten by several young men. There are few tourist-oriented sites in these neighborhoods—the Watts Towers being a notable exception—though they are, without question, quite unique.

The Neighborhoods in Brief

The Neighborhoods in Brief

HOLLYWOOD

Yes, they still come. Young aspirants are attracted to this town like moths fluttering in the glare of neon lights. But Hollywood is now much more a state of mind than a glamour center. Many of the neighborhood's former studios have moved to less expensive, more spacious venues; Hollywood Boulevard is one of the city's seediest strips. The area is now just a less-than-admirable part of the whole of

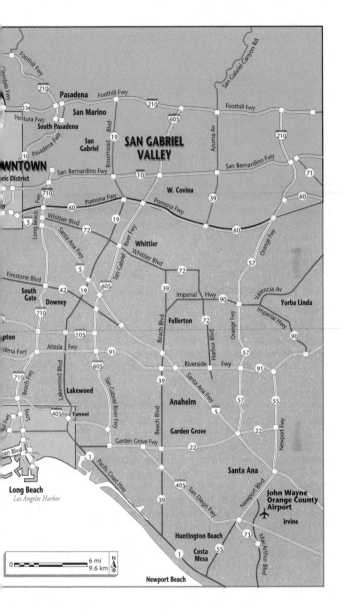

Los Angeles, but the legend of the neighborhood as the movie capital of the world endures.

For our purposes, the label "Hollywood" extends beyond the worn central neighborhood of Hollywood itself to surrounding neighborhoods. It encompasses basically everything between Western Avenue to the east and Fairfax Avenue to the west and from the Hollywood Hills (with their dazzling homes and million-dollar views) south, including the mid-Wilshire district (home to the newly named Museum Mile) and the famous, funky shopping district of Melrose Avenue. Also included here is expansive Griffith Park.

Seedy **Hollywood** centers around Hollywood and Sunset boulevards. It's home to several important attractions, such as the Walk of Fame and Mann's Chinese Theatre.

Melrose Avenue, a scruffy but fun neighborhood, is the city's funkiest shopping district.

The stretch of Wilshire Boulevard that runs through the southern part of Hollywood is known as the **Mid-Wilshire** district. This Wilshire corridor has had its commercial ups and downs in recent years, but is still considered to be one of Los Angeles's primary thoroughfares. It's lined with contemporary apartment houses and office buildings; the stretch just east of Fairfax Avenue, newly christened the Museum Mile, is home to the Los Angeles County Museum of Art, the La Brea Tar Pits, and that brand-new shrine to L.A. car culture, the Petersen Automotive Museum.

Griffith Park, up Western Avenue in the northernmost reaches of Hollywood, is one of the country's largest urban parks, and home to the Los Angeles Zoo and the famous Griffith Observatory.

WESTSIDE

The Westside, an imprecise, misshapen "L" sandwiched between Hollywood and the city's coastal communities, includes some of the Los Angeles's most prestigious neighborhoods, such as Beverly Hills, Bel Air, Brentwood, Century City, and Westwood. It's also home to West Hollywood, the primary center of gay life in L.A., and one of the city's best areas for shopping, eating, and nightlife.

Beverly Hills is roughly bounded by Olympic Boulevard on the south, Robertson Boulevard on the east, and Westwood and Century City on the west; it extends into the hills to the north. Politically distinct from the city of Los Angeles, this famously rich enclave is best known for its palm tree–lined streets of palatial homes and high-priced shops. But it's certainly not all glitz and glamour; the streets are crowded with a healthy mix of filthy rich, tourists, and wannabes that creates a unique—and sometimes bizarre—atmosphere.

West Hollywood is a key-shaped community (go ahead, look at your map) whose epicenter is the intersection of Santa Monica and La Cienega boulevards. It's bounded on the west by Doheny Drive and the south roughly by Melrose at its widest part; the tip of the key extends east for several blocks north and south of Santa Monica Boulevard as far as La Brea Avenue, but it's primarily located to the west of Fairfax Avenue. Nestled between Beverly Hills and Hollywood, this politically independent town can feel either tony or tawdry, depending on which end of the city you're in; but the oppressed appearance of some eastern areas is part of the authenticity of its distinctive urban-village feel. In addition to being home to the city's best restaurants, shops, and art galleries, West Hollywood is the center of L.A.'s gay community.

Impressions

I'm kind of excited because I just bought a house in the Hollywood Hills, which, it turns out, just slid into Bel Air, so it just quadrupled in value.
—Greg Kinnear, comedian and late-night talk show host

Bel Air and **Holmby Hills,** located in the hills north of Westwood and west of the Beverly Hills city limits, make up a wealthy residential area that is featured prominently on most maps to the stars' homes.

Brentwood, the world-famous backdrop for the O. J. Simpson melodrama, is really just a tiny, quiet, relatively upscale neighborhood with the typical L.A. mixture of homes, restaurants, and strip malls. It's west of I-405 and north of Santa Monica and West Los Angeles.

Westwood, an urban village that the University of California, Los Angeles (UCLA) calls home, is bounded by I-405, Santa Monica Boulevard, Sunset Boulevard, and Beverly Hills. The village is especially busy at night, when it sometimes seems as though half of L.A. has come here to catch dinner and a movie.

Century City is a compact and busy high-rise area sandwiched between West Los Angeles and Beverly Hills that bustles with businesses, shops, cinemas, and theaters. Once the backlot of 20th Century Fox, Century City is home to the Shubert Theatre and the outdoor Century City Marketplace shopping mall. It's a good, central place to locate, but it won't overwhelm you with personality. Its three main thoroughfares are Century Park East, Avenue of the Stars, and Century Park West; it's bounded on the north by Santa Monica Boulevard and on the south by Pico Boulevard.

West Los Angeles is a label that basically applies to everything that isn't one of the other Westside neighborhoods. It's basically the area south of Santa Monica Boulevard, north of Venice Boulevard, east of Santa Monica and Venice, and west and south of Beverly Hills and Century City.

THE BEACHES

These are my favorite L.A. communities. The 72-mile beachfront stretching from Malibu to Long Beach has milder weather and less smog than the inland communities, and traffic is nominally lighter—except on summer weekends, of course. The towns along the coast each have their own mood and charm; they're listed below from north to south.

Malibu, at the northern border of Los Angeles County, 25 miles from downtown, was once a privately owned ranch—purchased in 1857 for 10¢ an acre. Today its particularly wide beaches, sparsely populated hills, and relative remoteness from the inner city make it extremely popular with rich recluses. Indeed, the resident lists of Malibu Colony and nearby Broad Beach—oceanfront strips of closely packed mansions—reads like a who's who in Hollywood. With plenty of green space and dramatic rocky outcroppings, Malibu's rural beauty is unsurpassed in L.A. Except for the renowned J. Paul Getty Museum, Malibu is a cultural desert—but that's the whole idea.

Santa Monica, Los Angeles's premier beach community, is one of the most dynamic, fun, and pretty places in the entire city. The town is known for its long ocean pier, artsy atmosphere, and somewhat wacky residents. It's also noted for its particularly acute homeless problem. Santa Monica has the highest concentration of good restaurants in L.A. The town's Third Street Promenade, a pedestrian-only thoroughfare lined with great shops and restaurants, is one of the country's most successful revitalization projects. Main Street, which runs parallel to the ocean south to Venice, is also crammed with creative shops and eateries.

Venice, a planned community in the spirit of its Italian forebear, was constructed with a series of narrow canals connected by quaint one-lane bridges as its main arteries. With the discovery of oil in the 1940s, however, most of its canals were filled in and it was largely left to disrepair. The area has been infested with grime and crime, but gentrification is in full swing: There are scores of great restaurants and boutiques, the existing canals are lined with quaint homes and apartment duplexes, and real estate values are soaring. Some of L.A.'s most innovative and interesting architecture lines funky Main Street. Without question, Venice is best known for it's Ocean Front Walk, a sand-front sidewalk that's a nonstop circus of skaters, sellers, and posers of all ages, colors, types, and sizes.

Marina del Rey, just south of Venice, is a somewhat quieter, more upscale community that's best known for its small-craft harbor, one of the largest of its kind in the world. You can watch the boats negotiate their way through a maze of piers while strolling along the town's Restaurant Row, a waterfront path packed with an assortment of eateries.

Manhattan, Hermosa, and Redondo Beaches and Rancho Palos Verdes are all quiet residential neighborhoods with modest homes, mild weather, and easy parking. Other than excellent beaches for volleyballers, surfers, and sun-worshippers, there's not much about these relatively sleepy South Bay suburbs for visitors to get very excited about. When it comes to good restaurants or cultural activities, pickings in these parts are quite slim indeed. The drive to downtown can easily take 45 minutes.

Long Beach, one of America's busiest commercial ports, is also the fifth-largest incorporated city in California. True to its name, the city does in fact have a very long beach—$5^1/_2$ miles of sand—along with lots of restaurants and recreation, including tennis, golf, sailing, fishing, and boating. The city is best known as the permanent home of the *Queen Mary,* and for its nine-mile breakwater, an artificial rock jetty constructed in the twenties and thirties to create a calm harbor. Although there are some attractive areas, many of the neighborhoods are poorly maintained, and there's a decided dearth of cultural activities. On the plus side, Long Beach is well connected to downtown by the MetroRail, and the city is moving forward with a $650 million waterfront renovation.

THE VALLEYS

There are three distinct valleys surrounding the Los Angeles basin. To L.A.'s hipsters, visiting the valleys ranks right up there with root canals and the sound of nails scratching blackboards, but there's really lots worth seeing there, particularly in the San Fernando Valley and Pasadena, in the San Gabriel Valley.

The **San Fernando Valley,** known locally as *the* Valley, was nationally popularized in the eighties by the notorious mall-loving "Valley Girl" stereotype. About 1.5 million residents brave the Valley's oppressive summer heat (the average August high is 93.5 degrees) and smog that sometimes comes in designer colors. Snuggled between the Santa Monica and San Gabriel mountain ranges, most of the Valley, such as the communities of North Hollywood, Sherman Oaks, Encino, Tarzana, and Woodland Hills, is residential and commercial, and off the beaten tourist track. But there are some attractions that are bound to draw you over the hill: **Universal City,** located west of Griffith Park between U.S. 101 and Calif. 134, is home to Universal Studios and the trippy shopping and entertainment complex known as CityWalk. And you may make a trip to **Burbank,** just west of these other suburbs and north of Universal City, to see one of your favorite TV shows being filmed at NBC or Warner Bros. Studios. There are also a few good restaurants and shops along Ventura Boulevard in and around **Studio City.**

Glendale is a largely residential community north of downtown, sandwiched between the San Fernando and San Gabriel valleys. You'll find the city's best sightseeing cemetery, Forest Lawn, there.

The **San Gabriel Valley,** located northeast of downtown, is also largely residential. With the notable exception of Pasadena (see Chapter 11, "Easy Excursions from Los Angeles"), arts and entertainment opportunities are sorely lacking here; you could find more culture in a petri dish. The San Gabriel is a Death Valley of fine dining and, in summer, is dangerously laden with heavy wheeze-and-sneeze smog.

2 Getting Around

BY PUBLIC TRANSPORTATION

I've heard rumors about visitors to Los Angeles who have toured the city entirely by public transportation, but they can't be more than that—rumors. It's hard to believe that anyone can comprehensively tour Auto Land without a car of their own. Still, if you're in the city for only a short time, are on a very tight budget, or don't expect to be moving around a lot, public transport might be for you. The city's trains and buses are operated by the **Los Angeles County Metropolitan Transit Authority (MTA)** (425 S. Main Street, Los Angeles, CA 90013; ☎ **213/626-4455**). In addition to offering schedule and trip information, the MTA office publishes a handy pamphlet outlining about two dozen self-guided MTA tours, including visits to Universal Studios, Beverly Hills, and Disneyland. A second, more convenient MTA office is located in the ARCO Towers at 515 S. Flower Street.

BY BUS Spread-out sights, sluggish service, and frequent transfers make extensive touring by bus impractical. For short hops and occasional jaunts, however, buses are both economical and environmentally correct. Be sure to take a good book along to while away ride time (*War and Peace,* perhaps?).

The basic bus fare is $1.35 for all local lines, with transfers costing 25¢. Express buses, which travel along the freeways, and buses on intercounty routes charge higher fares; phone for information.

The **Downtown Area Short Hop (DASH)** shuttle system operates buses throughout downtown and the west side of L.A. Service runs every 5 to 20 minutes, depending on the time of day, and costs just 25¢. Phone the MTA for schedules and route information.

BY RAIL The **Metro Blue Line,** an underused aboveground rail system, connects downtown Los Angeles with Long Beach. Trains operate daily from 6am to 9pm; the fare is $1.35.

The **Metro Red Line,** L.A.'s first subway, opened in 1993 and currently covers just 4.4 miles, making five stops in the downtown area. The line begins at Union Station, the city's main train depot, and travels to Wilshire Boulevard and Alvarado Street in just seven minutes. The fare is 25¢. The Red Line will be extended to Hollywood and the San Fernando Valley by 1999.

The **Metro Green Line,** opened in 1995, runs for 20 miles along the center of the new I-105 Glenn Anderson (Century) Freeway, and connects Norwalk in eastern Los Angeles County to LAX. A connection with the Blue Line offers visitors access from LAX to the city's urban center.

Call the MTA for information on all Metro lines.

BY CAR

Need I tell you that Los Angeles is a car city? An elaborate network of freeways connects this incredible urban sprawl, and roads are generally well maintained. The golden rule of Los Angeles is this: Always allow more time to get to your destination than you reasonably think it will take, especially during morning and evening rush hours.

RENTALS Los Angeles is one of the cheapest places in America to rent a car. Although no self-respecting Angeleno would ever be caught dead in one, major national car-rental companies usually rent Geo Metros and similar tin cans for about $35 per day and $120 per week with unlimited mileage. If you're thinking of splurging, however, at the other end of the spectrum is **Budget Rent-a-Car of Beverly Hills** (9815 Wilshire Blvd., Beverly Hills; ☎ 310/274-9173) rents Mercedes, BMWs, and Porsches for up to $450 per day.

The best-known firms, with locations throughout the city, include Alamo (☎ 800/327-9633), Avis (☎ 800/331-1212), Budget (☎ 800/527-0700), Dollar (☎ 800/421-6868), General (☎ 800/327-7607), Hertz (☎ 800/654-3131), National (☎ 800/328-4567), and Thrifty (☎ 800/367-2277).

Most rental firms pad their profits by selling Loss/Damage Waiver (LDW), which usually costs an extra $9 per day. Before agreeing to this, however, check with your insurance carrier and credit- and charge-card companies; many people don't realize that they are already covered by either one or both.

For renters, the minimum age usually falls somewhere between 19 to 25. Some agencies have also set maximum ages. If you're concerned that these limits may affect you, ask about rental requirements at the time of booking to avoid problems later.

Finally, think about splurging on a convertible. Few things in life can match the feeling of flying along warm California freeways with the sun smiling on your shoulders and the wind whipping through your hair.

PARKING Parking space in L.A. is usually ample, but in some sections—most notably downtown and in Santa Monica, West Hollywood, and Hollywood—finding a space can be wrought with frustration. In most places you'll be able to find metered street parking— carry plenty of quarters. When you can't, expect to valet or garage your car for somewhere between $4 and $10. Many restaurants and nightclubs, and even some shopping centers, offer valet parking; they usually charge about $5. Most of the hotels listed in this book offer off-street parking, for which they charge up to $20 per day.

DRIVING TIPS Los Angeles has the most extensive freeway system in the world. In addition to a number, each freeway also has a name, or series of names, as it passes through various communities. See "Orientation," above, and its accompanying map for a listing of major highways and freeways, along with their locally known names.

Many Southern California freeways have designated car-pool lanes, also known as High Occupancy Vehicle (HOV) lanes. Some require two passengers, others three. The minimum fine for an HOV violation is $246.

When it comes to radio traffic reporter jargon, the names of L.A.'s freeways (as opposed to their numbers) are usually used. A "SigAlert" is the term used for an unplanned freeway crisis (i.e., a serious accident) that will affect the movement of traffic for 30 minutes or more. (They're named after Lloyd Sigmon, a traffic reporter in the 1950s.) When you hear "A big rig is blocking the number one lane," you can determine the lane by counting out from the center divider.

On surface roads, you may turn right at a red light (unless otherwise indicated) after making a complete stop and yielding to traffic and pedestrians. Pedestrians have the right-of-way at intersections and crosswalks.

BY TAXI

Distances are long in L.A., and cab fares are high; even a short trip can cost $10 or more. Taxis charge $1.90 at the flagdrop, plus $1.60 per mile. A service charge is added to fares originating at LAX.

Except in the heart of downtown, passing cabs will usually not pull over when hailed. Cab stands are located at airports, at downtown's Union Station, and at major hotels. To assure a ride, order a taxi in advance from **Checker Cab** (☎ 213/221-2355), **L.A. Taxi** (☎ 213/627-7000), or **United Independent Taxi** (☎ 213/483-7604).

BY BICYCLE

If you care about your life, you won't try to bicycle in the city as a means of transport. Traffic is heavy, and often you just can't get there by bike. Cycles are terrific for recreation, however, especially along the car-free beach bike path in Venice and Santa Monica. See "Outdoor Activities" in Chapter 7 for details.

FAST FACTS: Los Angeles

American Express   In addition to those at 327 N. Beverly Dr., Beverly Hills, and 901 W. 7th St., downtown, offices are located throughout the city. To report lost or stolen cards, call **800/528-4800.** To report lost or stolen traveler's checks, call **800/221-7282.**

Area Code   There are three area codes in Los Angeles. Most numbers—all of those east of La Cienega Boulevard, including Hollywood and downtown—are within the 213 code. Phone numbers west of La Cienega, including the city's beach communities, begin with a 310 area code. Many inland suburbs, including Pasadena and towns of the San Fernando Valley, are within the 818 calling area.

Baby-sitters   If you're staying at one of the larger hotels, the concierge can usually recommend a reliable baby-sitter. If not, contact the Baby-Sitters Guild (P.O. Box 3418, South Pasadena, CA 91031; ☎ **818/441-4293**). This company, in business since 1948, provides mature, bonded sitters, on call 24 hours.

Computer Rentals   PCR Personal Computer Rentals (5777 W. Century Blvd., Suite 110, Los Angeles, CA 90045; ☎ **310/417-3007** or 800/322-1001; fax 310/645-8765) rents laptops, printers, and peripherals on a short-term basis on short notice.

Dentists   Hotels usually have a list of dentists in case you need one. For other referrals, you can call the Los Angeles Dental Society (☎ **800/422-8338**).

Doctors   For referrals, you can contact the Los Angeles Medical Association (☎ **213/483-6122**), or call **800/922-0000** for a free, confidential physician referral.

Emergencies   For police, fire, highway patrol, or in case of life-threatening medical emergencies, dial **911.**

Library   Gutted by fire in 1986, the Los Angeles Central Library (630 W. 5th St.; ☎ **213/228-7000**) reopened in 1993 to become the third largest in America.

Liquor Laws   Liquor and grocery stores can sell packaged alcoholic beverages between 6am and 2am. Most restaurants, nightclubs, and bars are licensed to serve alcoholic beverages during the same hours. The legal age for purchase and consumption is 21; proof of age is required. In California you can purchase packaged liquor with your credit or charge card; most stores, however, usually have a minimum dollar amount for charging.

Newspapers/Magazines   The *Los Angeles Times* is a plump high-quality daily with strong local and national coverage, and meager international offerings. Its Sunday "Calendar" section is an excellent and interesting guide to the world of entertainment in and around L.A. The free weekly events magazine *L.A. Weekly* is packed with news of events and a calendar of happenings around town; it's available from sidewalk newsracks and in many stores and restaurants around the city. *Los Angeles Magazine* and *Buzz* are hip monthlies with good listings and entertainment news.

Melrose News, at the corner of Melrose and Martel avenues, is one of the city's best outdoor newsstands. World Book & News Co., at 1652 N. Cahuenga Boulevard, near Hollywood and Vine and Mann's Chinese Theater, is equally terrific. Located here for almost 70 years, the shop stocks lots of out-of-town and foreign papers and magazines. No one minds if you browse through the magazines, but you'll be reprimanded for thumbing through the newspapers. It's open 24 hours.

Police   See "Emergencies," above. For nonemergency police matters, phone **213/485-2121** or, in Beverly Hills, 213/550-4951.

Post Office   Call **213/586-1467** to find the one closest to you.

Radio Stations   There are literally dozens of radio stations in L.A. FM classical music stations include KCSN (88.5), KCPB (91.1), KUSC (91.5), and KKGO (105.1). Country music stations include KFOX (93.5), KIKF (94.3), and KFRG (95.1). Rock music stations include KUCI (88.9), KLOS (95.5), KLSX (97.1), and KROQ (106.7). The top AM news and information station is KNX (1070).

Taxes   The combined Los Angeles County and California state sales taxes amount to 8.25%; hotel taxes add another 14 to 17%.

Television Stations   All the major networks and several independent stations are represented. They are KCBS, Channel 2; KNBC, Channel 4; KTLA, Channel 5; KABC, Channel 7; KCAL, Channel 9; KTTV (Fox), Channel 11; and KCOP, Channel 13.

Time   Call for the correct time at **213/853-1212.**

Weather   Call Los Angeles Weather Information (☎ **213/554-1212**) to find out if the sun will ever stop shining.

5

Accommodations

In sprawling Los Angeles, location is everything. Choosing the right neighborhood as a base can make or break your vacation; if you plan to while away a few days at the beach but base yourself downtown, for example, you're going to lose a lot of valuable relaxation time on the freeway. For business travelers, choosing a location is easy: Pick a hotel near your work—don't commute if you don't have to. For vacationers, though, the decision about where to stay is a more difficult one. Take into consideration where you'll be wanting to spend your time before you commit yourself to a base. But, wherever you stay, count on doing a good deal of driving—no hotel in Los Angeles is convenient to everything.

In general, downtown hotels are business oriented; they're sometimes popular with groups, but are largely ignored by independent tourists. The top hotels here are very good, but cheaper ones can be downright nasty. If you're on a budget, locate elsewhere.

There are fewer hotels in Hollywood than the visitor would expect. The accommodations here, usually moderately priced, are generally well maintained but otherwise unspectacular. Hollywood is very centrally located between downtown and Beverly Hills, and it's within easy reach of Santa Monica. It's a great base if you're planning to do a lot of touring.

Most visitors stay on the city's Westside, a short drive from the beach and close to most of L.A.'s most colorful sights. The city's most elegant—and expensive—accommodations are in Beverly Hills and Bel Air; a few of the hotels in this neighborhood have become visitor attractions themselves. You'll find the city's best hotel values in West Hollywood, an exciting and convenient place to base yourself.

The relatively smogless coastal areas are understandably popular with visitors. Trendy Santa Monica and its neighbors are home to lots of hotels; book ahead, because they fill up quickly in the summer, when everyone wants to be by the water. Santa Monica also enjoys convenient freeway access to the popular tourist sights inland. Malibu and the South Bay communities (Manhattan, Hermosa, and Redondo beaches) are more out of the way, and hence quieter.

Families might want to head to the San Fernando Valley to be near Universal Studios, or straight to Anaheim or Buena Park for easy access to Disneyland and Knott's Berry Farm (see Chapter 11, "Easy Excursions from Los Angeles," for places to stay in the Anaheim area).

The hotels listed below are categorized first by area, then by price: under "Very Expensive," you'll find double rooms for more than $200; under "Expensive," doubles are $150 to $199; "Moderate" doubles are $100 to $149; and "Inexpensive" doubles are below $100. Rates given are the rack rates for a standard room for two with private bath (unless otherwise noted); you can often do better. Ask about weekend packages and discounts, corporate rates, family plans, and any other special rates that might be available. The prices given do not include state and city hotel taxes, which run from 14% to a whopping 17%. Be aware that most hotels make additional charges for parking (with in-and-out privileges, except where noted) and levy heavy surcharges for telephone use.

Most L.A. hotels have their own on-site health facilities; they can vary from a small room with just a few free weights to full-service spas. Hotels without facilities often have an arrangement with a nearby club, at which you can pay to use their facilities on a per-day basis; charges are usually $8 to $15.

All the top-quality, business-oriented chain hotels (including Four Seasons, Hilton, Hyatt, Sheraton, and Wyndham) offer rooms on exclusive "Club" or "Executive" floors, and most of the city's better hotels offer no-smoking rooms; these special rooms should be requested when making reservations.

Chain-operated toll-free numbers can also help you in your search for accommodations. These "800" numbers will save you time and money when inquiring about rates and availability. Best Western (☎ 800/528-1234), Days Inn (☎ 800/325-2525), Holiday Inn (☎ 800/465-4329), Motel 6 (☎ 800/437-7486), Quality Inn (☎ 800/228-5151), Ramada Inn (☎ 800/272-6232), and Travelodge (☎ 800/421-3939) all have locations in the Los Angeles area.

RESERVATIONS SERVICES

Several hotel reservations services offer one-stop shopping; they'll tell you what's available at many of L.A.'s hotels and book you into the one of your choice, all at no additional charge. These services are particularly helpful for last-minute reservations, when rooms are often scarce—or discounted. The following companies serve the L.A. area:

Central Reservation Service, 505 Maitland Ave., Suite 100, Altamonte Springs, FL 32701 (☎ 417/339-4116 or 800/548-3311; fax 407/339-4736).

Hotel Reservations Network, 8140 Walnut Hill Lane, Suite 203, Dallas, TX 75231 (☎ 214/361-7311 or 800/96-HOTEL; fax 214/361-7299).

1 Best Bets

- **Best Luxury Hotel:** The **Hotel Bel-Air** (☎ 310/472-1211 or 800/648-4097) wins my vote hands down. Nestled in eleven lush acres of private parkland, this opulent castle-away-from-home is an oasis in the middle of the urban jungle.

- **Best Historic Hotel:** While many might argue that the nearby Biltmore is L.A.'s grand dame, it can hardly match the comparative intimacy of the **Wyndham Checkers Hotel** (☎ 213/624-0000 or 800/996-3426). Rooms have all the modern amenities that you'd expect from a hotel of this caliber, but the hotel's cultural integrity— including an abundance of original 1927 detail—is intact, so much so that the Wyndham Checkers has been preserved by the city as a cultural landmark.

- **Best for Business Travelers:** The **Hyatt Regency Los Angeles** (☎ 213/683-1234 or 800/233-1234) is designed to meet the needs of today's business traveler. It has a central downtown location, a particularly well staffed business center, a state-of-the-art fitness club, and room service until midnight. Two floors of Regency Club rooms have dedicated concierges, and complimentary breakfast and afternoon cocktails are served to Regency Club guests.

- **Best for a Romantic Getaway:** If a luxurious oceanfront room at **Shutters on the Beach** (☎ 310/458-0030 or 800/334-0000) doesn't put a spring in your relationship, it's hard to imagine that any place will. Walk on the beach, watch the sun set over the Pacific, and order breakfast in bed from One Pico, Santa Monica's finest hotel restaurant.

- **Best Trendy Hotel:** The **Peninsula Beverly Hills** (☎ 310/551-2888 or 800/462-7899) is the hotel of the moment. Celebrities and industry insiders from around the globe have abandoned their long-standing allegiances to stalwarts like the Regent Beverly Wilshire in order to pow-wow at this new power spot. The Peninsula's more than a bit contrived, but what else would you sexpect from today's high-profile trendsetters?

- **Best for Families:** Because it's both close to the beach and the boardwalk and offers great summertime children's programs, the **Loews Santa Monica Beach Hotel** (☎ 310/458-0030 or 800/334-9000) tops our list as L.A.'s best family hotel.

- **Best Moderately Priced Hotel:** The well-maintained, double-decker **Casa Malibu** (☎ 310/456-2219 or 800/831-0858) has a terrific beachfront location and rates left over from more carefree days. I love Casa Malibu; it's L.A.'s best kept secret—until now, of course.

- **Best Budget Hotel:** The **Hotel del Capri** (☎ 310/474-3522 or 800/444-6835)isn't the cheapest hotel in town, but it's well located and a great buy in an expensive neighborhood. It's also very comfortable—more so than its rate card would suggest.

- **Best Alternative Accommodation:** The casual party atmosphere at **Banana Bungalow** (☎ 213/851-1129 or 800/4-HOSTEL) isn't for everybody, but if you're looking for an unusual place to hang your hat, this is it. Daily activities and free transportation to many of the city's top attractions make this the best place for fun-loving but frugal explorers.

- **Best Service:** The Regent hotel chain built its reputation on the quality of its service, and the tony **Regent Beverly Wilshire** (☎ 310/275-5200 or 800/421-4354) is one of its crown jewels. Stewards are at your service on every floor, and you can summon a butler at any time with the bell that sits beside your bed. The service is doting if you want it, discrete if you don't.

- **Best Location: Le Montrose Suite Hotel** (☎ 310/855-1115 or 800/776-0666), located in West Hollywood, gets marks not only for its convenience to restaurants, clubs, and attractions, but also for its manageable size—which means you won't have to wait forever for your car to be delivered from the valet.

- **Best Health Club:** The state-of-the-art health club at the Biltmore (☎ 213/624-1011 or 800/245-8673) is L.A.'s best hotel facility. It's packed with treadmills, StairMasters, Lifecycles, and other cardio and weight machines, as well as a full complement of free weights.

2 Downtown

VERY EXPENSIVE

The Biltmore

506 S. Grand Ave. (between 5th and 6th sts.), Los Angeles, CA 90071. ☎ **213/ 624-1011** or 800/245-8673. Fax 213/612-1545. 700 rms, 40 suites. A/C MINIBAR TV TEL. $215–$275 double; suites from $325. AE, CB, DC, EURO, MC, V. Parking $18.

Built in 1923, the historic—and opulent—Biltmore is considered the grand dame of L.A. hotels. During the 1930s and 1940s, the Academy Awards were held in the spectacular Crystal Ballroom—the first sketch of the Oscar statuette was scrawled on a linen napkin here—and the hotel was the top choice for presidents and the elite. You've seen the Biltmore in many movies, including *The Fabulous Baker Boys, Beverly Hills Cop,* and Barbra Streisand's *A Star is Born;* the Crystal Ballroom appeared upside down in *The Poseidon Adventure.*

The 11-story hotel sparkles with Italian marble and traditional French-reproduction furnishings, but the hotel's overall elegance has been compromised by an ugly office tower that was added in the mid-1980s. Still, the sense of refinement and graciousness endures, with a vaulted, hand-painted lobby ceiling, attentively decorated—though small—rooms with marble baths, and some enchanting Old World suites with lofty living rooms and nonworking fireplaces.

Dining/Entertainment: Bernard's features high-quality continental cuisine. Smeraldi's serves homemade pastas and lighter California fare. The sophisticated, velvet-wrapped Grand Avenue Bar showcases top-name jazz talent. Afternoon tea and evening cocktails are served in the lobby's stately Rendezvous Court.

Services: Concierge, 24-hour room service, dry cleaning, laundry service, newspaper delivery, nightly turndown, express checkout, valet parking.

Facilities: Beautiful, original 1923 tile-and-brass–inlaid swimming pool, state-of-the-art health club, Jacuzzi, sauna, well-staffed business center.

Sheraton Grande

333 S. Figueroa St. (between 3rd and 4th sts.), Los Angeles, CA 90012. ☎ **213/617-1133** or 800/325-3535. Fax 213/613-0291. 469 rms, 69 suites. A/C MINIBAR TV TEL. $200–$235 double; suites from $275. AE, CB, DC, DISC, EURO, MC, V. Parking $17.

The 14-story Sheraton Grande, with its magnificent smoky-mirrored facade, is located right in the heart of the downtown hustle. The airy, skylit lobby and lounge are as spacious and warm as the attractive guestrooms. A 1994 renovation updated already well chosen room furnishings and refurbished public areas. Floor-to-ceiling windows in every room offer impressive city views.

Dining/Entertainment: The gourmet California-style Scarlatti is helmed by chef Trey Foshee, formerly of Röckenwagner and Abiquiu. There's casual dining at the Back Porch, and a pianist performs daily in the lounge.

Services: Concierge, 24-hour room service, laundry service, nightly turndown, express checkout, valet parking.

Facilities: Four movie theaters, downtown's best heated outdoor pool, access to an off-premises health club, sundeck.

Wyndham Checkers Hotel

535 S. Grand Ave., Los Angeles, CA 90071. ☎ **213/624-0000** or 800/996-3426. Fax 213/626-9906. 188 rms, 15 suites. A/C TEL TV. $205 double; suites from $350. AE, DC, DISC, EURO, MC, V. Parking $18 Mon–Fri, $10 Sat–Sun.

The atmosphere at the Wyndham Checkers, a "boutique" version of the Biltmore across the street, is as removed from "Hollywood" as a top L.A. hotel can get. Built in 1927, the hotel is protected by the City Cultural Heritage Commission as a Historic Cultural Monument. It has the feel of a grand old home, with cozy (and freshly upgraded) public areas such as a wood-paneled library. The top-of-the-line accommodations are outfitted with oversize beds and coffeemakers.

Dining/Entertainment: Checkers Restaurant is one of downtown's finest dining rooms (see review in Chapter 6).

Services: Concierge, 24-hour room service, dry cleaning, laundry service, nightly turndown, express checkout, valet parking.

Facilities: Rooftop spa, heated lap pool, Jacuzzi, sundeck.

EXPENSIVE

Hyatt Regency Los Angeles

711 S. Hope St. (at 7th St.), Los Angeles, CA 90071. ☎ **213/683-1234** or 800/233-1234. Fax 213/612-3179. 484 rms, 40 suites. A/C TV TEL. $174–$234 double; suites from $225. AE, CB, DC, DISC, EURO, MC, V. Parking $13.50.

This 24-story Hyatt is one of the "anchors" of Broadway Plaza, a 35-store shopping complex in the heart of downtown near the Convention Center, the Music Center, and Dodger Stadium. This Hyatt is functional but sterile, outfitted like any other upscale chain hotel catering to the business traveler. Its most outstanding features are absolutely enormous windows that offer great views of downtown from every room. Two floors of Regency Club rooms come with dedicated concierges and complimentary breakfast and afternoon cocktails.

Dining/Entertainment: The Brasserie is nothing to write home about, but the view from the more opulent, distinctive Pavan will keep you lingering for hours.

Services: Concierge, room service (6am to midnight), laundry service, express checkout, valet parking.

Facilities: State-of-the-art fitness club, well-staffed business center.

Inter-Continental Los Angeles

251 S. Olive St., Los Angeles, 90012. ☎ **213/617-3300.** Fax 213/617-3399. 469 rooms. A/C TV TEL. $170–$200 double. AE, DC, DISC, EURO, MC, V. Valet parking $18.

Opened in 1992, this large, ultra-contemporary, 17-story hotel is the first to be constructed downtown in over a decade. Adjacent to the Museum of Contemporary Art and within walking distance of the Music Center, this member of the internationally prestigious Inter-Continental chain is the best-managed property in the neighborhood, run by a doting, eager-to-please staff. Conservatively styled, amenity-packed rooms boast floor-to-ceiling views and oversize baths with separate dressing areas. Public areas are decorated with works of art on loan from the Museum of Contemporary Art.

Dining/Entertainment: Two restaurants, one offering California cuisine (dinner only), the other serving more casual American fare all day.

Services: Concierge, 24-hour room service, dry cleaning, laundry service, newspaper delivery, nightly turndown, express checkout, valet parking.

Facilities: Large outdoor heated pool, small health club, sundeck, well-staffed business center.

New Otani Hotel and Garden

120 S. Los Angeles St. (at 1st St.), Los Angeles, CA 90012. ☎ **213/629-1200** or 800/421-8795, 800/273-2294 in California. Fax 213/622-0980. 434 rms, 15 suites. A/C MINIBAR TV TEL. $170–$230 double; Japanese-style suites from $340. Cultural packages available. AE, CB, DC, EURO, MC, V. Parking $11.

Most of the plush rooms in this anonymous 21-story concrete tower are Western style and comparable to other top downtown hotels in quality (and price). The best reason to stay here is to experience the New Otani's unique Japanese-style suites, outfitted with futons on tatami floors, Ofuro baths, and sliding rice-paper shoji screens. Hotel guests have exclusive use of the half-acre rooftop classical tea garden. One- and two-night Japanese Experience cultural packages include suite accommodations, sake and Japanese appetizers served at check-in by a kimono-clad waitress, dinner in any of the hotel's restaurants, shiatsu massages, and a live bonsai tree to take home with you.

Dining/Entertainment: There are two Japanese restaurants, one California-style dining room, and a coffee shop (fresh-baked breads and pastries are a specialty). The beautiful Garden Grill, a Tokyo-style Teriyaki grill featuring rare Japanese Kobe beef (which is beer-fed and massaged daily!). Chefs prepare seafood and prime steaks.

Downtown Area Accommodations & Dining

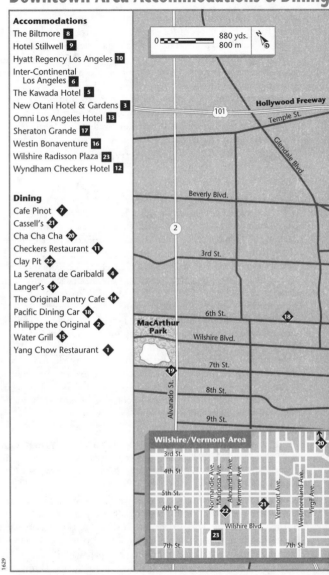

Accommodations

The Biltmore **8**
Hotel Stillwell **9**
Hyatt Regency Los Angeles **10**
Inter-Continental
  Los Angeles **6**
The Kawada Hotel **5**
New Otani Hotel & Gardens **3**
Omni Los Angeles Hotel **13**
Sheraton Grande **17**
Westin Bonaventure **16**
Wilshire Radisson Plaza **23**
Wyndham Checkers Hotel **12**

Dining

Cafe Pinot **7**
Cassell's **21**
Cha Cha Cha **20**
Checkers Restaurant **11**
Clay Pit **22**
La Serenata de Garibaldi **4**
Langer's **19**
The Original Pantry Cafe **14**
Pacific Dining Car **18**
Philippe the Original **2**
Water Grill **15**
Yang Chow Restaurant **1**

0 ┅┅┅┅ 880 yds.
        800 m

Hollywood Freeway
101
Temple St.
Glendale Blvd.
Beverly Blvd.
2
3rd St.
6th St.
18
MacArthur Park
Wilshire Blvd.
19
7th St.
Alvarado St.
8th St.
9th St.

Wilshire/Vermont Area
3rd St.
4th St.
Normandie Ave.
Mariposa Ave.
Alexandria Ave.
Kenmore Ave.
Vermont Ave.
Westmoreland Ave.
Virgil Ave.
5th St.
6th St.
20
21
22
Wilshire Blvd.
23
7th St.   7th St.

1629

Services: Concierge, room service (6am–11pm), same-day laundry service, nightly turndown, airport limousine service, valet parking.

Facilities: Japanese-style health club (with saunas, baths, and shiatsu massages). Golf and tennis are available at a nearby country club. Car rental desk, arcade with more than 30 shops.

Omni Los Angeles Hotel

930 Wilshire Blvd. (at Figueroa St.), Los Angeles, CA 90071. ☎ **213/629-4321** or 800/843-6664. 900 rms, 32 suites. A/C MINIBAR TV TEL. $167–$197 double; suites from $375. AE, CB, DC, EURO, MC, V. Parking $16.50.

Omni Hotels took over this huge hotel from the Hilton chain in 1995. It's still too early to tell what (if any) improvements will be made, but we can only hope that restyling will warm the impersonal lobby and utilitarian guest rooms, which seem to assume that all business travelers are strictly right-brained. The best rooms overlook the oval swimming pool. The hotel is centrally located, near many downtown attractions. The premium Towers rooms (on the 15th and 16th floors) offer separate check-in facilities, a dedicated concierge, and complimentary continental breakfast and afternoon cocktails.

Dining/Entertainment: Of the hotel's three restaurants, Cardini, serving northern Italian cuisine, is the only one worth staying in for. The popular City Grill serves breakfast and burgers.

Services: Concierge, room service (6am–11pm), dry cleaning, laundry service, express checkout, valet parking.

Facilities: Large outdoor heated pool, small cardio and weight room, sundeck, car rental desk, tour desk, beauty salon.

Westin Bonaventure

404 S. Figueroa St. (between 4th and 5th sts.), Los Angeles, CA 90071. ☎ **213/624-1000** or 800/228-3000. Fax 213/612-4800. 1,368 rms, 94 suites. A/C MINIBAR TV TEL. $175–$215 double; suites from $335. AE, CB, DC, EURO, MC, V. Parking $18.

The 35-story Bonaventure is the hotel that locals most love to hate. It's certainly architecturally unique: The hotel's five gleaming glass silos—like giant mirrored rolls of paper towels—constitute one of downtown's most distinctive landmarks. This is an enormous convention hotel, designed on the scale of a mini-city. The 6-story skylit lobby houses splashing fountains, gardens, trees, even a large lake. There's a tangle of concrete ramps and 12 glass-enclosed, high-speed elevators that appear to rise from the reflecting pools. Guest rooms begin on the 10th floor; each has a wall of windows offering good views, but are smaller than similarly priced rooms in the neighborhood. One of the towers is a completely remodeled all-suite facility where rooms come with an additional parlor room and half-bath. There's also an Executive Club level with upgraded facilities and services.

Dining/Entertainment: The rooftop Top of Five features panoramic views along with adequate, but not distinctive, continental cuisine. Ask for an exterior table, they're the only ones with the view. The views from the Bona Vista cocktail lounge are worth the price of a drink. There's nightly entertainment—jazz combos, cocktail-hour dancing—at the Sidewalk Cafe, a California bistro, and the adjacent Lobby Court.

Services: Concierge, 24-hour room service, nightly turndown, express checkout, valet parking.

Facilities: Large outdoor pool, sundeck, business center open Monday through Friday, conference rooms, car rental desk, five levels of shops and boutiques.

MODERATE

Wilshire Radisson Plaza

3515 Wilshire Blvd. (at Normandie Ave.), Los Angeles, CA 90010. ☎ **213/381-7411** or 800/333-3333. Fax 213/386-7379. 396 rms, 5 suites. A/C TV TEL. $120–$160 double; suites from $250. AE, DC, DISC, EURO, MC, V. Valet parking $10, self-parking $8.

Close to both Hollywood and downtown, this 12-story hotel is popular with business travelers for its push-button comfort and convenient location. The otherwise nondescript hotel earned a bit of notoriety during the 1981 World Series, when Yankees owner George Steinbrenner broke his hand and busted his lip in a supposed altercation with Dodger fans in the elevator; most people believe he did it to himself, through beating up the elevator in frustration over the third-game loss. The functional, modern rooms are attractively furnished; each has a glass-brick wall. One-and two-bedroom suites have two baths and a living room. There's a heated outdoor pool, a small fitness center, and a business center.

INEXPENSIVE

The Kawada Hotel

200 S. Hill St. (at 2nd St.), Los Angeles, CA 90012. ☎ **213/621-4455** or 800/752-9232. Fax 213/687-4455. 116 rms, 1 suite. A/C TV TEL. $74–$80 double; $145 suite. AE, DISC, EURO, MC, V. Parking $6.60.

This pretty, well-kept, and efficiently managed hotel is a pleasant oasis in the otherwise gritty heart of downtown. Behind the clean three-story, red-brick exterior are over a hundred pristine rooms, all with handy kitchenettes and simple furnishings. The rooms aren't large, but they're extremely functional, each outfitted with a VCR (movies are available free of charge) and two phones. No-smoking rooms are available. The hotel's lobby-level restaurant features an eclectic international menu all day.

Hotel Stillwell

838 S. Grand Ave. (between 8th and 9th sts.), Los Angeles, CA 90071. ☎ **213/627-1151** or 800/553-4774. Fax 213/622-8940. 250 rms. A/C TV TEL. $45–$60 double. AE, DC, EURO, MC, V. Parking $5.

It's far from fancy, but the Stillwell's modestly priced rooms are a good option in an otherwise expensive neighborhood. This relatively clean, basic hotel is conveniently located, close to the Civic Center, the Museum of Contemporary Art, and Union Station. Rooms are simply decorated; some are large enough for families. No smoking rooms are available. There are two lobby-level restaurants, a business center, and a tour desk.

3 Hollywood

MODERATE

Holiday Inn Hollywood

1755 N. Highland Ave. (between Franklin and Hollywood blvds.), Hollywood, CA 90028. ☎ **213/462-7181** or 800/465-4329. Fax 213/466-9072. 470 rms, 22 suites. A/C TV TEL. $100–$145 double; suites from $135. AE, DC, DISC, EURO, MC, V. Parking $5.50.

This 23-story hotel in the heart of Hollywood offers perfectly acceptable rooms that are both pleasant and comfortable—as long as you don't mind being on a busy thoroughfare and sharing the pavement with bikers, wannabe rockers, and the other colorful characters that

Hollywood Area Accommodations & Dining

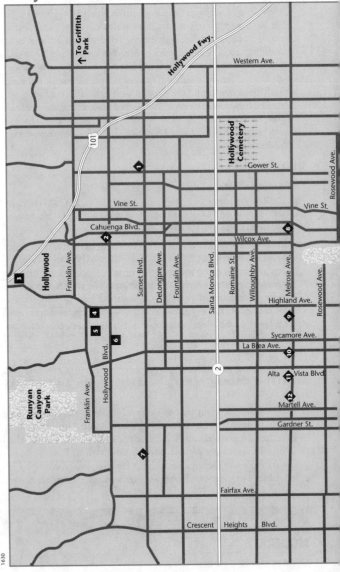

make up the neighborhood mélange. A major guest room renovation was completed in 1995, so the hotel's standard furnishings are now stain-free. Suites, which include small kitchenettes, are particularly good buys. There's a swimming pool, a sundeck, and a revolving rooftop restaurant.

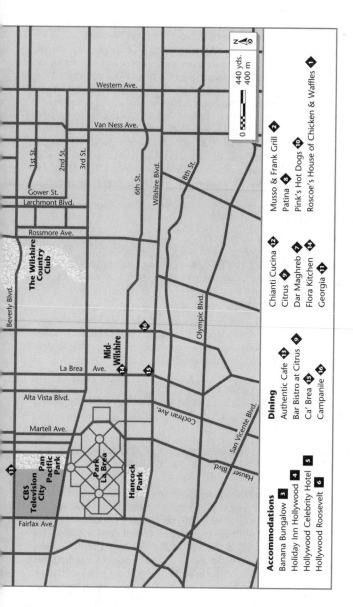

Dining
Authentic Cafe 13
Bar Bistro at Citrus 9
Ca' Brea 14
Campanile 15
Chianti Cucina 12
Citrus 9
Dar Maghreb 7
Flora Kitchen 11
Georgia 11
Musso & Frank Grill 2
Patina 8
Pink's Hot Dogs 10
Roscoe's House of Chicken & Waffles 1

Accommodations
Banana Bungalow 3
Holiday Inn Hollywood 4
Hollywood Celebrity Hotel 5
Hollywood Roosevelt 6

$ Hollywood Roosevelt

7000 Hollywood Blvd., Hollywood, CA 90028. ☎ **213/466-7000,** 800/950-7667, or 800/333-3333. 311 rms, 19 suites. $99–$110 double, suites from $150. AE, CB, DC, DISC, EURO, MC, V. Valet parking $9.50.

A movie-city landmark, this 12-story hotel is located on a slightly scary, very touristy part of Hollywood Boulevard, across from Mann's

Chinese Theatre and just down the street from the Walk of Fame. The Roosevelt (home to the first Academy Awards ceremony) was one of the city's grandest hotels when it opened its doors in 1927. But, like the starlets who once filled the lobby, its beauty faded; until a relatively recent nip-and-tuck, it seemed well on its way to Forest Lawn. The exquisitely restored two-story lobby features a Hollywood minimuseum. Rooms, however, are typical of chain hotels, far less appealing—in size and decor—than the public areas; but a few are charmed with their original 1920s-style bathrooms. Suites are named after stars who stayed in them during the glory days; some have grand verandas. High floors have unbeatable skyline views. David Hockney decorated the famous Olympic-size pool. The Cinegrill supper club draws locals with a zany cabaret show that's really worth staying in for.

INEXPENSIVE

Hollywood Celebrity Hotel

1775 Orchid Ave. (north of Hollywood Blvd.), Hollywood, CA 90028. ☎ **213/850-6464** or 800/222-7017, 800/222-7090 in California. Fax 213/850-7667. 38 rms. A/C TV TEL. $60–$65 double. All rates include continental breakfast. AE, CB, DC, DISC, EURO, MC, V. Free parking.

This small but centrally located hotel is one of the best budget buys in Hollywood. Located just half a block behind Mann's Chinese Theatre, it offers spacious, comfortable, art deco–style units. Breakfast is delivered to your door along with the newspaper every morning. Small pets are allowed, but a $50 deposit is required.

4 Westside

VERY EXPENSIVE

The Argyle

8358 Sunset Blvd., West Hollywood, CA 90069. ☎ **213/654-7100** or 800/225-2637. Fax 213/654-9287. 63 rms. MINIBAR TV TEL. $230 double; suites from $285. AE, CB, DC, EURO, MC, V.

Completed in 1929, this landmark 15-story hotel is one of the most pristine art-deco buildings in the city; it was designed in the Streamline Moderne style, with a gun-metal gray facade, rounded corners, and an intricate stepped pediment that's reminiscent of classical designs. It's also terrifically located, at the base of the Hollywood Hills between Beverly Hills and Hollywood. Formerly the St. James Club (and, before that, Sunset Tower), the hotel has been home to Jean Harlow, Errol Flynn, and John Wayne (who once kept a cow on his balcony so he could have fresh milk every day). More recently, it has made an appearance in *The Player*. Purchased in 1995 by the Lancaster Group (which owns the Jefferson in Washington and the Tremont in Chicago), the Argyle is slated for interior renovation and a dusty rose face-lift. Rooms are on the small side, but they're lovely, with deco reproductions and specially commissioned hand-crafted Italian furnishings, such as unique gondola-like beds. Corner rooms have marvelous rounded windows and spectacular city views.

Dining/Entertainment: Book a table at Fenix when you reserve your room. Ken Frank, one of the area's most respected restaurateurs, sold his celebrated French restaurant La Toque in order to cook here; it's likely to become one of the neighborhood's most prominent dining rooms.

Services: Concierge, 24-hour room service, laundry service, secretarial services.

Facilities: Heated outdoor pool, small exercise room with free weights and cardio machines, sundeck, car rental desk.

✪ Beverly Hills Hotel & Bungalows

9641 Sunset Blvd. (at Rodeo Dr.), Beverly Hills, CA 90210. ☎ **310/276-2251** or 800/283-8885. Fax 310/281-2905. 194 rms, 21 bungalows and garden suites. A/C TV TEL. $300–$350 double; bungalows from $300; suites from $595. AE, DC, EURO, MC, V. Parking $15.

After a $4^1/_2$-year, $100 million restoration, the Pink Palace is back. The famous stucco facade, impeccably landscaped grounds, and grand lobby have been restored to their former over-the-top glory, and then some: Despite declarations that the custom pink color has been painstakingly re-created, most everyone will tell you—myself included—that the hotel should now be known as the "Salmon Palace." Despite this controversy, the reborn hotel is glorious again. This is the kind of place where legends are made—and many were; this was center stage for deal—and star—making in Hollywood's golden days. Howard Hughes long maintained quite a complex here (he even kept a separate room for his personal food-taster). Dean Martin and Frank Sinatra once got into a big fistfight with other guests at the bar. In 1969, John Lennon and Yoko Ono checked into the most secluded bungalow under assumed names, only to station so many armed guards around their cozy hideaway that they might as well have put up a neon sign announcing their arrival. The stories go on and on. What attracted all the glitterati? For one thing, each other. Once you've arrived, this is where you stood in the proverbial spotlight and took your well-deserved bow. But the hotel has a lot of catching up to do after a $2^1/_2$-year absence: It's too early yet to tell if it will be able to regain its place as Hollywood's epicentral clubhouse again.

The hotel was reconfigured to compete in today's luxury market: The room count was reduced so that rooms could become more spacious. The new models come loaded with modern amenities, but the best original touches have been retained as well: A butler is at your service at the touch of a button. Gone is the sorry plumbing and tiny bathrooms of yesteryear; today's larger ones are outfitted with double Grecian marble sinks, TVs, and telephones for sink-side deal making. The bungalows are more luxurious than ever—and who knows who you'll have as a neighbor?

Dining/Entertainment: The iconic Polo Lounge, with the return of its original atmosphere and traditional comfort fare (like Dutch apple pancakes and its signature guacamole), hopes to regain its pre-closure popularity. The adjacent Polo Grill takes up the nouvelle torch, specializing in California cuisine. The famous Fountain Coffee Shop is back. The Tea Lounge is another new addition.

Westside Accommodations

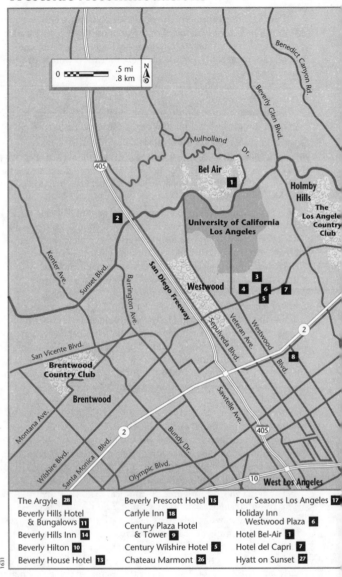

The Argyle **28**	Beverly Prescott Hotel **15**	Four Seasons Los Angeles **17**
Beverly Hills Hotel & Bungalows **11**	Carlyle Inn **18**	Holiday Inn Westwood Plaza **6**
Beverly Hills Inn **14**	Century Plaza Hotel & Tower **9**	Hotel Bel-Air **1**
Beverly Hilton **10**	Century Wilshire Hotel **5**	Hotel del Capri **7**
Beverly House Hotel **13**	Chateau Marmont **26**	Hyatt on Sunset **27**

Services: Concierge, 24-hour room service, dry cleaning, laundry service, nightly turndown, airport limo service, massage, valet parking.

Facilities: VCRs, Video rentals delivered to room, large outdoor heated pool, fitness room with cardio machines, Jacuzzi, sundeck, car rental desk, beauty salon, boutiques.

e Mondrian Hotel **29**	The Peninsula Beverly Hills **12**	Summerfield Suites **22**
e Montrose Suite Hotel **20**	Radisson Bel-Air Summit Hotel **2**	Sunset Marquis Hotel & Villas **24**
e Parc Hotel **23**	Ramada Limited Hotel **4**	Westwood Marquis Hotel & Gardens **3**
os Angeles West Travelodge **8**	Regent Beverly Wilshire **16**	Wyndham Bel Age Hotel **21**
ark Sunset Hotel **25**	San Vicente Inn **19**	

Beverly Hilton

9876 Wilshire Blvd. (at Santa Monica Blvd.), Beverly Hills, CA 90210. ☎ **310/
274-7777** or 800/445-8667. Fax 310/285-1313. 581 rms, 90 suites. A/C MINIBAR
TV TEL. $225–$275 double; suites from $300. AE, CB, DC, DISC, EURO, MC, V.
Parking $15.

Easily one of the best in the Hilton chain, this huge convention hotel, owned by Merv Griffin, has been attracting professionals—and a smattering of tourists—since 1955. The eight-story hotel is a self-contained mini city, complete with shopping mall, Olympic-size swimming pool, and indoor tennis and racquetball courts. It's been six years, though, since the hotel has seen a major renovation, and it's showing some wear. And beware: The cookie-cutter rooms are not all alike—only some have balconies and/or are decidedly larger than others.

Dining/Entertainment: It's hard to beat a pu-pu platter and a rum-spiked pineapple punch at the Polynesian-style Trader Vic's. This probably isn't the best place in Beverly Hills for dinner, but it's about the atmosphere, not the food. Grif's is best for Sunday brunch.

Services: Concierge, 24-hour room service, express checkout, valet parking.

Facilities: Two outdoor heated pools, small exercise room with cardio machines, sundeck, business center, shops.

Four Seasons Los Angeles

300 S. Doheny Dr. (at Burton Way), Los Angeles, CA 90048. ☎ **310/273-2222.** Fax 310/859-3824. 179 rms, 106 suites. A/C MINIBAR TV TEL. $310–$360 double; suites from $430. AE, DC, EURO, MC, V. Valet parking $8; free self-parking.

Four Seasons operates terrific hotels. As the unofficial superintendent of the monied elite, the ultraconservative Canadian chain can always be counted on for impeccable service and the highest standards. This means attention to the slightest details, top-quality food and decor, and a concierge that's famously well-connected. This 16-story hotel attracts both old money and new, so you'll see pin-striped financiers and rock stars sharing the elevator. Both groups favor the European art, bathroom TVs, and oversize private balconies. Guest rooms are sumptuous but nevertheless dull; their designs and muted colors won't win any style awards. And bathrooms have only single sinks, and bedrooms are devoid of stereos or VCRs—increasingly common accoutrements in deluxe hotels.

Dining/Entertainment: The Gardens is a terrific California-French restaurant that's often overlooked by locals; service and food are first rate, and Sunday brunch is worth leaving your room for.

Services: Concierge, 24-hour room service, overnight laundry, complimentary shoeshine, nightly turndown, valet parking.

Facilities: Large outdoor heated pool, small exercise room, Jacuzzi, sundeck, car rental desk, gift shop, florist.

✪ Hotel Bel-Air

701 Stone Canyon Rd. (north of Sunset Blvd.), Bel Air, CA 90077. ☎ **310/472-1211** or 800/648-4097. Fax 310/476-5890. 52 rms, 40 suites. $315–$435 double, suites $495–$2,500. AE, DC, MC, V. Parking $12.50.

"Hotel Bel" is your address when you want to impress. This Mission-style hotel is truly one of the finest—and most beautiful—hotels in Southern California. It regularly wins praise for its attentive service and luxurious rooms. The grounds—eleven acres of private park—are strikingly magical, lush with ancient trees, fragrant flowers, and a swan-filled pond. The welcoming, richly traditional public rooms are filled with fine antiques. Guest villas dot the property, decorated Mediterranean style, with compulsive attention to detail. Rooms and garden suites are equally stunning; all have two phones, a VCR, and a CD player. Some units have wood-burning fireplaces. The hotel is a natural for honeymooners and other celebrants.

Dining/Entertainment: It's worth having dinner at The Restaurant. Even if you're not staying, stop in for drinks at the cozy bar.

Services: Concierge, 24-hour room service, evening turndown, valet parking, welcome tea upon arrival.

Facilities: VCRs, large outdoor heated pool, health club with treadmills, StairMasters, Lifecycles, sundeck, nature trails.

The Peninsula Beverly Hills

9882 Little Santa Monica Blvd. (at Wilshire Blvd.), Beverly Hills, CA 90212. ☎ **310/551-2888** or 800/462-7899. Fax 310/788-2319. 162 rms, 48 suites. A/C MINIBAR TV TEL. $280–$425 double; suites from $500. AE, CB, DC, DISC, EURO, MC, V. Parking $17.

This is an excellent hotel that strives to be more opulent and personalized than its competition, but ends up feeling more than a bit contrived. The squat Renaissance-style hotel, fronted by a flower-hedged circular motorcourt, has a small, postcard-perfect lobby and large, luxurious rooms fitted with antiques, marble floors, and magnificent rugs. The best suites are in the two-story villas; they have their own fireplaces, spa tubs, and terraces.

Dining/Entertainment: Breakfast at the Belvedere is a tradition among agents and clients from nearby CAA. Insiders order the nowhere-on-the-menu banana-stuffed Brioche French Toast, topped with strawberries and powdered sugar. The restaurant also serves lunch and dinner. Light lunches are served seasonally on the 5th floor Roof Garden Terrace—a treat. There's a clublike cocktail lounge, and afternoon tea and cocktails are poured in the Living Room.

Services: 24-hour concierge, 24-hour room service, overnight dry cleaning, courtesy Rolls-Royce service in the area.

Facilities: Outdoor heated rooftop lap pool; tiny exercise room; Jacuzzi; a well-equipped day spa offering body treatments, saunas, and steam rooms; sundeck; business center; sundry shop.

✪ Regent Beverly Wilshire

9500 Wilshire Blvd. (east of Santa Monica Blvd.), Beverly Hills, CA 90210. ☎ **310/275-5200** or 800/421-4354. Fax 310/274-2851. 300 rms, 144 suites. A/C TV TEL. $255–$315 standard double; $335-$405 deluxe double; suites from $425. AE, CB, DC, DISC, EURO, MC, V. Parking $15.

If the Beverly Hills Hotel is where new money exhibits itself, then this is the place for seasoned sophisticates. But that doesn't mean that it hasn't seen its share of color: Actor Warren Beatty earned his playboy reputation while living here, and parts of *Pretty Woman* were filmed in one of the palatial suites. You just can't beat the location, close to Rodeo Drive shops and an easy cruise down Wilshire to just about anywhere else. Nobody lingers in the spacious, ornate lobby; tell your friends to meet you in the more private lounge. Rooms are refined, with a mix of period furniture, three phones, three TVs, and special double-glazed windows that ensure absolute quiet. Wilshire Wing rooms are unusually huge, but those on the Beverly side are prettier, and include balconies overlooking the pool. Bathrooms have an extra-deep soaking tub and a glass-enclosed shower that's large enough for two (or more). There's steward service on every floor and butlers can be called from a bedside bell.

Dining/Entertainment: The elegant dining room here—one of the hottest of the moment—is the only place on the Westside offering fine dining and live dance music. The Lounge, a European-style salon, serves a terrific tea from 3 to 5pm, light menus, and cocktails; at night, it's packed with media moguls and beautiful hangers-on.

Services: Concierge, 24-hour room service, overnight shoeshine, nightly turndown, express checkout, valet parking.

Facilities: Small outdoor heated pool, large health club with cardio and weight machines and free weights, hot tubs, sundeck, massage, business center, shops.

Sunset Marquis Hotel and Villas

1200 N. Alta Loma Rd. (one block south of Santa Monica Blvd.), West Hollywood, CA 90069. ☎ **310/657-1333** or 800/858-9758. Fax 310/652-5300. 9 rms, 96 suites, 12 villas. TV TEL. $215–$295 double; two-bedroom suites from $430; villas from $1,500. AE, DC, EURO, MC, V. Free parking.

This is the ultimate music-industry hostelry, regularly hosting the biggest names in rock. Sometimes they even record in the Mediterranean-style hotel's basement studios, retiring afterward to the lobby bar, where their session can be piped in directly. It's a short walk from rowdy Sunset Strip, but the hotel feels a world away, with lush gardens, koi ponds, exotic birds, and tropical foliage. Standard rooms are done in traditional motel style; they're not particularly special, just overpriced. But each comes with a sitting area and a good-size refrigerator. The private villas take hospitality to a totally different level—they even have their own baby grand pianos and butlers. This is where Mick stays.

Dining/Entertainment: The Whiskey is one of L.A.'s most exclusive bars; the likes of Axl Rose and Robert Plant turn it into a celebrity fest Wednesday through Saturday nights. Unless you're staying at the hotel, though, you'll probably never get in. Notes, a seafood and pasta restaurant, is nothing special.

Services: Concierge, room service, dry cleaning, laundry service, in-room massage, valet parking.

Facilities: VCRs, two outdoor heated swimming pools, small exercise room, health spa offering beauty treatments, Jacuzzi, sauna, sundeck, 24-hour business and message center, access to the hotel's 48-track/112-channel automated studio.

Westwood Marquis Hotel and Gardens

930 Hilgard Ave., Los Angeles, CA 90024-3025. ☎ **310/208-8765** or 800/ 421-2317. Fax 310/824-0355. 238 suites, 20 penthouse suites. A/C MINIBAR TV TEL. $220–$450 suite; penthouse suites from $475. AE, DC, DISC, EURO, MC, V.

This terrific all-suite hotel near UCLA, which attracts behind-the-scenes Industry types, offers accommodations that are straightforward without being boring. Hidden behind a severe concrete exterior, each stylish room is unique and loaded with amenities. The 15-story hotel underwent a major renovation in 1995; each suite was outfitted with multiline speakerphones and fresh textiles. South-facing suites have the best city and ocean views. Beware: The hotel can be noisy during graduation and other large school events.

Dining/Entertainment: The Garden Terrace serves breakfast, lunch, and Sunday champagne brunch; dinner is served in the Dynasty Room. There are cocktails and afternoon tea in the lounge, and cocktails and casual fare at the outdoor cafe.

Services: Concierge, 24-hour room service, dry cleaning, laundry service, nightly turndown, valet parking.

Facilities: Two outdoor heated pools, Jacuzzi, small fitness center, sundeck, flower shop, gift shop.

Wyndham Bel Age Hotel

1020 N. San Vicente Blvd. (between Sunset and Santa Monica blvds.), West Hollywood, CA 90069. ☎ **310/854-1111** or 800/434-4443. Fax 310/854-0926. 188 suites. A/C MINIBAR TV TEL. $200–$500 double. AE, CB, DC, EURO, MC, V. Parking $14.

Disguised as an ugly stucco apartment building, the Bel Age is actually one of West Hollywood's best luxury hotels, and an all-suite darling of the entertainment world. You've seen it pretty regularly on *90210*. The spacious, amenity-filled suites are fitted with dark pecan and rosewood retro furnishings. The best rooms face south; on a clear day, you can see all the way to the Pacific from their large balconies. The hotel was recently acquired by the Wyndham chain and is slated for a $5 million renovation—including an exterior face-lift—in 1996.

Dining/Entertainment: Make reservations long before check-in at the Franco-Russian Diaghilev (see review in Chapter 6). The Brasserie is less formal and offers great city views; its bar—which regularly draws top jazz performers—is one of the neighborhood's prettiest.

Services: Concierge, 24-hour room service, laundry service, valet parking.

Facilities: Rooftop outdoor heated pool, small fitness room, Jacuzzi, sundeck, hair salon, gift shop, art gallery, florist.

EXPENSIVE

Beverly Prescott Hotel

1224 S. Beverwil Dr. (P.O. Box 3065) (north of Pico Blvd.), Beverly Hills, CA 90212. ☎ **310/277-2800** or 800/421-3212. Fax 310/203-9537. 128 rms, 12 suites. A/C TV TEL. $145–$195 double; suites from $250. AE, DC, DISC, EURO, MC, V. Parking $12.

This hotel opened its doors in 1993, after a multimillion-dollar renovation that rendered the former Beverly Hillcrest unrecognizable. Managed by the Kimpton Group, owners of about a dozen top-quality "boutique" hotels in San Francisco, the Prescott is knowledgeably run and joyfully decorated; its comfortable, colorful, funky furnishings were carefully chosen by a confidently quirky designer. Thus, it was in perfect character for the hoteliers to commission legendary rock musician and neckwear designer Jerry Garcia to remodel one of the suites. The resulting Garcia Suite is surprisingly sedate, designed with fish themes, subtly psychedelic fabrics, a top-of-the-line sound system, and an eclectic art collection that includes a dozen pieces by Captain Trips himself. Each room has an oversize TV screen, cordless phones, and a private balcony with good city views.

Dining/Entertainment: Sylvie is not as good as the restaurant it replaced, but it's still worth staying in for.

Services: Concierge, 24-hour room service, overnight laundry/shoeshine, free morning newspaper, nightly turndown, massage and manicure services, complimentary shuttle service to nearby business centers and shopping.

Facilities: Large outdoor heated pool, fitness room with cardio machines, sundeck, business services.

Century Plaza Hotel and Tower

Ave. of the Stars (south of Santa Monica Blvd.), Century City, CA 90067. ☎ **310/277-2000** or 800/228-3000. Fax 310/551-3355. 1,072 rms, 76 suites. A/C TV TEL. $150–$220 double; suites from $350. AE, CB, DC, EURO, MC, V. Valet parking $18, self-parking $10.

This Westin-managed property is an imposing, 30-story high curved glass-and-concrete complex located on 10 of L.A.'s most centrally located acres, a former Twentieth Century Fox backlot. It's so close to film and TV's Century City nerve center that it has become the de facto home-away-from-home for countless rank-and-file industry execs and creative types. Because it's so huge, the hotel is also a natural for conventions and meetings; there's always something going on here. All this makes it the antithesis of warm and cozy, but rooms are large, the freeways nearby, and your anonymity is assured. Rooms on the Tower side are nominally nicer—and pricier—than those in the Hotel side. Tower suites are head and shoulders above Hotel ones.

Dining/Entertainment: The hotel has five restaurants and two lounges, but dine in only if you have to.

Services: Concierge, 24-hour room service, same-day laundry service, evening turndown, complimentary car service to and from Beverly Hills, valet parking.

Facilities: Two large outdoor heated pools, a children's pool, free access to an off-premises health club, three Jacuzzis, sundeck, business center, conference rooms, car rental desk, airline desk, ticket agency, tour desk.

✪ Chateau Marmont

8221 Sunset Blvd. (between La Cienega and Crescent Heights blvds.), West Hollywood, CA 90046. ☎ **213/656-1010** or 800/242-8328. Fax 213/655-5311. 63 rms, 53 suites, 4 bungalows. A/C TV TEL. $160 double; suites from $210; bungalows from $495. AE, CB, DC, EURO, MC, V. Free parking.

The Norman-style Chateau Marmont has been hosting film stars and Industry power brokers since its inception in the 1920s; it's now a historical monument. Greta Garbo regularly checked in as "Harriet Brown," and Howard Hughes maintained a suite here for a while; Jim Morrison was only one of the many to call this home in later years. Situated on a cliff just above the Sunset Strip, the hotel built its reputation on exclusivity and privacy, a posture that was shattered when

John Belushi overdosed in Bungalow No. 2. Chateau Marmont is popular because it's close to the Hollywood action and a luxurious world away at the same time. The standard rooms have views of the city and the Hollywood Hills; some have kitchenettes. Their faux English and formica furnishings are not too rustic—just enough that you'll enjoy their kitsch. Suites are large, and most come with cloth-canopied balconies. The poolside Cape Cod bungalows—large, secluded, cozy, with full kitchens—are some of the most coveted in town. The hotel's underutilized baronial living room is a wonderful place to sample the fruits of the famous wine cellar.

Services: Concierge, 24-hour room service, laundry service, nightly turndown.

Facilities: Large outdoor heated pool, small fitness room, sundeck.

Le Mondrian Hotel

8440 Sunset Blvd., West Hollywood, CA 90069. ☎ **213/650-8999** or 800/525-8029. Fax 213/650-5215. 224 suites. A/C MINIBAR TV TEL. $160–$200 suite. AE, CB, DC, EURO, MC, V. Parking $17.

You can't miss this hotel's monumental exterior, a 100,000-square-foot mural by Israeli artist Yaacov Agam. The work—indeed, the entire hotel—is a tribute to Dutch painter Piet Mondrian. The 12-story all-suite hotel—like Mondrian's art, designed with few curves and lots of primary colors—caters primarily to creative-type business travelers; it's often filled with New York advertising execs and a smattering of entertainment people. Upscale, functional, amenity-packed accommodations—dressed in solid colors, of course—have a crisp showroom quality. The hotel sits on the highest part of the Strip; on clear days, you can see all the way to the ocean.

Dining/Entertainment: The cafe is open all day, and the adjoining lounge presents live jazz nightly.

Services: Concierge, 24-hour room service, nightly turndown, voice mail, currency exchange.

Facilities: Heated outdoor pool, well-equipped fitness center, sauna, steam room, whirlpool, sundeck.

⑤ Le Montrose Suite Hotel

900 Hammond St., West Hollywood, CA 90069. ☎ **310/855-1115** or 800/776-0666. Fax 310/657-9192. 37 junior suites, 60 executive suites, 13 one-bedroom suites. $145–$195 suite. AE, CB, DC, EURO, MC, V. Parking $17.

Nestled on a quiet residential street just two blocks from the bustling Strip, this all-suite hotel features large one-bedroom apartments that feel more like upscale condos than standard hotel rooms. Each has a large bedroom, kitchen, and bathroom, as well as a sizable sunken living room complete with gas fireplace, fax machine, and Nintendo games. You have to go up to the roof for anything resembling a view, but once you're up there, you can swim in the pool or play on the lighted tennis court. For location, quality, and price, this is one of L.A.'s best values. Le Montrose is currently constructing an on-site music and sound studio in order to attract music industry clientele; let's hope that when this place catches on, prices will stay reasonable and reservations won't be hard to come by.

Dining/Entertainment: The Library Restaurant serves continental meals all day. Light bites are served poolside.

Services: Concierge, room service (7am–10:45pm), nightly turn-down, voice mail, currency exchange.

Facilities: VCRs, video library, outdoor heated pool, small exercise room, Jacuzzi, sauna, sundeck, one lighted tennis court, complimentary bicycles.

Summerfield Suites

1000 Wesmount Dr. (one block west of La Cienega Blvd.), West Hollywood, CA 90069. ☎ **310/657-7400.** Fax 310/854-6744. 103 suites. A/C TV TEL. $149–$199 suite. AE, CB, DC, EURO, MC, V. Parking $8.

Situated in a residential West Hollywood neighborhood, this all-suite property (formerly known as Le Dufy Hotel de Luxe) looks and feels much like a high-quality apartment building. A relatively unassuming interior and quiet public areas are hallmarks of value—less flash for less cash. Likewise, accommodations are detailed and plush without being excessive in either size or style. Most of the pastel-paletted suites have sunken living rooms, gas fireplaces, contemporary furnishings, and petite balconies overlooking Hollywood or Beverly Hills. All have kitchenettes and pretty good original art.

Dining/Entertainment: There's a California-style cafe with an adjacent bar.

Services: Concierge, room service (7am–11pm), laundry service, newspaper delivery.

Facilities: Outdoor heated pool, small exercise room with cardio machines, rooftop Jacuzzi, sauna, sundeck.

MODERATE

Beverly Hills Inn

125 South Spalding Dr., Beverly Hills, CA 90212 ☎ **310/278-0303** or 800/463-4466. Fax 310/273-6614. 52 rms. 11 suites. $110–$160 double; suites from $160. All rates include breakfast. AE, DC, EC, EURO, MC, V. Free parking.

Once the nondescript Beverly Crest Hotel—so dull that you could pass it a hundred times without ever noticing it—this property underwent an enormous year-long renovation and reopened in 1995; it's now a terrific place to stay. The Beverly Hills Inn is well located, within walking distance of both Rodeo Drive and Century City. Rooms are thoughtfully designed in a slightly Asian style. They tend to be on the small side, but you get what you pay for here; prices go up for the larger rooms. The best accommodations overlook the pool and courtyard; those on the other side can keep an eye on their cars in the parking lot. Every room has a refrigerator. There's a sauna and exercise room, and a small bar aptly named the Garden Hideaway. At press time, a new bar and restaurant were scheduled to open shortly.

☉ Carlyle Inn

119 S. Robertson Blvd. (south of Wilshire Blvd.), Los Angeles, CA 90035. ☎ **310/275-4445** or 800/322-7595. Fax 310/859-0496. 32 rms, 10 suites. A/C MINIBAR TV TEL. $95–$140 double; $160 suite. AE, DC, DISC, EURO, MC, V. Free parking.

Hidden on an uneventful stretch of Robertson Boulevard, just south of Beverly Hills, this four-story inn is one of the best-priced finds in Los Angeles. The hotel's exceedingly clever design has transformed an ordinary square lot in a high-density district into an delightfully airy hostelry. Despite its small size and unlikely location, architects have managed to create a multistory interior courtyard, which almost every room faces. Well-planned, contemporary interiors are fitted with recessed lighting, deco wall lamps, pine furnishings, and well-framed classical architectural monoprints. Amenities include coffeemakers and VCRs. The hotel's primary drawback is that it lacks views; curtains must remain drawn at all times to maintain any sense of privacy. Suites are only slightly larger than standard rooms.

Holiday Inn Westwood Plaza

10740 Wilshire Blvd. (at Selby Ave.), Los Angeles, CA 90024. ☎ **310/475-8711** or 800/472-8556. Fax 310/475-5220. 295 rms, 8 suites. A/C MINIBAR TV TEL. $130-$140 double; suites from $225. AE, CB, DC, DISC, EURO, MC, V. Free parking.

This is your standard Holiday Inn, with a good Westwood location and comfortable guest rooms that were updated in late 1994. Special touches include marble sinks and complimentary morning newspapers delivered to your door. The hotel also provides complimentary shuttle service to anyplace within a $2^1/_2$-mile radius. There's a large outdoor heated pool, exercise room with cardio machines, sauna, Jacuzzi, sundeck, car rental desk, tour desk, and gift shop. Cafe Le Dome is best known for its cocktail lounge; it's popular with the basketball and football players who frequently stay here.

Hyatt on Sunset

8401 Sunset Blvd. (two blocks east of La Cienega Blvd.), West Hollywood, CA 90069. ☎ **213/656-1234** or 800/233-1234. Fax 213/650-7024. 262 rms, 28 suits. A/C TV TEL. $140-$160 double; $350-$550 suite. Special weekend rates available. AE, CB, DC, DISC, EURO, MC, V. Parking $10.

This aging 13-story chain hotel is favored by newly signed rock bands and other Industry types for its Sunset Strip location: close to Tower Records, the Whiskey A-Go-Go, The Roxy, and Spago. Except for its art deco lobby, there's nothing exceptional here. The rectangular rooms are spacious; some have private balconies, and those on high floors enjoy skyline views. There's a heated rooftop swimming pool, business center, and room service from 6am to midnight. There's a restaurant and a sports bar/deli that serves sandwiches and pastas.

Le Parc Hotel

733 N. West Knoll Dr., West Hollywood, CA 90069. ☎ **310/855-8888** or 800/5-SUITES. Fax 310/659-7812. 154 suites. A/C TV TEL. $105-$165 suite. AE, DC, EURO, MC, V. Parking $10.

Situated on a quiet residential street, Le Parc is a high-quality all-suite hotel with a pleasantly mixed clientele. Designers stay here because it's a few minutes' walk to the Pacific Design Center; patients and medical consultants check in because it's close to Cedars-Sinai Medical Center; and tourists enjoy being near Farmer's Market and Museum Row. The nicely furnished, apartment-like units each have a kitchenette, dining area, living room with fireplace, and balcony.

There's a swimming pool, a basketball hoop, and a tennis court (recently resurfaced and lit for night play) on the roof. What this hotel lacks in cachet it more than makes up for in value. Although your L.A. friends may not have heard of this place, they'll be impressed when you invite them up for drinks. Request one of their 50 newly updated suites.

Radisson Bel-Air Summit Hotel

11461 Sunset Blvd., Los Angeles, CA 90049. ☎ **310/476-6571** or 800/333-3333. Fax 310/471-6310. 162 rms, 6 suites. A/C MINIBAR TV TEL. $129–$179 double; suites from $189. AE, CB, DC, DISC, EURO, MC, V. Parking $5.

This two-story hotel on eight garden acres has one thing going for it: location, location, location. It's just minutes away from Beverly Hills, Brentwood, Westwood Village, and Century City. Otherwise, it's the standard chain-hotel fare: conservatively styled rooms and suites that are spacious, airy, and comfortably fitted with furniture that was obviously purchased in bulk; each has a large balcony. Suites were substantially updated in 1995. The hotel has a heated swimming pool, a single unlit tennis court, a recently renovated lobby restaurant and bar, and an advanced facial salon, Hathaway Renewal Center.

INEXPENSIVE

⑤ Banana Bungalow

2775 Cahuenga Blvd. (north of U.S. 101), West Hollywood, CA 90068. ☎ **213/851-1129** or 800/4-HOSTEL. Fax 213/851-2022. 200 beds, 25 doubles. $40 double; $15 per person in multibed room. EURO, MC, V. Free parking.

If you're under 35, this is a great choice. It's probably the most fun place to stay in the city; it's often filled with international guests and the atmosphere is always upbeat. Nestled in the Hollywood Hills a short drive from the Walk of Fame and Universal Studios, Banana Bungalow has double and multishare rooms, kitchen facilities, a restaurant, a lounge, a movie theater, and an arcade/game room. The hostel offers free airport pickup and regular excursions to the beach, Disneyland, and other L.A.–area destinations. Last time I was there, a huge beer party was going on by the swimming pool, complete with a rock band.

Beverly House Hotel

140 S. Lasky Dr., Beverly Hills, CA. ☎ **310/271-2145** or 800/432-5444. Fax 310/276-8431. 50 rms. A/C. $88–$98 double. All rates include breakfast. AE, CB, EURO, MC, V. Free parking.

This is a small, clean, and quiet bed-and-breakfast–style hotel situated in the heart of Beverly Hills, an easy walk from restaurants, fashionable shops, and department stores. The rooms are charming enough to warrant a brief stay, but you wouldn't want to live in them. They're on the small side, but big enough to accommodate a king bed, a table, and two chairs. A few of the bathrooms have stall showers only. Continental breakfast is served in a pleasant dining room.

⑤ Hotel del Capri

10587 Wilshire Blvd. (at Westholme Ave.), Los Angeles, CA 90024. ☎ **310/474-3511** or 800/444-6835. Fax 310/470-9999. 36 rms, 45 suites. A/C TV TEL.

🏨 Family-Friendly Accommodations

The highest concentration of family-friendly accommodations—those that make families with kids their primary concern—are found close to Disneyland (see "Anaheim" in Chapter 11, below). That doesn't mean that families aren't welcome in L.A. hotels—in fact, a few welcome kids with open arms.

Loews Santa Monica Beach Hotel *(see p. 76)* offers comprehensive children's programs throughout the summer. More like a resort than any other L.A. hotel, Loews boasts an unbeatable location; it's right by the beach and the boardwalk. What more could make the kids happy? They also offer baby-sitting services, so you can enjoy a kid-free evening on the town.

Century Plaza Hotel and Tower *(see p. 70)* offers spacious, family-sized rooms and lots of facilities, including a children's pool adjacent to the two larger ones. Because it's a veritable city unto itself, older kids love to explore this labyrinthine hotel.

The **Sheraton Universal** *(see p. 84)* enjoys a terrifically kid-friendly location, adjacent to Universal Studios and the enormously fun CityWalk mall. Baby-sitting services are available and there's a large game room on the premises.

Le Parc Hotel *(see p.73),* **Le Mondrian Hotel** *(see p. 71)*, and **Le Montrose Suite Hotel** *(see p. 71)* are fairly comparable all-suite hotels centrally located in West Hollywood. Multiple rooms means privacy for parents, and kitchenettes can cut down on restaurant and room-service bills.

$85–$105 double; suites from $110. Rates include continental breakfast. AE, CB, DC, EURO, MC, V. Free parking.

The del Capri is one of the best values in trendy Westwood. This well-located and fairly priced hotel is popular with tourists, business travelers, and parents visiting their UCLA offspring. There are two parts to the property: a four-story building on the boulevard, and a quieter two-story motel that surrounds a kidney-shaped swimming pool. Each unit is slightly different from the next, but all are of good quality and have electrically adjustable beds—a decidedly novel touch. The more expensive rooms are slightly larger, and have whirlpool baths and an extra phone in the bathroom. Most of the suites have kitchenettes. The hotel provides free shuttle service to nearby shopping and attractions in Westwood, Beverly Hills, and Century City.

Park Sunset Hotel

8462 Sunset Blvd., West Hollywood, CA 90069. ☎ **213/654-6470** or 800/821-3660. Fax 213/654-6470, ext. 555. 84 rms, 20 suites. A/C TV TEL. $75–$80 double; $150 suite. AE, CB, DC, DISC, EURO, MC, V. Valet parking $5.

You would think that the Park Sunset's location—right on the Strip—would make this one of the noisiest places to sleep in L.A. But all the guest rooms are in the back of the modest three-story hotel, away from the cars and cacophony. The rooms are well kept and surprisingly well decorated; some have balconies and/or kitchens, and corner rooms have panoramic city views. There's a small heated pool in a lush courtyard, and a Thai restaurant on the lobby level.

San Vicente Inn

837 N. San Vicente Blvd., West Hollywood, CA 90069. ☎ **310/854-6915.** 9 rms, 4 suites. TV TEL. $78–$98 double; suites from $89. All rates include breakfast. AE, CB, DC, EURO, MC, V. Free parking.

West Hollywood's only bed-and-breakfast caters to a gay clientele. It's a thoroughly charming place, with rooms that are individually and cozily decorated. Some rooms have kitchens, but you won't really need one; lots of restaurants (and shops and bars) are just steps away. Guests have use of the garden patio and swimming pool.

Century Wilshire Hotel

10776 Wilshire Blvd. (between Malcolm and Selby aves.), Los Angeles, CA 90024. ☎ **310/474-4506** or 800/421-7223 (outside CA). Fax 310/474-2535. 100 rms, 58 suites. TV TEL. $85 double; $95 junior suite; $125-$150 one-bedroom suite. All rates include continental breakfast. AE, CB, DC, EURO, MC, V. Free parking.

The units here are large, sparsely decorated, and well located, near UCLA and Beverly Hills. Most of the rooms in this three-story hotel have kitchenettes, and some have French doors that open onto balconies. The hotel surrounds a quiet courtyard and has an Olympic-size swimming pool. Breakfast is served each morning either inside or out in the courtyard. For the money, it's hard to do better in Westwood.

Los Angeles West Travelodge

10740 Santa Monica Blvd. (at Overland Ave.), Los Angeles, CA 90025. ☎ **310/ 474-4576.** Fax 310/470-3117. 36 rms. A/C TV TEL. $66–96 double. AE, CB, DC, EURO, MC, V. Free parking.

This clean and friendly establishment offers good value in a high-priced area. The pleasant, modern rooms come with coffeemakers and refrigerators, and there's an enclosed, heated swimming pool with a sundeck.

Ramada Limited Hotel

1052 Tiverton Ave. (near Glendon Ave.), Los Angeles, CA 90024. ☎ **310/208-6677** or 800/631-0100. Fax 310/824-3732. 36 rms, 6 suites. A/C TV TEL. $66–$76 double; suites from $96. AE, CB, DC, DISC, EURO, MC, V. Free parking.

This place isn't a fancy place by any stretch of the imagination, but the rooms are comfortable and have recently been updated. Some have stoves, refrigerators, and stainless-steel countertops; others have microwave ovens. Bathrooms have marble vanities. Facilities include an exercise room, a lounge, and an activities desk.

5　The Beaches

VERY EXPENSIVE

Loews Santa Monica Beach Hotel

1700 Ocean Ave. (south of Colorado Blvd.), Santa Monica, CA 90401. ☎ **310/ 458-6700** or 800/223-0888. Fax 310/458-6761. 349 rms, 22 suites. A/C MINIBAR

TV TEL. $215–$265 double; suites from $305. AE, CB, DC, EURO, MC, V. Valet parking $15, self-parking $13.

If it weren't for Shutters, this would be the finest hotel in Santa Monica. Loews isn't exactly beachfront; it's on a hill less than a block away, but the unobstructed ocean views are fabulous. Terrific location aside, this is still a great hotel. A dramatic, multistory glass and green-steel atrium lobby gives way to ample cookie-cutter rooms that are out-fitted with the latest luxury-hotel amenities. This popular hotel doesn't need my recommendation to stir business; the hotel has become some-thing of a darling for Industry functions, and it's booked to capacity in the summer months.

Dining/Entertainment: There are two restaurants and poolside snack service. A pianist performs in the lounge nightly. Comedians often perform on Sunday nights (admission is $6).

Services: Concierge, 24-hour room service, overnight shoeshine, nightly turndown, baby-sitting, valet parking.

Facilities: VCRs on request, outdoor heated pool, Jacuzzi, fitness center with cardio machines, summer children's program, business center, bike and roller skate rental.

Miramar Sheraton Hotel

101 Wilshire Blvd. (between Ocean Ave. and 2nd St.), Santa Monica, CA 90401. ☎ 310/576-7777 or 800/325-3535. Fax 310/458-7912. 301 rms, 61 suites. A/C MINIBAR TV TEL. $195–$225 double; suites from $275. AE, CB, DC, EURO, MC, V. Parking $11.

Miramar is Spanish for "ocean view"—perched on a cliff above Santa Monica Beach, that's just what this 10-story hotel offers. It was origi-nally built in the 1920s; even after an extensive and beautiful 1994 renovation, the elegance of that era remains. The approach is particu-larly impressive: Wrought-iron gates open to a majestic Moreton Bay fig tree. Inside, the spacious rooms have been thoughtfully redecorated; they feel classically stylish and contemporary at the same time. Top floors have great views of the bay clear to Malibu. The lush gardens and pretty pool area have led some to refer to the Miramar as the "little Beverly Hills Hotel by the beach."

Dining/Entertainment: The Miramar Grille, a California-style bistro, is open for lunch and dinner; a cafe serves casual fare all day.

Services: Concierge, 24-hour room service, same-day laundry service, complimentary newspaper, nightly turndown, valet parking.

Facilities: Large outdoor heated pool, small health center, sundeck, bicycle rental, car rental desk, beauty salon, gift shop, women's boutique.

✪ Shutters on the Beach

1 Pico Blvd. (at the beach), Santa Monica, CA 90405. ☎ 310/458-0030 or 800/334-9000. Fax 310/458-4589. 186 rms, 12 suites. MINIBAR TV TEL. $230–$350 double; suites from $550. AE, DC, DISC, EURO, MC, V. Parking $15.

Light and luxurious Shutters enjoys one of the city's most prized locations: directly on the beach (this is the only fine hotel to enjoy such a distinction in L.A.), one block from Santa Monica Pier. Opened in 1993, the gray-shingled hotel, designed to optimize its costly real

Accommodations at the Beaches

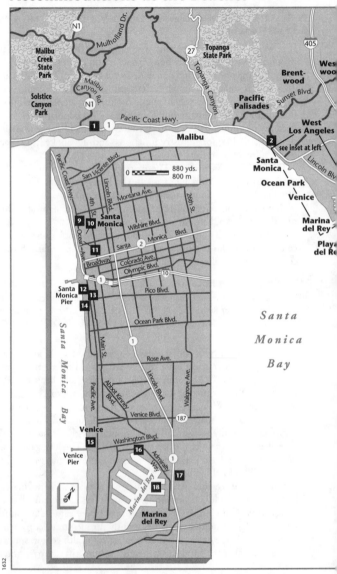

estate, is divided into two parts separated by a small pool: squat beachfront cottagelike accommodations and a taller tower. Although the beach-cottage rooms are plainly more desirable, when it comes to rates, the hotel doesn't distinguish between them. The views and sounds of the ocean are the most outstanding qualities of the rooms, some of which have fireplaces and Jacuzzis; all have floor-to-ceiling windows that open. Showers come with waterproof radios, toy duckies,

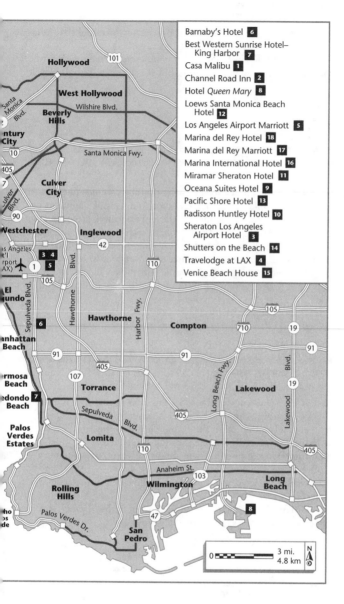

Barnaby's Hotel **6**

Best Western Sunrise Hotel– King Harbor **7**

Casa Malibu **1**

Channel Road Inn **2**

Hotel *Queen Mary* **8**

Loews Santa Monica Beach Hotel **12**

Los Angeles Airport Marriott **5**

Marina del Rey Hotel **18**

Marina del Rey Marriott **17**

Marina International Hotel **16**

Miramar Sheraton Hotel **11**

Oceana Suites Hotel **9**

Pacific Shore Hotel **13**

Radisson Huntley Hotel **10**

Sheraton Los Angeles Airport Hotel **3**

Shutters on the Beach **14**

Travelodge at LAX **4**

Venice Beach House **15**

and biodegradable bath supplies. Despite this welcome whimsy, there's a relaxed and elegant atmosphere throughout the contemporary art–filled hotel.

Dining/Entertainment: One Pico, the hotel's premier restaurant, is very well regarded. The best meals at the more casual Pedals are prepared on the wood-burning grill. The overdesigned Handle Bar offers good happy-hour specials.

Services: Concierge, 24-hour room service, overnight laundry, evening turndown, in-room massage, valet parking.

Facilities: VCRs, outdoor heated pool, exercise room with cardio machines, Jacuzzi, sauna, sundeck, beach equipment rental, bicycle rental.

EXPENSIVE

Barnaby's Hotel

3501 Sepulveda Blvd. (at Rosecrans), Manhattan Beach, CA 90266. ☎ **310/ 545-8466** or 800/552-5285. 126 rms. A/C. $159–$200 double. AE, DC, DISC, EURO, MC, V. All rates include breakfast. Valet parking $4.

The most unusual hotel on the coast, Barnaby's sounds like a guest house, operates like a bed-and-breakfast, and feels like a quaint old hotel. The hotel's stuccoed pink facade and trademark green awnings give way to European-styled guest rooms; each is uniquely decorated with antique headboards, lace curtains, and 19th-century prints. The best rooms are in back and overlook the courtyard, where weddings and other functions are held. Romantic Barnaby's is an excellent place for couples and celebrants. Full English breakfasts are served buffet style.

Services: Complimentary airport service.

Facilities: Glass-enclosed heated pool and Jacuzzi, sundeck.

Los Angeles Airport Marriott

Century Blvd. (at Airport Blvd.), Los Angeles, CA 90045. ☎ **310/641-5700** or 800/ 228-9290. Fax 310/337-5358. 1,020 rms, 19 suites. A/C TV TEL. $150–$175 double; suites from $375. AE, CB, DC, DISC, EURO, MC, V. Parking $9.

Built in 1973 and renovated in 1987, this is no cutting-edge hotel, but it's a good airport choice. The hotel is designed for travelers on the fly; there's a laundry room, and ironing boards, irons, and hairdryers are available for use. Rooms are cheerfully decorated.

Dining/Entertainment: There are two serviceable restaurants and a coffee shop.

Services: Concierge, room service, complimentary airport limousine service.

Facilities: Giant outdoor heated pool, swim-up bar, Jacuzzi, garden sundeck, business center, car rental desk, tour desks.

Marina del Rey Hotel

13534 Bali Way (west of Lincoln Blvd.), Marina del Rey, CA 90292. ☎ **310/ 301-1000** or 800/882-4000, 800/862-7462 in California. Fax 310/301-8167. 154 rms, 6 suites. A/C TV TEL. $140–$205 double; suites from $350. Packages available. AE, CB, DC, EURO, MC, V. Free parking.

This hotel, on a pier jutting into the harbor, is bounded on three sides by one of the world's largest marinas. A garish lobby gives way to first-class guest rooms that are surprisingly well decorated, with fine contemporary furnishings and a few nautical nods. Most rooms have balconies or patios; some have harbor views.

Dining/Entertainment: The Crystal Seahorse, overlooking the marina, serves California-style cuisine all day.

Services: Concierge, room service, complimentary airport limousine.

Facilities: Outdoor heated waterside pool, sundeck, nearby tennis and golf, putting green, car rental desk.

Marina International

4200 Admiralty Way, (west of Lincoln Blvd.), Marina del Rey, CA 90292. ☎ **310/ 301-2000** or 800/882-4000, 800/862-7462 in California. Fax 310/301-6687. 135 rms, 24 suites, 25 bungalows. A/C TV TEL. $125–$298 double; suites from $130; bungalows from $150. AE, CB, DC, EURO, MC, V. Free parking.

This hotel's lovely rooms are bright, contemporary, and very, very private. Most rooms are decorated in a casual California style, with soft pastels and textured fabrics; many have balconies or patios with unobstructed water views. Suites have an additional sitting room and an extra phone in the bathroom. The bungalows are plush and absolutely huge (they're larger than the suites—some are even split-level duplexes), with sitting areas that can double as second bedrooms.

Dining/Entertainment: The Crystal Fountain, open for breakfast and lunch, serves continental fare indoors or out.

Services: Concierge, room service, complimentary airport shuttle.

Facilities: Outdoor heated pool, whirlpool, sundeck, nearby golf and tennis, business center, tour desk.

MODERATE

✪ Casa Malibu

22752 Pacific Coast Hwy. (about a quarter-mile south of Malibu Pier), Malibu, CA 90265. ☎ **310/456-2219** or 800/831-0858. Fax 310/456-5418. 21 rms. TV TEL. $90–$110 double with garden view, $130 double with ocean view, $145–$155 oceanfront double. Room with kitchen $10 extra. AE, EURO, MC, V. Free parking.

I'm hesitant to crow too loudly about Casa Malibu—one of my favorite L.A. hotels—for fear that it will be even harder to get a room here. The modest two-story motel wraps around a palm-studded inner courtyard with well-tended flowerbeds and cuppa d'oro vines climbing the facade. Just past the garden is the blue Pacific and a large swath of private Malibu beach for the exclusive use of hotel guests. Rooms are surprisingly contemporary and cheerful, with top-quality mattresses, bathrobes, coffeemaker, and refrigerator. The king-bedded oceanfront rooms have balconies directly over the sand; they're some of the city's most coveted accommodations. If you've got a room without a view, you can only see the ocean from the communal balcony; but since the sound of the waves will put you soundly to sleep in any of the rooms, that criticism seems like complaining that the caviar is too cold.

Channel Road Inn

219 W. Channel Road, Santa Monica, CA 90402. ☎ **310/459-1920** or 310/ 454-7577. Fax 310/454-9920. 12 rms, 2 suites. TV TEL. $95-$160 double; suites from $165. EURO, MC, V. All rates include breakfast. Valet parking $8.

Built in 1910, this charming inn has just a dozen individually decorated rooms, fitted with pine furnishings, a smattering of antiques, and four-poster beds covered with hand-sewn Amish quilts. Located just one block from the beach, many rooms enjoy ocean views. There's a hot tub on the property, and a few bicycles for guests' use.

Hotel *Queen Mary*

1126 Queen's Hwy. (off I-710 south), Long Beach, CA 90802-6390. ☎ **310/435-3511** or 310/432-6964, or 800/437-2934. Fax 310/437-453. 348 rms, 17 suites. A/C TV TEL. $75–$160 double; suites from $350. AE, DC, EURO, MC, V. Parking $5.

This is considered the most luxurious ocean liner ever to sail the Atlantic, but that doesn't make it a great hotel. While the rooms are the largest ever built aboard a ship, they're not exceptional when compared to those on terra firma, and only the most expensive ones have portholes. And while the charm and elegance of the art deco era are still present in each stateroom's decor, modern amenities, like TVs and carpeting, are overdue for replacement. For nostalgia or novelty, however, a stay here is thoroughly recommendable; the ship's beautifully carved interior is a festival for the eye and fun to explore. And the weekday rates are hard to beat. Sir Winston's, the hotel's top dining room, offers a great view of the coastline, but the food can't match it. A terrific Sunday Champagne brunch is served in the ship's Grand Salon, and it's always worth having a cocktail in the art deco Observation Bar.

Oceana Suites Hotel

849 Ocean Ave., Santa Monica, CA 90403. ☎ **310/393-0486** or 800/777-0758. 60 apts. TV TEL. $139–$199 one- and two-bedroom apts. Lower rates off season. All rates include breakfast. AE, DISC, DC, MC, V. Parking $5.

This ocean-view, apartment-style hotel is a great value for families, and it's excellently located, in a residential neighborhood across from Pacific Palisades. The furniture is worn, but clean; all units have terraces. A small continental breakfast is provided every morning, along with the daily newspaper. Coffee is available in the lobby at all times.

Pacific Shore Hotel

1819 Ocean Ave. (at Pico Blvd.), Santa Monica, CA 90401. ☎ **310/451-8711** or 800/622-8711. Fax 310/394-6657. 168 rms. A/C TV TEL. $125–$135 double. AE, EURO, MC, V. Free parking.

A rectanglular, eight-story glass and concrete monolith located about a block from the beach, this is a good choice for those who want to be in the heart of Santa Monica. There's nothing to get too excited about, but the rooms are decent and well priced. Every room is chain-hotel identical. Great sunsets can be seen from the ocean-facing rooms on the high floors, but you'll have to look over busy Ocean Avenue, a vacant lot, and the roofs of Shutters on the Beach. There are ice and soft-drink machines on every floor, a busy cocktail lounge downstairs, and a heated swimming pool and Jacuzzi out back.

Radisson Huntley Hotel

1111 2nd St. (north of Wilshire Blvd.), Santa Monica, CA 90403. ☎ **310/394-5454** or 800/333-3333. Fax 310/458-9776. 213 rms, 6 suites. A/C TV TEL. $135–$160 double; suites from $150. Ask about the "Supersaver Rates" promotion. AE, CB, DC, DISC, EURO, MC, V. Parking $5.50.

This hotel, one of Santa Monica's tallest buildings, offers nondescript, moderate-quality accommodations close to the Third Street Mall and just two blocks from the beach. Rooms are basic but comfortable, with either ocean or mountain views. Toppers, the rooftop Mexican restaurant, has a great view, serves very good margaritas, and hosts live entertainment nightly. There's also a classy coffee shop serving American standards.

Sheraton Los Angeles Airport Hotel

6101 W. Century Blvd. (near Sepulveda Blvd.), Los Angeles, CA 90045. ☎ **310/ 642-1111** or 800/325-3535. Fax 310/410-1267. 807 rms, 91 suites. A/C MINIBAR TV TEL. $135–$175 double; suites from $300. AE, CB, DC, DISC, EURO, MC, V. Parking $9.

This 15-story hotel is one of the newer additions to the airport area. Rooms have a California look, with rattan chairs and greenery. It's just a Sheraton, but the location makes it equally popular with business and leisure travelers. There's a large heated outdoor pool, an exercise room with Universal equipment, and a Jacuzzi. The hotel also offers 24-hour room service, a rarity in this price range.

✪ Venice Beach House

15 30th Ave. (off Pacific Ave.), Venice, CA 90291. ☎ **310/823-1966.** Fax 310/ 823-1842. 4 rms, 5 suites. TV TEL. $85–$95 double w/shared bath; $130–$165 suite. All rates include continental breakfast. AE, EURO, MC, V. Free parking.

This former family home, built in 1911, is now one of the area's finest bed-and-breakfasts. The interiors of this Victorian, with its hardwood floors, bay windows, lattice porch, and large Oriental rugs, will make you forget the hustle and bustle of the beach that's just steps away. Each of the nine guest rooms is different, outfitted with white rattan or antique wood furnishings; some are punctuated with country prints, others with shelves packed with worn hardcover books. One particularly romantic room has an ocean view and a fireplace. Continental breakfast—cereal, breads, juice, and coffee—is served in the comfortable downstairs sitting room; afternoon tea or cool lemonade is served with fresh-baked cookies every day. The inn can prepare picnic baskets for day excursions. *Beware:* The inn can get noisy, and despite its relative homeyness, it's not for everyone. Smoking is not permitted.

INEXPENSIVE

Best Western Sunrise Hotel-King Harbor

400 N. Harbor Dr., Redondo Beach, CA 90277. ☎ **310/376-0746** or 800/ 334-7384. Fax 310/376-7384. 111 rms. A/C TV TEL. $80–$125 double, children under 12 stay free. AE, DISC, DC, MC, V. Free parking.

Although the rooms are a bit outdated, this Best Western offers clean and comfortable accommodations close to Hermosa and Redondo beaches. The hotel is directly across the street from King Harbor; some rooms even have views of the ocean. There's a pool and a whirlpool if you don't want to make your way to the beach; baby-sitting, airport transportation, and bicycle rentals are available.

Marina del Rey Marriott

13480 Maxella Ave., Marina del Rey, CA 90292. ☎ **310/822-8555** or 800/ 228-9290. Fax 310/823-2996. 281 rms. A/C MINIBAR TV TEL. $79–$129 double. Children under 10 stay free. AE, DISC, DC, MC, V.

This resortlike hotel is conveniently located only a few blocks from the marina and the Villa Marina Center, where you'll find good dining options and shopping. The rooms are outfitted with English-style mahogany furniture; many have patios or balconies. Take advantage of the spa, pool, sauna, steam room, and whirlpool; you'll also have free use of a nearby fitness center.

Travelodge at LAX

5547 W. Century Blvd., Los Angeles, CA 90045. ☎ **310/649-4000** or 800/421-3939. Fax 310/649-0311. 147 rms. A/C TV TEL. $74 double. Extra person $8; children under 18 stay free. Lower rates off season. AE, DISC, DC, MC, V. Free parking.

The lobby is nondescript and the rooms standard, but there's a surprisingly beautiful tropical garden surrounding the pool area. Some units have terraces. No-smoking rooms are available. Services include free airport transportation, baby-sitting, 24-hour room service (a rarity for a hotel in this price range), and a car rental desk. A Denny's is attached to the hotel.

6 San Fernando Valley

MODERATE

Radisson Valley Center

15433 Ventura Blvd., Sherman Oaks, CA 91403. ☎ **818/981-5400.** Fax 818/981-3175. 215 rms, 3 suites. A/C TV TEL. $115 double Sun–Thurs, $90 double Fri–Sat; suites from $225. Special discount packages available. AE, CB, DC, EURO, MC, V. Parking $5.

This hotel conveniently sits at the crossroads of two major freeways, the San Diego (I-405) and Ventura (U.S. 101). Universal Studios, NBC, Magic Mountain, Griffith Park, Hollywood, and Beverly Hills are all nearby. The spacious rooms have private balconies and are attractively decorated; the baths and furnishings are just beginning to show their age. This Radisson is a comfortable enough place to sleep, and even have a swim or Jacuzzi after a long day of sightseeing. The cafe is open all day and has an adjacent cocktail lounge.

Sheraton Universal

333 Universal Terrace Pkwy., Universal City, 91608. ☎ **818/980-1212** or 800/325-3535. Fax 818/985-4980. 424 rms, 18 suites. A/C MINIBAR TEL TV. $130–$160 double; suites from $245. AE, CB, DC, DISC, EURO, MC, V. Valet parking $12.50, self-parking $9.50.

This 21-story concrete rectangle, situated on the grounds of Universal Studios, is a good-quality, mixed-use hotel catering to tourists, businesspeople, and Industry folks visiting the studios' production offices. A major 1994 renovation updated every room with contemporary fabrics and floor-to-ceiling windows that actually open; each is equipped with Nintendo games. The hotel is very close to the Hollywood Bowl, and you can practically roll out of bed and into the theme park.

Sportsmen's Lodge

12825 Ventura Blvd. (west of Coldwater Canyon), Studio City, CA 91604. ☎ **818/ 769-4700** or 800/821-8511, 800/821-1625 in California. Fax 213/877-3898. 193 rms, 13 suites. A/C TV TEL. $111–$140 double; poolside executive studio $175, $180 suite. AE, DC, DISC, EURO, MC, V. Free parking.

Walking around the ponds and waterfalls in back of this sprawling motel, it's hard to imagine that busy Ventura Boulevard is just across the parking lot. Rooms are large and comfortable, but not luxurious; many have balconies, and refrigerators are available. The poolside executive studios are the largest and best located of the accommodations here. The hotel has a heated, Olympic-size swimming pool, a large sundeck, a well-equipped exercise room, and a variety of shops and service desks, and both bowling and golf are available nearby. Complimentary afternoon tea is served in the lobby at 4pm. Caribou, a stunning glass-enclosed dining room, has been winning rave reviews.

6

Dining

Any way you look at it—food, decor, service—Los Angeles is one of the world's great dining cities. When it comes to culinary innovation and architectural design, L.A.'s restaurants are tops.

It wasn't always this way. Barely more than a dozen years ago, back in the days when the cream of the L.A. crop stuck to traditional French fare and chefs didn't venture beyond the kitchen, it was hard to get a memorable meal here. Today, many of the city's outstanding eateries—Citrus, Matsuhisa, Patina, and Michael's, to name a few—have built culinary reputations that extend far beyond city limits. Others—like the Wolfgang Puck Cafe, Planet Hollywood, and Lawry's The Prime Rib—have won international fame from franchising and product merchandising. Even Spago—unarguably L.A.'s most famous eatery, whose influence has been felt in kitchens the world over—has started branching its way across the country, setting up shop in Las Vegas.

The scene that was so erratic in its youth is now leveling out as it matures. Fewer new restaurants have made their way during the past few recessionary years (Abiquiu is probably the finest exception to that rule), and those that were the new kids on the block in the 1980s have now firmly entrenched themselves. While some diners are lamenting this fact, most are not-so-secretly toasting a trend that has put value (and doggie bags) in vogue. Going with the flow—leaving the "more-is-more" 1980s behind for the "less-is-more" 1990s—many of the city's top restaurants have simplified their menus, lowered prices, and begun to offer prix-fixe meals that are cheaper than putting together the same meal à la carte. And it's now easier to procure tables, too. On a recent Friday afternoon at 4pm, you could still reserve a table for that night at Campanile, Citrus, Drai's, The Ivy, Locanda Veneta, Matsuhisa, Patina, Pinot Bistro, and all of Wolfgang Puck's restaurants—in short, the best restaurants in town.

For food lovers with less cash to spend, these are exciting times indeed. Owners of many of the city's most celebrated restaurants have recently opened more informal (and less expensive) sister eateries. Piero Selvaggio (Valentino) opened moderately priced Posto in Sherman Oaks; Michel Richard (Citrus) split his dining room in two to create the value-priced Bar Bistro; Joachim Splichal (Patina and Pinot Bistro) opened Patinette in the Museum of Contemporary Art and Cafe Pinot in the gardens of the L.A. Public Library; and Wolfgang Puck

(Spago, Chinois on Main, and Granita) debuted a chain of Wolfgang Puck's Cafes in Los Angeles and elsewhere.

The city's restaurants are categorized below first by area, then by price, according to the following guide: "Expensive," main courses average more than $20; "Moderate," main courses average between $10 and $20; and "Inexpensive," main courses average under $10. Keep in mind that many of the restaurants listed as "expensive" are moderately priced at lunch. Reservations are recommended almost everywhere.

1 Best Bets

- **Best Spot for a Romantic Dinner: Camelions** (246 26th St., Santa Monica; ☎ 310/395-0746) unabashedly appeals to lovers: Most of the tables at this intimate restaurant only seat two, and there's not a cold seat in the house. Each of the three 1920s stucco cottages enjoys its own crackling fireplace. On warm nights, you can eat on the ivy-trellised brick patio, where it's not hard to imagine you're in the south of France.

- **Best Spot for a Power Lunch:** New York transplant **Barney Greengrass** (on the top floor of Barney's New York, 9570 Wilshire Blvd., Beverly Hills; ☎ 310/777-5877) has quickly become the a darling of the entertainment industry. Combining Jewish standards with high style, this super-upscale deli appeals to the sensibilities of dealmakers who appreciate the sizzle as much as the matzoh-ball soup.

- **Best Spot for a Celebration:** There are so many restaurants in L.A. that are suitable for celebrating, it's hard to pick just one. **Citrus** (6703 Melrose Ave., Hollywood; ☎ 213/857-0034) gets my vote, though, because it's open and airy, has large tables suited to good-size parties, and a fun and friendly atmosphere. And the food's terrific.

- **Best Spot for People Watching:** Nowhere in L.A. is the people watching better than on Venice's Ocean Front Walk, and no restaurant offers a better seat for the action than **Sidewalk Cafe** (1401 Ocean Front Walk, Venice; ☎ 310/399-5547). Unobstructed views of parading skaters, bikers, skateboarders, muscle men, breakdancers, buskers, sword swallowers, and other participants in the daily carnival overshadow the food here, which is a whole lot better than it needs to be.

- **Best Spot for Celebrity Sighting:** Although stars can regularly be spotted at any of the city's best eateries, dinner at **Matsuhisa** (129 N. La Cienega Blvd., Beverly Hills; ☎ 310/659-9639) can almost guarantee a top celebrity sighting most any night of the week. Other Hollywood-heavy restaurants include Morton's and Drai's (on Mondays), Eclipse (Mondays and Tuesdays), and The Ivy and Maple Drive (from Wednesdays to Saturdays).

- **Best Outdoor Dining:** Alfresco dining is surprisingly rare in this balmy town; maybe because so much of L.A. is smoggy and downright unattractive. A short drive to verdant Topanga Canyon and the **Inn of the Seventh Ray** (128 Old Topanga Canyon Rd., Topanga Canyon; ☎ 310/455-1311), however, and the city's ills are only distant memories.

- **Best Decor: Campanile** (624 S. La Brea Ave., Hollywood; ☎ 213/938-1447), built by Charlie Chaplin in 1928 as his private offices, was beautifully designed in an understated, postmodern style that takes full advantage of the building's intrinsic charm. The restaurant is both elegantly vintage and crisply contemporary, an imaginative amalgam that makes it one of L.A.'s most beautiful dining rooms.

- **Best View: Cafe Del Rey** (4451 Admiralty Way, Marina del Rey; ☎ 310/823-6395) delivers, with an unparalleled panorama of Marina del Rey's beautiful harbor enhanced by a lively, upbeat atmosphere. Both the restaurant and the views are best at lunch; be sure to reserve a table by the window.

- **Best Wine List:** Wine lovers nationwide felt his pain when restaurateur Piero Selvaggio lost over 20,000 bottles during the 1994 earthquake. Despite the loss, **Valentino** (3115 Pico Blvd., Santa Monica; ☎ 310/829-4313) still boasts L.A.'s best cellar, and has been honored with *Wine Spectator*'s highest rating.

- **Best Value:** Almost every top restaurateur in L.A. has recently opened a more informal eatery, but none is more value packed than Michel Richard's **Bar Bistro** (6703 Melrose Ave., Los Angeles; ☎ 213/857-0034), which serves essentially the same food as its parent restaurant, Citrus, at drastically reduced prices. Don't miss this one—make reservations in advance.

- **Best for Kids:** More theme park than restaurant, **Dive!** (in the Century City Marketplace, 10250 Santa Monica Blvd., Century City; ☎ 310/788-3483) is a festive submarine-theme eatery that's packed with child-pleasing special-effects gadgetry of all kinds. Dive! is a nonstop party for the eyes and ears, but the same can't be said for the palate—the nouveau subs are nothing special.

- **Best American Cuisine:** Chef Leonard Schwartz cooks the city's greatest meatloaf, chili, and veal chops. Period. He grills a great burger, too. **Maple Drive** (345 N. Maple Dr., Beverly Hills; ☎ 310/274-9800) isn't cheap, but if you'd like to prove to your European friends that American fare isn't all McDonald's and Coca-Cola, this will wordlessly do the trick.

- **Best California Cuisine:** Chef/owner Michael McCarty has had his personal ups and downs in recent years, but his eponymous Santa Monica restaurant, **Michael's** (1147 3rd St., Santa Monica; ☎ 310/451-0843), hasn't suffered because of it. In fact, humbled by a restaurant closing in D.C., Michael's has actually improved. A visit to this ground-breaking eatery makes it clear why McCarty is considered an originator of California cuisine.

- **Best Chinese Cuisine:** For more than thirty years, **Yang Chow Restaurant** (819 N. Broadway, Chinatown; ☎ 213/625-0811) has been serving some of the best Chinese food this side of Hong Kong. The kitchen's Mandarin and Szechuan recipes go far beyond traditional family fare, but prices remain well within reach.

- **Best Continental Cuisine: Chaya Brasserie** (8741 Alden Dr., Los Angeles; ☎ 310/859-8833), best known for superb grilled fish and meats, takes Continental staples and raises them to a new art form using local flavorings and some Asian techniques. Chef Shigefumi Tachibe is far from traditional, but then again, this *is* Los Angeles.

- **Best French Cuisine:** Joachim Splichal, one of L.A.'s very best chefs, serves fabulous French fare with a distinctive California twist at **Patina** (5955 Melrose Ave., Los Angeles; ☎ 213/467-1108). The wintertime game dishes are unequaled, and the mashed potatoes and potato truffle chips are second to none.

- **Best Italian Cuisine:** *New York Times* food critic Ruth Reichl called **Valentino** (3115 Pico Blvd., Santa Monica; ☎ 310/829-4313) the best Italian restaurant in America. This restaurant is very traditional and unusually formal—for L.A.—but the wonderful dining experience you'll have here is worth dressing up for.

- **Best Mexican Cuisine:** It's one thing for a restaurant to have a loyal local following; it's quite another to have fanatical regulars who live miles away, particularly in a city full of top Mexican eateries. But **La Serenata de Garibaldi** (1842 E. 1st St., Boyle Heights; ☎ 213/265-2887) is the Big Enchilada. It was also a regular lunch spot for O. J. Simpson's "dream team."

- **Best Seafood: Water Grill** (544 S. Grand Ave., downtown; ☎ 213/891-0900), a beautiful contemporary fish house, serves imaginative dishes influenced by America's regional cuisines. An absolutely huge raw bar features the best clams, crabs, shrimp, and oysters available, and the fish is so fresh it practically jumps on the plate.

- **Best Burgers: Cassell's** (3266 W. 6th St., downtown; ☎ 213/480-8668) is little more than a shabby burger bar, but this downtown spot has been flipping the finest patties around since time immemorial. Don't let the lunch crowd scare you away; arrive with a hearty appetite, and dig in.

- **Best Desserts:** Before French chef Michel Richard ever stirred a sous he was a baker extraordinaire, creating some of the best desserts anywhere. **Citrus** (6703 Melrose Ave., Hollywood; ☎ 213/857-0034) is a great place for dinner, but no one will mind if you show up late just for sweets. Nancy Silverton's creations at Campanile come in a close second.

- **Best Afternoon Tea:** One of the most elegant teas this side of the Thames is served afternoons from 3 to 5pm in the lounge at the **Regent Beverly Wilshire** (9500 Wilshire Blvd., Beverly Hills; ☎ 310/275-5200). A fine selection of Chinese and Indian teas is served with the requisite finger sandwiches, scones, and crumpets in one of L.A.'s most sumptuous salons.

- **Best Fast Food:** The food at **La Salsa** (9631 Little Santa Monica Blvd., Beverly Hills; ☎ 310/276-2373; other locations throughout the city) is not only fast, it's freshly cooked to order, relatively lean, and delicious. This bright, spotless, tasty alternative is more than a cut above most McTaco stands.

- **Best Picnic Fare:** Open since 1917, **Grand Central Market** (317 S. Broadway, downtown; ☎ 213/622-1763) is L.A's largest and oldest food hall, selling everything from morning-fresh bread to local and exotic produce, raw fish to smoked meats, Chinese noodles to chili. And the cultural experience of a visit here is a terrific precursor to any picnic.

2 Restaurants by Cuisine

AMERICAN
Flora Kitchen (Hollywood)
The Ivy (Westside)
Maple Drive (Westside)
Musso & Frank Grill
(Hollywood)
The Original Pantry Cafe
(Downtown)
Roscoe's House of Chicken
'n' Waffles (Hollywood)
72 Market Street
(The Beaches)
Sidewalk Cafe (The Beaches)

BARBECUE
Benny's Bar-B-Q
(The Beaches)

BREAKFAST
Barney Greengrass (Westside)
Campanile (Hollywood)
Cava (Westside)
Cha Cha Cha (Downtown)
Chez Melange (The Beaches)
Flora Kitchen (Hollywood)
Gratis (Westside)
Jerry's Famous Deli (San
Fernando Valley)
Langer's (Downtown)
Nate & Al's (Westside)
The Original Pantry Cafe
(Downtown)
Pacific Dining Car (Downtown)
Philippe the Original
(Downtown)
Roscoe's House of Chicken
'n' Waffles (Hollywood)
Sidewalk Cafe (The Beaches)
The Source (Westside)

CALIFORNIAN
Alice's (The Beaches)
Bar Bistro at Citrus
(Hollywood)
Cafe Del Rey (The Beaches)
Chez Melange (The Beaches)
Citrus (Hollywood)
Eclipse (Westside)
Four Oaks (Westside)
Granita (The Beaches)
Michael's (The Beaches)
Morton's (Westside)
Spago (Westside)

CALIFORNIAN/FRENCH
Cafe Pinot (Downtown)
Camelions (The Beaches)
Carrots (The Beaches)
Patina (Hollywood)
Pinot Bistro (San Fernando
Valley)

CARIBBEAN
Cha Cha Cha (Downtown)

CHINESE
Yang Chow Restaurant
(Downtown)

CONTINENTAL
Checkers Restaurant
(Downtown)

CUBAN
Versailles (Westside)

DELIS
Barney Greengrass (Westside)
Jerry's Famous Deli (San
Fernando Valley)

Langer's (Downtown)
Nate & Al's (Westside)

FRANCO-CHINESE
Chinois on Main
(The Beaches)

FRANCO-JAPANESE
Chaya Brasserie (Westside)

FRANCO-RUSSIAN
Diaghilev (Westside)

FRENCH (CLASSIC)
Drai's (Westside)

HEALTH FOOD/VEGETARIAN
Gratis (Westside)
Inn of the Seventh Ray
(The Beaches)
The Source (Westside)

INDIAN
Bombay Cafe (Westside)
Clay Pit (Downtown)

ITALIAN
Ca' Brea (Hollywood)
Campanile (Hollywood)
Chianti Cucina
(Hollywood)
Il Pastaio (Westside)
Locanda Veneta (Westside)
Mezzaluna (Westside)
Rösti Rosticceria Toscana
(Westside)
Valentino (The Beaches)

JAPANESE
Ginza Sushi-Ko (Westside)
Matsuhisa (Westside)
Mishima (Westside)

MEXICAN
La Salsa (Westside)
La Serenata de Garibaldi
(Downtown)

MIDDLE EASTERN
Noura Cafe (Westside)

MOROCCAN
Dar Maghreb (Hollywood)

SANDWICHES/BURGERS
The Apple Pan (Westside)
Cassell's (Downtown)
Dive! (Westside)
Jodi Maroni's Sausage
Kingdom (The Beaches)
Philippe the Original
(Downtown)
Pink's Hot Dogs (Hollywood)

SEAFOOD
Water Grill (Downtown)

SOUTHERN
Aunt Kizzy's Back Porch
(The Beaches)
Georgia (Hollywood)

SOUTHWESTERN
Abiquiu (The Beaches)
Authentic Cafe (Hollywood)

SPANISH
Cava (Westside)

STEAKS
Lawry's The Prime Rib
(Westside)
Pacific Dining Car
(Downtown)
The Palm (Westside)

3 Downtown

EXPENSIVE

Checkers Restaurant

535 S. Grand Ave. (in the Wyndham Checkers Hotel, between 5th and 6th sts.).
☎ 213/624-0000. Reservations recommended. Main courses $18–$28; lunch $15–
$19; weekend brunch $9–$18. AE, DC, MC, V. Mon–Fri 11:30am–2:30pm; Sat–Sun
10:30am–2:30pm; daily 5:30–9:30pm. CONTEMPORARY CONTINENTAL.

Nine-to-fivers looking to grab a quick, inexpensive bite are the bread and butter of most eateries in this neighborhood. Not so at Checkers; this peaceful restaurant represents the pinnacle of elegance. The warm, velvet-lined formal dining room is so plush and conservatively ornate that it feels like you're dining inside a Fabergé egg. The food is very good; complex concoctions are well within the capablilities of the kitchen. At lunch or dinner, you might begin with smoked duck breast carpaccio or rum-soaked salmon terrine layered with cream cheese and capers. Main courses include lentil and caraway–crusted pork tenderloin and tiger prawns with soba noodles. A la carte brunches mean everything from granola with sun-dried fruit to duck hash with rosemary and poached eggs.

Pacific Dining Car

1310 W. 6th St. (at Witmer St.). ☎ **213/483-6000.** Reservations recommended. Main courses $20–$42; lunch $14–$29; breakfast $11–$20. AE, MC, V. Daily 24 hours (breakfast 11pm–11am). STEAKS.

It's 4am and you're in the mood for a well-marbled, patiently aged New York steak. Well, even in these health-conscious times, there are still enough nocturnal carnivores in Los Angeles to justify not one, but two all-night Pacific Dining Car steakhouses. The flagship location, just a few short blocks from the epicenter of downtown , is dark and clubby, a vestige of an age when diners guiltlessly indulged in fist-sized medallions of beef. The mesquite-charred steaks are terrific indeed, a cut above the restaurant's other hearty offerings, like lamb and chicken. There's a good wine selection. A separate breakfast menu features egg dishes, salads, and mini-steaks.

A second restaurant is located in Santa Monica, at 2700 Wilshire Blvd., one block east of 26th Street (☎ 310/453-4000).

Water Grill

544 S. Grand Ave. (between 5th and 6th sts.). ☎ **213/891-0900.** Reservations recommended. Main courses $15–$25; lunch $9–$12. AE, DC, DISC, MC, V. Mon–Wed 11am–5pm, Thurs 11am–10pm, Fri 11am–11pm, Sat 5–11pm, Sun 4:30–9pm. SEAFOOD.

Popular with the suit-and-tie crowd at lunch, the restaurant attracts concertgoers en route to the Music Center by night. The dining room is a stylish and sophisticated fusion of wood, leather, and brass, but it gets a lighthearted lift from cavorting papier-mâché fish that play against an aquamarine ceiling painted with bubbles. Water Grill, considered by many to be L.A.'s best seafood house, is best known for its shellfish. Among the appetizers are a dozen different oysters. Discovery Bay Flats and Goosepoints (both from Washington State), two of my favorites, are particularly sweet and clean. Main courses are imaginative dishes influenced by the cuisines of Hawaii, the Pacific Northwest, New Orleans, and New England. Black linguine is topped with calamari, rock shrimp, and bay scallops in a spicy sauce; Dungeness crab is stuffed into a Maine lobster; grilled mahimahi is served with zucchini noodles; and seared sea scallops are paired with house-smoked salmon.

MODERATE

§ Cafe Pinot

700 West 5th. St. (between Grand and Flower sts.). ☎ **213/239-6500.** Reservations recommended. Main courses $13–$22; lunch $9–$18. AE, MC, V. Mon–Sat 11:15am–2:30pm, Mon 5–9pm, Tues–Sat 5–9:30pm. CALIFORNIAN/FRENCH.

Chef Joachim Splichal is quickly becoming the most dominant force on the L.A. restaurant scene. Modeled after his top-ranked restaurant, Patina, Cafe Pinot is designed to be less formal in atmosphere and lighter on the plate—and the pocketbook—than his flagship eatery. Opened in 1995 in the gardens of the L.A. Public Library, Cafe Pinot has a cool, contemporary dining room with panoramic windows. The restaurant's location makes it a natural for downtown business folk; at night, there's free shuttle transportation to The Music Center. Splichal has installed a giant rotisserie in the kitchen, and the best meals come from it. The moist, tender mustard-crusted roast chicken is your best bet unless its Friday night, when you can order the roast suckling pig with its unique crackling skin. Other recommendable dishes include duck leg confit, grilled calf's liver, and seared peppered tuna.

Cha Cha Cha

656 N. Virgil Ave. (at Melrose Ave.), Silver Lake. ☎ **213/664-7723.** Reservations recommended. Main courses $8–$15; breakfast and lunch $5–$9. AE, DC, DISC, MC, V. Sun–Thurs 8am–10:30pm; Fri–Sat 8am–11:30pm. CARIBBEAN.

Cha Cha Cha serves the West Coast's best Caribbean food in a fun and funky space on the seedy fringe of downtown. The restaurant is a festival of flavors and colors that are both upbeat and offbeat. It's impossible to feel down when you're part of this eclectic hodgepodge of pulsating Caribbean music, wild decor, and kaleidoscopic clutter; still, the intimate dining rooms cater to lively romantics, not obnoxious frat boys. Claustrophobes should choose seats in the airy covered courtyard. The very spicy black-pepper jumbo shrimp gets top marks, as does the paella, a generous mixture of chicken, sausage, and seafood blended with saffroned rice. Other Jamaican/Haitian/Cuban/Puerto Rican–inspired recommendations include jerk pork and mambo gumbo, a zesty soup of okra, shredded chicken, and spices. Hardcore Caribbeanites might visit for breakfast, when the fare ranges from plantain, yucca, onion, and herb omelettes to scrambled eggs with fresh tomatillos served on hot grilled tortillas.

A second restaurant is located in Long Beach, at 726 Pacific Ave. (☎ 310/436-3900).

Clay Pit

3465 W. 6th St. (in Chapman Market, between Normandie and Vermont aves.). ☎ **213/382-6300.** Reservations recommended on weekends. Main courses $12–$17; lunch $7–$11; weekday lunch buffet $7.75; Sunday brunch buffet $9.95. AE, CB, DC, DISC, MC, V. Mon–Sat 11:30am–2:30pm; daily 5:30–10pm; Sun 11:30am–2:30pm. NORTH INDIAN.

When you're in the mood for very good, inexpensive North Indian cooking, you can do no better than this cozy and reliable mid-Wilshire tandoori room. Physically, Clay Pit is just an unremarkable neighbor-hood place, with standard furnishings and decor. But, in nice weather, you can dine on an outdoor patio overlooking the action in the landmark Chapman Market arcade. Doting waiters serve flavorful traditional curries, some with California twists. If you're in the mood for authentic, order creamy saag paneer (spinach and homemade cheese), chunky aloo motor kabi (potato and peas in a coriander-based tomato sauce), or juicy lamb tikka (marinated in a yogurt sauce and cooked in the clay oven). If you're not, order rosemary-scented lamb, succulent pork chops, or moist ahi. Excellent breads and unbeatable all-you-can-eat buffets keep this value-packed place popular.

La Serenata de Garibaldi

1842 E. 1st St. (between Boyle and State sts,), Boyle Heights. ☎ **213/265-2887.** Reservations recommended on weekends. Main courses $9–$18; lunch $6–$11. MC, V. Tues–Sun 11am–10pm. MEXICAN.

It's no small accomplishment to be considered L.A.'s top Mexican restaurant, but that's exactly what this place is to its faithful legions. Los Angeles's relatively high menu prices, along with its close proximity to the border, attract Mexico's best chefs and top ingredients; both meet in La Serenata's hard-working kitchen, where seafood is the focus. Trademark dishes include shrimp in cilantro sauce and Mexican sea bass fillets in a tangy chipotle sauce. There are the traditional rice-and-beans meals, too, including soft tacos and chicken mole, which are superb. The simple storefront eatery would certainly be even more popular if it weren't smack in the center of a somewhat dodgy East L.A. neighborhood, but it's directly across from the Hollenbeck Police Station, so the location adds nothing more than a further air of authenticity.

INEXPENSIVE

Cassell's

3266 W. 6th St. (west of Vermont Ave.). ☎ **213/480-8668.** Hamburgers $4–$7. No credit cards. Mon–Sat 10:30am–4pm. BURGERS.

Cassell's yellow Formica tables and linoleum floors are the definitions of "dive"; but when the product in question is a great burger, a white-trash dining room is the appropriate milieu. Despite a few recent protests to the contrary, Cassell's continues to flip one of the best burgers in town. And regulars rave about the restaurant's homemade mayonnaise, used to create superior potato and egg salads. Also praise-worthy are the deliciously crispy onion rings, which, like the rest of the artery-clogging menu, are made fresh in-house. The restaurant is only open for lunch.

Langer's

704 S. Alvarado St. (at 7th St.). ☎ **213/483-8050.** Reservations not accepted. Main courses $6–$14. MC, V. Mon–Sat 8am–4pm. DELI.

A leader in L.A.'s long-running deli war, Langer's makes some of the best stuffed kishka and matzoh-ball soup this side of the Hudson. For many, however, it's the fresh chopped liver and lean and spicy hot pastrami sandwiches that make Langer's L.A.'s best deli. Langer's has been serving the business community and displaced New Yorkers for almost 50 years. After the riots, when things got dicey around this neighborhood, the restaurant began a curbside delivery service: Phone in your order with an ETA, and they'll be waiting for you at the curb—with change.

The Original Pantry Cafe

877 S. Figueroa St. (at 9th St.). ☎ **213/972-9279.** Reservations not accepted. Main courses $6–$11. No credit cards. Daily 24 hours. AMERICAN.

An L.A. institution if there ever was one, this place has been serving huge portions of comfort food around the clock for more than 60 years; they don't even have a key to the front door. Owned by L.A. Mayor Richard Riordan, the Pantry is especially popular with politicos, who come here for weekday lunches, and conference-goers en route to the nearby L.A. Convention Center. The well-worn restaurant is also a welcoming beacon to late-night clubbers (downtown becomes a virtual ghost town). A bowl of celery stalks, carrot sticks, and whole radishes greets you at your Formica table, and creamy coleslaw and sourdough bread come free with every meal. Famous for quantity rather than quality, the Pantry serves huge T-bone steaks, densely packed meatloaf, macaroni and cheese, and other American favorites. A typical breakfast (served all day) might consist of a huge stack of hotcakes, a big slab of sweet cured ham, home fries, and coffee.

Philippe the Original

1001 N. Alameda St. (at Ord St.). ☎ **213/628-3781.** Reservations not accepted. Main courses $3–$7. No credit cards. Daily 6am–10pm. SANDWICHES/AMERICAN.

Good old-fashioned value is what this legendary landmark cafeteria is all about. Popular with both South-Central projects dwellers and Beverly Hills elite, Philippe's decidedly unspectacular dining room is a microcosm of the entire city; it's one of the few places, it seems, where everyone can get along. Philippe's claims to have invented the French-dipped sandwich at this location in 1908; these remain the most popular menu items. Patrons push trays along the counter and watch while their choice of beef, pork, ham, turkey, or lamb is sliced and layered onto crusty French bread that's been dipped in meat juices. Other menu items include homemade beef stew, chili, and pickled pigs' feet. A hearty breakfast, served daily until 10:30am, is worth attending if only for Philippe's uncommonly good cinnamon-dipped French toast. Beer and wine are available.

Yang Chow Restaurant

819 N. Broadway (at Alpine St.), Chinatown. ☎ **213/625-0811.** Reservations recommended on weekends. Main courses $8–$12. AE, MC, V. Daily 11:30am–2:30pm; Sun–Thurs 5–9:30pm, Fri–Sat 5–10:30pm. MANDARIN/SZECHUAN.

Open for more then thirty years, family-operated Yang Chow is well-known among local foodies as one of L.A.'s best Chinese restaurants. It's not the restaurant's bland and functional decor that accrues accolades, however; what makes Yang Chow so popular is an interesting, value-packed menu where complex flavors mingle on most every plate. After covering the Mandarin and Szechwan basics—sweet and sour pork, shrimp with broccoli, moo shu chicken—the kitchen leaps into

L.A.'s Coolest Chefs and Their Hot Restaurants

With the explosion of the Los Angeles restaurant scene, top chefs have joined movie stars as L.A.'s most celebrated residents. Increasingly, the city's chefs have become stars—and scenemakers—in their own right, signing multimillion-dollar, multi-restaurant deals, often with celebrity backers. But the top gourmets tend to be held to a different standard than their celluloid-friendly counterparts; the public, happy to forgive and forget a flop of a movie, are much less understanding when it comes to their stomachs. Thus, the chefs who have made it in L.A. tend to be the real thing, culinary Michelangelos who can turn the harshest, most cynical gourmands into their biggest fans.

L.A.'s "Old Guard" are the heavyweight chefs who have been around a dozen years or so—they're the DeNiros, the Stallones, the Schwarzeneggers of the city's kitchens. They're far from formulaic, however; in a scene that will stand for no less, they remain as inventive as ever. In this group is the venerable Piero Selvaggio, whose Valentino is one of America's best Italian restaurants. His signature dish, risotto with white truffles, almost smells too good to eat. Sicilian-born Celestino Drago headed other people's kitchens for years before opening his successful pasta palace, Il Pastaio, in Beverly Hills. French chef Michel Richard's Citrus has proved so consistently popular, it's practically a license to print money. Richard knows a good thing when he sees it, and is currently running around the country opening multiple spin-offs, each called Citronelle. And German-born Wolfgang Puck—the most famous of this group, best known for the gourmet pizzas he began serving at the popular-as-ever Spago over a dozen years ago—has moved into the populist cafe market, as well as into national supermarket freezers.

The "New Guard"—the Brad Pitts, Johnny Depps, Chris O'Donnells of the culinary scene—includes Joachim Splichal (Patina, Pinot Bistro, Cafe Pinot, Patinette), who is nosing in on Puck as L.A.'s most successful culinary entrepreneur. John Sedlar of Abiquiu is a young American with one of cookery's brightest futures; his innovative cone-shaped tacos will continue to be the talk of the town in 1996. Antonio Tommasi (Ca' Brea, Locanda Veneta, and Ca' Del Sole), one of the country's best northern Italian chefs, keeps them coming with updated versions of classics like butter squash–stuffed ravioli and shrimp risotto. Mark Peel and Nancy Silverton of Campanile are Puck alumni and the city's top husband-and-wife team. Their La Brea Bakery, next door, has a devoted following, and delivers to eateries as far away as Santa Barbara. Nobuyuki Matsuhisa (Matsuhisa) is often called L.A.'s most creative chef for his innovative combinations of Japanese flavors with South American spices and salsas. Success has finally gone to his head: Matsuhisa opened a second restaurant (Nobu) in New York.

uncharted territories, concocting dishes like spicy Dungeness crab; a tangy and hot sautéed squid; and beef kidneys, which are cooked firm and served with a garlicky soy sauce. House specialties include particularly well-spiced and textured cold noodles in sesame sauce, and sautéed shellfish with a pungent hoisin-based dipping sauce. Portions are large and served promptly by an uncharacteristically kind waitstaff.

4 Hollywood

EXPENSIVE

✪ Campanile

624 S. La Brea Ave. (north of Wilshire Blvd.). ☎ **213/938-1447.** Reservations required. Main courses $18–$28; breakfast $7–$11; lunch $7–$15; AE, MC, V. Mon–Fri 7:30am–2:30am, Sat–Sun 8am–1:30pm; Mon–Thurs 6–10pm, Fri–Sat 5:30–11pm. ITALIAN CONTEMPORARY.

Built as Charlie Chaplin's private offices in 1928, this lovely building has a multilevel layout, with flower-bedecked interior balconies, a bubbling fountain, and a skylight through which diners can see the campanile (bell tower). Crisply contemporary, the dining rooms are successful amalgams of vintage and modern, making this one of the most attractive spaces in Los Angeles. The kitchen, headed by Spago alumnus chef/owner Mark Peel, gets a giant leg up from baker (and wife) Nancy Silverton, who runs the now-legendary La Brea Bakery next door. Meals here might begin with fried zucchini flowers drizzled with melted mozzarella, or lamb carpaccio surrounded by artichoke leaves—a dish that arrives looking like one of Van Gogh's sunflowers. Chef Peel is particularly known for his grills and roasts; try braised beef shanks with olive and garlic sauce or papardelle with braised rabbit, roasted tomato, and collard greens. Oh, yes—and don't skip dessert here; the restaurant's many enthusiastic sweets fans have turned Nancy Silverton's dessert book into a best seller. An egg menu is available mornings, but local power-breakfasters usually opt for the ginger scones and espresso wheels.

✪ Citrus

6703 Melrose Ave. (west of Highland Ave.). ☎ **213/857-0034.** Reservations recommended. Main courses $25–$30; lunch $10–$16. AE, MC, V. Mon–Fri noon–2:30pm; Mon–Thurs 6–10pm, Fri–Sat 6–10:30pm. CALIFORNIAN.

Second in culinary celebrity only to Wolfgang Puck, innovative French chef Michel Richard originally made his mark as a pastry wunderkind, wowing the most refined sweet tooths on two continents. Richard's seamless transition to main courses is showcased nightly at this popular glass-wrapped bistro, which has matured into a cherished L.A. institution. When he's not gallivanting around the world opening spin-off Citronelles or cooking at international benefits, the portly, bearded Richard personally works wonders in the kitchen, which overlooks the dining room's umbrella-topped tables. Beautifully presented contemporary bistro fare includes starters like shiitake mushroom and garlic napoleon, escargot in a potato basket, sautéed scallops with onion rings, and enoki mushrooms with malossol caviar. Roasted duck with couscous and lemon sauce, Chilean sea bass with crayfish and pearl pasta, and roasted venison loin with potato risotto are typical main courses. Citrus has one of the best-selected wine lists (offering several good buys) in town. Whatever you do, save room for dessert; it's still Richard's best course.

✪ Patina

5955 Melrose Ave. (west of Cahuenga Blvd.). ☎ **213/467-1108.** Reservations required. Main courses $18–$26; lunch $8–$12. AE, DC, DISC, MC, V. Tues–Fri 11:30am–2pm; Sun–Thurs 6–9:30pm, Fri–Sat 6–10:30pm. CALIFORNIAN/FRENCH.

Joachim Splichal is one of the city's very best chefs. He's also a genius at choosing and training top chefs to cook in his kitchens, no small talent for a celebrity who's regularly jetting around the world. Patina routinely wins the highest praise from demanding gourmands, who are happy to empty their bank accounts for unbeatable meals that almost never miss their intended mark. The dining room is straightforwardly attractive, low key, well lit, and professional, without the slightest hint of stuffiness. The menu is equally disarming: "Mallard Duck with Portobello Mushrooms" gives little hint of the brilliant colors and flavors that appear on the plate. Splichal is one of the few L.A. chefs daring enough to have an offal section on the menu—brains, kidneys, cock's combs, and the like. The seasonal menu features partridge, pheasant, venison, and other game in winter and spotlights exotic local vegetables in warmer months. Seafood is always available; if Maine lobster cannelloni or asparagus-wrapped John Dory is on the menu, order it. Patina is justifiably famous for its mashed potatoes and potato truffle chips; be sure to include one (or both) with your meal.

MODERATE

✪ Bar Bistro at Citrus

6703 Melrose Ave. (west of Highland Ave.). ☎ **213/857-0034.** Reservations recommended. Main courses $12–$16; lunch $7–$12. AE, MC, V. Mon–Fri noon–2:30pm; Mon–Thurs 6–10pm, Fri–Sat 6–10:30pm. CALIFORNIAN.

The recent partition of the dining room at Michel Richard's venerable Citrus to make way for this downscale upstart was the most conspicuous illustration of how top restaurateurs are dealing with the changing economic climate. Serving what is essentially the same food as Citrus at drastically reduced prices, this place became an overnight success, and remains one of Los Angeles' very best buys. Prices are kept low with less expensive meats, and without the use of time-consuming stock reductions. The atmosphere is also less weighty and more jovial than that at Citrus.

✪ Ca' Brea

346 S. La Brea Ave. (north of Wilshire Blvd.). ☎ **213/938-2863.** Reservations required. Main courses $9–$21; lunch $7–$20. AE, CB, DC, MC, V. Mon–Sat 11:30am–2:30pm; Mon–Thurs 5:30–10:30pm, Fri–Sat 5:30pm–midnight. NORTHERN ITALIAN.

With Ca' Brea opened in 1991, its talented chef/owner Antonio Tommasi was catapulted into a public spotlight that's shared by only a handful of L.A. chefs—Wolfgang Puck, Michel Richard, Joachim

Splichal. Since then, Tommasi has opened two other celebrated restaurants, Locanda Veneta in Hollywood and Ca' Del Sole in the Valley, but, for many, Ca' Brea remains tops. The restaurant's refreshingly bright two-story dining room is a happy place, hung with colorful, oversize contemporary paintings and backed by an open prep-kitchen where you can watch as your seafood cakes are sautéed and your Napa cabbage braised. Booths are the most coveted seats; but with only 20 tables in all, be thankful you are sitting anywhere. Detractors might complain that Ca' Brea isn't what it used to be since Tommasi began splitting his time between three restaurants. But Tommasi stops in daily and keeps a very close watch over his hand-picked staff. Consistently excellent dishes include the roasted pork sausage, butter squash–stuffed ravioli, and duck served with a light honey-balsamic vinaigrette.

Chianti Cucina

7383 Melrose Ave. (between Fairfax and La Brea aves.). ☎ **213/653-8333.** Reservations recommended. Main courses $12–20. AE, CB, DC, MC, V. Chianti Cucina: Mon–Thurs, Sun 11:30am–11:30pm, Fri–Sat 11:30am–midnight. Ristorante Chianti: Sun–Thurs 5:30–10:30pm, Fri–Sat 5:30–11pm. ITALIAN/TUSCAN.

Innocent passersby, and locals in search of a secret hideaway, go to the dimly lit, crimson-colored Ristorante Chianti, where waiters whip out flashlights so customers can read the menu. Cognoscenti, on the other hand, bypass this 60-year-old standby and head straight for Chianti Cucina, the bright, bustling eat-in "kitchen" of the more formal restaurant next door. Chianti Cucina features excellent meals at fair prices. The menu, which changes frequently, is always interesting and often exceptional. Hot and cold appetizers range from fresh handmade mozzarella and prosciutto to lamb carpaccio with asparagus and marinated grilled eggplant filled with goat cheese, arugula, and sun-dried tomatoes. As for main dishes, the homemade pasta is both superior and deliciously inventive. Try the black tortellini filled with fresh salmon, or the giant ravioli filled with spinach and ricotta.

Dar Maghreb

7651 Sunset Blvd. (between Fairfax and La Brea aves.). ☎ **213/876-7651.** Reservations recommended. Fixed-price dinners $18–$30. CB, DC, MC, V. Daily 6–11pm. MOROCCAN.

If you're a lone diner in search of a quick bite, this isn't the place for you. Dinner at Dar Maghreb is an entertaining dining experience that increases exponentially the larger your party is and the longer you linger. Leave your shoes at the door and enter an exotic Arab world of genie waitresses who wash your hands with lemon water and belly dancers who shimmy around an exquisite fountain in the center of a Koranic patio. The rustic Berber Room, dressed with mountain rugs and brass furniture from Marrakech, is not quite as cozy as the richly carpeted Rabat room, which has the exotic atmosphere of an upscale opium den. In both dining rooms, guests sit at traditional tables on either low sofas or goatskin cushions. Nothing is available à la carte; the fixed-price meal is a multicourse feast, including a choice of chicken, lamb, turkey, beef, squab, quail, or shrimp, eaten with your hands and hunks of bread, and shared from the same dish with other members of your party. Chicken cooked with pickled lemons, onions, and fresh coriander, and couscous with lamb, squash, carrots, tomatoes, garbanzo beans, turnips, onions, and raisins are two of the most popular dishes, but everything is delicious. Most meals come with Moroccan salads and b'stilla, an appetizer of shredded chicken, eggs, almonds, and spices wrapped in a flaky pastry shell and topped with powdered sugar and cinnamon. Invite only friends with good personal hygiene, wear your freshest socks, and come prepared for an adventure.

Georgia

7250 Melrose Ave. (at Alta Vista Ave.). ☎ **213/933-8420.** Reservations recommended. Main courses $13–$19; lunch $6–$15. AE, MC, V. Mon–Fri noon–3pm; Mon–Sat 6:30–11pm, Sun 5:30–11pm. SOUTHERN.

Soul food and power ties come together at this calorie-unconscious ode to southern cooking in the heart of Melrose's funky shopping district. Owned by a group of investors that includes Denzel Washington and Eddie Murphy, the restaurant is popular with Hollywood's African-American crowd and others who can afford L.A.'s highest-priced pork chops, fried chicken, and grits. It's great for people watching. The antebellum-style dining room is built to resemble a fine southern house, complete with mahogany floors, Spanish moss, and wrought-iron gates; a bourbon bar continues the theme. Smoked baby back ribs are particularly good and, like many other dishes, are smothered in onion gravy or remoulade, and sided with corn pudding, grits, string beans, or an excellent creamy garlic coleslaw. Other recommendations include turtle soup, grilled gulf shrimp, and a Creole-style catfish that is more delicately fried than it would traditionally be.

Musso & Frank Grill

6667 Hollywood Blvd. (at Cahuenga Blvd.). ☎ **213/467-7788.** Reservations recommended. Main courses $13–$22. AE, CB, DC, MC, V. Tues–Sat 11am–11pm. AMERICAN/CONTINENTAL.

A survey of Hollywood eateries that leaves out Musso & Frank is like a study of Las Vegas showrooms that fails to mention Wayne Newton. It's not that this is the best restaurant in town, nor is it the most famous; but as L.A's oldest eatery (since 1919), Musso & Frank is the paragon of Old Hollywood grill rooms, an almost kitschy glimpse into a meat-and-potatoes world that's remained the same for generations. This is where Faulkner and Hemingway drank during their screenwriting days, where Orson Welles used to hold court. The restaurant is still known for their bone-dry martinis and perfectly seasoned Bloody Marys. The setting is what you'd expect: oak-beamed ceilings, red-leather booths and banquettes, mahogany room dividers (complete with coathooks), chandeliers with tiny shades. The extensive menu is a veritable survey of American/continental cookery. Hearty dinners include veal scaloppine marsala, roast spring lamb with mint jelly, and broiled lobster. Grilled meats are the restaurant's specialties, as is a chicken potpie that has as much salt as it has heft. There is an extensive wine selection along with the full bar; nobody minds if you show up just for drinks.

INEXPENSIVE

ⓢ Authentic Cafe

7605 Beverly Blvd. (at Curson Ave.). ☎ **213/939-4626.** Reservations not accepted. Main courses $8–$13; lunch $5–$9. MC, V. Mon–Thurs 11:30am–10pm, Fri 11:30am–11pm, Sat 10am–11pm, Sun 10am–10pm. SOUTHWESTERN.

True to its name, this excellent restaurant serves authentic southwestern food in a casual atmosphere; it's a winning combination that has made it an L.A. favorite. The trendy dining room is known for hip people-watching, large portions, and good food; that translates into long waits almost every night of the week. You'll sometimes find an Asian flair to Chef Roger Hayot's southwestern-style meals. Look for Brie, papaya, and chili quesadillas; other worthwhile dishes are the chicken casserole with a cornbread crust; fresh corn and red peppers in chili-cream sauce; and meatloaf with caramelized onions. Lunches—gourmet pizzas, grilled sandwiches, salads—are lighter.

Flora Kitchen

460 S. La Brea Ave. (at 6th St.). ☎ **213/931-9900.** Reservations not accepted. Main courses $5–$10. AE, MC, V. Sun–Thurs 8am–10pm, Fri–Sat 8am–11pm. AMERICAN.

Picture an upscale, funky Carrow's or Denny's and you've imagined Flora Kitchen. Known for its tuna and chicken salads served on exalted La Brea Bakery breads, the restaurant is equally comfortable dishing out more eclectic fare like cayenne-spiced potato soup, poached salmon with dill sauce, and seared ahi with roast vegetables. Flora is popular with art-gallery strollers by day, and with music lovers, who take the restaurant's dinners, boxed, to the Hollywood Bowl, on warm summer nights. Unfortunately, service at Denny's is better.

Pink's Hot Dogs

709 N. La Brea Ave. (at Melrose Ave.) ☎ **213/931-4223.** Hot dogs $2. Sun–Thurs 9:30am–2am, Fri–Sat 9:30am–3am. HOT DOGS.

Pink's isn't your usual guidebook recommendation, but then again, this crusty corner stand is not your usual doggery. The heartburn-inducing chili dogs are so decadent that otherwise upstanding, health-conscious Angelenos crave them; so seductive are these artificially orange goo–topped dogs that they don't mind being seen at this diminutive shanty shack. Pray the bulldozers stay away from this little nugget of a place.

Roscoe's House of Chicken 'n' Waffles

1514 N. Gower St. (at Sunset Blvd). ☎ **213/466-7453.** Reservations not accepted. Main courses $4–$11. No credit cards. Sun–Thurs 9am–midnight, Fri–Sat 9am–4am. AMERICAN.

It sounds like a bad joke: Only chicken and waffle dishes are served here, a rubric that also encompasses eggs and chicken livers. Its close proximity to CBS Television City has turned this simple restaurant into a kind of de facto commissary for the network. A chicken-and-cheese omelette isn't everyone's ideal way to begin the day, but it's de rigueur at Roscoe's. At lunch, few calorie-unconscious diners can resist the chicken smothered in gravy and onions—a house specialty that's served with waffles or grits and biscuits. Large chicken-salad bowls and chicken sandwiches also provide plenty of cluck for the buck. Home-made cornbread, sweet potato pie, homemade potato salad, and corn on the cob are available as side orders, and wine and beer are sold.

Roscoe's can also be found at 4907 W. Washington Blvd. (at La Brea Ave, ☎ 213/936-3730); and 5006 West Pico Blvd. (☎ 213/934-4405).

5 Westside

EXPENSIVE

Diaghilev

1020 N. San Vicente Blvd. (in the Wyndham Bel Age Hotel), West Hollywood. ☎ **310/854-1111.** Reservations accepted. Main courses $23–$27. AE, CB, DC, DISC, MC, V. Tues–Sat 6:30–11pm. FRANCO-RUSSIAN.

In a world where most hoteliers are tearing their hair out trying to persuade guests to spend their dinner dollars in-house, Diaghilev finds itself in the enviable position of having to regularly turn away would-be diners, most of whom aren't even sleeping upstairs. Tucked away in the Wyndham Bel Age Hotel, Diaghilev is a sumptuous turn-of-the-century Franco-Russian theme restaurant where guests lounge on overstuffed loveseats and dine to the soulful strums of a mandolinist. Gilt-framed landscapes hang on silk-covered walls, imported caviar is spooned with ceremony, and seemingly endless varieties of flavored vodkas are sipped from fine crystal. On most nights, host Dimitri hands every lady a long-stemmed rose. Each diner is treated like a czar by a fawning waitstaff that never lets a glass empty or a cleaned plate lie. For starters, sample the blini topped with Russian vodka and caviar. Better yet, order the zakuski combination plate, which includes smoked salmon, a twirl of egg noodles mixed with veal, and a plump mini–cabbage roll. Main courses include a truffled chicken Kiev and braised veal chop in raspberry vinegar; a moist salmon croquet is wrapped in a wonderful flaky pastry. Diaghilev is delicious, but not cheap; complimentary chocolates served before the check arrives softens the blow.

Drai's

730 N. La Cienega Blvd. (between Melrose Ave. and Santa Monica Blvd.). ☎ **310/358-8585.** Reservations required. Main courses $17–$25. AE, MC, V. Daily 6–10:30pm. CLASSIC FRENCH.

Drai's is the kind of attitude-heavy restaurant that insiders love and outsiders love to hate. Owned by producer-turned-restaurateur Victor Drai, the restaurant is currently going head to head with Morton's for the hip Hollywood Monday night crowd and—at least according to some observers—it's winning. Located on the site of L'Ermitage, a once-famous temple of French haute cuisine, Drai has lightened the menu and turned the front room into a lounge, where diners wait for tables; they're shuttled back after dinner for rushed desserts. The bistro-style offerings include smoked duck salad, baked sweet-breads, beef bourguignonne, and the like. Chef Claude Segal, who's as talented—and confident—as any of the stars in his dining room, doesn't shy away from risk, but he's not always successful. Drai's is a destination restaurant, not just a place for a quick bite; make reservations well in advance, and think about renting a limousine.

Eclipse

8800 Melrose Ave. (at Robertson Blvd.), West Hollywood. ☎ **310/724-5959.** Reservations required. Main courses $18–$30. AE, DC, DISC, MC, V. Daily 5:30–10:30pm. CALIFORNIAN.

One of Hollywood's hottest new restaurants, Eclipse boasts a flawless pedigree that includes celebrity backers Steven Seagal and Whoopi Goldberg and Spago alumnus maître d' Bernard Erpicum. The restaurant is located in the old Morton's space (Morton's has relocated across the street); on most nights, Eclipse attracts just as many stars and studio heads as its heavyweight neighbor. The restaurant's A-room is both exciting and romantic: It features terra-cotta tones, a high chalet-style ceiling, and large picture windows overlooking a faux forest. On any given night, you can get whiplash while rubbernecking to see the likes of Ovitz, Geffen, or Guber schmoozing with celebs like De Niro, Cruise, or Stone. Unfortunately for most mortals, reservations are required up to one month in advance on weekends, and you're likely to be seated in Siberia. Star power aside, the food is excellent, sometimes even superlative. Chef Serge Falesitch's California Provençal menu emphasizes seafood that's gloriously simple and artfully presented. A bounteous shellfish platter, translucent sashimi, and sesame-studded seared scallops are all great starters. Whole striped bass and John Dory are aromatically infused with basil, tarragon, and fennel and roasted in a brick oven. There's also a superb artichoke risotto, orecchiette with duck ragout, and a thick, perfectly grilled veal chop.

✪ Four Oaks

2181 No. Beverly Glen Blvd., Los Angeles. ☎ **310/470-2265.** Reservations required. Main courses $22–$29. Main courses $22–$29. AE, MC, V. Tues–Sat 11:30am–9:30pm, Sun 10:30am–2pm; daily 6–10pm. CALIFORNIAN.

Just looking at the menu here makes me swoon. The country-cottage ambiance and chef Peter Roelant's supperlative blend of fresh ingredients with luxurious Continental flourishes make a meal at the Four Oaks one of my favorite luxuries. Dinner is served beneath trees festooned with twinkling lights. Appetizers like lavender-smoked salmon with crisp potatoes and horseredish crème fraîche complement mouth-watering dishes like roasted chicken with sage, Oregon forest mushrooms, artichoke hearts, and port-balsamic sauce. If you're looking for someplace special, head to this canyon hideaway—you won't be disappointed.

Ginza Sushi-Ko

218 N. Rodeo Dr. (in the Two Rodeo complex), Beverly Hills. ☎ **310/247-8939.** Reservations required. Sushi $7–$25 per piece, main courses about $35. MC, V. Mon–Sat 6–10pm. JAPANESE/SUSHI.

It seems that most every restaurant in L.A. needs some kind of hook. For Ginza Sushi-Ko that twist is cost: This is far and away the city's most expensive eatery. You have to be missing Nippon pretty badly to spend upwards of $200 per person for fresh fish flown in daily from

Westside Dining

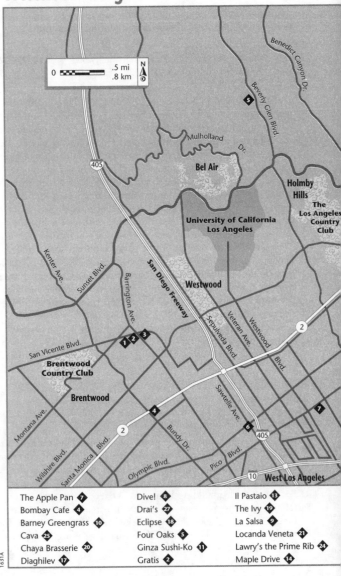

The Apple Pan 7	Dive! 8	Il Pastaio 13
Bombay Cafe 4	Drai's 27	The Ivy 19
Barney Greengrass 10	Eclipse 18	La Salsa 9
Cava 25	Four Oaks 5	Locanda Veneta 21
Chaya Brasserie 20	Ginza Sushi-Ko 11	Lawry's the Prime Rib 24
Diaghilev 17	Gratis 2	Maple Drive 14

Tokyo's famed Tsukiji Market. During a time when the emphasis at most area restaurants is on local ingredients and price consciousness, Ginza Sushi-Ko is bucking the trend. Located on the second floor of one of the world's most exclusive shopping malls, it's the epitome of modesty, and just oh so Japanese. Announced by a simple sign, the dining room seats but 20, either at the bar or in one of several private

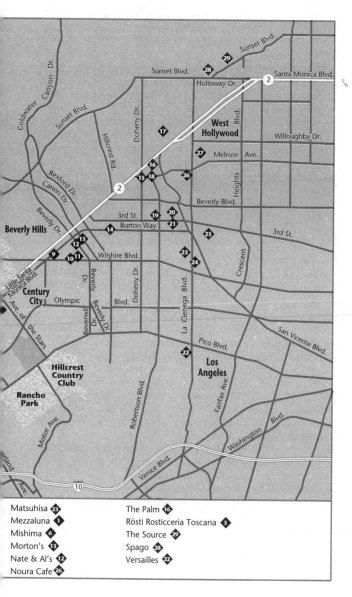

Matsuhisa **23**	The Palm **16**
Mezzaluna **1**	Rösti Rosticceria Toscana **3**
Mishima **6**	The Source **29**
Morton's **13**	Spago **28**
Nate & Al's **12**	Versailles **22**
Noura Cafe **26**	

tatami rooms. There is no printed menu; diners are told what's fresh, order their favorite cuts, and sit back for the escapade of artful flavor, in which not one grain of rice or dot of roe is ever out of place.

The Ivy

133 N. Robertson Blvd. (between 3rd St. and Beverly Blvd.), West Hollywood. ☎ **310/274-8303.** Reservations recommended on weekends. Main courses

$22–$38; lunch $10–$25. AE, DC, DISC, MC, V. Mon–Sat, 11:30am–3pm, Sun 11am–3pm. Mon–Thurs 6–11pm, Fri–Sat 6–11:30pm, Sun 5:30–10:30pm. AMERICAN CONTEMPORARY.

The Ivy attracts one of the most Industry-heavy crowds in the city; it's wildly popular with agents, producers, and plenty of stars. If you like nightclubs with velvet ropes and pick-and-choose doormen, you'll feel at home at this snobby eatery, which treats celebrities and nobodies as differently as Brahmans and Untouchables. Just past the cool reception lies two disarmingly down-home dining rooms furnished with rustic antiques, Navajo rugs, hanging baskets, and huge roses planted in antique pewter pots; there's also a thoroughly charming patio. The food is excellent. The Ivy's Caesar salad is perfect, as are the plump and crispy crab cakes. Recommended dishes include spinach linguine with a peppery tomato-basil sauce, prime rib dusted with Cajun spices, and succulently tender lime-marinated grilled chicken. They also do a great burger. The wine list is particularly notable, and there's always a terrific variety of desserts. Too bad about the attitude.

Lawry's The Prime Rib

55 N. La Cienega Blvd. (north of Wilshire Blvd.), Beverly Hills. ☎ **310/652-2827.** Reservations required. Main courses $19–$26. AE, CB, DC, DISC, MC, V. Mon–Thurs 5–11pm, Fri–Sat 5pm–midnight, Sun 3–10pm. STEAKS.

Most Americans know Lawry's only as a brand of seasoned salt; the seasoning was invented here, conceived to flavor this restaurant's meats. Opened in 1938 by Lawrence Frank, Lawry's remains a serious family enterprise. Going to Lawry's is an Old World event; the only menu offerings are four cuts of prime rib that vary in size from two fingers to an entire hand. Every standing rib roast is dry aged for two to three weeks, sprinkled with Lawry's famous seasoning, then roasted on a bed of rock salt. A carver wheels the cooked beef tableside, then slices it properly, rare to well done. The result is incredibly tender and juicy prime rib, some of the nation's very best. All dinners come with very mushy mashed potatoes, whipped creamy with horseradish, and York-shire pudding. Each dinner also comes with the Original Spinning Bowl Salad: While mixed greens, hard-boiled eggs, and chopped beets are spinning on a bed of crushed ice, they're drenched with dressing poured straight from the Lawry's bottle. Lawry's moved across the street from its original location a few years ago, but retained its throwback-to-the-thirties clubroom atmosphere, complete with Persian-carpeted oak floors, high-backed chairs, and original European oils. Couples should opt for a table in either the Vintage or Oval rooms (the latter seats larger parties as well).

Maple Drive

345 N. Maple Dr. (at Burton Way), Beverly Hills. ☎ **310/274-9800.** Reservations recommended. Main courses $17–$25; lunch $7–$15. AE, MC, V. Mon–Sat lunch 11:30am–2:30pm, dinner 6–10pm. AMERICAN.

Owned by Liza Minelli, Dudley Moore, and producer/director Tony Bill (the same celebrity trio that brought 72 Market Street to Venice), Maple Drive is one of the best traditional American restaurants in, well, America. Chef Leonard Schwartz cooks the great meatloaf, terrific chili, and out-of-this-world veal chops, (which regulars ask for Milanese style—lightly breaded and served with a squeeze of lemon). The restaurant attracts the biggest celebrities—Barbra, Elton, Arnold, and others who have enjoyed fame for so long they often seem tired of the attention; they enter through a second, more discrete, door and sit in relatively secluded booths in back of the multilevel dining room. That's a bonus for us nobodies; on warm nights, the best seats are out on the patio. Maple Drive is a classy place with great food, high prices, and live dinnertime jazz. Even if Clint isn't at the next table, it's worth lingering for the extraordinary desserts.

Matsuhisa

129 N. La Cienega Blvd. (north of Wilshire Blvd.), Beverly Hills. ☎ **310/659-9639.** Reservations required. Main courses $14–$22; good sushi assortment $20–$30; lunch $7–$13. AE, DC, MC, V. Mon–Fri 11:45am–2:45pm; nightly 5:45–10:15pm. JAPANESE/PERUVIAN.

Japanese chef/owner Nobuyuki Matsuhisa arrived in Los Angeles via Peru and opened what may be the most creative restaurant in the entire city. A true master of fish cookery, Matsuhisa creates fantastic, unusual dishes by combining Japanese flavors with South American spices and salsas. Broiled sea bass with black truffles, sautéed squid with garlic and soy, and Dungeness crab tossed with chilies and cream are good examples of the masterfully prepared delicacies that are available in addition to thickly-sliced nigiri and creative sushi rolls. Matsuhisa is also known for having some of the most hard-to-get tables in town. Both tight and bright, the restaurant's small, crowded main dining room suffers from bad lighting and precious lack of privacy. There's lots of action behind the sushi bar, and a frenetic service staff keeps the restaurant humming at a fiery pace. Stars are commonplace, though many are just walking through on their way to a private room. Matsuhisa is fantastically popular with hardcore foodies, who continually return for the savory surprises that come with every bite. Reserve early, unless you are happy starting your meal at 6 or 10pm.

Morton's

8764 Melrose Ave. (east of Santa Monica Blvd.), West Hollywood. ☎ **310/ 276-5205.** Reservations required. Main courses $17–$29; lunch $7–$15. AE, MC, V. Mon–Fri noon–11:30pm, Sat 6–11:30pm. CALIFORNIAN.

Dining at Hard Rock Cafe–founder Peter Morton's eponymous restaurant has become something of a rite of passage for any Industry insider worthy of the label. Indeed, the restaurant's clientele reads like a who's-who. For years now, on Monday nights, entertainment's high and mighty have considered these the most coveted tables in the city. But this could be changing; after a move across the street and two chef changes, regulars are mumbling that, although the space has improved, the food has been better. Phoning on a recent Friday, I easily got a reservation for the following Monday—at 8:30pm. The restaurant's seating policy ensures that "nobodies" are placed "in the trees" (by the tall potted plants near the back wall). For those lucky enough not to face the wall, the lofty dining room provides good sightlines, yet remains dark enough to keep it feeling personal. Meals at Morton's are straightforward and good. The menu isn't intimidating, and plates are assembled without a lot of visual froufrou. The emphasis on simplicity, quality, and freshness translates into appetizers like fresh Maryland crab cakes, tuna sashimi, and chopped shrimp and black bean quesadillas. Typical main courses on the seasonal menu include lime-grilled free-range chicken, grilled swordfish, sautéed veal chop, and New York steak. Desserts include hot fudge sundaes and warm fruit tarts.

The Palm

9001 Santa Monica Blvd. (between Doheny Dr. and Robertson Blvd.), West Hollywood. ☎ **310/550-8811.** Reservations required. Main courses $16–$28; lobsters $18 per pound; lunch $8–$15. AE, CB, DC, DISC, MC, V. Mon–Fri noon–3pm, Mon–Sat 5–10pm, Sun 5–9:30pm. STEAK/LOBSTER.

Every great American city has a great steakhouse; in Los Angeles, it's the Palm. The child of the famous New York restaurant of the same name, the Palm is widely regarded by local foodies as one of the best traditional American eateries in the city. The glitterati seem to agree, as stars and their handlers are regularly in attendance. In both food and ambiance, this west coast apple hasn't fallen far from the proverbial tree. The restaurant is brightly lit, extremely noisy, and casually decorated, with caricatures on the walls and sawdust on the floor. Live Nova Scotia lobsters are flown in almost daily, then broiled over charcoal and served with big bowls of melted butter. Most are an enormous three to seven pounds and, although they're obscenely expensive, can be shared. Steaks are similarly sized, and some of the choicest cuts of beef available anywhere: New York sirloin, filet mignon, porterhouse, and prime rib are all perfectly grilled to order and served à la carte. Diners also swear by the celebrated Gigi Salad, a mixture of lettuce, shrimp, bacon, green beans, pimento, and avocado. Unfortunately, the wine list is poor and desserts are worse.

✪ Spago

1114 Horn Ave. (at Sunset Blvd.), West Hollywood. ☎ **310/652-4025.** Reservations required. Main courses $18–$28. DC, DISC, MC, V. Daily 6–11:30pm. CALIFORNIAN.

Wolfgang Puck is more than a great chef: He's also a masterful businessman and publicist who has made Spago one of the best-known restaurants in America. Despite all the hoopla—and more than 15 years of service—Spago remains one of L.A.'s top-rated eateries. The bright, clean, colorful dining room is noisy and upbeat. German-born Puck originally won fame serving imaginative "gourmet" pizzas. These individual-size, thin-crust pies are baked in a wood-burning oven, topped with goodies like duck sausage, shiitake mushrooms, leeks, and artichokes, and other combinations once considered to be on the culinary edge. Puck, it seems, is rarely in the kitchen, but the superchef has an uncanny knack for hiring kitchen help as smart and creative as himself; Spago alumni have gone on to open other top restaurants, Campanile, Eclipse, and Carrots among them. Spago's pastas are great because the combinations are perfect: black-pepper fettuccine with Louisiana shrimp, roasted garlic, and basil; or angel hair with goat cheese and broccoli. Of meat dishes, roast Sonoma lamb with braised shallots and grilled chicken with garlic and parsley are two perennial favorites. The celebrated (and far from secret) off-menu meal is Jewish Pizza, a crispy pie topped with smoked salmon, crème fraîche, dill, red onion, and dollops of caviar. As in most star-heavy restaurants, the rest of us sit in back; but even at a table that doesn't overlook the boulevard, you can expect completely unpretentious, expert service.

MODERATE

Barney Greengrass

9570 Wilshire Blvd. (in Barney's New York), Beverly Hills. ☎ **310/777-5877.** Reservations not accepted. Main courses $12–$23; breakfast $5–$11; lunch $8–$15. AE, DC, MC, V. Mon–Thurs 7:30am–7pm, Fri 7:30am–8pm, Sat 9am–7pm, Sun 9am–6pm. DELI.

It was a big deal in Beverly Hills when the celebrated New York clothier Barney's opened a satellite store here. But it was a *very* big deal in Hollywood when New York's celebrated "sturgeon king," Barney Greengrass, opened on the department store's top floor. This upscale deli has quickly become an important power lunch spot for the Industry crowd. Famous for sturgeon and smoked fish—at caviar prices—Barney Greengrass seems more than a bit like a fish out of water here. As soon as you get off the elevator you can tell that the restaurant is joyful, clean, and bright, without the attitude—and none of the atmosphere—of New York's nosheries. In addition to having a separate caviar, champagne, and vodka bar, the restaurant makes its own oven-baked matzos, claims to import their bagels from New York's famed H&H bagelry, and sets its paper-covered tables with designer utensils and stemware. The many smoked specialties include Nova Scotia salmon, sable, chubs, rainbow trout, whitefish, and, of course, sturgeon. The best meals are matzo brei with onions and wild mushrooms, orange-challah french toast, and smoked-salmon soufflé.

Bombay Cafe

12113 Santa Monica Blvd. (at Bundy Dr.) ☎ **310/820-2070.** Reservations recommended on weekends. Main courses $9–$15. MC, V. Tues–Sun 11am–4pm, Tues–Thurs 4–10pm, Fri–Sat 4–11pm. SOUTH INDIAN.

Indian is the cuisine of the moment in L.A., and nowhere is it done better than at Bombay Cafe. The unlikely McRestaurant interior and storefront location (on the second floor of a nondescript mini-mall) belie excellent curries and kormas that are typical of South Indian street food. Once seated, immediately order sev puri for the table; these crispy little chips topped with chopped potatoes, onions, cilantro, and chutneys are the perfect accompaniment to what is sure to be an extended menu-reading session. Also recommended are the burrito-like "frankies," juicy little bread rolls stuffed with lamb, chicken, or cauliflower. The best dishes come from the 800-degree tandoor, and include spicy yogurt-marinated swordfish, lamb, and chicken. Tandoori chicken sausages are unique, as is tandoori chicken salad, which is heavily mixed with cilantro and scallions. The food is served authentically spicy, unless you specify otherwise. The restaurant is phenomenally popular, and gets its share of celebrities: Meg Ryan and Dennis Quaid hired Bombay Cafe to cater an affair at their Montana ranch. Only beer and wine are served.

Cava

8384 W. 3rd St. (in the Beverly Plaza Hotel, at Orlando Ave.). ☎ **213/658-8898.**
Reservations recommended on weekends. Main courses $8–$17; breakfast $3–$9;
lunch $4–$14. AE, CB, DC, DISC, MC, V. Daily 6:30am–midnight. SPANISH.

Trendy types in the mood for some fun are attracted to Cava's great
mambo atmosphere, made festive with flamboyant colors, long shared
tables, and loud, lively flamenco that's live on weekends. People get
drunk here, eat too much, then dance it off until midnight. The
majority of main courses—including beef-stuffed green peppers, pork
with sautéed apples, crispy red snapper with garlic, and sherry-glazed
orange chicken—are very good. But the large variety of tapas is even
more recommendable; order a good assortment and you'll be rewarded
with a party of flavors and textures. Top picks include grilled shrimp
in garlic sauce, mussels steamed in sweet sherry, lamb riblets in red
wine, and eggplant rolled in cheese and chorizo. Paellas are available
with or without meat. If you have room for dessert, try the ruby-
colored pears poached in port, the rice pudding, or the flan.

Chaya Brasserie

8741 Alden Dr. (west of Robertson Blvd.). ☎ **310/859-8833.** Reservations recom-
mended on weekends. Main courses $11–$24; lunch $9–$16. AE, CB, DC, MC, V.
Mon–Fri 11am–2:30pm; Mon–Thurs 6–10:30pm, Fri–Sat 6–11pm, Sun 6–10pm.
FRANCO-JAPANESE.

Now open for a dozen years, Chaya has become well ensconced as one
of Los Angeles's finest restaurants. Popular with film agents during
lunch and a particularly beautiful assembly of stars at night, the restaurant is loved for its exceptionally good food and refreshingly
unpretentious atmosphere. Despite a high noise level, the stage-lit
dining room feels sensuous and swoony. On warm afternoons and
evenings, the best tables are on the outside terrace, overlooking the busy
street. A continental bistro with Asian overtones, Chaya is best known
for superb grilled fish and meats, like seared soy-marinated Hawaiian
tuna and Long Island duckling. Chef Shigefumi Tachibe's lobster
ravioli with pesto-cream sauce is both stylish and delicious, as is
a deceptively simple off-menu dish of spaghetti dressed in dry red
chilies, garlic, and olive oil. Hot and cold starters include seaweed salad
with ginger-soy rice vinaigrette, escargots with chopped mushrooms,
and sautéed foie gras over hearts of daikon.

⑤ Il Pastaio

400 N. Canon Dr. (at Brighton Way), Beverly Hills. ☎ **310/205-5444.** Reservations
not accepted. Main courses $12–$23; lunch $7–$12. AE, MC, V. Mon–Sat 11:30am–
11pm. ITALIAN.

Sicilian-born Celestino Drago is an terrific chef who has been helm-
ing the kitchens of high-profile L.A. restaurants for years. Branching
out on his own, Chef Drago hit the jackpot with this hugely successful, value-priced eatery. The restaurant is a simple pasta place with
white walls, a long bar, and a pasta-making area. It's as narrow as a
bowling alley and almost as loud. Only starters, pastas, and risottos
are served, but the selections are vast and great for grazing. Swordfish carpaccio with shaved fennel and blood oranges, and seafood

"spaghetti" in a flaky envelope are Drago's signature dishes. Chef Drago offered a sautéed foie gras appetizer with a buttery balsamic vinegar glaze when he worked at Chianti, and he continues to serve it here—to those who know enough to ask for it. Pastas include lobster-stuffed ravioli in a silky lobster reduction, and garganelli: wheat pasta curls in amatriciana sauce (pureed tomato, pancetta, percorino, and onion). Two risotti are offered nightly, and both usually hit the proverbial bull's-eye. Unfortunately, Il Pastaio is too small. There's almost always a wait, and an uncomfortable one at that. But by meal's end, it always seems worth it.

A second Il Pastaio, on South Lake Street in Pasadena (☎ 818/795-4006), opened in early 1995.

✪ Locanda Veneta

8638 W. 3rd St. (between San Vicente and Robertson blvds.). ☎ **310/274-1893.** Reservations required. Main courses $10–$22. AE, DC, DISC, MC, V. Mon–Fri 11:30am–2:30pm; Mon–Sat 5:30–11:30pm. ITALIAN/VENETIAN.

Locanda Veneta's citywide renown belies its tiny size and unpretentious setting. Its location, across from the unsightly white monolith that is Cedars-Sinai Hospital, is a far cry from Venice's Grand Canal. And the single, loud, tightly packed dining room can sometimes feel like Piazza San Marco at the height of tourist season. But the sensible prices reflect the restaurant's efficient decor, and while the dining room is decidedly unfancy, the kitchen is dead serious. The restaurant has become a kind of temple for knowledgeable foodies, who flock here to sample the latest creations of chef/owner Antonio Tommasi, a gifted artist and culinary technician who's building a national reputation. Soups are excellent, seafood dishes extraordinary, and pastas are as good as they can get. Signature dishes include pasta and bean soup, veal chops, lobster ravioli, shrimp risotto, and perfectly grilled vegetables. Insiders order linguine with rock shrimp, baby asparagus, and tomatoes—an uncharacteristically light off-menu meal.

Mezzaluna

11750 San Vicente Blvd., Brentwood. ☎ **310/447-8667.** Reservations required. Main courses $10–$22; lunch $7–$13. AE, DC, DISC, MC, V. Mon–Sat 11:30am–10pm, Sun dinner only 5–10pm. ITALIAN.

Thanks to windfall P.R., this once-trendy little neighborhood restaurant is now bursting at the seams with tourists. Everyone, it seems, wants to taste a bit of history, no matter how macabre. Mezzaluna, you'll recall, is where Ronald Goldman waited tables, and where Nicole Brown Simpson, a regular customer, ate her last meal—rigatoni melanzane. Theatrically lighted, colorfully tiled, and stylishly furnished, Mezzaluna has the same upper middle–class atmosphere as its sister restaurants in New York and Aspen. Gastronomically speaking, the restaurant is best known for its crispy pizzas, topped in traditional California style with smoked meats, porcini mushrooms, pestos, and the like. Pastas are equally creative and good, but not great. The carpaccios are more likable, paired with sautéed olives and tomatoes or hearts of palm and avocado. There's a full bar—don't order anything with "O.J."

INEXPENSIVE

The Apple Pan

10801 Pico Blvd. (east of Westwood Blvd.). ☎ **310/475-3585.** Reservations not accepted. Main courses $6–$7. No credit cards. Tues–Thurs, and Sun 11am–midnight; Fri–Sat 11am–1am. SANDWICHES/AMERICAN.

There are no tables, just a U-shaped counter, at this classic American burger shack and L.A. landmark. Open since 1947, The Apple Pan is a diner that looks—and acts—the part. It's famous for juicy burgers, bullet service, and its authentic frills-free atmosphere. The hickory burger is best, though the tuna sandwich also has its huge share of fans. Ham, egg salad, and swiss cheese sandwiches round out the menu. Definitely order fries and, if you're in the mood, the banana cream pie, too.

Dive!

10250 Santa Monica Blvd. (in the Century City Marketplace). ☎ **310/788-3483.** Reservations accepted only for parties of 10 or more. Main courses $6–$15. AE, DC, MC, V. Sun–Thurs 11:30am–11pm, Fri–Sat 11:30am–midnight. SANDWICHES/ AMERICAN.

"Prepare to dive!" the public address system cries without warning. Red lights flash, the room darkens, water bubbles through "portholes," video monitors go black . . . and a waitress casually delivers another coke to an adjacent table. Owned by Steven Spielberg and Jeffrey Katzenberg, two thirds of the new mega-company Dreamworks SKG, Dive! is the first of what the investors hope to be a series of submarine-themed restaurants. The restaurant-cum-theme-park's insulated underwater ambience is the ultimate in dining entertainment. Except for the fries and the thin-cut onion rings, however, the same cannot be said of the food, which is decent at best and bad at worst. The menu is mainly submarine sandwiches (get it?), along with salads and some wood-roasted dishes like salmon served with assorted dipping sauces, such as homemade ketchup and cheddar cheese sauce. Stick with the subs. The restaurant is perpetually packed; waiting patrons get a beeper that conveniently won't work outside, so they have to wait at the expensive bar, where there's a voyeuristic periscope exposing the goings-on down on Santa Monica Boulevard. At the requisite gift shop, you can purchase a souvenir menu sprinkled with puns and quotations. It costs $5, but it lights up.

Gratis

11658 San Vicente Blvd. (east of Barrington Ave.), Brentwood. ☎ **310/571-2345.** Reservations accepted only for parties of six or more. Main courses $6–$10. AE, MC, V. Daily 10:30am–10pm. VEGETARIAN FAT-FREE.

Gratis—an inevitable outgrowth of everything that is L.A.—whips up inventive pizzas, soups, salads, and vegetable-based dishes that are entirely fat and cholesterol free. Chef Richard Leveckis's eclectic menu has some winners, most notably the vegetable chili and barbecued zucchini, but most meals (like anything with cheese) are the bland concoctions most carnivores fear. Surprisingly, the fat-free triple-layer chocolate cake is the restaurant's best dish. There's a simple, bright dining room and a bustling take-away counter, where Glenn Close, Warren Beatty, Meryl Streep, and Publishers Clearing House pitchman Ed McMahon have all been spotted. It remains to be seen, however, if they'll return.

La Salsa

9631 Little Santa Monica Blvd. (between Camden and Bedford drs.), Beverly Hills. ☎ **310/276-2373.** Main courses $5–$7. MC, V. Mon–Fri 10:30am–9:30pm, Sat 10:30am–9pm, Sun 10:30am–7pm. MEXICAN.

L.A.'s best Mexican fast food is served at this bright and spotless taquaria chain, well-known throughout the city for its excellent, healthful, lard-free burritos and tacos. The Gourmet Burrito is a hefty mix of grilled chicken or steak, cheese, and guacamole; the Grande adds rice and beans. True to its name, La Salsa excels in the preparation of fresh sauces, offering four types varying in spiciness, texture, and flavor. The restaurants serve soda and beer, and (sometimes) orchata, a traditional Mexican drink made with rice flour and cinnamon. Order at the counter.

Other locations include 22800 Pacific Coast Highway, Malibu, ☎ 310/456-6299; 44 N. Fair Oaks Ave., Pasadena, ☎ 818/793-0723; downtown at 727 Flower St., ☎ 213/892-8227; and 245 Pine Ave., Long Beach, ☎ 310/491-1104.

Mishima

11301 Olympic Blvd. (at Sawtelle Blvd.). ☎ **310/473-5297.** Reservations not accepted. Main courses $4–$9. MC, V. Tues–Sun 11:30am–9pm. JAPANESE.

Hidden on the second floor of an unobtrusive strip mall, this small Japanese eatery has nevertheless become extraordinarily popular with neighborhood residents and workers. A dead ringer for any number of noodle shops in Tokyo, Mishima sports a contemporary Asian decor, complete with matte black tables and chairs, Japanese prints on white walls, and plastic reproductions of every menu item. A loyal clientele fills the small, bright dining room with noodle slurps and chopstick clacks. Udon (thick wheat noodles) or soba (narrow buckwheat linguine) are the main choices here; both are served either hot or cold in a variety of soups and sauces that true aficionados might find too bland and too thin. Sushi, chicken dishes, and a variety of tempuras are also available. It all seems so authentically Japanese—except, thankfully, for the prices.

Nate & Al's

414 N. Beverly Dr. (at Brighton Way), Beverly Hills. ☎ **310/274-0101.** Reservations not accepted. Main courses $8–$13. AE, DISC, MC, V. Daily 7:30am–9pm. DELI.

Nate & Al's is little more than a glorified coffee shop that has been slapping pastrami on fresh-baked rye for homesick New Yorkers since 1945. The deli is an established Industry hangout and claims zillions of loyalists who are ardent admirers of the chopped liver and chicken soup with matzoh balls. The menu, which is as thick as *War and Peace*, includes staples like lox, whitefish, herring, potato pancakes, blintzes, and borscht. Huge sandwiches come overstuffed with meats and cheeses. Wine and beer are available.

Noura Cafe

8479 Melrose Ave. (near La Cienega Blvd.). ☎ **213/651-4581.** Reservations accepted only for parties of 6 or more. Main courses $5–$11; salads and pitas $4–$7. MC, V. Daily 11am–11pm. MIDDLE EASTERN.

Noura Cafe is packed with beautiful, model types who love the restaurant's healthful, largely vegetarian Middle Eastern cuisine. Seating is either inside or out, beside a warm firepit. Most meals are served with pita bread, for stuffing with broiled lamb, beef, chicken, or any number of salads. Traditional Mediterranean salads include baba ghanoush (grilled eggplant with tahini and lemon), Turkish (tomatoes, green onions, and spices), and tabbouleh (cracked wheat, parsley, and tomatoes).

⑤ Rösti Rosticceria Toscana

908 S. Barrington Ave. (at San Vicente Blvd.), Brentwood. ☎ **310/447-8695.** Reservations not accepted. Main courses $7–$13; lunch $4–$9. AE, MC, V. Daily 7am–10pm. ITALIAN.

In Florence, one sees a lot of places like Rösti: Clean and bright, with sparkling white tiles, shelves of packaged pastas, oils, and other Italian foods, a few tables, and some sidewalk seating shaded with bright red umbrellas. The best dish here—by far—is the grilled rosemary-scented half chicken: The skin is crisp, the meat is juicy, and it's served with wonderful slow-roasted potatoes. Rösti is primarily a locals kind of place; many of the customers order their meals packaged to take home. For visitors, it's one of the best values in the neighborhood. Flaked tuna tossed with white cannellini beans is the best of the antipasti, and the creamy spinach-stuffed ravioli is the top pasta; the seafood risotto is a meaty mixture of rock shrimp, calamari, and fresh clams. The restaurant opens early for cappuccino and pastries.

The Source

8301 W. Sunset Blvd. (between La Cienega Blvd. and Fairfax Ave.), West Hollywood. ☎ **213/656-6388.** Reservations not accepted. Main courses $5–$11. AE, CB, DC, MC, V. Mon–Fri 8am–midnight, Sat–Sun 9am–midnight. CALIFORNIA HEALTH FOOD.

This is where Woody Allen met Diane Keaton for a typical L.A. lunch in *Annie Hall*—part of his New York-centric statement about health-crazy Los Angeles. The restaurant is painted with giant colorful sunflowers and daisies that sprout up against a green background; from the street it looks just like the 1960s throwback that it is. Today, Fabio eats here(!) along with other health-conscious Angelenos who enjoy the ultra-casual dining room. Some diners choose to sit on the covered patio that overlooks Sunset Boulevard; it's a lot more enjoyable than it sounds. Good salads and sandwiches are augmented by a small offering of cooked dishes, including cheese-walnut loaf and recommendable veggie burgers. Portions are huge, and homemade soups and whole-wheat rolls are included with most meals. Drinks include yogurt shakes, beer, and wine, and the date-nut cheesecake is worth sticking around for.

Versailles

1415 S. La Cienega Blvd. (south of Pico Blvd.). ☎ **310/289-0392.** Reservations not accepted. Main courses $5–$11. AE, MC, V. Daily 11am–10pm. CUBAN.

😊 Family-Friendly Restaurants

Prices notwithstanding, **Musso & Frank Grill** *(see p.100)*, Holly-wood's oldest restaurant, is a simple family place that offers something for everyone. Located directly on the Walk of Fame, the restaurant is in the heart of touristland. Kids are pleased by the extensive menu that offers something for everyone. For adults, the restaurant offers unmistakable quality. And who else will serve you peas and cubed carrots—with absolutely no irony—just like Mom used to?

On the other end of the scale is **Pink's Hot Dogs** *(see p.101)*, an institution in its own right that has been serving politically incorrect franks for what seems like forever. Everyone loves Pink's chili dogs, but you may never get the orange stains out of your kid's clothes.

Visiting **Lawry's The Prime Rib** *(see p.106)* is an event, and a thrill for everybody. The steak is served with such flourish that it's hard not to feel like you're someplace special.

Dive! *(see p. 112)* was created by Steven Spielberg and Jeffrey Katzenberg with kids specifically in mind. It's a fun place, with surroundings designed to take your mind off the food.

Outfitted with formica tabletops and looking something like an ethnic International House of Pancakes, Versailles feels very much like any number of Miami restaurants that cater to the exiled Cuban community. Because meals are good, bountiful, and cheap, there's often a wait to get in here. The menu reads like a veritable survey of Havana-style cookery and includes specialties like Moors and Christians (flavorful black beans with white rice), ropa vieja (a stringy beef stew), eastin lechón (suckling pig with sliced onions), and fried whole fish (usually sea bass). Shredded roast pork is particularly recommendable, especially when tossed with the restaurant's trademark garlic-citrus sauce. But what everyone comes for is the chicken—succulent, slow roasted for an eternity, smothered in onions and the garlic-citrus sauce or barbecue sauce. Most everything is served with black beans and rice. Wine and beer are available.

Additional Versailles restaurants are located in Culver City at 10319 Venice Blvd. (☎ 310/558-3168); and in Encino at 17410 Ventura Blvd. (☎ 818/906-0756).

6 The Beaches

EXPENSIVE

Chez Melange

1716 Pacific Coast Hwy (at the Palos Verdes Inn), Redondo Beach. ☎ **310/540-1222.** Reservations required. Main courses $18–$30; lunch $8–$11; breakfast $5–$8. AE, MC, V. Daily 7–11am; Mon–Fri 11:30am–3pm; Mon–Sat 5–11pm, Sun 5–10pm. CALIFORNIAN.

Redondo's appropriately named Chez Melange is not only the best restaurant in the South Bay, it's most eclectic, too. While the combination of sausages and sushi on the same menu should send up red flags in most restaurants, both are well within this kitchen's formidable abilities. Homemade sausages are made with veal, chicken, and lamb, and served with gourmet dipping sauces. Sushi is morning fresh and sliced thick. About a dozen daily specials might include braised rabbit simmered in chicken stock and white wine, or blackened chicken burritos. It's not on the menu, but cognoscenti come for fresh ahi, which is seared medium rare and blended with sun-dried tomatoes, chopped red onions, horseradish, and a little olive oil, then topped with capers and served on homemade crostini. Call ahead to make sure the fish came in. Required to serve breakfast by the hotel in which they're located, Chez Melange rises to the occasion with kippers and eggs, and scrambled eggs with fried oysters, bacon, and mushrooms. Conceived for serious eaters, the restaurant keeps its clientele with wonderful consistency, a clever newsletter, and lots of special dinners and events.

Chinois on Main

2709 Main St. (south of Pico Blvd.), Santa Monica. ☎ **310/392-9025.** Reservations required. Main courses $21–$29. AE, DC, MC, V. Wed–Fri 11:30am–2pm; daily 6–10:30pm. FRANCO-CHINESE.

Widely regarded as Wolfgang Puck's best restaurant, this Franco-Chinese eatery bustles nightly with locals and visitors who are wowed by the eatery's reputation, and rarely disappointed by the food. Groundbreaking in its time, the restaurant still relies on the same quirky East-meets-West mélange of ingredients and technique. The menu is just about equally split between Chinois' signature dishes and new creations by head chef Makoto Tanaka. The most famous of the former are the surprisingly tough baby pork ribs in a cloyingly tangy plum sauce, and farm-raised whole catfish that's perfectly deep fried and dramatically presented—but a bit bland, frankly. Terrific newer dishes include Louisiana shrimp in a mustard-fired plum sauce, and rare roasted loin of venison served in a ginger-spiced Port and sundried cherries sauce. Chef Tanaka will gladly prepare, on request, grilled squab on pan-fried noodles. This off-menu dish comes with a rich garlic-ginger sauce and sautéed shiitake and oyster mushrooms; it's said to be a favorite of regulars Luther Vandross and Shirley MacLaine. The dining room, designed by Puck's wife Barbara Lazaroff, is as colorful as it is loud. The noise level can be deafening, especially if a large party is in the house.

Granita

In the Malibu Colony Mall, 23725 W. Malibu Rd. (at Webb Way), Malibu. ☎ **310/456-0488.** Reservations required. Main courses $21–$26. CB, DC, DISC, MC, V. Mon–Wed 11:30am–2:30pm; daily 6–10:30pm; Sat–Sun 11am–2:30pm. CALIFORNIAN.

When Wolfgang Puck's Granita came to Malibu, local foodies were thrilled that they no longer had to drive all the way to Santa Monica just to have a decent dinner. The food here is great, sometimes even outstanding. But, after only five years, the over-the-top decor is feeling kind of dated, and I just can't imagine this surreal eruption of kaleidoscopic art as my regular dining room. The entire restaurant—floors, ceilings, walls—is a chromatic blast as varied as the fish swimming in the lighted aquariums. The happy underwater-acid-trip theme is reinforced by an energetic waitstaff outfitted in vests or ties that explode with color. The food here is as consciously contemporary as the surroundings; there's to be no doubt that Puck is a master of his craft, and a culinary artist to boot. House specialties are from the sea, and include grilled Atlantic salmon on roasted Chino corn salsa, Alaskan spot prawns with saffron risotto and crispy ginger, and roasted Chinese duck with Asian salad and ginger mango relish. Puck's signature pizzas are here, too. Insiders begin with the off-menu potato gazette with smoked salmon, or chicken soup made with roasted-chicken stock, angel-hair noodles, and designer veggies.

✪ Michael's

1147 3rd St. (west of Wilshire Blvd.), Santa Monica. ☎ **310/451-0843.** Reservations required. Main courses $15–$25; lunch $12–$21. AE, CB, DC, DISC, MC, V. Tues–Fri noon–2pm; Tues–Sat 6:30–9:30pm. CALIFORNIAN.

If Wolfgang Puck is the father of contemporary California cuisine, then Michael McCarty is the grandfather. Born in New York and schooled in France, McCarty opened this self-consciously modern American restaurant in 1979, when he was only 25 years old. Those were exciting times: Walls were irreverently hung with works by David Hockney, Cy Twombly, and Jasper Johns; staff uniforms were designed by Ralph Lauren; and the unusually casual dining room had the added novelty of a dining patio and rock garden. Several top L.A. restaurants have since caught up to Michael's—most notably Puck's Spago, Joachim Splichal's Patina, and Michel Richard's Citrus—but this fetching Santa Monica eatery remains one of the city's best. A recent price rollback has made dishes like Michael's simple grilled pork tenderloin with cream sauce and apples, and duck with Grand Marnier and oranges, even more appetizing. Spaghetti tossed in a creamy Chardonnay sauce with large sea scallops, roasted sweet peppers, baby asparagus, and American golden caviar is just one example of the restaurant's delicious, complex pastas. Don't miss Michael's famous goat cheese salad, served warm with walnuts and vinaigrette.

72 Market Street

72 Market St. (west of Pacific Ave.), Venice. ☎ **310/392-8720.** Reservations recommended on weekends. Main courses $18–$30; lunch $9–$18. AE, MC, V. Mon–Fri 11:30am–2:30pm; nightly 6–10:30pm; Sun 10am–2:30pm. AMERICAN.

Dudley Moore and Tony Bill's "Maple Drive by-the-sea" is a work of art, both architecturally and gastronomically. The single, large, skylit dining room is something of a modern art gallery, with a festival of angles that includes partitions disguised as modern sculpture. Once the trendiest place on the beach, the restaurant has matured; it now has all the hallmarks of permanency. A recent chef change came with a welcome menu revision, but the Franco-American staples that continue to draw loyal crowds haven't budged an inch. A terrific salad niçoise is

Dining at the Beaches

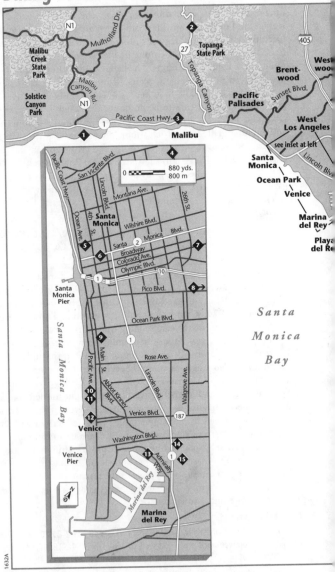

made with fresh rare-charred tuna, and Dover sole arrives flaky and moist. Meatloaf and chili remain favorites, often reaching the top of local "best" lists. Some regulars opt for the off-menu steak tartare—chopped beef tenderloin with egg, capers, shallots, parsley, mustard, radicchio, snow peas, and tomatoes. A dedicated oyster bar serves up many fresh half-shell selections, along with ceviches, Sevruga caviar, and combinations like calamari with tomatillos.

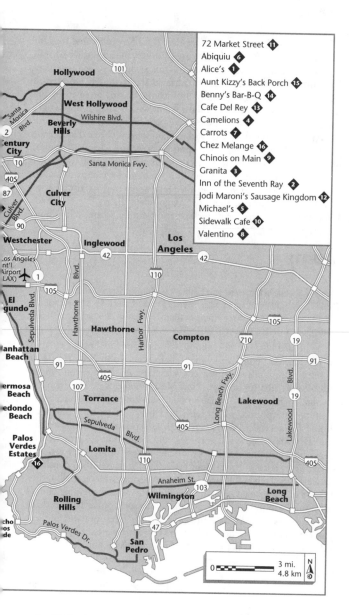

72 Market Street ⓫
Abiquiu ❻
Alice's ❶
Aunt Kizzy's Back Porch ⓯
Benny's Bar-B-Q ⓮
Cafe Del Rey ⓭
Camelions ❹
Carrots ❼
Chez Melange ⓰
Chinois on Main ❾
Granita ❸
Inn of the Seventh Ray ❷
Jodi Maroni's Sausage Kingdom ⓬
Michael's ❺
Sidewalk Cafe ❿
Valentino ❽

In 1995, the restaurant began offering exotic box lunches for air travelers. Dishes like Maine lobster salad and veal with wild rice ($18 to $39) are guaranteed to make your flight companions hate you.

✪ Valentino

3115 Pico Blvd. (west of Bundy Dr.), Santa Monica. ☎ **310/829-4313.** Reservations required. Pasta $12–$16, meat and fish $18–$25. AE, CB, DC, DISC, MC, V. Fri 11:30am–2:30pm; Mon–Thurs 5:30–10:30pm, Fri–Sat 5:30–11pm. ITALIAN.

What more can I say about a place that *Wine Spectator* rated tops for wine and *New York Times* food critic Ruth Reichl called the best Italian restaurant in America? The creations of owner Piero Selvaggio and his brilliant young chef, Angelo Auriana, are absolutely wonderful. Dinners here are always lengthy multicourse affairs, often involving several bottles of wine. You might begin with a crisp Pinot Grigio paired with caviar-filled cannoli; or crespelle, thin little pancakes with fresh porcini mushrooms and a rich melt of fontina cheese. Handmade pastas tossed with tender baby squid or sweet tiny clams are typical of first courses, though it really depends on what came to market the morning you visit. A rich Barolo is the perfect accompaniment to rosemary-infused roasted rabbit; the fantastically fragrant risotto with white truffles is one of the most magnificent dishes I've ever had. Jackets are all but required in the elegant dining room. What more can I say—go!

MODERATE

✪ Abiquiu

1413 5th St. (between Broadway and Santa Monica Blvd.), Santa Monica. ☎ **310/395-8611.** Reservations required. Main courses $13–$18; lunch $9–$16. AE, MC, V. Mon–Fri 11:30am–2:30pm; Mon–Thurs 6–10pm, Fri–Sun 6–10:30pm; brunch Sun 11:30am–2pm. CONTEMPORARY SOUTHWESTERN.

If you needed just one more morsel of proof that Los Angeles remains on the culinary edge, this is it. Chef/owner John Sedlar, one of the city's most gifted young chefs, named Abiquiu (pronounced "Ab-i-kyoo") after his northern New Mexico hometown. The dramatic, postmodern restaurant is Sedlar's vehicle for showing off his own brand of southwestern food, which relies heavily on yellow corn and green chilies. The specialty here is tamales, Mexican favorites that are traditionally made of meat and cornmeal and steamed in a cornhusk; but this is no traditional restaurant. Of the dozens of gourmet varieties served here, none is better than the salmon mousse–filled cornhusk tamale, or the crab and lobster tamale steamed in a lobster shell. Other dishes that have stolen onto the menu include an unbelievably fantastic lobster sushi roll with creamy green-chili sauce. Sedlar had his share of controversy when Catholics picketed his restaurant for serving dessert tamales on Madonna (not the pop star) plates. The chef just ordered more of this personally designed tableware, but has promised to quit stenciling shock messages like "D.O.A." on the plates' rims. Upstairs, there's a dedicated tamale and tequila bar, for light bites and strong margaritas. Abiquiu is underpriced and busy; go early and arrive hungry.

Alice's

23000 Pacific Coast Hwy. (a quarter-mile south of the Malibu Pier), Malibu. ☎ **310/456-6646.** Reservations required. Main courses $9–$18; lunch $7–$15. AE, MC, V. Mon–Fri 11:30am–10pm, Sat–Sun 11am–11pm. CALIFORNIAN.

Alice's has a long history as one of the loveliest restaurants in Malibu. The dining room is glassed in on three sides and faces Malibu Pier; rear tables sit on a raised platform so that everyone has ocean views. It's a light and airy place, with a mostly seafood menu to match. Admittedly, most people are here for the one-of-a-kind atmosphere, but the food is a lot better than it needs to be. Seared yellowtail tuna is seved simply, on a bed of spinach, with lemon and tarragon butter. Grilled chicken breast is marinated in garlic and soy and served with tomato-cilantro relish. Pastas and pizzas are also available, and there's a full bar.

Aunt Kizzy's Back Porch

4325 Glencoe Ave. (in the Villa Marina Shopping Center), Marina del Rey. ☎ **310/ 578-1005.** Reservations not accepted. Main courses $8–$13; Sun brunch $12. No credit cards. Mon–Sat 11am–4pm; Sun–Thurs 4–11pm, Fri–Sat 4pm–midnight; Sun 11am–3pm. SOUTHERN.

Aunt Kizzy's isn't about trends. This is a real southern restaurant, owned by genuine southerners from Texas and Oklahoma. Sticklers might complain that the farm-raised catfish they serve here just isn't as good as the ones pulled straight from the bayou, but they're sure a whole lot cleaner. Kizzy's chicken Creole, jambalaya, and smothered pork chops are just about as good as it gets in this city. Almost every-thing comes with vegetables, red beans and rice, and corn muffins. Fresh-squeezed lemonade is served by the mason jar. These are huge meals that, as corny as it sounds, are as filling as they are delicious. Sunday brunches are all-you-can-eat affairs, served buffet style. The biggest problem with Aunt Kizzy's is its location, hidden in a shopping center that has too few parking spaces to accommodate it. Look for the restaurant to the right of Vons supermarket.

Cafe Del Rey

4451 Admiralty Way (between Lincoln Blvd. and Washington St.), Marina del Rey. ☎ **310/823-6395.** Reservations required. Main courses $9–$18; lunch $10–$15. AE, DC, DISC, MC, V. Mon–Sat 11:30am–2:30pm; Sun 5–10:30pm, Mon–Thurs 5:30–10:30pm, Fri–Sat 5:30–11pm. Sun 10:30am–2:30pm. CALIFORNIAN.

This is a lively, open, high-tech space that makes a meal feel like an event, with a huge menu filled with unusual choices that make ordering fun. And there's a terrific view of the Marina, so you know you're someplace special. The kitchen focuses on creative preparations of fresh, seasonal foods. While most dishes are very good, some are too creative, and too contrived. Cuban black-bean soup, Angus rib-eye steaks, and quesadillas stuffed with wild mushrooms and grilled veg-etables are all winners; Peking duck with mango chutney, red-chili angel hair pasta with sautéed-shrimps, and penne with wild bacon and fresh tomatoes are not. Get a table by the window, choose wisely, and enjoy yourself.

✪ Camelions

246 26th St. (south of San Vicente Blvd.), Santa Monica. ☎ **310/395-0746.** Reservations required. Main courses $14–$22; lunch $10–$13. AE, CB, DC, MC, V. Tues–Sun 11:30am–2:30pm; Tues–Sun 6–9:30pm. CALIFORNIAN/FRENCH.

Either indoors or out, dining here is one of Los Angeles' most romantic dining experiences. Camelions' three 1920s stucco cottages, each with beamed ceilings and a crackling fireplace, are built around an ivy-trellised brick patio. Contrary to its Provençal setting, the tasty

French-inspired cuisine is plenty California trendy. Norwegian salmon carpaccio is prepared with soy sauce, dill, and a light squeeze of lemon; lightly browned potato crepes are topped with a dollop of golden caviar. The best dishes are baby chicken basted with a savory walnut-garlic sauce; swordfish zested with a marinade of paprika, coriander, and cumin; and grilled duck breast, sliced thin and fanned out on a plate of ginger sauce. A large selection of sandwiches and salads (like spinach with warm new potatoes, bacon, and mustard vinaigrette) are available at lunch.

✪ Carrots

2834 Santa Monica Blvd. (between 26th St. and Centinela Ave.), Santa Monica. ☎ **310/453-6505.** Reservations recommended on weekends. Main courses $14–$22; lunch $5–$7. MC, V. Wed–Fri 11:30am–2:30pm; Tues–Sun 6–10pm. CALIFORNIAN/FRENCH.

Chef/owner Fred Iwasaki, a former sous-chef at Spago and Chinois, was born in the year of the Rabbit—hence Carrots . . . get it? His tiny restaurant, set in an undistinguished mini-mall, is an understated setting for very good food at very fair prices. Dinners might begin with black mussels in a black bean sauce, shrimp wrapped with julienned potatoes, or a baby green salad with goat cheese. You can't go wrong by ordering grilled salmon, which is sautéed in an onion butter sauce, or New York steak, which is perfectly grilled and thinly sliced. As is the current trend, Carrots offers counter seating for singles; on weekends—even lone diners are happy if they can find a spot here.

Inn of the Seventh Ray

128 Old Topanga Canyon Rd. (on Calif. 27), Topanga Canyon. ☎ **310/455-1311.** Reservations required. Main courses $16–$25; lunch/brunch $7–$13. MC, V. Mon–Fri 11:30am–3pm, Sat 10:30am–3pm, Sun 9:30am–3pm; daily 6–10pm. CALIFORNIA HEALTH FOOD.

Topanga Canyon has long been the home of L.A.'s New Agers; it's a mountainous, sparsely populated area that is undeniably beautiful, even spiritual. This restaurant, a former church, is in the middle of the aura. No one comes here just to eat; people come for a romantic dining experience, far from the bright lights of the city. About half the seating is outdoors, at tables overlooking a creek and endless tangles of untamed vines and shrubs. Inside, the dining room is rustic, with a sloping roof and a glass wall offering mountain views. The inn was opened about 25 years ago by Ralph and Lucille Yaney, who preach some kind of mumbo-jumbo about the energy of food, and list menu items in order of their "esoteric vibrational value." Everything is prepared from scratch, and foods are organic and chemical and preservative free. The fish are caught in deep water far offshore and served the same day; they even sell unpasteurized wines. Ten main dishes are available daily, and all are served with hors d'oeuvres, soup or salad, and vegetables. The lightest dish, called Five Secret Rays, consists of lightly steamed vegetables served with lemon-tahini and caraway cheese sauces; the densest dish—vibrationally speaking—is a 10-ounce New York steak cut from naturally fed beef.

INEXPENSIVE

Benny's Bar-B-Q

4077 Lincoln Blvd. (south of Washington Blvd.), Marina del Rey. ☎ **310/821-6939.** Sandwiches $4–$6, dinner specials $7–$10. AE, MC, V. Mon–Sat 11am–10pm, Sun 2–10pm. BARBECUE.

It's mostly take-out at this divey cookshack, but there are a few tables, where diners gorge themselves on Los Angeles' best barbecued pork and beef ribs and hot link sausages. Like almost everything on the menu, barbecued chicken is bathed in a tangy hot sauce and served with baked beans and a choice of cole slaw, potato salad, fries, or corn on the cob. Beef, ham, and pork sandwiches are also available. To reach Benny's, find Lincoln Boulevard, then follow the heavy aroma.

Jodi Maroni's Sausage Kingdom

2011 Ocean Front Walk (north of Venice Blvd.), Venice. ☎ **310/306-1995.** Sandwiches $4–$6. No credit cards. Daily 10am–5:30pm. SANDWICHES/SAUSAGES.

Your cardiologist might not approve, but Jodi Maroni's all-natural, preservative-free sausages are some of the best weiners served anywhere. The grungy walk-up (or Rollerblade-up) counter looks fairly foreboding—you wouldn't know there was gourmet fare behind that aging hot dog–stand facade. At least fourteen different grilled sausage sandwiches are served here. Bypass the traditional hot Italian and try the Toulouse garlic, Bombay curried lamb, all-chicken apple, or orange-garlic-cumin. Each is served on a freshly baked onion roll and smothered with onions and peppers. Burgers, hot dogs, BLTs, and rotisserie chicken are also served, but why bother?

Other locations include 1000 Universal Center Drive, CityWalk, Suite 175, Universal City ☎ 818/622-JODY; and 1315 3rd St. Promenade, Santa Monica ☎ 310/393-9063.

Sidewalk Cafe

1401 Ocean Front Walk (between Horizon and Pacific aves.), Venice. ☎ **310/399-5547.** Reservations not accepted. Main courses $6–$13. MC, V. Sun–Thurs 8am–11pm, Fri–Sat 8am–midnight. AMERICAN.

Nowhere in L.A. is the people watching better than along Ocean Front Walk. The constantly bustling Sidewalk Cafe is ensconced in one of Venice's few remaining early 20th-century buildings. The best seats, of course, are out front, around overcrowded open-air tables, all with a perfect view of the crowd, which provides nonstop entertainment. The menu is extensive, and the food is a whole lot better than it has to be at a location like this. Choose from the seriously overstuffed sandwiches or other oversize American favorites: omelettes, salads, burgers.

7 San Fernando Valley

EXPENSIVE

✪ Pinot Bistro

12969 Ventura Blvd. (west of Coldwater Canyon Ave.), Studio City. ☎ **818/990-0500.** Reservations required. Main courses $16–$22; lunch $7–$13. AE, DC,

DISC, MC, V. Mon–Fri 11:30am–2:30pm; Mon–Thurs 6–10pm, Fri 6–10:30pm, Sat 5:30–10:30pm, Sun 5:30–9:30pm. CALIFORNIAN/FRENCH.

When the Valley crowd doesn't want to make the drive to Patina, they pack into Pinot Bistro, one of restaurateur Joachim Splichal's other hugely successful restaurants. The Valley's only great bistro is designed with dark woods, etched glass, and cream-colored walls that scream "trendy French" almost as loudly as the rich, straightforward cooking. The menu is a symphony of California and continental elements that includes a beautiful warm potato tart with smoked whitefish, and baby lobster tails with creamy polenta; both are studies in culinary perfection. The most popular dish here is Chef Octavio Becerra's Frenchified Tuscan bean soup, infused with oven-dried tomatoes and roasted garlic and served over crusty ciabatta bread. Generously portioned main dishes continue the gourmet theme: baby lobster risotto; braised oxtail with parsley gnocchi; and puff pastry stuffed with bay scallops, Manila clams, and roast duck. The service is good, attentive and unobtrusive. Many regulars prefer Pinot Bistro at lunch, when a less expensive menu is served to a more easygoing crowd.

MODERATE

Jerry's Famous Deli

12655 Ventura Blvd. (at Coldwater Canyon Blvd.), Studio City. ☎ **818/980-4245.** Main courses $9–$14; breakfast $2–$11; sandwiches and salads $4–$12. AE, MC, V. Daily 24 hours. DELI.

Just east of Coldwater Canyon Avenue there's a simple yet sizable deli where all the Valley's hipsters go to relieve their late-night munchies. This place probably has one of the largest menus in America—a tome that spans cultures and continents, from Central America to China to New York. From salads to sandwiches to steak and seafood platters, everything, including breakfast, is served all day. Jerry's is not the best deli in the world, but it's consistently good, and an integral part of Los Angeles's cultural landscape. It also has a full bar.

There's another Jerry's at 13181 Mindinao Way (in the Villa Marina Shopping Center), Marina del Rey, ☎ 310/821-6626.

What to See & Do in Los Angeles

These are exciting times in Los Angeles. The city is currently enjoying the same fame, fortune, and power that London had in the 18th century, Paris possessed in the 19th century, and New York enjoyed at the turn of this century. Museums are opening, culture is flourishing, and the entire world is fascinated by what's going on in L.A.

New museums, such as the Petersen Automotive Museum and the Museum of Tolerance, have popped up over the last few years, and many of the older ones are expanding and improving: The Los Angeles County Museum of Art, the Petersen, George C. Page Museum of Tar Pit Discoveries, the Museum of Miniatures, and the Craft & Folk Art Museum were united along their common stretch of Wilshire Boulevard under the auspices of the newly named Museum Mile; the Hammer has just merged with UCLA; and the Getty is putting the finishing touches on a new $750 million complex in the Brentwood hills.

But it's not just the museums that are experiencing a renaissance. The city and its planners know what side their bread is buttered on: The Walk of Fame, the Hollywood sign, Santa Monica Pier, and other traditional tourist draws are being spruced up; new ones, like Universal CityWalk, have been added to L.A.'s repertoire; and L.A.'s theme parks are continually adding new attractions.

Bisected by the Santa Monica Mountains and fronted by long stretches of beach, Los Angeles is also one of the best cities in the world for nature and sports lovers. Where else can you hike in the mountains, in-line skate along the beach, take a swim in the ocean, enjoy a gourmet meal, then take in a football or basketball or ice hockey or baseball game—all in the same day?

There's plenty to do in L.A.; the problem is, you have to drive everywhere to do it. To get the most out of the city, advance planning is necessary, as is a good map. Think out your day's activities; if you plan to spend your morning along the Walk of Fame, your afternoon at the Getty, and your evening taking in Olvera Street, you'll probably end up wasting a lot of valuable time on the freeway, sitting in traffic.

Plan your days geographically to get the most from them; for instance, couple a morning at the Getty with an afternoon on Venice's Ocean Front Walk, an afternoon at a TV taping in Burbank with an evening at Universal CityWalk.

To find out what's going on while you're in town, pick up a copy of the tabloid *L.A. Weekly*, the monthly magazine *Los Angeles*, or the Sunday *Los Angeles Times* "Calendar" section.

SUGGESTED ITINERARIES

If You Have One Day

Spend the morning in Hollywood. See the Walk of Fame, Mann's Chinese Theatre, and the Frederick's of Hollywood and Max Factor museums. Cruise Sunset Boulevard, lunch in West Hollywood, take your obligatory stroll along Beverly Hills' Rodeo Drive, then head for the ocean. Spend your afternoon and evening in Santa Monica. Don't miss a stroll along Venice's Ocean Front Walk. At night, depending on what you like, head either downtown to the Music Center, or return to Hollywood and West Hollywood to check out the club and music scene.

If You Have Two Days

Spend the first day as above. On your second day, tour a TV or film studio, or go shopping on Melrose Avenue. Have lunch at Farmer's Market. Visit the La Brea Tar Pits, then take in one of the adjacent museums on Museum Row, perhaps the Petersen Auto Museum. At sunset, cruise Mulholland Drive, or watch the sun sink from a secluded seaside cove in Malibu. After dark, take in a spectacular city view from Mount Hollywood's Griffith Observatory.

If You Have Three Days

Spend your third day exploring the city's beach communities. Take a hike up to Inspiration Point in Will Rogers' State Historic Park, then rent a surfboard and hit the waves, or just relax, at Zuma Beach. Explore Santa Monica's Third Street Promenade or skate along the Ocean Front Walk that stretches for 22 miles, from Pacific Palisades to Torrance. Have dinner at one of Santa Monica's many restaurants.

If You Have Five Days

On your fourth and fifth days, take in the following: Visit a theme park—Universal Studios or Disneyland—or try out as a contestant on a TV game show. Perhaps join a studio audience and watch your favorite show being taped. Visit Forest Lawn Cemetery in Glendale, or check out the J. Paul Getty Museum, El Pueblo de Los Angeles Historic District, or the Los Angeles County Museum of Art. Make a reservation and have dinner at one of LA.'s top restaurants, maybe Spago, Patina, or Abiquiu.

1   The Top Attractions

DOWNTOWN

El Pueblo de Los Angeles Historic District

Bounded by Alameda, Arcadia, Spring, and Macy sts. ☎ 213/628-1274.

This Los Angeles Historic District was built in the 1930s, on the site where the city was founded, as an alternative to the wholesale razing of a particularly unsightly slum. The result is a contrived nostalgic fantasy of the city's beginnings, a kitschy theme park anthologizing Latino culture in a Disneyesque fashion. Nevertheless, El Pueblo has proven wildly successful, because L.A.'s Latinos have adopted it as an important cultural monument.

El Pueblo is not entirely without authenticity. This was the site of an 18th-century Mexican settlement; some of L.A.'s oldest extant buildings are located here, and the area really does exude the ambiance of Old Mexico. At its core, the 44-acre Historic District is a Mexican-style marketplace where you can stroll along narrow terra cotta–tiled pathways past souvenir stands, food stalls, clothing shops, and cafes. The carnival of sights and sounds is heightened by mariachis, colorful piñatas, and more than occasional folklorico dancing. Olvera Street, the district's primary pedestrian thoroughfare, and adjacent Main Street, are home to about two dozen 19th-century buildings. Stop in at the Visitor's Center (622 N. Main St., ☎ 213/628-1274; Mon–Sat 10am–3pm), located in a large Victorian boardinghouse built in 1887. Don't miss Avila Adobe (E-10 Olvera St.; Mon–Sat 10am–5pm); built in 1818, it's the oldest building still standing in Los Angeles.

HOLLYWOOD

Hollywood Sign

At the top of Beachwood Dr., Hollywood.

These 50-foot-high white sheet-metal letters have come to symbolize both the movie industry and the city itself. Erected in 1923 as an advertisement for a fledgling real estate development, the full text originally read *Hollywoodland*. Actress Peg Entwistle leapt to her death from the "H" in 1932; an earthquake-monitoring seismograph is now buried near its base. The recent installation of motion detectors around the sign just made this graffiti tagger's coup a target even more worth boasting about. A thorny hiking trail leads to it from Durand Drive near Beachwood Drive, but the best view is from down below, at the corner of Sunset Boulevard and Bronson Avenue.

Hollywood Walk of Fame

Hollywood Blvd., between Gower St. and La Brea Ave.; and Vine St., between Yucca St. and Sunset Blvd. ☎ 213/469-8311. From U.S. 101, exit onto Highland Blvd. and turn left onto Hollywood Blvd.

Over 2,500 celebrities are honored along the world's most famous sidewalk. Each bronze medallion, set into the center of a granite star, pays homage to a famous television, film, radio, theater, or recording personality. Although about a third of them are just about as obscure as

Los Angeles Attractions at a Glance

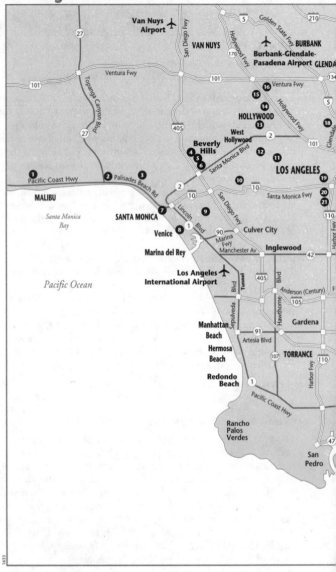

Andromeda—their fame simply hasn't withstood the test of time—millions of visitors are thrilled by the sight of famous names like James Dean (at 1719 Vine St.), John Lennon (at 1750 Vine St.), Marlon Brando (at 1765 Vine St.), Rudolph Valentino (at 6164 Hollywood Blvd.), Greta Garbo (6901 Hollywood Blvd.), Louis Armstrong (7000 Hollywood Blvd.), and Barbra Streisand (6925 Hollywood Blvd.).

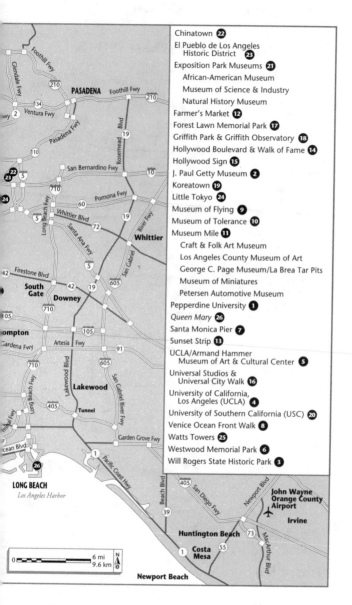

The sight of leather-clad bikers, long-haired metalheads, druggies, hookers, and hordes of disoriented tourists, all treading on memorials to Hollywood's greats, makes for quite a bizarre tribute indeed. But the Hollywood Chamber of Commerce has been doing a terrific job sprucing up the pedestrian experience with filmstrip crosswalks, rows of swaying palms, accent lighting, and landscaped medians. And at least one weekend a month, a privately organized group of fans calling

Downtown Area Attractions

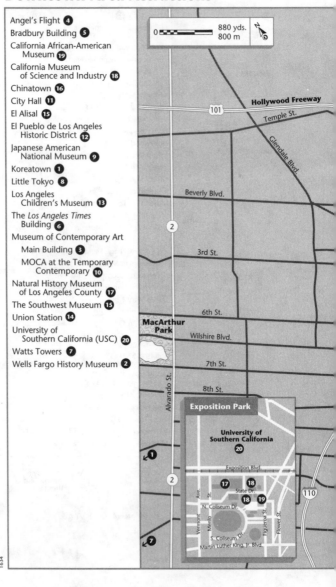

Angel's Flight **4**
Bradbury Building **5**
California African-American Museum **19**
California Museum of Science and Industry **18**
Chinatown **16**
City Hall **11**
El Alisal **15**
El Pueblo de Los Angeles Historic District **12**
Japanese American National Museum **9**
Koreatown **1**
Little Tokyo **8**
Los Angeles Children's Museum **13**
The *Los Angeles Times* Building **6**
Museum of Contemporary Art
  Main Building **3**
  MOCA at the Temporary Contemporary **10**
Natural History Museum of Los Angeles County **17**
The Southwest Museum **15**
Union Station **14**
University of Southern California (USC) **20**
Watts Towers **7**
Wells Fargo History Museum **2**

0 ━━━ 880 yds.
      800 m

Hollywood Freeway
101
Temple St.
Glendale Blvd.
Beverly Blvd.
2
3rd St.
6th St.
MacArthur Park
Wilshire Blvd.
7th St.
Alvarado St.
8th St.

Exposition Park

University of Southern California
20

Exposition Blvd.
17
State Dr.
18
18 **19**
N. Coliseum Dr.
Vermont Ave.
Menlo St.
S. Coliseum Dr.
Figueroa St.
Flower St.
Martin Luther King, Jr. Blvd.
110
1
2
7

themselves Star Polishers busy themselves scrubbing tarnished medallions.

Recent subway digging under Hollywood Boulevard has caused the street to sink several inches. When actor John Forsythe's star cracked, authorities removed many others to prevent further damage. In the next few years, up to 250 stars, including those of Marilyn Monroe (6744 Hollywood Blvd.) and Elvis Presley (6777 Hollywood Blvd.) will be temporarily removed as the subway project expands.

The legendary sidewalk is continually adding new names. Celebrities (or their fan clubs) pay about $4,000 for the honor of a star. But not anyone can buy one; the honoree has to be deemed worthy. The public is invited to attend dedication ceremonies; the celebrity honoree is usually in attendance. Write or phone the Hollywood Chamber of Commerce (6255 Sunset Blvd., Suite 911, Hollywood, CA 90028; ☎ 213/469-8311) for information on who's being honored this week.

Mann's Chinese Theatre

6925 Hollywood Blvd. ☎ **213/461-3331.** Movie tickets $7.50. Call for show times. From U.S. 101, exit onto Highland Blvd. and turn right onto Hollywood Blvd. The theater is three blocks ahead on your right.

This is one of the world's great movie palaces, and one of Hollywood's finest landmarks. The Chinese Theatre was opened in 1927 by entertainment impresario Sid Grauman, a brilliant promoter who's credited with originating the idea of the paparazzi-packed movie "premiere." Outrageously conceived, with both authentic and simulated Chinese embellishments, gaudy Grauman's theater was designed to impress. Original Chinese heaven doves top the facade, and two of the theater's exterior columns once propped up a Ming Dynasty temple.

Visitors flock to the theater by the millions, not for its architectural flamboyance, but for its world-famous entry court, where stars like Elizabeth Taylor, Paul Newman, Ginger Rogers, Humphrey Bogart, Frank Sinatra, Marilyn Monroe, and about 160 others set their signatures and hand- and footprints in concrete. It's not always hands and feet, though. Betty Grable made an impression with her shapely leg, Gene Autry with the hoofprints of his horse Champion, and Jimmy Durante and Bob Hope used their trademark noses.

The **Egyptian Theater** (6712 Hollywood Blvd.; ☎ **213/467-6167**), another of the string of picture palaces built by Sid Grauman, is two blocks down the boulevard. Opened in 1922, this theater's over-the-top architecture was inspired by the then-recent discovery of King Tut's tomb. Its glory days are past, but the structure— with its trademark scarab—is still worth checking out.

Farmer's Market

6333 W. 3rd St. (near Fairfax Ave.). ☎ **213/933-9211.** Mon–Sat 9am–6:30pm, Sun 10am–5pm. From U.S. 101, exit Santa Monica Blvd. west. Turn left at Fairfax Ave.; the market is at the corner of Fairfax and 3rd St.

During the Depression, growers from throughout Southern California came to the center of Los Angeles and set up a cluster of stands in order to sell their produce directly to city dwellers. In the 60-plus years since that time, mom-and-pop farms have gone the way of the cattle plow, and L.A. has grown so big that a farmer would have to drive all day to get from the orchards to Hollywood and back.

Almost all that's left of the original Farmer's Market is its history-laden name. Recognizable by its trademark shingled 10-story clocktower, the squat, sprawling market has evolved into a food marketplace with a carnival atmosphere, a kind of "turf" version of San Francisco's surfy Fisherman's Wharf. About 100 restaurants, shops, and grocers cater to a mix of workers from the adjacent CBS Television City complex, locals, and tourists, who are brought here by the busload. Retailers sell pet supplies, clothing, books, and art, but everyone comes here for the food stands, selling oysters, Cajun gumbo, fresh-squeezed orange juice, roast-beef sandwiches, and all kinds of international fast foods. You can still buy fruits and vegetables here, but they're mostly imported from Latin America, and prices are higher than in the local supermarkets.

Griffith Observatory

2800 E. Observatory Rd. (in Griffith Park, at the end of Vermont Ave.). ☎ **213/664-1191.** (☎ 213/663-8171 for the Sky Report, a recorded message on current planet positions and celestial events.) Admission $4 adults, $2 children, $3 seniors. Sept–May Tues–Fri 2–10pm, Sat–Sun 12:30–10pm; Jun–Aug daily 12:30–10pm. From U.S. 101, take Vermont Ave. north into Griffith Park.

Made world famous in the film *Rebel Without a Cause*, Griffith Observatory's bronze domes have been Hollywood Hills landmarks since 1935. Most visitors never actually go inside; they come to this spot on the south slope of Mt. Hollywood for unparalleled views of Los Angeles, which sometimes reach all the way to the ocean. On warm nights, with the city lights twinkling below, this is one of the most romantic places in L.A.

The main dome houses a planetarium, where narrated projection shows reveal the stars and planets that are hidden from the naked eye by the city's lights and smog. Mock excursions into space search for extraterrestrial life, or examine the causes of earthquakes, moonquakes, and starquakes. Presentations last about an hour, and showtimes vary; call for information.

The adjacent Hall of Science holds exhibits on galaxies, meteorites, and other cosmic objects, including a telescope trained on the sun; a Foucault Pendulum; and 6-foot-diameter earth and moon globes. On clear nights you can gaze at the heavens through the powerful 12-inch telescope.

WESTSIDE

Rancho La Brea Tar Pits/George C. Page Museum

5801 Wilshire Blvd., Hancock Park, Los Angeles. ☎ **213/857-6311.** Admission $6 adults, $3.50 seniors (62 and older) and students with I.D., $2 children 5–12, kids 4 and under free; free to all the second Tuesday of every month. Museum, Tues–Sun 10am–5pm; paleontology laboratory, Wed–Sun 10am–5pm; tar pits, Sat–Sun 10am–5pm. From the Santa Monica Fwy. (I-10), exit onto La Brea Ave. north, continue for three miles, and turn left onto Wilshire Blvd. The museum and tar pits are about 10 blocks ahead, between Fairfax and La Brea aves.

An odorous, murky swamp of congealed oil continuously oozes to the earth's surface in the middle of Los Angeles. No, it's not a low-budget horror movie set: It's the La Brea Tar Pits, an awesome, primal pool right on Museum Mile, where hot tar has been bubbling from the earth for over 40,000 years. The glistening pools, which look like murky water, have enticed thirsty animals throughout history. Thousands of mammals, birds, amphibians, and insects—many of which are now extinct—mistakenly crawled into the sticky sludge and stayed forever. In 1906 scientists began a systematic removal and classification of entombed specimens, including ground sloths, giant vultures, mastodons, camels, bears, lizards, even prehistoric relatives of today's beloved super-rats. The best finds are on display in the adjacent George C. Page Museum of La Brea Discoveries, where an excellent 15-minute film documenting the recoveries is also shown. Archeology work is ongoing; you can watch as scientists clean, identify, and catalog new finds in the paleontology laboratory.

The tar pits themselves are only open on weekends; guided tours are given Saturdays and Sundays at 1pm. Swimming is prohibited.

THE BEACHES

J. Paul Getty Museum

17985 Pacific Coast Hwy., Malibu. ☎ **310/458-2003.** Admission free. Tues–Sun 10am–5pm (last entrance at 4:30pm). From Santa Monica, take Calif. 1 (Pacific Coast Highway) north about five miles to the museum entrance.

When it opened in 1974, the Getty Museum was mocked as a filthy-rich upstart with a spotty art collection. Generously endowed by an oil baron, the Getty was ridiculed by competitors out of both envy and fear of its art-buying potential. It didn't help that the museum was pompously designed to imitate a 1st-century Roman villa buried at Pompeii. With about $60 million a year to spend, the Getty has repeatedly made headlines by paying record prices for some of the art world's trophies. But far from snatching up everything, the museum is buying intelligently and selectively—perhaps realizing its detractors' worst fears—methodically transforming what was once a rich man's pastime into a connoisseur's delight.

The most notable piece in the rich antiquities collection is *The Victorious Athlete*, a 4th-century B.C. Greek sculpture known as the Getty Bronze; it's believed to have been crafted by Lysippus, court sculptor to Alexander the Great. But the most compelling antiquity is the *Kouros*, a Greek sculpture of a nude youth. It's now largely believed to be fake, but, after years of scientific testing and international scholarly debate, the legitimacy of the statue has yet to be resolved. In a classic example of turning lemons into lemonade, rather than shirking the controversial spotlight, the museum has turned the debate into the focal point of their exhibit, displaying all the evidence both for and against the statue's authenticity.

The Getty is beginning to win respect for its 19th-century paintings collection. Regular multimillion-dollar purchases make this collection one of the world's most exciting works in progress. The museum's most famous 19th-century work, van Gogh's *Irises,* is hung in the second-floor gallery. The continually expanding Renaissance collection includes Titian's *Venus and Adonis,* Andrea Mantegna's *Adororation of the Magi,* and two recently acquired early Rembrandts.

Docent orientation lectures depart from the ocean end of the main garden every 15 minutes from 9:30am to 3:15pm. Don't pass by the very unusual bookstore without a look-see.

Important: Parking is free, but you must phone for a parking reservation 7 to 10 days in advance. If you can't get a reservation, your best bet is to park in the lot of any restaurant on P.C.H. and phone a cab (see "Getting Around," in Chapter 4). Due to an agreement with local homeowners, walk-in visitors are not permitted.

Venice Ocean Front Walk

On the beach, between Venice Blvd. and Rose Ave.

This has long been one of L.A.'s most colorful areas. Founded at the turn of the century, the town was a theme development inspired by its

Italian namesake. Authentic Venetian gondolas plied miles of inland waterways lined with rococo palaces. In the 1950s Venice became the celebrated stomping grounds of Jack Kerouac, Allen Ginsberg, William S. Burroughs, and other beats. In the sixties this was the epicenter of L.A.'s hippie scene.

Today, Venice is still one of the world's most engaging bohe-mias. It's not an exaggeration to say that no visit to L.A. would be complete without a stroll along the famous beach path, an almost surreal assem-blage of every L.A. stereotype—and then some. Among stalls and stands selling cheap sunglasses, Mexican blankets, and "herbal ecstasy" pills swirls a carnival of humanity that includes bikini-clad rollerskaters, tattooed bikers, muscle-bound pretty boys, panhandling vets, urban gangbangers, beautiful wannabes, and plenty of tourists and gawkers. On any given day, you're bound to come across all kinds of perform-ers: white-faced mimes, breakdancers, buskers, chainsaw jugglers, talk-ing parrots, an occasional apocalyp-tic evangelist. Last time I was there, a man stood behind a table and railed against the evils of circumcision. "It's too late for us, guys, but we can save the next generation." But a chubby guy singing "Kokomo"—out of tune but with all his heart—cheered me up.

Queen Mary

Pier J, Long Beach. ☎ **310/435-3511.** Admission free; tours, $5 adults, $3 children. Parking $5. Daily 10am–6pm (last entry at 5:30pm). Take the Long Beach Fwy. (I-710) to its terminus at the Marina.

Launched in England in 1934 and permanently docked here since 1967, the *Queen Mary* is the most luxurious of oceanliners—a history-laden art deco gem that shuttled the rich between continents before crumpets and caviar were served on airplanes. There's something magi-cal about this ship, with it's mammoth black-and-white hull and three bright red stacks. The *Queen* operates as a hotel (see Chapter 5 for details), restaurant, shopping complex, tourist attraction, and even chapel for weddings "at sea." It's a yawn of a combination that, financially, has left the ship nearly dry-docked.

On board, visitors can tour the *Queen Mary's* engine rooms and bridge as well as re-creations of all classes of staterooms. In addition to an extensive World War II display (in which the ship took part as a troop carrier), there's a fine exhibit on model ships and ship-building, and an unspectacular sound-and-light show that reenacts a near colli-sion at sea. Just do like most everybody else and have a free look at all the public areas, then peek in at some of the 20 shops selling histori-cal newspapers and other dust-collectors. The mahogany and crystal Observation Bar is a great place to have a drink.

The giant dome adjacent to the *Queen Mary* once housed Howard Hughes's enormous Spruce Goose airplane, but it proved so unpopular as a tourist attraction that it was shipped to an Oregon museum. The dome was converted into a Warner Brothers studio; much of *Batman Forever* was filmed on sets housed here. Visitors are not allowed inside the dome, but keep your eyes peeled for the *Baywatch* crew, which films here in Long Beach.

SAN FERNANDO VALLEY

Universal Studios

Hollywood Fwy. (Lankershim Blvd. exit), Universal City. ☎ **818/508-9600.** Admission $31 adults, $25 seniors (65 and older) and children 3–11, kids under 3 free. Parking is $5. Summer daily 7am–11pm; rest of the year daily 9am–7pm. From U.S. 101 (Hollywood Fwy.), take the Lankershim Blvd. exit to the park entrance.

Believing that filmmaking itself was a bona fide attraction, Universal Studios began offering tours to the public in 1964. The concept worked. Today, Universal is more than just one of the largest movie studios in the world—it's one of the biggest amusement parks, attracting more than five million visitors a year. After walking through the trippy Universal CityWalk mall (see "The Shopping Scene" in Chapter 9), visitors descend into a valley of rides via a set of lengthy outdoor escalators.

The main attraction continues to be the Studio Tour, a one-hour guided tram ride around the company's 420 acres. En route, you pass stars' dressing rooms and production offices before visiting famous back-lot sets that include an eerily familiar Old West town, a clean New York City street, and the famous town square from the *Back to the Future* films. Along the way, the tram encounters several staged "disasters" that I won't divulge here, lest I ruin the surprise for you.

Other attractions are more typical of high-tech theme park fare, but all have a film-oriented slant. On "Back to the Future—The Ride," you're seated in a mock time-traveling DeLorean and thrust into a fantastic multimedia rollercoasting extravaganza—it's far and away Universal's best ride. The "Backdraft" ride surrounds visitors with brilliant balls of very real fire spewing from imitation ruptured fuel lines. Kids love it. Like the movie that inspired it, the "E.T. Adventure" appeals to the heart; you ride simulated bicycles on an extraordinary special-effects adventure through principal parts of the film. The new "Flintstone Show" is another multi-media carnival, combining film with an array of live-action "prehistoric" electronic models of pterodactyl planes, flame spewing volcanoes, and stone age "celebrities." Shows based on the movies *An American Tail* and *Back to the Future* showcase innovative moviemaking techniques and are educational in spirit. You can be part of a live audience for a TV show taping, but there's so much to do here that you should probably save that for another day (see "TV Tapings," below).

Universal Studios is really a fun place. But, just like any theme park, lines can be long; a wait for a five-minute ride can sometimes last more than one hour. In summer, the stifling Valley heat can dog you all day. To avoid the crowds, skip weekends, school vacations, and Japanese holidays.

2 TV Tapings

Being part of the audience for the taping of a television show might be the quintessential L.A. experience. This is a great way to see Hollywood at work, to find out how your favorite sitcom or talk show is made, and to catch a glimpse of your favorite TV personalities. But you might end up with tickets to a show that may never make an appearance in your *TV Guide* rather than for one of your favorites, like *Mad About You* or *Friends*. Tickets to top shows are in greater demand than others, and getting your hands on them usually takes advance planning—and possibly some time waiting on line.

Request tickets as far in advance as possible. Several episodes may be shot on a single day, so you may be required to remain in the theater for up to four hours. If you phone at the last moment, you may luck into tickets for your top choice. More likely, however, you'll be given a list of shows that are currently filming, and you won't recognize many of the titles; studios are always taping pilots, few of which end up on the air. But you never know who may be starring in them—look at all the famous faces that have launched new sitcoms in the past couple of years. Tickets are always free, usually limited to two per person, and are distributed on a first-come, first-served basis. Many shows do not admit children under the age of 10; in some cases, no one under the age of 18 is admitted.

Audiences Unlimited (☎ 818/506-0043) distributes tickets for the top sitcoms, including *Murphy Brown, Seinfeld*, and *Frasier*. **Television Tickets** (☎ 213/467-4697) distributes tickets for the most popular talk and game shows. Their services are free, and you can reserve by phone. Or you can get tickets directly from the networks:

ABC, 4151 Prospect Avenue, Hollywood, CA 90027 (☎ 310/557-7777; ticket information hotline 818/506-0067). Taped messages on the hotline let you know what's currently going on. Order tickets for a taping either by writing three weeks in advance or by showing up the day of the taping.

CBS, 7800 Beverly Boulevard, Los Angeles, CA 90036 (☎ 213/852-2345; ticket information hotline 213/852-2458). Call to see what's being filmed while you're in town. Tickets for tapings are distributed on a first-come, first-served basis; you can write in advance to reserve them or pick them up directly at the studios up to an hour before taping.

NBC, 3000 West Alameda Avenue, Burbank, CA 91523 (☎ 818/840-4444 or 818/840-3537). Call to see what's on while you're in L.A. Tickets for NBC tapings, including the *Tonight Show with Jay Leno*, can be obtained in two ways: Pick them up on the day of the show you want to see at the NBC ticket counter—they're distributed on a first-come, first-served basis at the ticket counter off California Avenue; or, at least three weeks before your visit, send a self-addressed, stamped envelope with your ticket request to the address above.

3 More City Sights & Attractions

ARCHITECTURAL HIGHLIGHTS

Los Angeles is a veritable Disneyland of architecture. The city is home to an amalgam of distinctive styles, from art deco to Spanish revival to coffee-shop kitsch to suburban ranch to postmodern—and much more.

Confessions of a Former Game Show Contestant

People are still impressed when they hear that I was a game show contestant, even though it's been more than eight years since I won $28,224 on *The $25,000 Pyramid*. There's definitely a pop-culture cachet to a game show appearance: shaking hands with Alex Trebek or Wink Martindale . . . maybe matching wits with up-and-coming or has-been sitcom stars . . . pulling out bits of grade-school logic or otherwise worthless pop trivia from the vast recesses of your brain . . . your friends and family watching your winnings tally up on the LED readout from home.

Perhaps you've been thinking of taking a chance on fame and fortune next time you're in L.A. Both are more attainable than you might think—actress Markie Post's career began with her audition for a game show; and as far as fortune goes, *someone* has to win the $100,000 *Jeopardy* championship!

If you're serious about trying to get on a show, be sure you have some flexibility in your schedule; although most production companies go out of their way to give priority to out-of-town contestants, you should be prepared to return to Los Angeles one or more times for a final audition and/or taping. My own journey from first interview to a victory hug from host Dick Clark took four months. Here are some tips that might help you prepare:

The Bubblier the Better: Be friendly, cheerful, and bright at your audition as well as during taping. Be good-natured when you lose or make mistakes and, above all, be exuberant if you win the "big money." When you're onstage, nothing feels quite real; I really did have to remind myself to look thrilled when I suddenly had *25 grand* more than I had 60 seconds earlier.

Dress for Success, Part One: Contestant coordinators look for players who won't put off viewers. It's awfully hard for a granny in the heartland to relate to a trendy big-city type. So dress as conservatively as possible for your auditions.

The movie industry, more than anything else, has defined Los Angeles. The process of moviemaking isn't—and never has been—confined to studio offices and back lots; it's staged in the city's public spaces, it spills out into the streets. The city is an extension of the movie set, and Angelenos have always seen it—and used it—that way. Thus, all of Los Angeles has an air of Hollywood surreality about it that plays itself out in the architecture; the whole city seems a bit larger than life. Cutting-edge, over-the-top styles that would be out of place in other cities, from Tail o' the Pup to the mansions lining the streets of Beverly Hills, are perfectly at home in L.A. The world's top architects, from Frank Lloyd Wright to Frank Gehry, have flocked to L.A.,

Dress for Success, Part Two: Have you ever noticed that women contestants are always clad in solid blue, red, or green dresses? Producers will dissuade you from wearing white, black, neutrals, stripes, large prints, or metallics, most of which require lighting and camera adjustments they'd rather not make just for you. Men have an easier time of it; most of you guys already own a suitable jacket or suit.

Most Unglamorous Advice: Remember income taxes. Should you be lucky enough to win big, bear in mind that the *retail* value of all your prizes will be reported to the IRS as earnings, as well as any cash winnings.

Some Game Shows Currently in Production

In addition to those listed below, shows sometimes advertise for contestants on the front page of the *Los Angeles Times* classified section.

The Price Is Right (Network)   Contestants are chosen from the studio audience to test their shopping expertise. Write for tickets to *The Price Is Right,* CBS Television City, 7800 Beverly Blvd., Los Angeles, CA 90036.

Supermarket Sweep (Cable)   Do this one with a partner—teams of two use their knowledge of trivia and their supermarket navigation skills to win. ☎ **213/960-2444.**

Shop Till You Drop (Cable)   Pairs compete in games of skill in a replica shopping-mall setting, in which they "shop" to acquire prizes. ☎ **213/463-7677.**

Jeopardy (Syndicated)   Trivia quiz not for the fainthearted (contestant, that is. It doesn't hurt nearly so much to watch!). ☎ **310/280-5367.**

Wheel Of Fortune (Syndicated)   Less about your skill with the "hangman"-style puzzles than your luck spinning the carnival wheel. ☎ **213/520-5555.**

—Stephanie Avnet

reveling in the artistic freedom they have here. Los Angeles has taken some hard criticism as not being a "serious" architectural center, but in terms of innovation and personal style, the city couldn't get higher marks.

Although much of it is gone, you'll still find some prime examples of the roadside art that defined L.A. in earlier days. The famous Brown Derby is gone, but you can still find a giant doughnut (Randy's Donuts), an oversize hot dog (the aforementioned Tail o' the Pup), and a stack of 45s (Capitol Records), in addition to some new structures carrying on the tradition, like Melrose Avenue's The Hamburger That Ate L.A., and the Chiat-Day offices in Venice.

DOWNTOWN

Bradbury Building

304 S. Broadway (at 3rd St.). ☎ **213/626-1893.**

Built in 1893, this National Historic Landmark is Los Angeles's oldest commercial building, and one of the city's most revered architectural achievements. Capped by a magical five-story skylight, Bradbury's courtyard combines glazed brick, Mexican tile, rich Belgian marble, handsome oak paneling, and lacelike wrought-iron railings. The glass-topped atrium is often used as a movie and TV set; you've seen it in *Chinatown* and *Blade Runner.* Open Monday to Friday 9am to 5pm, Saturday 9am to 4pm.

Central Library

630 W. 5th St. (between Flower St. and Grand Ave.). ☎ **213/228-7000.**

This is one of L.A.'s early architectural achievements. The city rallied to save the library when an arson fire nearly destroyed it in 1986; the triumphant result has returned much of its original splendor. Working in the early 1920s, architect Bertram G. Goodhue employed the Egyptian motifs and materials popularized by the recent discovery of King Tut's tomb, and combined them with a more modern use of concrete block to great effect.

City Hall

200 N. Spring St.

Built in 1928, the 27-story triangular Los Angeles City Hall remained the tallest building in the city for over 30 years. The structure's distinctive ziggurat roof was featured in the film *War of the Worlds,* but is probably best known as the headquarters of the *Daily Planet* in the *Superman* TV series. When it was built, City Hall was the sole exception to an ordinance outlawing buildings taller than 150 feet. On a clear day, the top floor observation deck (open Monday to Friday 10am to 4pm) offers views to Mount Wilson, 15 miles away.

El Alisal

200 E. Avenue 43, Highland Park. ☎ **213/222-0546.**

El Alisal is a small, rugged, two-story "castle," built from 1889 to 1910 from large rocks and telephone poles purchased from the Santa Fe Railroad. The architect and creator was Charles F. Lummis, a Harvard graduate, archeologist, and writer, who walked from Ohio to California and coined the slogan "See America First." A fan of Native American culture, Lummis is credited with popularizing the concept "Southwest," referring to New Mexico and Arizona. He often lived the lifestyle of the Indians, and founded the nearby Southwest Museum, a repository of Indian artifacts. In his castle, Lummis held fabulous parties for the theatrical, political, and artistic elite; his guest list often included Will Rogers and Teddy Roosevelt. The most outstanding feature of his house is the fireplace, which was carved by Mount Rushmore creator Gutzon Borglum. The home's lawn has been turned into an experimental garden of water-conserving plants. Open Friday to Sunday noon to 4pm.

Union Station
Macy and Alameda sts.

Union Station, completed in 1939, is one of the finest examples of California mission-style architecture. The fantastic cream-colored structure, built with cathedral-size proportions, hardly justifies the infrequent train service. When strolling through these grand historic halls, it's easy to imagine the glamorous movie stars who once boarded *The City of Los Angeles* and *The Super Chief* to journey back East during the glory days of rail travel.

✪ Watts Towers
1765 E. 107th St., Los Angeles. ☎ **213/569-8181.** Call for directions.

Ghettoized by its inland location, three long miles from the nearest freeway, Watts is one of America's most infamous slums. The district became notorious as the site of violent riots in the summer of 1965, in which 34 people were killed and over 1,000 injured. Today, a visit to Watts is a lesson in inner-city life; it's a high-density land of gray strip malls, well-guarded check-cashing shops, nail salons, and fast-food restaurants. There's not much for the casual tourist here, and some visitors might not feel comfortable motoring around gangland. But the Towers warrant a visit. They are colorful, 99-foot-tall cement and steel sculptures ornamented with mosaics of bottles, sea shells, cups, plates, generic pottery, and ceramic tiles. They were completed in 1954 by folk artist Simon Rodia, an immigrant Italian tilesetter who worked on them for 33 years. Rodia retired to the San Francisco Bay Area in disgust after protracted battles over the Towers' safety. They are now designated an official cultural monument. Tours are offered on Saturday and Sunday.

HOLLYWOOD

In addition to those listed below, don't miss the Griffith Observatory and Mann's Chinese Theatre (see "Top Attractions," above), and the Hollywood Roosevelt Hotel (see Chapter 5).

Capitol Records Building
1750 Vine St. ☎ **213/462-6252.**

Opened in 1956, this 12-story tower near the corner of Hollywood and Vine is one of the city's most recognizable buildings. At the suggestion of singer Nat "King" Cole and songwriter Johnny Mercer, Capitol's headquarters was designed to resemble a stack of records, topped with a giant turntable stylus. Cole, Mercer, and other 1950s Capitol artists populate a giant exterior mural.

Department Store
3050 Wilshire Blvd. (at Vermont Ave.)

Formerly Bullock's, then I. Magnin, this classy art-deco gem features a stylish interior with mottled marble wall panels, Cubist wall reliefs, and luxurious wood veneers. The main entrance faces the parking lot in the rear; the street-side facade was meant to be admired while flying past.

Freeman House

1962 Glencoe Way. ☎ **213/850-6278.**

Frank Lloyd Wright's Freeman House, built in 1924, was designed as an experimental prototype of mass-produced affordable housing. The home's richly patterned "textile-block" exterior was Wright's invention, and is the most famous aspect of the home's design. Situated on a dramatic site overlooking Hollywood, Freeman House is built with the world's first glass-to-glass corner windows. Dancer Martha Graham, musician Xavier Cugat, art collector Galka Sheye, photographer Edward Weston, and architects Philip Johnson and Richard Neutra all lived or spent significant time at this house, which became known as an avant-garde salon. The house is open to the public for tours every Saturday at 2pm and 4pm.

Hollyhock House

4800 Hollywood Blvd. (in Barnsdall Park). ☎ **213/485-4581.**

Built between 1917 and 1920, this was the first Frank Lloyd Wright residence to be constructed in Los Angeles. Designed as the centerpiece of an art-filled park, the house was commissioned by oil heiress Aline Barnsdall, yet another in a long line of rich eccentrics who hosted artistic salons in L.A.. Today the house is owned by the city and operates as a small gallery.

WESTSIDE

In addition to the design center, don't miss the Argyle and Beverly Hills Hotels (see Chapter 5), and be sure to wind your way through the streets of Beverly Hills off Sunset Boulevard (see driving tour, below).

Pacific Design Center

8687 Melrose Ave., West Hollywood. ☎ **310/657-0800.**

Designed by Argentinean architect Cesar Pelli, the bold architecture and overwhelming scale of the Pacific Design Center aroused plenty of controversy when it was erected in 1975. Sheathed in cobalt-blue glass that's designed with a gentle curve, the seven-story building houses over 750,000 square feet of wholesale interior design showrooms, and is known to locals as "the blue whale." When the property for the design center was acquired in the 1970s, almost all of the small businesses that lined this stretch of Melrose Avenue were demolished. Only tenacious Hugo's Plating, which still stands in front of the center, successfully resisted the wrecking ball. In 1988 a second box, dressed in equally dramatic sea green, was added to the design center and surrounded by a protected outdoor plaza.

✪ Tail o' the Pup

San Vicente Blvd. (between Beverly Blvd. and Melrose Ave.), West Hollywood. ☎ **310/652-4517.**

At first glance, you might not think twice about this hot dog–shaped bit of kitsch just across from the Beverly Center. But locals adored this closet-sized wiener dispensary so much that when it was threatened by the developer's bulldozer, they spoke out en masse to save it. One of the last remaining examples of '50s representational architecture, the "little dog that could" also serves up a great Baseball Special.

THE BEACHES

Chiat/Day/Mojo Headquarters

340 Main St., Venice.

What would otherwise be an unspectacular contemporary office building is made fantastic by a three-story pair of binoculars that frames the entrance to this advertising agency. The sculpture is modeled after a design created by Claes Oldenburg and Coosje van Bruggen.

The Narrowest House

708 Gladys Ave., Long Beach.

This narrow English Tudor-style home was built in 1932. Its construction was the result of a bet in which builder Nelson Rummond boasted that he could build a habitable residence on a lot measuring only 10 feet wide by 50 feet deep. The three-story, 860-square-foot structure is featured in "Ripley's Believe It or Not" as the nation's narrowest home.

SAN FERNANDO VALLEY

Walt Disney Corporate Offices

500 S. Buena Vista St. (at Alameda Ave.), Burbank. ☎ **818/560-1000.**

At first glance, this is just another neoclassical building. But wait a minute: Those aren't Ionic columns holding up the building's pediment—they're the Seven Dwarfs (giant-size, of course).

CHURCHES & CEMETERIES
WESTSIDE

Westwood Memorial Park

1218 Glendon Ave., Westwood. ☎ **310/474-1579.**

This is the final resting place of Truman Capote, Roy Orbison, Donna Reed, Buddy Rich, Dorothy Stratton, Natalie Wood, and lots of other celebrities, but the main attraction is the grave of film goddess Marilyn Monroe (1926–62). Marilyn died alone in her modest bungalow at 12305 Fifth Helena Drive, near Sunset Boulevard.

Church of the Good Shepherd

505 N. Bedford Dr., Beverly Hills.

Built in 1924, this is Beverly Hills's oldest house of worship, and it has seen its share of public tragedy. In 1950, Elizabeth Taylor and her first husband, Nicky Hilton, were married here, and the funerals of Alfred Hitchcock, Gary Cooper, and Jimmy Durante were all held here.

THE BEACHES

Wayfarers Chapel

5755 Palos Verdes Dr. S., Rancho Palos Verdes. ☎ **310/377-1650.**

Constructed on a broad cliff with a steep face, the Wayfarers Chapel enjoys a fantastic spot overlooking the lashing waves of the Pacific. Designed by Frank Lloyd Wright, Jr., son of the more celebrated architect, the church is constructed of glass, redwood, and native stone. Known locally as the "glass church," Wayfarers is a memorial to

Emanuel Swedenborg, an 18th-century Swedish philosopher who claimed to have visions of spirits and heavenly hosts. Rare plants, some of which are native to Israel, surround the building. Open daily 9am to 5pm. Phone in advance to arrange a free escorted tour.

THE VALLEYS

✪ Forest Lawn Memorial Park

1712 S. Glendale Ave., Glendale. ☎ **213/254-3131** or 800/204-3131. From U.S. I-5, exit east onto Los Feliz Blvd., turn right on Glendale Ave.; the entrance is two blocks ahead.

The cemetery of the rich and famous, Forest Lawn boasts even more stars in the ground than Hollywood's Walk of Fame. Pick up a map to prominent resting places at the information booth located at the cemetery's entrance, then tour the rolling 300 acres at your leisure. Some of the most celebrated interees include Humphrey Bogart, Nat "King" Cole, Sammy Davis, Jr., W. C. Fields, Errol Flynn, Clark Gable, Karen Carpenter, Gummo Marx, Gracie Allen, Jean Harlow, Alan Ladd, Carole Lombard, and Walt Disney (whom, contrary to popular belief, is not cryogenically frozen).

Conceived in 1917 as a memorial park of sculpture and lush landscaping, the cemetery was built with 1,000 full-scale reproductions of Renaissance statuary, and an enormous Great Mausoleum. There's even an oversize stained-glass re-creation of Leonardo's *The Last Supper*. The result is the tacky place comic Lenny Bruce called "Disneyland for the dead" and Evelyn Waugh brutally parodied in *The Loved One*. When you're ready to sit down, follow the other tourists to the narrated cemetery show, in which two of Forest Lawn's most prized paintings are exhibited: *The Resurrection* and *The Crucifixion*, the latter of which Pope John Paul II called "deeply inspiring." The show is staged daily, every hour from 10am to 4pm, in a specially built theater.

Other sights in the cemetery include the Wee Kirk o' the Heather, a church modeled after a 14th-century Scottish chapel, and the Church of the Recessional, a surprisingly popular place for marriages—including that of Ronald Reagan and Jane Wyman. The nearby Forest Lawn Museum displays stained glass from a 14th-century European cathedral and reproductions of world-famous artworks, including Michelangelo's *David*. Open daily 8am to 5pm.

COLLEGES AND UNIVERSITIES
DOWNTOWN

University of Southern California (USC)

Bounded by Figueroa, Jefferson, Exposition, and Vermont aves. ☎ **213/740-2300.**

Founded by the Methodist Episcopal Church in 1879, the University of Southern California (USC) is the West Coast's oldest private university, and is one of the West's best schools. The campus was the cultural center of an otherwise rural area when the school was founded over 100 years ago. Today this downtown site, adjacent to Exposition Park, is more than a bit dodgy, and not high on most tourists' sightseeing lists. If you do go, seek out Widney Hall, a two-story clapboard from 1880 that's the oldest building on campus. Free one-hour campus tours are offered Monday through Friday from 10am to 2pm. They depart on the hour from the Admissions Center. USC's aptly named football Trojans play in the adjacent Los Angeles Coliseum.

WESTSIDE

University of California, Los Angeles (UCLA)

Bounded by LeConte St., Sunset Blvd., Gayley Ave., and Hilgard Ave., Westwood. ☎ **310/206-8147.**

UCLA enjoys a parklike setting in swanky Westwood and makes for a nice stroll. Most of UCLA's buildings are unspectacular, but you might want to seek out the romanesque Royce Hall, and Morgan Center Hall of Fame, where trophies and memorabilia of the Bruins athletic departments are on display. The prettiest section is North Campus, where you can walk through the Franklin Murphy Sculpture Garden, home to works by Gaston Lachaise and Henry Moore. Although the school only became a full-fledged institution in 1927, UCLA inherited Berkeley's rich academic tradition and is, qualitatively, that top school's peer. Like USC, UCLA is well known for its film school, and end-of-the-year student screenings are some of the hottest tickets in town. Free 90-minute tours are offered Monday to Friday; reservations are required.

THE BEACHES

Pepperdine University

24255 W. Pacific Coast Highway, Malibu. ☎ **310/456-4000.**

If you drive up the Pacific Coast Highway, you can't miss the Malibu campus of Pepperdine University. The school's enormous rolling green lawn is the size of several football fields—and as inviting as seats at the 50-yard line. Pepperdine is affiliated with the Churches of Christ, and has campuses in both Los Angeles and Heidelberg, Germany. There are about 6,000 students at Pepperdine, but never have I seen a single one of them lounging on the lawn.

MISSIONS

In the late 18th century, Franciscan missionaries established twenty-one missions up the California coast, from San Diego to Sonoma. Each uniquely beautiful mission was built one day's trek from the next, along a path known as El Camino Real (the Royal Road), remnants of which still exist today. Their construction marked the end of the Indian era and the beginning of the European age. The two L.A. area missions are located in the valleys that took their names. In addition to the one listed below, see Mission San Gabriel in "Pasadena & the San Gabriel Valley" in Chapter 11.

Mission San Fernando

15151 San Fernando Mission Blvd., Mission Hills. ☎ **818/361-0186.** Admission $4 adults, $3 seniors and children under 13. Daily 9am–5pm. From I-5, exit at San Fernando Mission Blvd. east and drive five blocks to the mission.

Established in 1797, Mission San Fernando once controlled more than 1.5 million acres, employed 1,500 Native Americans, and boasted over 22,000 head of cattle and extensive orchards. The mission complex was destroyed several times, but was always faithfully rebuilt with low buildings surrounding grassy courtyards. The aging church was replaced in the 1940s, and again in the 1970s after a particularly destructive earthquake. The Convento, a 250-foot-long colonnaded structure dating from 1810, is the compound's oldest remaining part. Some of the mission's rooms, including the old library and the private salon of the first bishop of California, have been restored to their late 18th-century appearance,. A half-dozen padres and many hundreds of Shoshone Indians are buried in the adjacent cemetery.

MUSEUMS & GALLERIES
DOWNTOWN

The first three museums listed below are located in Exposition Park, just southwest of downtown.

California African-American Museum

600 State Dr., Exposition Park. ☎ 213/744-7432. Admission free; donation requested. Tues–Sun 10am–5pm. Closed Thanksgiving, Christmas, New Year's Day. Parking $3.

This small museum is both a celebration of successful African-Americans and a living showplace of contemporary culture. The best exhibits are temporary, and touch on themes as varied as the human experience. Recent shows have included a sculpture exhibit examining interpretations of home; a survey of African puppetry; and a look at black music in Los Angeles in the 1960s. Multimedia biographical retrospectives are also commonplace: An exhibit honoring jazz genius Duke Ellington included his instruments and hand-written music. In the gift shop you'll find Sub-Saharan wooden masks and woven baskets, as well as hand-embroidered Ethiopian pillows. There are also posters, children's books, and calendars. The museum offers a full calendar of lectures, concerts, and special events; call for the latest.

California Museum of Science and Industry

700 State Dr., Exposition Park. ☎ 213/744-7400; IMAX theater ☎ 213/744-2014. Admission free to the museum; IMAX theater $6 adults, $4.75 ages 18–21, $4 seniors and children. Multishow discounts available. Daily 10am–5pm.

Celebrating Los Angeles's longstanding romance with the aerospace industry, this museum is best known for its collection of airplanes and other flying objects, including a Boeing DC-3 and a DC-8, and several rockets and satellites. Other industrial science exhibits include a working winery, and a behind-the-scenes look at a functioning McDonald's restaurant. Exhibits on robotics and fiber optics thrill kids, as does the hatchery, where almost 200 chicks are born daily. Temporary exhibits are well planned and thoughtfully executed. One recent pro–Evolution theory exhibit compared the development of chicks, frogs, and humans. The museum's IMAX theater shows up to three different films daily, from about 10am to 9pm. Most of the films are truly awesome exposés of events on earth and in space; the early shows are often packed with school groups. The two gift shops are brimming with science and aviation toys, model kits, Slinkys, gemstones, and freeze-dried astronaut snacks.

Natural History Museum of Los Angeles County

900 Exposition Blvd., Exposition Park. ☎ **213/744-3466.** Admission $8 adults; $5.50 children 12–17, seniors, and students with ID; $2 children 5–12; kids under 5 free; free to all the first Tues of every month. Tues–Sun 10am–5pm, and some Mons and holidays. Free docent-led tours are offered daily at 1pm. From the Pasadena Fwy. (Calif. 110), exit onto Exposition Blvd. east; the museum is three blocks ahead, one block west of Hoover Street.

Natural history museums tend to be huge and unwieldy, and this 35-hall behemoth is no exception. Opened in 1913 in a beautiful columned and domed Spanish Renaissance building, the museum is a warehouse of Earth's history, chronicling the planet and its inhabitants from 600 million years ago to the present day. There's a mind-numbing number of exhibits of prehistoric fossils, bird and marine life, rocks and minerals, and North American mammals. The best permanent displays include the world's rarest shark, a walk-through vault of priceless gems, and an Insect Zoo. Dioramas depict animals in their natural habitats, and other exhibits explore human cultures, including one on North Americans from 1660 to 1914. The Dinosaur Shop sells ant farms and exploding volcano and model kits. The Ethnic Arts Shop has one-of-a-kind folk art and jewelry from around the world. The bookstore has an extensive selection of scientific titles and hobbyists' field guides.

Museum of Contemporary Art

250 S. Grand Ave. and 152 N. Central Ave. ☎ **213/621-2766.** Admission $6 adults, $4 seniors and students, children under 12 free. Tues–Wed and Fri–Sun 11am–5pm, Thurs 11am–8pm.

This is Los Angeles's only institution exclusively devoted to art from 1940 to the present. The museum has good-quality collections of art in most media; all are displayed on a rotating basis. The museum is particularly strong in works by Cy Twombly, Jasper Johns, and Mark Rothko, and shows are often superb. In a terrific recent exhibition, nearly 30 room-size installations were on view simultaneously, a rare event anywhere. For many experts, MOCA's collections are too spotty to be considered world class, and the conservative museum board blushes when offered controversial shows (they passed on a Whitney exhibit that included photographs by Robert Mapplethorpe); but I've seen some excellent exhibitions here. MOCA is one museum with two buildings in the same neighborhood, but not within walking distance. The Grand Avenue main building is an appropriately contemporary red sandstone structure designed by renowned Japanese architect Arata Isozaki. The museum restaurant, Patinette (☎ **213/626-1178**), located here, is the casual-dining creation of celebrity chef Joachim Splichal (see Patina and Pinot Bistro in Chapter 6); lunch runs from $9 to $15. The museum's second space, on Central Avenue, is confusingly called MOCA at the Temporary Contemporary, but draws its art from the same pool as the main building. Phone to find out what's on, then make sure you go to the right building.

Japanese American National Museum

369 E. First St. (at Central Ave.). ☎ **213/625-0414.** Admission $4 adults, $3 seniors and children ages 6–17, $2 students. Tues–Thurs, and Sat–Sun 10am–5pm, Fri 11am–8pm.

Located in a beautifully restored historic building in Little Tokyo, the Japanese American National Museum is a private nonprofit institute created to document and celebrate the history of Japanese in America. The museum's fantastic permanent exhibition chronicles Japanese life in America, while temporary exhibits highlight distinctive aspects of Japanese-American culture. The newest exhibit, "America's Concentration Camps: Remembering the Japanese-American Experience," traces the experiences of the 120,000 Americans of Japanese ancestry who were forced into camps during World War II; when permitted to leave after close to three years, about four-fifths rebuilt their lives in the L.A. area.

Wells Fargo History Museum

333 S. Grand Ave. ☎ **213/253-7166.** Admission free. Mon–Fri 9am–5pm. Closed bank holidays.

Wells Fargo—the Federal Express of its day—was founded just after the Gold Rush as a fast freight and passenger line of horse-pulled stagecoaches; the firm of Henry Wells and William Fargo then branched out into banking. The company's history is inextricably intertwined with the opening of the West; that's proven to be this bank's most fetching marketing gimmick. This compact museum is not as large as the one at the company's main office in San Francisco, but it's worth stopping in for a quick peek at the authentic 19th-century Concord stagecoach and the Challenge nugget—a two-pound gold lump of 76% purity found in 1975. Visitors can also sit inside a half-built coach and listen to taped excerpts from the diary of a young Englishman who made the arduous journey across America in a similar carriage.

The Southwest Museum

234 Museum Dr., in the Highland Park District. ☎ **213/221-2164,** or 213/221-2163 for a recording. Admission $5 adults, $3 seniors (over 55) and students, $2 children 7–18, kids under 7 free. Tues–Sun 11am–5pm. From the Pasadena Fwy. (Calif. 110), exit onto Ave. 43; turn right onto Figueroa and follow the signs zigzagging up the hill to the museum at Museum Drive.

Located on top of a steep hill northeast of downtown, this is the city's oldest museum. Founded in 1907 by amateur historian and Native American expert Charles F. Lummis, this privately funded anthropological museum contains one of the finest collections of Native American art and artifacts found anywhere, including rare paintings, weapons, and a Cheyenne summer tepee. The largest exhibition chronicles 10,000 years of history of the people of the American Southwest. The California Hall focuses on the lifestyles of the first Californians; a separate two-level hall is dedicated to the culture of cold-climate tribes. The museum has a particularly active events calendar that includes a Native American Film Festival, regular lectures, and special children's programs. Phone for the latest. In the shop you'll find authentic Native American drums, kachina dolls, pottery, and sterling-silver jewelry by Native American artist Vernon Begaye.

HOLLYWOOD

The first four museums listed below are clustered around Hancock Park, adjacent to the La Brea Tar Pits (see "Top Attractions," above) on Wilshire Boulevard's "Museum Mile."

Craft & Folk Art Museum

5800 Wilshire Blvd. (at Curson Ave.). ☎ **213/937-5544,** or 213/243-0469 for a recording. Admission $4 adults, $2.50 seniors students, children under 12 free. Open Tues–Sat 11am–5pm, Fri 11am–8pm.

In 1965 a small restaurant and gallery called the Egg and the Eye began serving up small arts and crafts exhibitions along with modest meals. The restaurant no longer exists, but the gallery has grown into one of the city's largest, opening in a prominent Museum Mile building in 1995. "Craft and folk art" is quite a large rubric that encompasses everything from clothing, tools, religious artifacts, and other everyday objects to wood carvings, papier-mâché, weaving, and metalwork. The museum displays folk objects from around the world, but its strongest collection is masks from India, America, Mexico, Japan, and China. A recent exhibition of more than 100 painted clay figurines included a set of miniatures depicting the New York Yankees battling the L.A. Dodgers, with Fernando Valenzuela on the mound. The museum is best known for its annual International Festival of Masks, held each October in Hancock Park, across the street.

✪ Los Angeles County Museum of Art

5905 Wilshire Blvd. ☎ **213/857-6111,** or 213/857-6000 for a recording. Admission $6 adults, $4 students and seniors (62 and over); $1 children 6–17, kids under 6 free; regular exhibitions free to all the second Wed of every month. Wed–Thurs 10am–5pm, Fri 10am–9pm, Sat–Sun 11am–6pm. From the Hollywood Fwy. (U.S. 101), take the Santa Monica Blvd. exit west to Fairfax Ave., then turn left onto Wilshire Blvd.; follow it to the museum.

This is one of the finest art museums in the United States. The huge complex was designed by three very different architects over a span of 30 years; the architectural fusion can be migraine inducing, but this city landmark is well worth delving into. If you fear getting lost forever, head straight for the Japanese Pavilion, designed specifically to accommodate Japanese works, which holds the museum's highest concentration of great art. Its exterior walls are made of Kalwall, a translucent material that, like shoji screens, permits the entry of soft natural light. Inside is an internationally known collection of Japanese Edo paintings that's rivaled only by the holdings of the emperor of Japan.

The Anderson Building, the museum's contemporary wing, is home to 20th-century painting and sculpture. Here you'll find works by Matisse, Magritte, and a good number of Dada artists.

The Ahmanson Building houses the rest of museum's permanent collections. Here you'll find everything from 2,000-year-old pre-Columbian Mexican ceramics to John Singer Sargent's *Portrait of Mrs. Edward L. Davis and her son, Livingston Davis* (1890), one of the museum's most important holdings. There's a unique glass collection, spanning Roman times to the 19th century, as well as a renowned

Hollywood Area Attractions

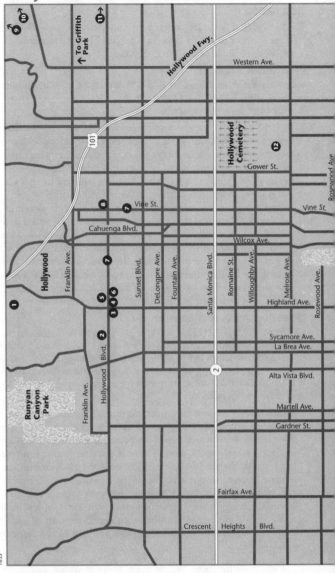

collection of mosaics and monumental silver. The museum also has one of the nation's largest holdings of costumes and textiles, and an important Indian and Southeast Asian art collection.

The Hammer Building is primarily used for major special loan exhibitions. Free guided tours covering the museum's highlights depart on a regular basis from this building. The museum shop is located here, too, and sells merchandise related to current exhibits. You can usually

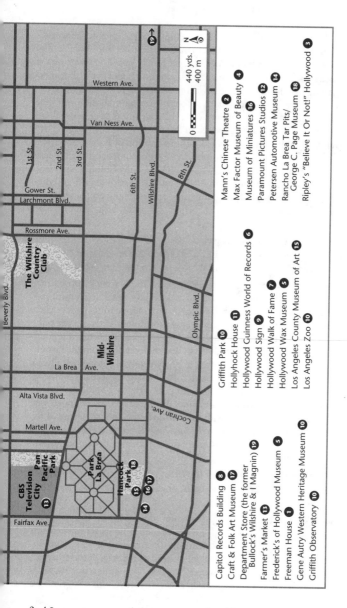

Western Ave.

Van Ness Ave.

1st St. 2nd St. 3rd St.

Gower St.
Larchmont Blvd.

Rossmore Ave.

6th St.

Wilshire Blvd.

8th St.

The Wilshire Country Club

Beverly Blvd.

Olympic Blvd.

Mid-Wilshire

La Brea Ave.

Alta Vista Blvd.

Martell Ave.

Cochran Ave.

Park La Brea

Hancock Park

CBS Television City

Pan Pacific Park

Fairfax Ave.

N

0   440 yds.
0   400 m

Mann's Chinese Theatre **2**
Max Factor Museum of Beauty **4**
Museum of Miniatures **16**
Paramount Pictures Studios **12**
Petersen Automotive Museum **14**
Rancho La Brea Tar Pits/
George C. Page Museum **18**
Ripley's "Believe It Or Not!" Hollywood **3**

Griffith Park **10**
Hollyhock House **11**
Hollywood Guinness World of Records **6**
Hollywood Sign **9**
Hollywood Walk of Fame **7**
Hollywood Wax Museum **5**
Los Angeles County Museum of Art **15**
Los Angeles Zoo **10**

Capitol Records Building **8**
Craft & Folk Art Museum **17**
Department Store (the former
Bullock's Wilshire & I Magnin) **19**
Farmer's Market **13**
Frederick's of Hollywood Museum **5**
Freeman House **1**
Gene Autry Western Heritage Museum **10**
Griffith Observatory **10**

find Japanese teapots, ikebana vases, and sushi accoutrements, as well as interesting jewelry.

The Bing Center has a 600-seat theater and a 116-seat auditorium where lectures, films, and concerts are held.

Museum of Miniatures

5900 Wilshire Blvd. ☎ **213/937-6464.** Admission $7.50 adults, $6.50 seniors, $5 students, $3 children. Tues–Sat 10am–5pm, Sun 11am–5pm.

With almost 200 exhibits, the Museum of Miniatures is the world's largest repository of diminutive mansions, pint-size automobiles, and intricately decorated mini-rooms. Completely unbeknownst to most Angelenos, miniatures-making is a thriving and popular art; almost everything here has been created within the last 15 years. And we're not talking mere doll houses here (though they have those too.): The Museum of Miniatures has perfect 1/12-scale minis of an antebellum mansion, a Benedictine abbey, and an entire Victorian village. They even have an intricately detailed mini re-creation of Judge Lance Ito's now famous courtroom, complete with prosecutors and the defense "dream team." Miniature 18K-gold train cars full of rubies, sapphires, and emeralds are pulled by an engine encrusted with almost 200 diamonds. The wonderful museum gift shop has lilliputian tea sets, very small clocks, and tiny Louis XV "chair" brooches; bring your life-size wallet.

✪ Petersen Automotive Museum

6060 Wilshire Blvd. (at Fairfax Ave.). ☎ **213/930-2277.** Admission $7 adults, $5 seniors and students, $3 children 5–12, kids under 5 free. Tues–Sun 10am–6pm.

When the Petersen opened in 1994, many locals were surprised that it had taken this long for the City of Freeways to salute its most important shaper. Indeed, this museum says more about the city than probably any other one in L.A. Named for Robert Petersen, the publisher responsible for *Hot Rod* and *Motor Trend* magazines, the four-story museum displays over 200 cars and motorcycles, from the historic to the futuristic. Cars on the first floor are depicted chronologically, in period settings. Other floors are devoted to frequently changing shows of race cars, early motorcycles, and famous movie vehicles. Recent exhibits have included the Flintstones' fiberglass and cotton movie car; a customized dune buggy, with seats made from surfboards, created for the Elvis Presley movie *Easy Come, Easy Go;* and a three-wheeled scooter that folds into a Samsonite briefcase, created in competition by a Mazda engineer.

The Frederick's of Hollywood Museum

6608 Hollywood Blvd. ☎ **213/466-8506.** Admission free. Mon–Sat 10am–6pm, Sun noon–5pm.

God bless Frederick Mellinger, inventer of the push-up bra, originally known as the "Rising Star." Frederick's of Hollywood opened this world-famous purple-and-pink art deco panty shop in 1947, and dutifully installed a small exhibition saluting all the stars of stage, screen, and television who glamorized lingerie. The collection includes Madonna's pointy-breasted corset, a pair of Tony Curtis's skivvies, and a Cher-autographed underwire bra (size 32B). Some exhibits were lost during the 1992 L.A. riots, when looters ransacked the exhibit. Mercifully, the bra worn by Milton Berle on his fifties TV show was saved. Stop in for a smile, check out Frederick's extensive collection of crotchless panties, and pick up a catalog.

✪ The Gene Autry Western Heritage Museum

4700 Western Heritage Way, in Griffith Park. ☎ **213/667-2000.** Admission $7 adults, $5 seniors (60 and over) and students 13–18, $3 children 2–12, kids under

2 free. Tues–Sun 10am–5pm. From I-5, exit at Zoo Drive and follow the signs to Griffith Park; the museum is located opposite the zoo.

If you're under the age of 45, you might not be familiar with Gene Autry, a Texas-born actor who starred in 82 Westerns and became known as the "Singing Cowboy." Autry also wrote about 300 songs, starred in his own television series, and, until 1995, was the majority owner of the California Angels. Opened in 1988, Autry's museum is one of L.A.'s best. The enormous collection of art and artifacts of the European conquest of the West is remarkably comprehensive and intelligently displayed. Evocative exhibits illustrate the everyday lives of early pioneers, not only with antique firearms, tools, saddles, and the like, but with many hands-on exhibits that successfully stir the imagination and the heart. There's footage from Buffalo Bill's Wild West Show, movie clips from the silent days, contemporary films, the works of Wild West artists, and plenty of memorabilia from Autry's own film and television projects. The "Hall of Merchandising" displays Roy Rogers bedspreads, Hopalong Cassidy radios, and other items from the collective consciousness—and material collections—of baby boomers. The very unusual museum shop sells western wear and jewelry. The life-size bronze equestrian sculpture at the museum's entrance is of Gene Autry and his faithful horse, Champion.

Max Factor Museum of Beauty

1666 North Highland Ave. (at Hollywood Blvd.). ☎ **213/463-6668**. Admission free. Mon–Sat 10am–4pm.

Max Factor moved his wig and cosmetics shop from Russia to Hollywood in 1904, where his specially thinned, tinted face cream became the first choice of film directors. The early boom years of moviemaking made Factor rich enough to open this art deco shop in 1935; it has been a Hollywood landmark ever since. Today the Max Factor Museum of Beauty takes a campy self-congratulatory stroll through almost a century of motion picture makeup history, reliving the glory days with movie stills and antique cosmetic samples. One installation "re-creates" a star's dressing room; nearby, you'll find a toupee worn by John Wayne.

WESTSIDE

Museum of Tolerance

9786 W. Pico Blvd. (at Roxbury Dr.). ☎ **310/553-8403**. Admission $8 adults, $6 seniors, $5 students, $3 children 3–12, children under 3 free. Advance purchase recommended. Mon–Thurs 10am–5pm, Fri 10am–3pm (to 1pm Nov–Mar), Sun 11am–5pm.

This is an extraordinary new museum with a mission: The Museum of Tolerance is designed to expose prejudices and teach racial and cultural tolerance. The museum is located in the Simon Wiesenthal Center, an institute founded by the legendary Nazi-hunter. While the Holocaust figures prominently here, this is not just a Jewish museum; it's an academy that broadly campaigns for a live-and-let-live world. Tolerance is an abstract idea that's hard to display, so most of this $50-million museum's exhibits are high tech and conceptual in nature. Fast-paced interactive displays are designed to touch the heart as well as the mind, and engage both serious investigators and the MTV crowd. This is one of the most unique museums in America, and definitely worth a visit.

UCLA/Armand Hammer Museum of Art and Cultural Center

10899 Wilshire Blvd. (in Westwood Village). ☎ **310/443-7000.**

Created in 1990 by the former Chairman and CEO of Occidental Petroleum, the Armand Hammer Museum has had a hard time winning the respect of critics and the public alike. Barbs are usually aimed at both the museum's relatively flat collection and its patron's tremendous ego. Ensconced in a two-story Carrara marble building attached to the oil company's offices, the Hammer is known for its firm attachment to the traditional Western European and Anglo-American art that was favored by its wealthy founder.

The collection's strengths lie mostly in late 19th-century works, with exceptional paintings by Toulouse-Lautrec, Degas, and van Gogh. Several canvases warrant special notice: John Singer Sargent's dramatic *Dr. Pozzi at Home* (1881) feels as though the doctor were an actor about to go on stage; it's a sophisticated masterpiece of Salon painting. Rembrandt's *Juno* (1662), painted as a loving tribute to the artist's mistress, is one of the museum's most important pieces, and one of the finest Dutch paintings in any American collection. The Impressionist-inspired *Lilacs* (1887) was painted with entrancing chromatic beauty by van Gogh. And a codex by Leonardo da Vinci is ensconced in its own dimly lit room; densely scribbled pages are filled with drawings and notations on theories of water and hydraulics.

In 1994 the Hammer effectively merged with UCLA's Wight Gallery, a feisty gallery with a reputation for championing contemporary political and experimental art. The new team quickly staged a controversial exhibition imported from New York's Whitney, winning early praise for their daring, if not for the show itself.

THE BEACHES

Museum of Flying

Santa Monica Airport, 2772 Donald Douglas Loop North, Santa Monica. ☎ **310/392-8822.** Admission $7 adults, $5 seniors, $3 children. Thurs–Sun 10am–5pm.

Once headquarters to the McDonald Douglas corporation, the Santa Monica Airport is the birthplace of the DC-3 and other pioneers of commercial aviation. The museum celebrates this bit of local history with 24 authentic aircraft displays and some interactive exhibits. In addition to antique Spitfires and Sopwith Camels, there's a new kid-oriented learning area, where "hands-on" exhibits detail airplane parts, pilot procedures, and the properties of air and aircraft design. The shop is full of scale models of World War II birds; the coffee-table book *The Best of the Past* beautifully illustrates 50 years of aviation history.

NEIGHBORHOODS

The following ethnic districts are all located downtown.

Chinatown

Bounded by North Broadway, North Hill St., Bernard St., and Sunset Blvd.

Hordes of Chinese settled in this once rural area during the second half of the 19th century. Today most Angelenos of Chinese descent are well integrated into the city's suburbs; few can be found living in this rough pocket of downtown. Reconstructed in 1938, a few blocks from its original site just south of Dodger Stadium, Chinatown centers on a mall, Mandarin Plaza, at 970 N. Broadway. Though it hardly compares in quality or size to the Chinese quarters of London, San Francisco, or New York, Chinatown's bustling little mom-and-pop shops and profusion of ethnic restaurants provide an interesting downtown diversion. Go on a Sunday morning for a dim sum brunch (try family-owned Yang Chow; see Chapter 6), then browse through the curious collection of shops jammed with Chinese slippers, cheap jewelry, and china. Amongst the wreckage, you'll find some upscale stores specializing in inlaid furniture, Asian art, fine silks, and other quality imports.

Chinatown is especially worth going out of your way for during Chinese New Year, a month-long celebration that usually begins in late January. The neighborhood explodes into a colorful fantasy of sights and sounds with the Golden Dragon Parade, a beauty pageant, and 5K/10K run. There are plenty of firecrackers and all the Lin Go New Year's cakes you can eat.

Little Tokyo

Bounded by 1st, Alameda, 3rd, and Los Angeles sts.

Like nearby Chinatown, this redeveloped ethnic neighborhood southeast of the Civic Center is not home to the majority of Angelenos of Japanese ancestry; suburban Gardena has that distinction. But Little Tokyo still functions as the community's cultural focal point, and is home to several small-scale paved malls filled with bakeries, bookshops, restaurants, and boutiques, as well as the occasional Buddhist temple. The Japanese American National Museum (see "Museums," above) is here, as is the Japanese American Cultural and Community Center (244 S. San Pedro St., ☎ 213/628-2725), where traditional Kabuki dramas and modern music concerts are regularly performed.

Little Tokyo is shabbier than most any district in the Japanese capital, and has difficulty holding a visitor's attention for much longer than the time it takes to eat lunch. Exceptions to this rule come twice yearly, during the Cherry Blossom Festival in spring, and Nisei Week in late summer. Both heritage festivals celebrate Japanese culture with parades, traditional Ondo street dancing, a carnival, and an arts fair.

Koreatown

Bordered by Olympic Blvd., Western Ave., and the 10 and 110 fwys.

Unlike Chinatown or Little Tokyo, Koreatown is not a contrived cultural theme park; it's the living, breathing hub of a relatively new Korean-American population, Los Angeles's largest Asian community. Koreans are well known in L.A. as hardworking shopkeepers who have penetrated every corner of the city, operating nail salons, souvenir shops, groceries, and many other businesses. Many of the shops in Koreatown are run by and for Koreans, often displaying signs only written in their native language. A cruise along Olympic Boulevard, between Vermont and Western avenues, discloses strip malls full of food, video, laundry, pet supply, and other workaday shops oriented to Korean tastes.

PIERS & PLAZAS
THE BEACHES

Santa Monica Pier
Ocean Ave. at the end of Colorado Blvd., Santa Monica. ☎ **310/458-8900.**

Slightly raffish and somewhat shabby, Santa Monica Pier is everything an old wharf is supposed to be. Built in 1909 as a passenger and cargo ship pier, the wooden wharf is now home to seafood restaurants and amusement arcades, as well as a gaily-colored turn-of-the-century indoor wooden carousel (which Paul Newman operated in *The Sting*). This is the last of the great pleasure piers, offering rides, romance, and perfect panoramic views of the bay and mountains. The pier is about one mile up Ocean Front Walk from Venice; it's a great round-trip stroll.

SAN FERNANDO VALLEY

Universal CityWalk
At Universal Studios, Universal Center Drive, Universal City. ☎ **213/251-4638.** From U.S. 101, take the Universal City exit and follow the signs. Open daily 11am–11pm; some restaurants stay open later.

Los Angeles's newest shopping-and-entertainment complex is an ultrastylized urban street that looks like it's Toontown's main thoroughfare. More than three dozen shops and specialty restaurants, including the Museum of Neon Art, B.B. King's Blues Club, and the Wolfgang Puck Cafe, hide behind oversize, cartoonish facades along the car-free promenade. This visual feast is definitely worth a look.

PARKS

Public parks are not L.A's strong suit. The city's ratio of approximately three acres of open parkland for every 1,000 residents is particularly dismal. The largest green areas in the flatlands around downtown, Hollywood, and the Westside are private country clubs and golf courses. Most of the public green spaces are limited to a single square block, and they're not the most pleasant places in the city for strolling or picnicking. The city's largest parks are located in the mountains and foothills surrounding the L.A. basin.

HOLLYWOOD

Griffith Park
Entrances from Feliz Blvd, Vermont Ave., and Western Ave. ☎ **213/665-5188.**

Mining tycoon Griffith J. Griffith donated these 4,000 acres of parkland to the city in 1896. Today, Griffith Park is the largest city park in America. There's a lot to do here, including hiking, horseback riding, golfing, swimming, biking, and picnicking (see "Outdoor Activities," below). For a general overview of the park, drive the mountainous loop road that winds from the top of Western Avenue, past Griffith Observatory, and down to Vermont Avenue. For a more

👫 Family-Friendly Attractions

Much of larger-than-life L.A. is as appealing to kids as it is to adults. Most of the city's best attractions, like downtown's Los Angeles Historic District, Hollywood's Farmer's Market, and Long Beach's *Queen Mary*, have a kid-friendly carnival-like atmosphere. The novelty of sights such as the Walk of Fame and Mann's Chinese Theatre appeals to all ages. The La Brea Tar Pits and Griffith Observatory interest the curious, as do studio tours (see "Organized Tours," below).

The **Los Angeles Children's Museum** (310 N. Main St., downtown; ☎ 213/687-8800) is a thoroughly enchanting place where kids learn by doing. Everyday experiences are demystified with interesting interactive exhibits displayed in a playlike atmosphere. In the Art Studio, kids are encouraged to make finger puppets from a variety of media, and shiny rockets out of Mylar. Turn the corner, and you're in an unrealistically clean and safe City Street, where kids can sit on a policeman's motorcycle or pretend to drive a bus or a firetruck. Kids of all ages can see their shadows freeze in the Shadow Box, board a mock METRO subway train complete with a real ticket machine and video maps, and play with giant foam-filled, Velcro-edged building blocks in Sticky City. And, because this is Hollywood, the museum wouldn't be complete without its own recording and TV studios, where kids can have a taste of fame. Many of the exhibits let kids dress up in costumes and play with stuff that's off-limits to them in real life. The museum hosts many special activities, from cultural celebrations to T-shirt decorating and musical instrument–making workshops. There is a 99-seat theater, where live performances are scheduled every weekend.

The **Los Angeles Zoo** (5333 Zoo Dr., in Griffith Park; ☎ 213/666-4090) is an easy place to tote the kids around. Animal habitats are divided by continent. The best features are the zoo's walk-in aviary and Adventure Island, an excellent children's zoo that re-creates mountain, meadow, desert, and shoreline habitats.

In addition to these kid-specific attractions, young tourists will also love the wacky **Universal CityWalk,** the carousel at **Santa Monica Pier,** the **Travel Town Transportation Museum** in Griffith Park, and the daily carnival of humanity along **Venice's Ocean Front Walk.** And if all this doesn't keep the kids happy, there are always the theme parks and beaches.

extensive foray, turn north at the loop road's midsection, onto Mt. Hollywood Drive. To reach the golf courses or Los Angeles Zoo (see "Zoos," below), take Los Feliz Boulevard to Griffith Park Drive, which runs along the park's western edge.

Near the Zoo, in a particularly dusty corner of the park, you'll find the Travel Town Transportation Museum, 5200 Zoo Drive (☎ **213/662-5874**), a little-known outdoor museum with a small collection of vintage locomotives and old airplanes. Kids love it. The museum is open Monday to Friday from 10am to 4pm, Saturday to Sunday from 10am to 5pm; admission is free.

THE BEACHES

Will Rogers State Historic Park

1501 Will Rogers State Park Rd., Pacific Palisades. ☎ **310/454-8212.** Park entrance $5 per vehicle, including all passengers. From Santa Monica, take PCH (Calif. 1) north; turn right onto Sunset Blvd., and continue to the park entrance.

Will Rogers (1879–1935) was born in Oklahoma and became a cowboy in the Texas Panhandle before drifting into a Wild West show as a folksy philosophizing roper. The "cracker-barrel philosopher" performed lariat tricks while carrying on a humorous deadpan monologue on current events. The showman moved to Los Angeles in 1919, where he become a movie actor as well as the author of numerous books detailing his down-home "cowboy philosophy."

Located between Santa Monica and Malibu, Will Rogers State Historic Park was once Will Rogers's private ranch and grounds. Willed to the state of California in 1944, the 168-acre estate is now both a park and historic site, supervised by the Department of Parks and Recreation. Visitors may explore the grounds, the former stables, and the 31-room house filled with the original furnishings, including a porch swing in the living room and many Native American rugs and baskets. Charles Lindbergh and his wife, Anne Morrow Lindbergh, hid out here in the 1930s during part of the craze that followed the kidnap and murder of their first son.

The park is open daily 8am to 7pm during the summer, until 6pm the rest of the year. Tours of the house are given Monday through Friday from 10:30am and continue every hour until 4:30pm. On Saturdays and Sundays the house is open continuously from 10am to 5pm. There are picnic tables, but no food is sold.

TOURIST TRAPS

You've heard of all of the following attractions, of course—but you should know exactly what you're in for before you part with your dollars. They're all located on Hollywood's most touristed strip.

Hollywood Guinness World of Records

6746 Hollywood Blvd., Hollywood. ☎ **213/463-6433.** Admission $7.95 adults, $4.95 children ages 6–10, $6.50 seniors. Sun–Thurs 10am–midnight, Fri–Sat 10am–2am.

Scale models, photographs, and push-button displays of the world's fattest man, biggest plant, smallest woman, fastest animal, and other superlatives don't make for a superlative experience.

The Hollywood Wax Museum

6767 Hollywood Blvd., Hollywood. ☎ **213/462-8860.** Admission $9 adults, $7.50 seniors, $7 children 6–12, free for kids under 6. Sun–Thurs 10am–midnight, Fri–Sat 10am–2am.

Cast in the Madame Tussaud mold, the Hollywood Wax Museum features dozens of lifelike figures of famous movie stars and events. The "museum" is not great, but it can be good for a cheeky laugh or two. A "Chamber of Horrors" exhibit includes the coffin used in *The Raven*, as well as a diorama from the Vincent Price classic *The House of Wax*. The "Movie Awards Theatre" exhibit is a short film highlighting Academy Award presentations from the last four decades.

Ripley's "Believe It Or Not!" Hollywood

6780 Hollywood Blvd., Hollywood. ☎ **213/466-6335**. Admission $8.95 adults, $7.95 seniors, $5.95 children ages 5–11.

Believe it or not, this amazing and silly "museum" is still open. A bizarre collection of wax figures, photos, and models depicts unnatural oddities from Robert Leroy Ripley's infamous arsenal. My favorites include the skeleton of a two-headed baby, a statue of Marilyn Monroe sculpted with shredded money, and a portrait of John Wayne made from laundry lint.

VIEWS

It's not always easy to get a good city view. Even if you've found a good vantage, the smog may keep you from having any kind of panorama. But, as they say, on a clear day you can see forever. One of the best views of the city can be had from Griffith Observatory (see "Top Attractions," above). The view of Santa Monica bay from the end of Santa Monica Pier is also great.

Angel's Flight

4th and Hill sts., downtown. ☎ **213/977-1794**.

A once-popular downtown landmark constructed in 1901, Angel's Flight was a tiny, open-car cable railway, or funicular, that transported passengers up the steep eastern slope of Bunker Hill, from Hill Street to Olive Street. Torn down in 1969, it's being rebuilt and will reopen in March of 1996. The projected fare to climb the hill is 25¢.

Mulholland Drive

Between Coldwater Canyon Dr. and U.S. 101.

Mulholland Drive coasts along the peaks of the Hollywood Hills, straddling Hollywood and the San Fernando Valley. The curvy road provides some amazing views of the city, and many opportunities to pull over and simply enjoy. Watch out for drag racers.

4 Organized Tours

STUDIO TOURS

HOLLYWOOD

Paramount Pictures

5555 Melrose Ave. ☎ **213/956-1777**. Tours $15 per person. Mon–Fri 9am–2pm.

Paramount's double-gated main entrance on Melrose Avenue may look familiar, but it's really an early-1980s reproduction of the original arched Bronson Street gate through which Gloria Swanson was driven in the cinema classic *Sunset Boulevard*. Paramount, originally known as the Famous Players Film Company, was founded in 1912 by motion picture pioneer Adolph Zukor; the producer merged with the

Jesse J. Lasky Feature Play Company and director Cecil B. DeMille to create *The Squaw Man,* the industry's first full-length feature.

Paramount's two-hour walking tour around their Hollywood headquarters is both a historical ode to filmmaking and a real-life look at a working studio. Tours depart hourly; the itinerary varies, depending on what productions are in progress. Visits might include a walk through the sound stages of TV shows like *Entertainment Tonight, Frasier,* and *Wings.* Cameras, recording equipment, and children under 10 are not allowed.

SAN FERNANDO VALLEY

NBC Studios

3000 W. Alameda Ave., Burbank. ☎ **818/840-3537.** Tours $6 adults, $5.50 seniors, $3.75 children ages 6–12. Weekdays 9am–3pm.

According to a security guard, John Wayne and Redd Foxx once got into a fight here after Wayne refused to ride in the same limousine as Foxx, who called the movie star a "redneck." Well, your NBC tour will probably be a bit more docile than that. The guided one-hour tour includes a behind-the-scenes look at the *Tonight Show* set, wardrobe, makeup, and set-building departments, and several sound studios. The tour includes some cool video demonstrations of high-tech special effects.

✪ Warner Brothers Studios

Olive Ave. (at Hollywood Way), Burbank. ☎ **818/954-1744.** Admission $27 per person. Mon–Fri 9am–4:30pm, Sat 10am–2pm.

Warner Brothers offers the most comprehensive—and the least theme park–like—of the studio tours. The tour takes visitors on a two-hour informational drive-and-walk jaunt around the studio's faux streets. After a brief introductory film, you'll pile into glorified golf carts and cruise past parking spaces marked "Clint Eastwood," "Michael Douglas," and "Sharon Stone," then walk through active film and television sets. Whether it's an orchestra scoring a film or a TV program being taped or edited, you'll get a glimpse of how it's done. Stops may include the wardrobe department or the mills where sets are made. Whenever possible, guests visit working sets to watch actors filming actual productions. Reservations are required; children under 10 are not admitted.

SIGHTSEEING TOURS

Oskar J's Tours (☎ 818/501-2217) operates regularly scheduled panoramic motorcoach tours of the city. Buses pick up passengers from major hotels for morning or afternoon 4½-hour tours of Sunset Strip, the movie studios, Farmer's Market, Hollywood, homes of the stars, and other attractions. Tours cost $42, and reservations are required.

Next Stage Tour Company offers a unique Insomniacs' Tour of L.A. (☎ 213/939-2688), a 3am tour of the predawn city that usually includes trips to the *Los Angeles Times;* flower, produce, and fish markets; and to the top of a skyscraper to watch the sun rise over the city. The fact-filled tour lasts about 6½ hours and includes breakfast. Tours depart twice monthly and cost $47 per person. Phone for information and reservations.

Stargazing in L.A.: Top Spots About Town for Sighting Celebrities

Celebrities pop up everywhere in L.A. If you spend enough time here, you'll surely bump into a few of them. If you're only in the city for a short time, however, it's best to go on the offensive.

Restaurants are your surest bet. Matsuhisa, The Ivy, and Maple Drive can almost guarantee sightings any night of the week. If you're not up to committing yourself to dining at one of these pricey hot spots, walk in confidently at 9pm and tell the maitre d' that you just want to take a look at the dining room. The trendiest clubs and bars—Whiskey, Viper Room, Tatou, and Roxbury—are second-best for star-sighting, but cover charges can be astronomical and the velvet ropes oppressive. And it's not always Mick and Rod and Madonna; a recent night on the town only turned up Yanni, Ralph Macchio, and Dr. Ruth.

Often, the best places to see members of the A-list aren't as obvious as a back-alley stage door or the front room of Spago. Shops along Sunset Boulevard, like Tower Records and the Virgin Megastore, are often star-heavy. Book Soup, that browser's paradise across the street from Tower, is usually good for a star or two. You'll often find them casually browsing the international newsstand (if they're not there to sign their latest tell-all autobiography). You might even pop into Sunset Strip Tattoo, where Cher, Charlie Sheen, Lenny Kravitz, and members of Guns 'n' Roses all got inked. A mid-afternoon stroll along Melrose Avenue might also produce a familiar face; check out Drake's Gift and Novelty Shop, Red Balls on Fire, Retail Slut, and Billy Martin's.

Keep your eyes peeled for celebrities—everyone does in L.A.—and you'll more than likely be rewarded. And don't feel bad if you only see Bob Denver. What greater sighting than Gilligan himself?

Grave Line Tours (☎ 213/469-4149) is a terrific journey through Hollywood's darker side. You're picked up in a renovated hearse and taken to the murder sites and final residences of the stars. You'll see the Hollywood Boulevard hotel where female impersonator-actor Divine died, the liquor store where John Belushi threw a temper tantrum shortly before his drug overdose, the telephone pole that Montgomery Clift crashed his car into, and the mansion where Sharon Tate was murdered by the Manson family. Tours cost $40 per person and last about $2^1/2$ hours. They depart daily at 9:30am from the intersection of Orchid Street and Hollywood Boulevard, by Mann's Chinese Theatre. Reservations are required.

LA Nighthawks (☎ 310/392-1500) runs specialized tours of L.A.'s nightclubs, usually for small groups traveling by limousine. A two-club, three-hour tour costs $500 for two; three clubs in 5 hours costs $600.

WALKING TOURS

The **L.A. Conservancy** (☎ 213/623-2489) hosts guided walks of downtown Los Angeles. The Conservancy conducts a dozen fascinating, information-packed tours of historic downtown L.A., seed of today's sprawling metropolis. The most popular is "Broadway Theaters," a loving look at movie palaces; other intriguing ones include "Marble Masterpieces," "Art Deco," "Mecca for Merchants," "Terra Cotta," and tours of the landmark Biltmore Hotel and City Hall. They're usually held on Saturday mornings, and cost $5. Call Monday through Friday between 9am and 5pm for exact schedule and information.

AIR TOURS

Heli L.A., Inc. (3200 Airport Ave., Santa Monica; ☎ **213/ 553-4354**), cruises the Paramount, Universal, Burbank, and Disney studios; hovers over the mega-estates of the stars in Beverly Hills and Bel Air; then winds up over Hollywood's Mann's Chinese Theatre, Sunset Strip, and the Hollywood sign. The cost of this helicopter "flightseeing" tour, including lunch or dinner, ranges from $99 to $149, depending on the itinerary. **Heli USA Helicopter Adventures** (3200 Airport Ave., Suite 6, Santa Monica; ☎ **800/443-5487**), offers similar services, both day and night.

Mile High Adventures (☎ 310/450-4447) actually takes passengers on a starlight flight over Los Angeles in a private cabin equipped with a featherbed, a down-filled duvet, king size pillows, music, a bottle of champagne, strawberries, and chocolate truffles. The flight takes one hour and departs from the Santa Monica airport; the price is $229 per couple. Only in L.A.!

BOAT TOURS

Spirit Cruises (Berth 75, Ports O' Call Village, San Pedro; ☎ **310/ 548-8080**) offers daily two-hour harbor cruises and spring whale-watching adventures. Harbor cruises cost $10 for adults and $5 for children. Whale-watching tours cost $15 for adults and $8 for children.

Gondola Getaway (5437 E. Ocean Blvd., Long Beach; ☎ **310/ 433-9595**) offers very romantic tours of Long Beach's Naples Island canals. One-hour excursions aboard authentic Venetian gondolas cost $55. They're perfect for lovebirds, provided you can keep the gondolier from singing.

RUNNING TOURS

Off 'N Running Tours (☎ 310/246-1418 or 800/523-TOUR) combines sporting with sightseeing, taking out-of-town joggers on guided jaunts through the streets of Los Angeles. One-on-one tours are customized to take in the most beautiful areas around your hotel, and can accompany any skill level for 4 to 12 miles. It's a smart way to get the most out of your first morning's jog. Tours cost about $35.

A NEWSPAPER TOUR

The *Los Angeles Times* (Times Mirror Square, 202 W. First St., downtown; ☎ 213/237-5757 or 800/528-4637), offers editorial tours of the nation's largest metropolitan newspaper. You'll see the newsroom, photo composition facilities, and the test kitchen, where recipes for the food section are developed. Tours of the paper's enormous Olympic Production Plant at 2000 E. Eighth Street are also available. You'll see the pressroom, newsprint storage area, platemaking center, and mailroom. Both tours are free; they're offered Monday to Friday at 11:15am and 3pm.

5 Beaches

Los Angeles County's 72-mile coastline sports over 30 miles of beaches, most of which are operated by the Department of Beaches & Harbors (13837 Fiji Way, Marina del Rey; ☎ 310/305-9503). County-run beaches usually charge for parking ($4 to $8). Lifeguards are on duty year-round during daylight hours. Alcohol, bonfires, and pets are prohibited, so you'll have to leave Fido at home. The following are the county's best beaches, listed from north to south:

NORTH COUNTY LINE BEACH

Located between Los Angeles and Ventura counties, immediately south of Point Mugu and north of Leo Carrillo Beach (see below) on PCH, this pristine beach is a popular surf spot. There are no facilities, and no parking or access road. Just pull over to the side of the highway; you'll see everyone else parked there.

LEO CARRILLO STATE BEACH

Located near the point at which Mulholland Drive meets the Pacific Coast Highway (Calif. 1), this beach is part of an adjacent inland state park, where camping is permitted. It's good for tidepool watching at low tide and for cookouts—fire pits are allowed.

EL PESCADOR, LA PIEDRA & EL MATADOR BEACHES

These relatively rugged and isolated beaches front a four-mile stretch of the Pacific Coast Highway between Broad Beach and Decker Canyon Roads. Very picturesque and perfect for picnicking, these beaches can be difficult to find, as they are marked only by small signs on the highway. Visitors are limited by a small number of parking spots atop the cliffs. Descend to the beach via stairs that cling to the cliffs.

ZUMA & POINT DUME BEACHES

Jam-packed on warm weekends, these two adjacent Malibu beaches offer wide stretches of sand, and plenty of parking and services. These are L.A.'s most popular beaches. Families go to Zuma, which is loaded with amenities—snack bars, restrooms, and jungle gyms—while younger people usually head for Point Dume.

PARADISE COVE

This private beach in the 28000 block of the Pacific Coast Highway charges $15 to park and $5 per person if you walk in. Changing rooms and showers are included in the price. The beach is often full by noon on weekends.

Beaches & Coastal Attractions

Beaches

El Pescador, La Piedra,
& El Matador Beaches **3**

Hermosa Beach **19**

Leo Carrillo Beach **2**

Long Beach **25**

Manhattan Beach **18**

Marina del Rey Beach **17**

North County Line Beach **1**

Paradise Cove **6**

Point Dume Beach **5**

Redondo Beach **20**

Santa Monica Beach **11**

Seal Beach **26**

Surfrider Beach **8**

Torrance Beach **21**

Venice Beach **15**

Zuma Beach **4**

Sights & Attractions

Chiat/Day/Mojo Headquarters **14**

J. Paul Getty Museum **9**

Museum of Flying **13**

The Narrowest House **23**

Pepperdine University **7**

Queen Mary **24**

Venice Ocean Front Walk **16**

Wayfarers Chapel **22**

Will Rogers State Historic Park **10**

Santa Monica Pier **12**

SURFRIDER BEACH

Without a doubt, these are L.A.'s best waves. One of the city's most popular surfing spots, this beach is located between the Malibu Pier and the lagoon. In surf lingo, few "locals only" wave wars are ever fought here—surfing is not as territorial here as it can be in other areas, where out-of-towners can be made to feel unwelcome. This is a pleasurable spot for visitors.

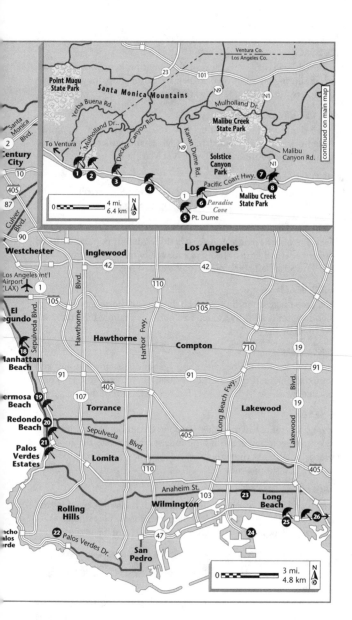

continued on main map

SANTA MONICA BEACH

The beaches on either side of the Santa Monica Pier are popular for their white sands and easy accessibility. There are big parking lots, eateries, and lots of well-maintained bathrooms. A paved beach path runs along here, allowing you to walk, bike, or skate to Venice and points south.

VENICE BEACH

The paved boardwalk gets most of the attention here, but the broad beach is alluring all on its own. Expensive parking lots abound on the small streets surrounding Windward Court.

MARINA DEL REY BEACH

Located right in the middle of del Rey, this covelike beach is popular with families, offering shaded picnic tables and rather calm waters. Parking is just off Admiralty Way, at Via Marina.

MANHATTAN BEACH

Locals sun south of the pier and park in lots on 26th Street or at the end of 45th Street. This is an excellent swimming beach.

HERMOSA BEACH

This is one of my favorite L.A. beaches. Hermosa is popular with the younger volleyball crowd. It offers wide sands and a paved boardwalk called The Strand. There's plenty of street parking.

REDONDO BEACH

Beach access here is south of King Harbor, at 200 Portofino Way. The Redondo Municipal Pier, located just north, is a family-oriented, fun-filled "mall by the sea."

TORRANCE BEACH

South of Redondo, the beaches are bigger and less crowded, but still offer excellent facilities, including food stands and toilets. Local snorkelers swear by Malaga Cove, located just south of the beach.

LONG BEACH

Running the entire length of the city along Ocean Boulevard, this calm, breakwater-protected beach is long indeed, and close to the good restaurants and shops that line Second Avenue. This is one of L.A. County's best sunning beaches.

SEAL BEACH

Both charming and quiet, smallish Seal Beach is a terrific place to steal away to from the city. A "Tot-Lot" has diversionary play structures for the kiddies. Parking is available both at the pier and on 1st Street.

6 Outdoor Activities

BICYCLING

Los Angeles is great for biking. If you're into distance pedaling, you can do no better than the flat 22-mile paved Ocean Front Walk that runs along the sand from Pacific Palisades in the north to Torrance in the south. The path attracts all levels of riders, so it gets pretty busy on weekends. For information on this and other city bike routes, phone the Metropolitan Transportation Authority (☎ 213/244-6539).

The best place to mountain bike is along the trails of Malibu Creek State Park (☎ 818/880-0350 or 800/533-7275), in the Santa Monica Mountains between Malibu and the San Fernando Valley. Fifteen miles

Fifteen miles of trails rise to a maximum of 3,000 feet and are appropriate for intermediate to advanced bikers. Pick up a trail map at the park entrance, four miles south of U.S. 101 off Las Virgenes Road, just north of Mulholland Highway. Park admission is $5 per car.

Sea Mist Rental (1619 Ocean Front Walk, Santa Monica; ☎ **310/ 395-7076**) rents 10-speed cruisers for $5 per hour and $14 per day; 15-speed mountain bikes rent for $6 per hour and $20 per day.

BUNGEE JUMPING

MegaBungee, at the Queen Mary Seaport (☎ **310/435-1880**), is a 210-foot, 21-story tower located alongside the historic *Queen Mary;* it's slightly higher than the ship's forward mast. The tallest freestanding bungee tower on the North American continent, MegaBungee uses especially scary New Zealand–style ankle restraints. At $85 per jump, the thrill is anything but cheap. The *Queen Mary* often offers lucrative hotel/jump packages; phone for details.

BOATING/SAILING

For both price and selection, the best place in the city from which to take to the water is Marina del Rey. Built in the sixties from a large swamp that was once an important rest stop for migratory birds on the Pacific Flyway, Marina del Rey is now one of the largest recreational harbors in the world. **Rent-A-Sail** (13719 Fiji Way; ☎ **310/ 822-1868**) rents powerboats for $28 per hour, and sailboats and catamarans for $15 to $30 per hour. The company provides renters with information, maps, and charts, and offers sailing lessons for $28 per hour.

The **Tallship Californian** (☎ **800/432-2201**), docked at Long Beach's Shoreline Village, offers four-hour, hands-on harbor sails. Barefooters help set sails, haul on the lines, and steer a 145-foot cutter-class sailboat. Sails cost $75 per person; reservations are required.

FISHING

Marina del Rey Sports Fishing (13759 Fiji Way; ☎ **310/822-3625**), known locally as "Captain Frenchy's," has four deep-sea boats departing daily on half- and full-day ocean fishing trips. Of course, it depends on what's running when you're out, but bass, barracuda, halibut, and yellowtail tuna are the most common catches on these party boats. Excursions cost from $20 to $25, and include bait and tackle. Phone for reservations.

No permit is required to cast from shore or drop a line from a pier. Local anglers will hate me for giving away their secret spot, but the best saltwater fishing spot in all of L.A. is at the foot of Torrance Boulevard in Redondo Beach. Centuries of tides and currents have created a deep underwater canyon here that's known among local fisherman as a glory hole.

FLYING

Air Combat USA (P.O. Box 2726, Fullerton; ☎ **800/522-7590;** fax 714/522-7592) lets pilots take the stick of an actual NATO tactical/ fighter trainer and engage in simulated aerial dogfighting with other combatants. For $695, wannabe top guns get a one-hour ground school "crash course," one hour of flight time, and a videotape of the entire experience. No flying experience is required. An instructor sits next to you the entire time, but even novices are in control of the plane about 95 percent of the time. Air Combat USA flies daily; reservations are required.

Crystal Soaring, at the Crystal Air Airport, Pear Blossom Hwy. (☎ 805/944-3341), offers piloted glider rides above the magnificent San Gabriel Mountains. Flights last from 20 to 40 minutes, and cost from $60 to $150. The airport is located about 90 minutes from downtown Los Angeles. Phone for reservations.

GOLFING

The greater Los Angeles area has more than 100 golf courses, which vary in quality from abysmal to superb. **American Golf Corp.** (1633 26th St., Santa Monica; ☎ 310/829-4653 or 800/863-3669; fax 310/829-4990) guarantees reserved tee times at more than 15 top area courses. The company can also arrange lessons and provide information on local tournaments.

It's best to book tee times at all of the following courses in advance:

Of the city's seven 18-hole and five 9-hole courses, you can't get more central than **Rancho Park Golf Course** (10460 W. Pico Blvd.; ☎ 310/838-7373), located smack-dab in the middle of L.A.'s Westside. The par-71 course has lots of tall trees, but not enough to dot out the towering Century City buildings next door. Greens fees are $17 Monday through Friday, and $21 on weekends.

✪ **Industry Hills Golf Club** (1 Industry Hills Pkwy., City of Industry; ☎ 818/810-4455) has two 18-hole courses designed by William Bell. Together they encompass 8 lakes, 160 bunkers, and long fairways. The Eisenhower Course, which consistently ranks among *Golf Digest*'s top 25 public courses, has extra-large uldulating greens and the challenge of thick kikuyu rough. An adjacent driving range is lit for night use. Greens fees are $45 on Monday through Friday and $60 on Saturday and Sunday.

It's a distance from the city, but the private **Monarch Bell Golf Course** (33080 Niguel Rd., Laguna Niguel; ☎ 714/240-8247), designed by Robert Trent Jones, Jr., is one of the most attractive and challenging courses in Southern California. Fronting the Pacific Ocean, Monarch Bell's beautiful elevated greens and exquisite rolling fairways are popular year-round. Greens fees are $75 Monday through Thursday and $100 Friday through Sunday, including the required cart rental. The course is located about an hour from downtown Los Angeles; it's definitely worth the trip to Orange County.

HANG GLIDING

Up and down the California coast, it's not uncommon to see people poised on the crests of hills, hanging from enormous colorful kites. You can, too. **Windsports International** (16145 Victory Blvd., Van Nuys; ☎ 818/988-0111) offers flight instruction and rentals for both novices and experts. A one-day lesson in a solo kite on a bunny hill costs $99. If it's more of a thrill you're looking for, choose the $125,

3,000-foot high-altitude tandem flight, where you are physically connected to an instructor. Lessons take off from varying spots in the San
Fernando Valley, depending on the winds. Phone for reservations.

HIKING

The Santa Monica Mountains, a small range that runs only 50 miles
from Griffith Park to Point Mugu, on the coast north of Malibu,
makes Los Angeles a great place for hiking. The mountains peak at
3,111 feet and are part of the Santa Monica Mountains National
Recreation Area (SMMNRA), a contiguous conglomeration of 350
public parks and 65,000 acres. Many animals make their homes in
the SMMNRA, including deer, coyote, rabbit, skunk, rattlesnake,
fox, hawk, and quail. The hills are also home to almost 1,000 drought-
resistant plant species, including live oak and coastal sage.

Hiking is best after spring rains, when the hills are green, flowers are
in bloom, and the air is clear. Summers can be very hot; hikers should
always carry fresh water. Beware of poison oak, a hearty shrub that's
common on the West Coast. Usually found among oak trees, poison
oak has leaves in groups of three, with waxed surfaces and prominent
veins. If you come into contact with this itch-producing plant, bathe
yourself in calamine lotion, or the ocean. If you're planning to do a lot
of hiking, phone the Mountain Parks Information Line (☎ **800/
533-7275**) and ask for a free trail map.

JRT International (14755 Ventura Blvd., Suite I-586, Sherman
Oaks; ☎ **818/501-1005**) offers personalized scenic hiking tours
around the SMMNRA lead by a ecology-oriented guide. The following are some of my favorite trails:

Santa Ynez Canyon, in Pacific Palisades, is a long and difficult
climb that rises steadily for about three miles. At the top, hikers are rewarded with fantastic views over the Pacific. Also at the top is Trippet
Ranch, a public facility providing water, restrooms, and picnic tables.
From Santa Monica, take Pacific Coast Highway (PCH) north. Turn
right onto Sunset Boulevard, then left onto Palisades Drive. Continue
for 2.5 miles, turn left onto Verenda de la Montura, and park at the
cul-de-sac at the end of the street, where you'll find the trailhead.

✪ **Temescal Canyon,** in Pacific Palisades, is far easier than the Santa
Ynez trail and, predictably, far more popular. A favorite of locals, this
is one of the quickest routes into the SMMNRA wilderness. Hikes here
are anywhere from one to five miles. From Santa Monica, take Pacific
Coast Highway (Calif. 1) north; turn right onto Temescal Canyon Rd.,
and follow it to the end. Sign in with the gatekeeper, who can also
answer your questions.

Will Rogers State Historic Park, Pacific Palisades, is also a terrific place for hiking. An intermediate-level hike from the park's entrance ends at Inspiration Point, a plateau from which you can see
a good portion of L.A.'s Westside. See "Parks," above, for complete
information.

HORSEBACK RIDING

There are surprisingly few stables in Los Angeles, which is unfortunate,
since there are plenty of great places to ride.

The **Los Angeles Equestrian Center** (480 Riverside Dr., Burbank; ☎ 818/840-9066) rents horses by the hour for western or English riding through Griffith Park's hills. There's a 200-pound weight limit, and children under 12 are not permitted to ride. Horse rental costs $13 per hour, and there's a two-hour rental maximum. The stables are open Monday through Friday 8am to 7pm and Saturday and Sunday 8am to 4pm.

Sunrise Downs Equestrian Center (11900 Big Tujunga Canyon Rd., Tujunga; ☎ 818/353-9410) offers two-, three-, and four-hour guided day or evening horseback tours through the San Gabriel Mountains and the scenic San Fernando Valley. They charge $25 per hour, per person; there's a two-person minimum.

JET SKIING

Nature Tours (1759 9th St., Suite 201, Santa Monica; ☎ 310/452-7508) offers intensive two-hour jet ski lessons, teaching all levels of riders how to get the most out of jet skis and wave runners. Beginners ski around Marina del Rey, while advanced jetters cruise up to Malibu. Midweek half-day trips to Pyramid Lake include jet-ski rental, lessons, and a lunchtime barbecue. The cost is about $150 per lesson or tour.

SEA KAYAKING

Sea kayaking is all the rage in Southern California; if you've ever tried it, you'll know why. Unlike river kayaks, in which your legs are actually inside the boat's hull, paddlers sit on top of sea kayaks, and can maneuver them more easily than canoes. **Southwind Kayak Center** (17855 Sky Park Circle, Suite A, Irvine; ☎ 714/261-0200 or 800/768-8494) combines sea kayaking with bird-watching on their tours of Upper Newport Bay. Trips cost $40 to $65. One-day Catalina Island kayaking trips are also arranged and cost about $120, including ferry ride.

Island Packers (1867 Spinnaker Dr., Ventura; ☎ 805/642-1393) arranges small group tours to Santa Cruz and the Anacapa Islands. One-day excursions last about 10 hours, include continental breakfast and a picnic lunch, and cost $135. Longer adventures can also be arranged, with camping or lodging included, for $215 to $445.

SCUBA DIVING

The best scuba diving and snorkeling in Los Angeles is off Catalina Island, and off Leo Carillo State Beach, near the Ventura County line. **Dive and Surf** (504 N. Broadway, Redondo Beach; ☎ 310/372-8423) arranges trips for all diving levels.

SKATING

The 22-mile-long Ocean Front Walk that runs from Pacific Palisades to Torrance is one of the premiere skating spots in the country. In-line skating is especially popular, but conventionals are often seen here, too. Roller-skating is allowed just about everywhere bicycling is, but beware that cyclists have the right of way. **Spokes 'n Stuff** (4175 Admiralty Way, Marina del Rey; ☎ 310/306-3332) is just one of many places to rent wheels near the Venice portion of Ocean Front Walk. Skates cost $5 per hour; knee pads and wrist guards come with every rental.

SURFING

Surfing was invented by the Polynesians. Captain Cook made note of it in Oahu in 1778. George Freeth (1883–1918) is widely credited with introducing the sport to California; he first surfed Redondo Beach in 1907. But the sport didn't catch on until the fifties, when California Institute of Technology graduate Bob Simmons invented a more maneuverable lightweight fiberglass board. International rules for surfing competitions were adopted in 1966, and the rest, as they say, is history.

Boards are rented at shops near all top surfing beaches in the L.A. area, including **Zuma Jay Surfboards** (22775 Pacific Coast Highway, Malibu; ☎ **310/456-8044**); you'll find the shop about a quarter mile south of Malibu Pier. Rentals are $20 per day.

TENNIS

While soft-surface courts are more popular on the East Coast, in California hard surfaces are most common. If your hotel doesn't have a court, and can't suggest any courts nearby, try the well-maintained, well lit **Griffith Park Tennis Courts,** on Commonwealth Road, just east of Vermont Avenue. Or, call the City of Los Angeles Department of Recreation and Parks (☎ **213/485-5555**) to make a reservation at a municipal court near you.

WINDSURFING

Invented and patented by Hoyle Schweitzer of Torrance in 1968, windsurfing, or sailboarding, is a fun sport that's much more difficult than it looks. The **Long Beach Windsurfing Center** (3850 E. Ocean Ave., Long Beach; ☎ **310/433-1014**) rents boards by the hour; it's open daily from 10am to 6pm.

At **Malibu Ocean Sports,** on the beach in front of Marina del Rey's Cheesecake Factory (☎ **310/821-8960**), windsurfer rentals— including board, wet suit, and flotation devices—are $15 per hour. Lessons are offered on weekends; the three-hour course costs $45 and is guaranteed to teach you the basics.

7 Spectator Sports

BASEBALL

Los Angeles has two major-league baseball teams. The **Los Angeles Dodgers** (☎ 213/224-1500) play at Dodger Stadium, 1000 Elysian Park, near Sunset Boulevard. If you're lucky, you just may get to see Hideo Nomo (the Dodgers' Japanese sensation) pitch before a hometown crowd (Hideo is actually the second Japanese player to play in the Big Leagues, but the first of any merit). If you go to a game, don't be surprised by the apparent apathy of the crowd; traffic is so bad getting to and from Dodger Stadium that the fans usually arrive late, around the second or third inning, and leave early—the stands empty out during the seventh inning. Dodgers' fans are an odd bunch.

The Disney-owned **California Angels** (☎ 714/634-2000) call Anaheim Stadium, at 2000 S. State College Boulevard (near Katella Avenue) in Anaheim, home. More often than not, games are populated by displaced fans there to see the visiting team rather than diehard Angels' supporters. If you go to cheer on your hometown Yankees, White Sox, or Twins, you'll probably be right at home in the crowd.

Since 1995's baseball strike, tickets to ball games have been very easy to get, though the best seats still go to season ticket holders.

BASKETBALL

Los Angeles has two National Basketball Association franchises: the **L.A. Lakers** (☎ 310/419-3100), who play at the Great Western Forum, 3900 W. Manchester Boulevard (at Prairie Avenue) in Inglewood; and the **L.A. Clippers** (☎ 213/745-0400), who hold court in the L.A. Sports Arena, 3939 S. Figueroa Street, near downtown. Good seats to Lakers games are all but impossible to acquire, though tickets in the nosebleed section are often available. They're practically giving away tickets to Clippers games—except for when they're playing the Lakers, of course.

FOOTBALL

Football fans are out of luck in L.A. now. The two former Los Angeles–area NFL teams both left town in 1995: the Raiders went back to Oakland, and the Rams ran for St. Louis.

HORSE RACING

The scenic **Hollywood Park Racetrack** (1050 S. Prairie Ave., Inglewood; ☎ **310/419-1500**), with its lakes and flowers, features thoroughbred racing from early April through July as well as in November and December. The $1 million Hollywood Gold Cup is also run here. Well-placed monitors project views of the back stretch as well as stop-action replays of photo finishes. The track restaurant, Citation (named after the Triple Crown-winning thoroughbred), features an eclectic menu that includes chicken, beef, pork, and ostrich dishes, but no horse meat, of course. Races are usually held Wednesday through Sunday. Post times are 1pm in summer (at 7pm on Friday), and 12:30pm in the fall. General admission is $6, $25 to the clubhouse.

One of the most beautiful tracks in the country, **Santa Anita Racetrack** (285 W. Huntington Dr., Arcadia; ☎ **818/574-7223**) offers thoroughbred racing from October through mid-November and December through late April. The track was featured in the Marx Brothers' film *A Day at the Races*, and in the 1954 version of *A Star Is Born*. On weekdays during the racing season the public is invited to watch morning workouts from 7:30 to 9:30am. Post time is 12:30 or 1pm. Admission is $3.

ICE HOCKEY

The NHL's **L.A. Kings** (☎ 310/673-6003) play at the Great Western Forum at 3900 W. Manchester Boulevard (at Prairie Avenue) in Inglewood. Gretsky's still worth seeing. The Disney-owned **Mighty Ducks** play at Arrowhead Pond, Anaheim (☎ 714/704-2500).

8

Hollywood at Home: A Driving Tour

by Stephanie Avnet

Ever since the days before talkies, visitors to Los Angeles have wanted to see just how the rich and famous live. Today it's big business—maps of dubious accuracy are sold on Sunset Strip street corners, and at least a dozen tour operators shuttle vanloads of looky-loos daily through Beverly Hills.

Sure, it's nice and easy to lay out your cash, climb on the bus, and sit back for the ride and the regular spiel. But it's much more fun to do it yourself. By setting your own pace, you can skip the cookie-cutter mansions—yes, there is such a thing—of yawn-inspiring celebs and take your time poking around the sites associated with the legendary (or just plain famous) folks that really give you a thrill.

Go where the tour vans can't—deep into the surrounding hillsides to spy on the rustic star retreats dating from Hollywood's Golden Age. Swaying palms silhouetted against a clear, sunny Los Angeles sky seem an unlikely backdrop for tragedy, but don't be fooled: Some of the homes you'll see are more than the humble abodes of their famous residents; they're the notorious stage sets for some of the movie world's greatest scandals. Behind their innocent facades and unassuming walls, a few even hide the truths to Hollywood mysteries that may never be solved.

Have fun!

Start: 8400 block of Santa Monica Boulevard in West Hollywood.
Finish: Sunset Boulevard at Beverly Glen in Bel-Air.
Time: Allow 3 to 4 hours, not including time spent dining.
Best/Worst Times: Anytime during daylight hours is good for the drive itself, but try to avoid the 12:30 to 1:30pm show-biz lunch rush at the eateries listed.
Related Tip: Notice the streetlamps all along the way—some of the city's loveliest and most elaborate fixtures line the route.

☕ **STARTING OUT**   Your mother was right, you know—the best way to start the day is with a "power" breakfast at one of these local hangouts:

You're as likely to see Hollywood names dining with their high-powered agents at **Hugo's** (8401 Santa Monica Blvd., at King's Rd.; ☎ 213/654-3993) as you are grungy struggling artists strolling in from the surrounding apartment buildings. Everyone is lured by the casual restaurant's legendary tasty breakfast fare, served throughout the day. Hugo's also offers a selection of pastas and other dishes, many imbued with a refreshingly unique Indian flavor.

Or, try another old Hollywood standby, **Barney's Beanery,** just west of Hugo's at 8447 Santa Monica Boulevard (☎ 213/654-2287). A reliable roadhouse since the days when old Route 66 passed this spot, Barney's draws crowds eager to enjoy a game of pool, a round of beers, and plates generously piled with chili burgers, seasoned fries, and other delicious diner fare (including all-day breakfast favorites). In keeping with the newly nutrition-conscious rock 'n' roll crowd, Barney's Beanery also serves great turkey and veggie burgers.

After fortifying yourself with a hearty meal, begin your adventure by heading west to:

1. **8563 Holloway Drive** and
2. **8573 Holloway Drive.** These apartment buildings share a garden courtyard as well as an infamous past. In 1976, washed-up actor Sal Mineo (best known for his role opposite James Dean in *Rebel Without a Cause)* was mysteriously stabbed to death in the carport beneath the fuschia-colored bougainvillea vines. Earlier, before these buildings were run down, Marilyn Monroe shared number 8573 with fellow starlet Shelly Winters. It would be only one of the dozens of places Marilyn lived in L.A. during her lifetime; you'll pass several more later on this tour.

Continue along Holloway to Sunset Boulevard and turn left, then left again on Larrabee. Follow Larrabee to Cynthia Street, and turn right; proceed to Doheny Drive. On the southeast corner of Doheny and Cynthia is:

3. **882 North Doheny Drive,** an austere white apartment building where Marilyn Monroe was living when she began her ill-fated courtship with her second husband, baseball great Joe DiMaggio.

Turn right onto Doheny, and take it past Sunset Boulevard into the hills, turning right onto tiny Cordell Drive to:

4. **9166 Cordell Drive.** This was the domicile of George Cukor, director of such classics as *The Philadelphia Story, Adam's Rib, Gaslight,* and *My Fair Lady.* The long privacy wall accented with palm trees once enclosed a compound of four houses, including one rented to Spencer Tracy. Katherine Hepburn continued living there for ten years following Tracy's death—in her arms in the kitchen—in 1967. This cozy enclave was beloved by Cukor; he entertained

often by the pool. After his death in 1982, the new owners swore they felt his presence haunting the halls he adored.

Take Doheny Drive back downhill, turning right on Cory Drive, and right again on Sunset Boulevard. As Sunset begins to veer left at the light, stay to the right and take Doheny Road to Schuyler Road. Make a right on Schuyler and follow it up the hill to Readcrest, turning left to:

5. 9377 Readcrest Drive, former home of actor Fernando Lamas and his wife, swimmer-actress–swimsuit designer Esther Williams.

Turn right when Readcrest meets Lindacrest, then right again onto Beverlycrest. You'll soon see:

6. 9402 Beverlycrest Drive, the home in which Rock Hudson died of AIDS, a sprawling estate he called "The Castle."

Beverlycrest will return you to Schuyler Road—follow it down the hill to Doheny Road and make a right turn, then curve left onto Foothill and find:

7. 915 Foothill Road, whose grand gates lead to an estate owned at one time by Mel Brooks, and most recently, by "Ol' Blue Eyes" himself, Frank Sinatra.

On the left side of the street, at the corner of Sunset Boulevard, is:

8. 9521 Sunset Boulevard, the childhood home of pint-size star Shirley Temple, who had her own miniature playhouse on the grounds.

Turn left onto Sunset, watching between Palm and Hillcrest on the left side of the street for:

9. 9419 Sunset Boulevard. Imagine MGM "boy wonder" executive Irving Thalberg and his actress wife, Norma Shearer, holding court behind these dense shrubbery walls; this was their estate until Thalberg's untimely death at age 37 in 1936.

Turn right on Hillcrest Road to Santa Monica Boulevard, right to Palm Drive, and right once again. Notice the pleasing symmetry of the landscaping on these streets in the "flats" of Beverly Hills—each north/south drive is planted with a different tree, though clearly not according to name (palm trees line Hillcrest Road, while Palm Drive displays the lavender blooms of jacaranda trees). On Palm you'll find:

10. 508 Palm Drive. This was home to Marilyn Monroe and Joe DiMaggio during their short marriage in 1954. Two houses up is:

11. 512 Palm Drive, a modest Mediterranean-style enclave that was blonde bombshell Jean Harlow's last home, where she died in 1937—at the age of 26—of sudden uremic poisoning.

Two blocks further is another former Marilyn Monroe home:

12. 718 Palm Drive. She briefly shared this ivy-covered house with William Morris agent Johnny Hyde in 1950, the year she began to make a name for herself with small, but pivotal, roles in *The Asphalt Jungle* and *All About Eve*.

Turn back toward Elevado Avenue, turn right to Rexford Avenue, and right again, following Rexford up past Sunset Boulevard to

Hollywood at Home: A Driving Tour

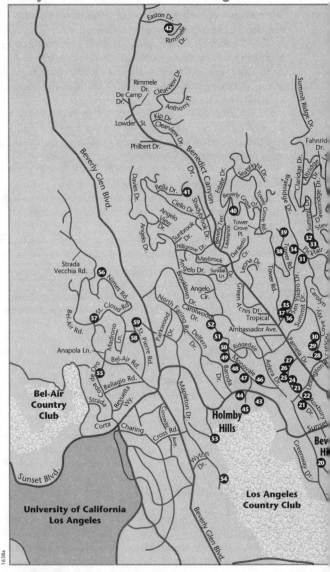

where it intersects Beverly Drive. Make a right turn and look to the left for:

13. **1011 Beverly Drive,** the opulent estate of actress and William Randolph Hearst mistress Marion Davies. Nearly as lavish and excessive as the Santa Monica beach house built for her by Hearst, this mansion is where he died in 1951 (and later she did, in 1961). The driveway is so enormous you might mistake it for a street; stone

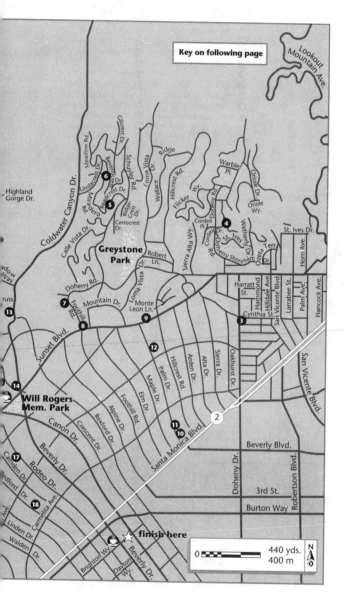

lions perch atop peach-colored walls guarding the gate, behind which you can see a broad road winding up the hill.

Turn around at Shadow Hill Way and slow down (if traffic allows) on the way back for another look. Turn right at the T-intersection, continuing south on Beverly Drive to Sunset Boulevard, then make a "hairpin" right turn onto Crescent Drive, where you'll come to:

Hollywood at Home: A Driving Tour

14. **904 Crescent Drive,** a former home of Gloria Swanson, silent film star and *Sunset Boulevard's* original Norma Desmond. Across the street are the:

15. **Beverly Hills Hotel and Bungalows,** secluded locale for many legendary trysts, including the rumored Marilyn Monroe/John F. Kennedy affair. Howard Hughes virtually lived here during his

Hollywood years, keeping several regular bungalows for his family and staff—including his private food-taster.

Continue to:

16. **1001 Crescent Drive,** an elegant mansion formerly occupied *Dynasty* star Linda Evans, and owned for many years by Blake Edwards and Julie Andrews.

Follow Crescent as it curves around, taking Oxford Way past Sunset Boulevard onto Rodeo Drive, which is residential here, but becomes Beverly Hills's most extravagant shopping avenue further south. At:

17. **725 Rodeo Drive** is the modest residence of the multitalented Gene Kelly.

Turn right on Carmelita, and right onto Bedford, and look for:

18. **620 Bedford Drive,** former residence of Marlene Dietrich. One block further is:

19. **730 Bedford Drive,** where, in 1958, Lana Turner's teenage daughter Cheryl Crane stabbed to death her mother's abusive boyfriend, gangster Johnny Stompanato.

Turn left onto Lomitas Avenue to Linden Drive, turn right, and proceed to:

20. **810 Linden Drive,** which looks exactly as it did the night in 1947 when hoodlum Benjamin "Bugsy" Siegel was gunned down through the living room window. A notorious gangster best remembered for creating Las Vegas from a patch of desert scruff, Siegel had been relaxing in the home of his girlfriend, small-time actress Virginia Hill.

Linden will merge into Whittier Drive; make a right turn onto Sunset Boulevard and take next left, onto Roxbury Drive, where you'll find:

21. **911 Roxbury Drive,** *Bewitched* star Elizabeth Montgomery's home until her tragic death in 1995, and:

22. **918 Roxbury Drive,** occupied by the actor James Stewart for decades. Stewart turned the adjoining corner lot into a walled garden to indulge his favorite hobby—gardening. Down the street is:

23. **1000 Roxbury Drive,** which was Lucille Ball's simple white home. Disturbed once too often by huge busloads of tourists pouring onto her front lawn, Lucy forced the city of Beverly Hills to create stringent guidelines for tour operators. Her neighbor for many years at:

24. **1002 Roxbury Drive** was another great comedian, Jack Benny. A few houses down and across the street is:

25. **1019 Roxbury Drive,** home of Rosemary Clooney (George's aunt, for all you *ER* fans). Next door is:

26. **1021 Roxbury Drive,** which was the modest home of composer Ira Gershwin, and:

27. **1023 Roxbury Drive,** a newer house built on the site where Spencer Tracy, and later Agnes Moorehead, once resided.

Stay on Roxbury, cross over Benedict Canyon Drive, and make the second left onto Cove Way, in front of:

28. **1000 Cove Way.** This stylish and traditional home was formerly the property of both movie villian Jack Palance and funny man W. C. Fields. Across the street is:

29. **1007 Cove Way,** home to Sidney Poitier, and:

30. **1011 Cove Way,** whose rough-hewn stone exterior suited the moniker of its previous owner, Rock Hudson.

Make a right turn on Summit Drive and follow it up the hill to:

31. **1143 Summit Drive,** former site of a Beverly Hills legend. When Douglas Fairbanks, Sr., and Mary Pickford—Hollywood's favorite couple in the 1920s—moved here, they lived in the only structure in sight, a small hunting lodge. They enlarged the dwelling, adding the first residential swimming pool in Beverly Hills; the gracious hilltop manor became known to the world as "Pickfair." Pickford continued to live here until her death in 1979. In 1990 singer Pia Zadora leveled the 42-room landmark to make way for the larger—and decidedly tackier—mansion you see today. About the only remnants of the glorious original are the stone cherubs adorning the front gate, a gift to the Fairbankses from Charlie Chaplin.

Veer to the right past 1143 and proceed up the street to:

32. **1167 Summit Drive,** home of actress and Elvis ex Priscilla Presley.

Turn around safely where you can; descending, you'll get a fine view of:

33. **1151 Summit Drive,** home of Sammy Davis, Jr., at the time of his death. Sadly, his family was forced to sell the home and auction off its contents to settle the debts he left behind.

Turn right on Pickfair Way (behind Pia Zadora's house). As Pickfair Way dips to meet San Ysidro Drive, glance straight ahead; atop the hill is:

34. **1155 San Ysidro Drive,** the former Fred Astaire estate. Make a left at the corner, and you'll see his winding driveway on the right. Further down the street is:

35. **1103 San Ysidro Drive,** the last home of Danny Kaye, of which only the impressive gateway is visible, and:

36. **1106 San Ysidro Drive,** the heavily remodeled former home of Rex Harrison. Across the street is:

37. **1100 Tower Road.** The overly theatrical Romanesque columns, gargoyles, and garden statuary must have suited Laurence Olivier and Vivien Leigh, who were living here when Leigh won her Best Actress Oscar for *Gone With The Wind.* Make a right turn around the house and continue up Tower to:

38. **1151 Tower Road.** Jay Leno lives here, and it's a sure bet the house has an extensive garage, for Jay lovingly maintains a spectacular collection of vintage automobiles; you might see him motoring about town in one.

Further up the hill, you'll see the short brick wall defines:

39. **1162 Tower Road,** the estate of the late Michael Landon. A devoted family man, the *Bonanza, Little House on the Prairie,* and *Highway to Heaven* star erected a full-size playground here for his many children and grandchildren; it's easy to see the swings, seesaws, and jungle gyms from the street.

You can turn around in the cul-de-sac at the end of Tower Road and gaze out at the extraordinary city view from what once was John Barrymore's vast estate on this hilltop, appropriately named "Bella Vista" (beautiful view). Backtrack down to where Tower Grove Drive heads up the hill to the right, and follow it up to Beverly Grove Drive; turn left. Just as you emerge at the next mini-canyon, look on the left for:

40. **9966 Beverly Grove,** Cary Grant's last home. Slow down, if you can, to look back through the gates to catch a glimpse of the gracious home (entirely remodeled by Grant in 1982), as well as his spectacular view of L.A. and the ocean.

Follow Beverly Grove down the hill to the T-shaped intersection with Beverly Estate Drive, taking it down to Beverly Glen Boulevard. Turn right on Beverly Glen, then left on Cielo Drive, following the road to where it widens slightly for the intersection with a tiny, overgrown spur called Bella Drive. Although technically a public road—and therefore fair game to the curious—there's only one home at the top of this nearly private driveway. But it's worth disturbing the wild rabbits to get to:

41. **1436 Bella Drive.** It has scarcely changed since 1925, when screen heartthrob Rudolph Valentino bought this white-walled estate and named it "Falcon Lair." Valentino's steel pennant emblazoned with the letter "V" still flies atop the house's red-tiled roof.

Looking down into the canyon from the summit, you can see the site of **10050 Cielo Drive,** infamous address of the August 1969 Manson family murder of pregnant actress Sharon Tate and four others. The house itself was torn down in 1994, just after Nine Inch Nails recorded their multi-platinum—and appropriately angst-ridden—album *The Downward Spiral* in it.

One unfortunate houseguest was jet-setting hairstylist Jay Sebring, visiting from further up the canyon, where he lived in a secluded house supposedly haunted by the ghost of movie studio head Paul Bern, who was newly married to starlet Jean Harlow at the time of his death. His death here in 1932 was officially called suicide, but many speculated about a scandalous murder and cover-up. You can reach the Bern/Sebring house if you're willing to ascend Easton Drive, a narrow and roughly paved alley: Return via Cielo Drive to Benedict Canyon, turn left, and proceed to Easton. Turn right to:

42. **9820 Easton Drive.** The address isn't really visible from the street, but if you go to the end and turn around, you can easily see the two-story Bavarian-style house on your left, set back and above the others.

Return via Benedict Canyon to Sunset Boulevard and make a right turn to:

43. **10000 Sunset Boulevard.** Both Howard Hughes and Vincente Minelli and Judy Garland owned this home, but today it gets the most attention for the whimsical statues adorning the front lawn. The sightseeing couple were the first installed, and tricked many passersby into thinking there was really someone looking over the wall!

Turn left at Carolwood, marked by the bubblegum-pink Spanish-style:

44. 10100 Sunset Boulevard. It has been owned by singer Rudy Vallee and later by Englebert Humperdinck, but its personality was indelibly stamped in the 1960s by Jayne Mansfield, who chose the color scheme and built a heart-shaped pool in the backyard.

The street dead-ends at:

45. 141 South Carolwood Drive, an English-style estate named "Owlwood" and owned at various times by Sonny and Cher, Tony Curtis, and movie mogul Joseph Schenck, at whose invitiation Curtis's future *Some Like It Hot* co-star Marilyn Monroe occupied a guest house during 1949.

Return to Sunset Boulevard and make a right, then a left onto Ladera Drive, and left on Monovale. You'll come to:

46. 144 Monovale Drive, the L.A. home of Elvis and Priscilla Presley, who purchased the white cottage in 1972 for a mere $335,000.

Follow Monovale as it merges with Carolwood, and proceed to:

47. 245 Carolwood Drive. This was the L.A. home of Burt Reynolds and Loni Anderson during their marriage; it once belonged to Beatle George Harrison. Down the street is:

48. 301 Carolwood Drive, the heavily guarded home of the very private Barbra Streisand, and:

49. 325 Carolwood Drive. Up the ivy garland–adorned driveway is Clark Gable's former abode. You can't miss:

50. 355 Carolwood Drive, Walt Disney's home, with its wrought iron mouse-ear motif on the gate. His widow, Lillian, still lives here. Next you'll see:

51. 375 Carolwood Drive, home to distinguished actor Gregory Peck, who was probably less than thrilled by the loud partying at:

52. 391 Carolwood Drive when it was owned by rocker Rod Stewart and his model wife, Rachel Hunter.

Return via Carolwood to Sunset Boulevard and turn right, then turn left onto Charing Cross. Slow down and smile for the sophisticated surveillance system (including cameras, microphones, and guards) at:

53. 10236 Charing Cross Road, an ostentatious stone manor known since 1971 as the "Playboy Mansion," now reincarnated as the family homestead of Mr. and Mrs. Hugh Hefner and their two small children.

Follow Charing Cross to Mapleton Drive, turn left, and proceed to:

54. 594 South Mapleton Drive. The community of Holmby Hills was outraged when Aaron Spelling, producer of such successful TV programs as *Charlie's Angels, The Love Boat, Beverly Hills, 90210,* and

Melrose Place—and Tori's dad—razed an estate overlooking the prestigious Los Angeles Country Club and erected this oversized, ostentatious monstrosity.

Past the Spelling residence, turn right on Club View Drive, and right again on Beverly Glen Boulevard. Take Beverly Glen past Sunset Boulevard, straight through the stately entrance to Bel-Air. Turn left at Bellagio Road, then right at Copa de Oro (cup of gold). Straight ahead is:

55. **363 Copa De Oro Road,** the ornate red brick mansion of heartthrob Tom Jones, at one time occupied by fellow Las Vegas headliner Dean Martin.

Veer right past the house to the intersection with Bel Air Road, turn right, and then left on St. Cloud Road to Nimes Road. As you approach:

56. **700 Nimes Road,** the exotic flowers in varying shades of purple and lavender provide the only clues to the glamorous owner who dwells behind this imposing gate . . . Elizabeth Taylor.

Follow Nimes around and back down to St. Cloud Road, turning left. On the left-hand side is:

57. **668 St. Cloud Road,** home to Mr. and Mrs. Ronald Reagan since his departure from the White House. Nancy had the original house number, 666, changed to a less demonic address. If the former President is in residence, the gatehouse will be staffed with armed Secret Service officers.

Continue past Nimes and turn left on St. Pierre. On the right-hand side is:

58. **345 St. Pierre Road,** a peach-colored house with green-patina iron fencework. Errol Flynn's alleged statutory rape—the scandal out of which the expression "in like Flynn" was born—took place here. Across the street, diagonally to the left is:

59. **414 St. Pierre Road,** which sits abandoned, its carved stone entryway and Mediterranean-tiled patio visible through the over-growth. As the street curves around the corner, peek into the neglected backyard at the spectacular swimming pool built for original owner Johnny Weissmuller. The athletic swimmer and on-screen Tarzan created a junglelike setting for his daily laps when he and this house were in their prime.

Continuing to the end of the block, you'll find yourself back at Beverly Glen Boulevard. A right turn will lead you to Sunset Boulevard.

WINDING DOWN   If all this sightseeing has left your stomach grumbling, stay in the neighborhood and visit one of these local watering holes:

Recently reopened after an extensive restoration, the **Beverly Hills Hotel** has been the unofficial "clubhouse" of the swank Hollywood crowd since it opened in 1912. Katherine Hepburn played tennis here daily, Marlene Dietrich shocked the staid Polo Lounge by strolling in wearing trousers, and Marilyn Monroe and Yves Montand emerged from their 1959 tryst in one of the secluded bungalows to smooch over a milkshake in the **Fountain Coffee Shop** (☎ 310/276-2251). Stopping in yourself for a sandwich and fountain treat at the shop's counter provides a perfect excuse to stroll these legendary grounds.

Or, try **Nate 'n Al Delicatessen,** at 414 North Beverly Drive (☎ 310/274-0101), a regular Beverly Hills fixture for ages. Despite its location among the boutiques of the "Golden Triangle," Nate 'n Al remains comfortably homey and unchanged, from the sweet condescension of the motherly waitresses to the best pastrami, pickles, and chopped liver in town. And you won't believe the famous faces lining the brown Naugahyde booths—many have had house accounts for decades!

9

Shopping

In the outlying suburbs of Los Angeles, giant malls are the center of the shopping universe. In L.A. proper, though—despite a few super-malls that have made it to downtown and the Westside—it's the strip mall that abounds, lining main thoroughfares throughout the city. In response to a public disgusted by the unchecked growth of this urban blight, the city is backpedaling from the previously undirected push toward a mini-mall–filled future: Conscious efforts are now being made to entice citizens out of their cars with well-conceived pedestrian thoroughfares and the development of unified retailing districts that bring buyers back into the neighborhoods.

Despite appearances, Southern California—even Los Angeles itself—is not entirely an upscale market, so don't worry that you'll be priced out of the shopping market. Like so much else that is Hollywood, the overwhelming sense of opulence is largely an illusion. In general, Southern California is still trailing the rest of the country in recovering from the recession—good news for visiting opportunists. Good buys and bargains abound.

Store hours are generally Monday through Saturday from 10am to 6pm and on Sunday from noon to 5pm. Most department stores and malls stay open later—usually Monday to Friday from 10am to 9pm, Saturday 10am to 6pm, and on Sunday 11am to 6pm. Shops along busy evening thoroughfares, such as Santa Monica's 3rd Street Promenade, West Hollywood's Sunset Strip, Westwood Village, and Universal CityWalk, usually stay open until 9pm throughout the week.

Sales tax in Los Angeles is 8.25%.

1 The Shopping Scene

HOLLYWOOD
MELROSE AVENUE (BETWEEN FAIRFAX AND LA BREA AVENUES)

It's showing some wear—some stretches have become downright ugly—but this is still one of the most exciting shopping streets in the country for cutting-edge fashions and eye-popping people watching. There are scores of shops selling the latest in clothes, gifts, jewelry, and accessories. Melrose is a playful stroll, dotted with plenty of hip restaurants and funky shops that are sure to shock. Where else could you find green patent-leather cowboy boots, a working 19th-century pocket watch, and an inflatable girlfriend in the same shopping spree?

HOLLYWOOD BOULEVARD (BETWEEN GOWER STREET AND LA BREA AVENUE)

One of Los Angeles's most famous streets is, for the most part, a sleazy strip. But along the Walk of Fame, between the T-shirt shops and greasy pizza parlors, you'll find some excellent poster shops, souvenir stores, and Hollywood memorabilia dealers. It's a silly, tourist-oriented strip that's worth getting out of your car for, especially if there's a chance of getting your hands on that long-sought-after Ethel Merman autograph or *200 Motels* poster.

WESTSIDE

WEST 3RD STREET (BETWEEN FAIRFAX AND ROBERTSON BOULEVARDS)

You can shop till you drop on this newly trendy strip, which is anchored on the east end by Farmer's Market. Many of Melrose Avenue's shops have relocated here, alongside some terrific up-and-comers, several cafés, and the much-lauded restaurant Locanda Veneta. "Fun" is more the catchword here than "funky," and the shops (including the vintage clothing stores) tend a bit more to the refined than they do along Melrose; you'd never find upscale bookshops dedicated to travel tomes and cookbooks in that neck of the woods, like you do here.

SUNSET STRIP (BETWEEN LA CIENEGA AND DOHENY DRIVE, WEST HOLLYWOOD)

The monster-size billboards advertising the latest rock god make it clear that this is rock 'n' roll territory. Tower Records and Virgin Megastore dominate a strip lined with trendy restaurants, industry-oriented hotels, and dozens of shops offering outrageous fashions and chunky stage accessories. Although the Strip isn't a great place for walking more than a block or two, you might cruise along and stop if something catches your eye.

LA BREA AVENUE (NORTH OF WILSHIRE BOULEVARD)

This is L.A.'s artiest shopping strip. Anchored by the giant American Rag, Cie., alterna-complex, La Brea is home to lots of great urban antique stores (dealing in deco, arts and crafts, 1950s modern, and the like; there's also a great antique hardware store), vintage clothiers, furniture galleries, and other warehouse-size stores, as well as some of the city's hippest restaurants, such as Campanile.

RODEO DRIVE AND BEVERLY HILLS'S GOLDEN TRIANGLE (BETWEEN SANTA MONICA BOULEVARD, WILSHIRE BOULEVARD, AND CRESCENT DRIVE)

Everyone knows about Rodeo Drive, the city's most famous shopping street. Couture shops from high fashion's Old Guard are located along these three hallowed blocks, along with plenty of newer high-end labels. Shops here include Cartier, Chanel, Giorgio Armani, Tiffany & Co., Van Cleef & Arpels, and Louis Vuitton. Many of these are clustered within two mini-malls called Rodeo Collection (421 N. Rodeo Dr.), and Two Rodeo (at Wilshire Blvd.).

The 16-square-block area surrounding Rodeo Drive is known as the "Golden Triangle." Shops off Rodeo are generally not as name conscious as those on the strip, but they're nevertheless plenty upscale. Little Santa Monica Boulevard has a particularly colorful line of specialty stores, and Brighton Way is as young and hip as relatively staid Beverly Hills gets.

WESTWOOD VILLAGE (BETWEEN WILSHIRE BOULEVARD, LE CONTE AVENUE, WESTWOOD BOULEVARD, AND BROXTON AVENUE)

A pedestrian-only area on weekends, Westwood Village is a college town catering to UCLA students and upscale couples. It can be a fun place to spend an afternoon or evening. There are dozens of chain stores, coffee shops, and restaurants, as well as bars and movie theaters. It's a colorful place, but the serious shopper will be disappointed; you're unlikely to find anything here that you wouldn't be able to find in any mall across America. Most of the shops here are open late throughout the week, including Sunday.

THE BEACHES

3RD STREET PROMENADE (3RD STREET, FROM BROADWAY TO WILSHIRE BLVD., SANTA MONICA)

Packed with chain stores and boutiques as well as dozens of restaurants and a large movie theater, Santa Monica's pedestrian-only 3rd Street is one of the most popular shopping areas in the city. The street bustles on into the evening with a seemingly endless assortment of street performers, and an endless parade of souls. This is pretty mainstream shopping territory, but you'll find a few gems—a clothier here, a bookstore there—that may make it worth your while.

MAIN STREET IN SANTA MONICA AND VENICE (BETWEEN PICO BOULEVARD AND ROSE AVENUE)

Another good strip for strolling, Main Street boasts a healthy combination of mall standards like Banana Republic and upscale, left-of-center individual boutiques. You'll also find plenty of casually hip cafes and restaurants. The primary strip connecting Santa Monica and Venice, Main Street has a relaxed, beach-community vibe that sets it apart from similar strips; the stores along it straddle the fashion fence between upscale trendy and beach-bum edgy.

MONTANA AVENUE (BETWEEN 7TH AND 17TH STREETS, SANTA MONICA)

Currently the most exciting shopping strip in the city, Montana is great for strolling, sipping cappuccinos, and stepping into boutique after boutique. The shopping isn't really much more sophisticated than that along Main Street, but the area and crowd make it seem so. This is probably what Beverly Hills was like before it went over the top.

SAN FERNANDO VALLEY

UNIVERSAL CITYWALK (UNIVERSAL CENTER DR., UNIVERSAL CITY, ☎ 818/622-4455)

Technically an outdoor mall rather than a shopping area, Universal CityWalk gets mention here because it is so utterly unique. A pedestrian promenade next door to Universal Studios, Universal CityWalk is dominated by brightly colored, outrageously surreal oversize storefronts. The heavily touristed faux street is home to an inordinate number of restaurants, including B.B. King's Blues Club, the newest Hard Rock Cafe, and a branch of the Hollywood Athletic Club featuring a restaurant and pool hall. This is consumer culture gone haywire.

2 Shopping A to Z

ANTIQUES

The Antique Guild

8800 Venice Blvd., near Culver City. ☎ 310/838-3131.

Billing itself as "the world's largest antique outlet," the Guild is a veritable warehouse of history, with more than two acres of antiques under one roof. Their buyers regularly purchase entire contents of European castles, beer halls, estates, and mansions. New shipments arrive weekly, so the merchandise is constantly changing. Look for everything from old armoires to chandeliers to stained glass, crystal, china, clocks, washstands, tables, mirrors, and much more. Open Monday to Saturday 10am to 6pm and Sunday noon to 6pm.

Arte de Mexico

5356 Riverton Ave., North Hollywood. ☎ 818/769-5090.

Seven warehouses full of carved furniture and wrought iron once sold only to moviemakers and restaurants is now open to the public. One of the most fascinating places in North Hollywood. Open daily 8:30am to 5:30pm.

Off the Wall

7325 Melrose Ave., Los Angeles. ☎ 213/930-1185.

Oversize antiques include kitschy statues, deco furnishings, carved wall reliefs, Wurlitzer jukeboxes, giant restaurant and gas station signs, pinball machines, and lots and lots of neon. Open Monday to Saturday 11am to 6pm.

✪ Piccolo Pete's

13814 Ventura Blvd., Sherman Oaks. ☎ 818/990-5421.

A lovely shop selling art nouveau, deco, and moderne furnishings and art, including clocks, radios, telephones, and lighting fixtures. Open Tuesday to Saturday 10:30 to 6pm, Sunday noon to 6pm.

Scavenger's Paradise

5453 Satsuma Ave., North Hollywood. ☎ 213/877-7945.

Rub elbows with set decorators and interior designers at this unusual shop. There's all kinds of antique housewares, like vintage doorknobs, cabinet pulls, and countless other treasures saved from the wrecking ball. Fixtures available from former stars' homes include Charlie Chaplin's wrought-iron light fixtures and Rock Hudson's window grill. Open Monday to Saturday noon to 4:30pm.

ART GALLERIES

Bergamot Station

2525 Michigan Ave., Santa Monica. ☎ **310/829-5854.**

Once a station for the Red Car trolley line, Bergamot Station is now home to about a dozen art galleries, a cafe, a bookstore, and offices. Don't miss the **Ernie Wolf Gallery** (☎ **310/582-1500**), specializing in works by Theophilus Nii Anum, the fantasy coffin maker Ghana, and Kenyan master painter Joseph Bertiers. Open Tuesday to Saturday 10:30 to 6pm, Sunday noon to 6pm.

The Broadway Gallery Complex

2022-2114 Broadway, Santa Monica. ☎ **310/829-3300.**

Ten galleries showing a wide range of works are housed in this single Santa Monica complex. Featured contemporary artists include Barbara Ackerman, Ruth Bloom, Mark Moore, and Sylvia White. Open Tuesday to Saturday 11am to 5:30pm.

The Eighth Muse

8713 Santa Monica Blvd., West Hollywood. ☎ **310/659-2545.**

This gallery specializes in gay- and lesbian-themed art. Sculpture, painting, ceramics, and jewelry shows are augmented by regular literary readings, performance art pieces, and musical concerts. Open Tuesday to Friday 11am to 6pm, Saturday 11am to 8pm, and by appointment.

Gallery of Functional Art

2525 Michigan Ave. (Bergamot Station), Santa Monica. ☎ **310/829-6990.**

Tables, chairs, beds, sofas, lighting, screens, dressers, and bathroom fixtures are some of the functional art pieces for sale here. Smaller items such as jewelry, watches, flatware, candlesticks, ceramics, and glass are also shown. All work is one of a kind or limited edition. Open Tuesday to Friday 11am to 7pm, Saturday 11am to 6pm, and Sunday noon to 5pm.

Murray Feldman Gallery

8687 Melrose Ave. (on the plaza at the Pacific Design Center), West Hollywood. ☎ **310/657-0800**, ext. 264.

This is one of the few L.A. galleries dedicated to the decorative arts and architectural design. It's a great excuse to visit the vast Pacific Design Center. Open Tuesday to Saturday noon to 6pm.

Name That Toon

8483 Melrose Ave., Los Angeles. ☎ **213/653-5633.**

Several L.A. galleries sell clay, computer, and cel animation art, but none has a better selection than this well-stocked shop, which specializes in original production cels from Disney, Warner Brothers, Hanna-Barbera, Dr. Seuss, and Walter Lantz. Original Ren and Stimpy and Simpsons art is also available. Phone for information on artists' receptions, lecturers, and other special events. Open Tuesday to Saturday 10am to 6:30pm, Sunday noon to 5pm.

BOOKS

Audubon Society Bookstore

7377 Santa Monica Blvd., West Hollywood. ☎ **213/876-0202.**

A terrific selection of books on nature, adventure travel, and ecology is augmented by birdwatching paraphernalia. Phone for information on L.A. nature walks. Open Tuesday to Saturday 10am to 4pm.

✪ Book Soup

8800 Sunset Blvd., West Hollywood. ☎ **310/657-1072.**

This has long been one of L.A.'s most celebrated bookshops, selling both mainstream and small-press books and hosting regular book signings and author nights. Book Soup is a great browsing shop. The owners recently annexed an adjacent cafe space so they can better cater to hungry intellectuals. There's an appealing bar, a charming outdoor patio, and an extensive menu that includes alphabet soup. Open Monday to Saturday noon to 10pm.

C. G. Jung Bookstore & Library

10349 W. Pico Blvd., Los Angeles. ☎ **310/556-1196.**

This bookshop specializes in analytical psychology, folklore, fairy tales, alchemy, dream studies, myths, symbolism, and other related topic. Tapes and videocassettes are also sold. Open Monday to Saturday noon to 5pm.

✪ The Cook's Library

8373 W. 3rd St., West Hollywood. ☎ **213/655-3141.**

There's a specialty bookshop for everyone in L.A.; this is where the city's top chefs find both classic and deliciously offbeat cookbooks and other food-oriented tomes. Browsing is welcomed, even encouraged, with tea, tasty treats, and rocking chairs.

Dutton's Brentwood Books

11975 San Vicente Blvd., Los Angeles. ☎ **310/476-6263.**

This huge bookshop is well known not only for an extensive selection of new books, but for its good children's section and an eclectic collection of used and rare. There are over 120,000 in-stock titles at any one time. They host regular author readings and signings, and sell cards, stationery, prints, CDs, and selected software. Open Monday to Friday 9am to 9pm, Saturday 9am to 6pm, Sunday 11am to 5pm.

Heritage Book Shop, Inc.

8340 Melrose Ave., Los Angeles. ☎ **310/659-3674.**

Specializing in rare books and manuscripts, Heritage is packed with first editions and special illustrations. Open Tuesday to Friday 9:30am to 5:30pm and Saturday 10am to 4:30pm.

L.A. (The Bookstore)

2433 Main St. (in the Edgemar Complex), Santa Monica. ☎ **310/452-2665.**

The ultimate in specialty bookstores, this creatively stocked shop includes city-related fiction, biography, maps, art, and photography. Current L.A.-oriented best-sellers share shelf space with hard-to-find scholarly histories of Venice, Santa Monica, and other neighborhoods. Open daily 10am to 10pm.

Midnight Special Bookstore

1318 3rd St., Santa Monica. ☎ **310/393-2923.**

This medium-size general bookshop, located on the 3rd Street Promenade, is known for its good small-press selection and regular poetry readings. Open Monday to Thursday and Sunday 10:30am to 11pm, Friday and Saturday 10:30am to 11:30pm.

Mysterious Bookshop

8763 Beverly Blvd., West Hollywood. ☎ **310/659-2959.**

Over 20,000 used, rare, and out-of-print titles make this the area's best mystery, espionage, detective, and thriller bookshop. Author appearances and other special events are regularly hosted. Open Monday to Saturday 10am to 6pm and Sunday noon to 5pm.

Samuel French Book Store

7623 Sunset Blvd., Hollywood. ☎ **213/876-0570.**

This is L.A.'s biggest theater and movie bookstore. Plays, screenplays, and film books are all sold here, as well as scripts for Broadway and Hollywood blockbusters. Open daily 10am to 9pm.

The Traveler's Bookcase

8375 W. 3rd St., West Hollywood. ☎ **213/655-0575.**

This store, one of the best travel bookshops in the West, stocks a huge selection of guidebooks and travel literature, as well as over 10,000 maps. Look for regular readings by well-known travel writers. Open Monday to Saturday 10am to 6pm, Sunday 11am to 4pm.

CIGARS

Churchill's Fine Cigars

5844 Naples Plaza, Naples Island, Long Beach. ☎ **310/433-3994.**

This suddenly trendy shop is one of the few places left where you can relax, get your shoes shined, play chess, and enjoy a stogie at the same time. Good Dominicans cost about $9, and are stored, along with dozens of other less-expensive choices, in a cedar-lined walk-in humidor. Open Monday to Friday 10am to 8pm, Saturday 10am to 6pm, and Sunday 10am to 5pm.

La Plata Cigars

1026 S. Grand Ave. (between 11th St. and Olympic Blvd.). ☎ **213/747-8561.**

Los Angeles' only cigar factory, this place has been hand rolling them since 1947. The public is welcome to visit the downtown factory and enter the shop's huge humidor to choose from thousands of fresh

cigars in all sizes—for about half what the fancy places charge. Open
Monday to Friday 7am to 4:30pm.

DEPARTMENT STORES

Barney's New York
9570 Wilshire Blvd., Beverly Hills. ☎ **310/276-4400.**

The celebrated New York clothier opened this Beverly Hills satellite
shop in 1994, and L.A. is already looking better. Saxophonist and
former *Tonight Show* bandleader Branford Marsalis gets his Gaultiers
here. Barney Greengrass, New York's "sturgeon king," has opened a
restaurant on the top floor (see Chapter 6 for details). Open Monday
to Wednesday and Friday to Saturday 10am to 7pm, Thursday 10am
to 8pm, and Sunday noon to 6pm.

The Broadway
8500 Beverly Blvd. (in the Beverly Center), Los Angeles. ☎ **310/854-7200.** Other
locations throughout the L.A. metropolitan area.

This Southern California–based chain sells moderately priced designer
clothes, sportswear, and casual clothing; it also has excellent cosmetics and cookware departments. Open Monday to Friday 10am to
9:30pm, Saturday 10am to 9pm, and Sunday 11am to 7pm.

Bullock's
10861 Weyburn Ave. (near Westwood Blvd.), Westwood. ☎ **310/208-4211.** Other
locations throughout the L.A. metropolitan area.

Upper-middle–class, fashion-conscious customers shop here for
imported designer fashions and good-quality private-label merchandise
in all departments. Open Monday to Friday 10am to 9pm, Saturday
10am to 7pm, and Sunday noon to 6pm.

Neiman Marcus
9700 Wilshire Blvd., Beverly Hills. ☎ **310/550-5900.**

Distinctive men's and women's fashions, world-famous furs, precious
jewels, unique gifts, and legendary personal service have made this one
of the area's most successful department stores. Open Monday to Saturday 10am to 6pm, Sunday noon to 6pm.

Nordstrom
10830 W. Pico Blvd. (in the Westside Pavilion), West Los Angeles. ☎ **310/
470-6155.**

Emphasis on customer service has won this Seattle-based chain a loyal
following. Equally devoted to women's and men's fashions, the store
has one of the best shoe selections in the city, and there are thousands
of suits in stock. Open Monday to Friday 10am to 9:30pm, Saturday
10am to 8pm, and Sunday 11am to 6pm.

Saks Fifth Avenue
9600 Wilshire Blvd., Beverly Hills. ☎ **310/275-4211.**

Los Angeles' oldest branch of this famous New York–based shop is as
opulent as any. Saks sells fashions and gifts for men, women, and
children, and has a well-respected restaurant on the top floor. Open

Monday to Wednesday and Friday to Saturday 10am to 6pm, Thursday 10am to 8:30pm, and Sunday noon to 6pm.

DISCOUNT SHOPPING

Nordstrom Rack

21490 Victory Blvd., Canoga Park. ☎ **818/884-6771.**

Top brands, after languishing too long on Nordstrom's racks, are deeply discounted and sold in this somewhat disorganized warehouse. A DKNY skirt marked down from $200 to $70 is par for the course; menswear deals are just as juicy. Open Monday to Friday 10am to 9pm, Saturday 10am to 8pm, and Sunday 11am to 7pm.

Cooper Building

860 S. Los Angeles St., downtown. ☎ **213/622-1139.**

The centerpiece of downtown's Garment District, the Cooper Building and surrounding blocks are full of shops selling clothes, luggage, and assorted goods at significantly discounted prices. Open Monday to Friday 9am to 6pm, Saturday 10am to 5pm.

EYEWEAR

L.A. Eyeworks

7407 Melrose Ave., Los Angeles. ☎ **213/653-8255.** Other locations throughout the L.A. metropolitan area.

This hometown design shop has become world famous for its innovative styles. This is the original storefront location. Open Monday to Friday 10am to 7pm, Saturday 10am to 6pm, and Sunday noon to 5pm.

FASHIONS

Battle Dress

7318C Melrose Ave., Los Angeles. ☎ **213/935-7350.**

This store sells some of the most unusual leather frocks, tops, pants, and boots I've ever seen; many of the handmade styles here were inspired by authentic Cherokee designs. Custom leather clothing is also available. Open Tuesday to Saturday noon to 8pm, Sunday 1 to 7pm.

Boy London

7519 Melrose Ave., Los Angeles. ☎ **213/655-0302.**

Once on the cutting edge of London's King's Road, Boy has toned down a bit, now selling shirts and other clothes emblazoned with its own logo. It's still cool, though. Open Monday to Friday 11am to 8pm, Saturday 11am to 9pm, and Sunday noon to 8pm.

Drake's Gift and Novelty Shop

7566 Melrose Ave., Los Angeles. ☎ **213/651-5600.**

Although it's not as hard core as some boutiques, Drake's is still definitely not for the timid. Quality sex-related items are available. Wearables include the latest in latex, plastic, and leather. Chains, whips, nipple clamps, and fetish fashion round out the fun. Open 24 hours.

Dressing the Part: Where to Find Hollywood's Hand-Me-Downs

Admit it: You've dreamed of being a glamorous movie or TV star—everyone has. Well, you shouldn't expect to be "discovered" during your L.A. vacation, but you can live out your fantasy by dressing the part. Costumes from famous movies, TV show wardrobes, castoffs from celebrity closets—they're easier to find (and more affordable to own) than you might think.

A good place to start is **Star Wares,** 2817 Main St., Santa Monica (☎ **310/399-0224;** open daily noon–6pm). This deceptively small shop regularly has leftovers from Cher's closet, as well as celebrity-worn apparel from the likes of Joan Rivers, Tim Curry, and Kathleen Turner. They also stock movie production wardrobes and genuine collector's items. If the $5,000 *Star Trek: The Next Generation* uniform or *Planet Of the Apes* military regalia you covet is out of your price range, don't worry: You can still pick up one of Johnny Depp's *Benny and Joon* outfits, dresses from the closets of Lucille Ball and Greer Garson, or ET's bathrobe, all of which are surprisingly affordable. Many pieces have accompanying photos or movie stills, so you'll know exactly who donned your piece before you.

That isn't the case, however, at **The Place & Co.,** 8820 S. Sepulveda Blvd., Westchester (☎ **310/645-1539;** open Mon–Sat 10am–6pm), where the anonymity of their well-heeled clientele (sellers *and* buyers) is strictly honored. Here you'll find men's and women's haute couture—always the latest fashions, gently worn—at a fraction of the Rodeo Drive prices. All the designers are here—Ungaro, Bill Blass, Krizia, Donna Karan. You may have even seen that Armani suit or Sonia Rykiel gown you find in the racks on an Academy Awards attendee last year!

For sheer volume, you can't beat **It's A Wrap,** 3315 W. Magnolia Blvd., Burbank (☎ **818/567-7366;** open Mon–Sat 11am–6pm, Sun 11am–4pm). Every item here is marked with its place of origin, and the list is staggering: *Beverly Hills, 90210; Melrose Place; Seinfeld; Baywatch; All My Children; Forrest Gump; The Brady Bunch Movie;* and so on. Many of these wardrobes (which include shoes and accessories) aren't outstanding but for their Hollywood origins: Jerry Seinfeld's trademark polo shirts, for instance, are standard

Gucci
347 N. Rodeo Dr., Beverly Hills. ☎ **310/278-3451.**

An elegant selection of apparel for men and women by one of the best known and most prestigious names in international fashion is showcased here. In addition to shoes, leather goods, and scarves beautiful enough for framing, the shop offers pricey accessories like a $7,000 mall-issue. Some collectible pieces, like Sylvester Stallone's *Rocky* stars-and-stripes boxers, are framed and on display.

When you're done at It's A Wrap, stop in across the street at **Junk For Joy,** 3314 W. Magnolia Blvd., Burbank (☎ **818/569-4903;** open Tues–Fri 10am–6pm, Saturday 11am–6pm). A Hollywood wardrobe coordinator or two will probably be hunting through this wacky little store right beside you. The emphasis here is on funky items more suitable as costumes than everyday wear (the store is mobbed each year around Halloween). At press time, they were loaded with seventies polyester shirts and tacky slacks, but you never know what you'll find when you get there.

The grand dame of all wardrobe and costume outlets is **Western Costume,** 11041 Vanowen St., North Hollywood (☎ **818/ 760-0900;** open for rentals Mon–Fri 8am–5:30pm, for sales Tues–Fri 10am–5pm). In business since 1912, Western Costume still designs and executes entire wardrobes for major motion pictures; when filming is finished, the garments are added to their staggering rental inventory. This place is perhaps best known for outfitting Vivien Leigh in *Gone With The Wind.* Several of Scarlett O'Hara's memorable gowns were even available for rent until they were recently auctioned off at a charity event. Western maintains an "outlet store" on the premises, where damaged garments are sold at rock-bottom (nothing over $15) prices. If you're willing to do some rescue work, there are definitely some hidden treasures here.

Finally, don't miss **Golyester,** 7957 Melrose Ave. (☎ **213/ 665-3393;** open Mon–Sat 11am–6pm). This shop is almost a museum of finely preserved (but reasonably priced) vintage clothing and fabrics. The staff will gladly flip through stacks of *Vogue* magazines from the thirties, forties, and fifties with you, pointing out the lavish, star-studded original advertisements for various outfits in their stock. Golyester is so overflowing with treasures that they're thinking of moving to a larger space nearby in early 1996, so check with them before you go.

—Stephanie Avnet

handmade crocodile bag. Open Monday to Saturday 10am to 6pm, and Sunday noon to 5pm.

Hermès
343 N. Rodeo Dr., Beverly Hills. ☎ **310/278-6440.**

This Beverly Hills branch of Paris's 160-year-old House of Hermès is known for its superlative handmade leather goods, hand-screened silk ties and scarves, perfumes, and other gift items. Open Monday to Saturday 10am to 6pm.

Hobie Sports

1409 3rd St., Santa Monica. ☎ **310/393-9995.**

In addition to swimwear, Hobie Sports specializes in colorful surfer dude–style shorts and T-shirts. Open Monday to Thursday 11am to 10pm, Friday and Saturday 11am to 11pm, and Sunday 11am to 8pm.

L.A. Equestrian Center's Dominion Saddlery

480 Riverside Dr., Burbank. ☎ **818/842-4300.**

One of L.A.'s largest collections of riding wear includes stretch Equijeans, leather lace-up boots, Lycra breeches, foxhunting jackets, and riding crops. Nothing's cheap. Open Monday and Saturday 9am to 5pm, Tuesday 9am to 8pm, Wednesday to Friday 9am to 6pm, and Sunday 9am to 4pm.

Leathers & Treasures

7511 Melrose Ave., Los Angeles. ☎ **213/655-7541.**

Amid rows of cowboy boots, skin lovers will find an abundance of bomber jackets, pants, vests, accessories, and hats. It's a crowded little shop with a good, unusual selection of goods. Open Monday to Saturday noon to 8pm and Sunday 1 to 7pm.

Louis Vuitton

307 N. Rodeo Dr., Beverly Hills. ☎ **310/859-0457.**

Carrying the largest selection of Vuitton items in the United States, this tony shop stocks luggage, handbags, wallets, and a seemingly endless variety of accessories. Open Monday to Saturday 10am to 6pm and Sunday 11am to 5pm.

Maxfield

8825 Melrose Ave., West Hollywood. ☎ **310/274-8800.**

Some of L.A.'s best-quality avant-garde designs include men's and women's fashions by Yamamoto, Comme des Garçons, Chrome Hearts, and the like. Furniture and home accessories are also sold.

Na Na

1228 3rd St., Santa Monica. ☎ **310/394-9690.**

This is what punk looks like in the nineties: clunky shoes, knit hats, narrow-striped shirts, and baggy streetwear. Open Monday to Thursday and Sunday 11am to 9pm and Friday and Saturday 11am to 11pm.

North Beach Leather

8500 W. Sunset Blvd., West Hollywood. ☎ **310/652-3224.**

This San Francisco–based shop has up-to-the-minute fashions from casual to elegant—particularly leather jackets and dresses—at high prices. Open Monday to Saturday 10am to 7pm, Sunday noon to 5pm.

Polo/Ralph Lauren

444 N. Rodeo Dr., Beverly Hills. ☎ **310/281-7200.**

This Beverly Hills shop is the exclusive Los Angeles outlet for Ralph Lauren's Polo collections for men, women, and children. Selected home furnishings are also sold. Open Monday to Wednesday and Friday and Saturday 10am to 6pm, Thursday 10am to 8pm, and Sunday noon to 5pm.

Red Balls on Fire

7708 Melrose Ave., Los Angeles. ☎ **213/655-3409.**

Outrageous stagewear and head-turning streetwear available here include funky jackets and the wildest stretch pants. Try them on in dressing rooms made of purple velvet-lined upright coffins. Open daily 11am to 8pm.

Retail Slut

7308 Melrose Ave., Los Angeles. ☎ **213/934-1339.**

You'll find new clothing and accessories for men and women at this famous rock 'n' roll shop. The unique designs are for a select crowd; don't expect to find anything for your next PTA meeting here. Open Monday to Saturday 11am to 7pm, Sunday noon to 6pm.

Studio Wardrobe Services

3953 Laurel Grove, Studio City. ☎ **818/508-7762.**

You may recognize some of the clothes here from movies you've seen; most were worn by extras before being turned over for public sale. Prices range from $25 to $1,500; new shipments arrive weekly. Open Monday to Saturday 10am to 6pm and Sunday noon to 5pm.

Texas Soul

7515 Melrose Ave., Los Angeles. ☎ **213/658-5571.** Second location at 14760 Ventura Blvd., Sherman Oaks (☎ **818/789-4935).**

Men's and women's boots, jackets, jewelry, and belts are peddled at this fun and funky western leather shop. Plenty of working and walking boots are sold, along with traditional cowboy styles. Open Monday to Saturday 11am to 8pm and Sunday noon to 7pm.

Trashy Lingerie

402 N. La Cienega Blvd., Hollywood. ☎ **310/652-4543.**

This shop will tailor-fit their house-designed clothes—everything from patent-leather bondage wear to elegant bridal underthings—for you. There's a $2 "membership" fee to enter the store, but, even for browsers, it's worth it. Open Monday to Saturday 10am to 7pm.

MEN'S

Bijan

420 N. Rodeo Dr., Beverly Hills. ☎ **310/273-6544.**

This top-quality menswear shop features exquisitely tailored clothing and accessories alongside Bijan's fragrance collection. Open Monday to Saturday 10am to 6pm.

Billy Martin's

8605 Sunset Blvd., West Hollywood. ☎ **310/289-5000.**

Founded by the legendary Yankee manager in 1978, this chic western shop—complete with fireplace and leather sofa—stocks hand-forged silver and gold belt buckles, Lucchese and Liberty boots, and stable staples like flannel shirts. Monday to Friday 10am to 7pm, Saturday 10am to 6pm, Sunday noon to 5pm.

Brooks Brothers

604 S. Figueroa St., downtown. ☎ **213/629-4200.**

Brooks Brothers introduced the button-down collar and single-handedly changed the standard of the well-dressed businessman. This multilevel shop also sells traditional casual wear, including sportswear, sweaters, and shirts. You'll find nothing cutting edge here; this is the quintessential conservative menswear store. Open Monday to Saturday 9:30am to 6pm.

Mark Michaels

4672 Admiralty Way, Marina del Rey. ☎ **310/822-1707.**

It's not easy to find designer duds when you're seven-foot-three, but Kareem Abdul-Jabbar and other tall guys find theirs at Mark Michaels, a specialty shop that tailor-makes suits, shirts, and slacks. Open Monday to Friday 10am to 6:30pm, Saturday 10am to 6pm.

WOMEN'S

Betsey Johnson Boutique

7311 Melrose Ave., Los Angeles. ☎ **213/931-4490.**

The New York–based designer has brought her brand of fashion—trendy, cutesy, body-conscious womenswear in colorful prints and faddish fabrics—to L.A. Open Monday to Saturday 11am to 7pm and Sunday noon to 6pm.

Chanel

400 N. Rodeo Dr., Beverly Hills. ☎ **310/278-5500.**

The entire elegant Chanel women's line— clothing, accessories, scents, cosmetics, jewelry—is under one roof here. Open Monday to Saturday 10am to 6pm and Sunday noon to 5pm.

Frederick's of Hollywood

6606 Hollywood Blvd., Hollywood. ☎ **213/466-8506.**

Behind the garish purple facade lies one of the most famous panty shops in the world. Everything from spandex suits to bikini bras and sophisticated nighties is here. Even if you're not buying, stop in and pick up one of their famous catalogs. Open Monday to Saturday 10am to 6pm, Sunday noon to 5pm.

Giorgio Beverly Hills

327 N. Rodeo Dr., Beverly Hills. ☎ **310/274-0200.**

Giorgio's signature yellow-and-white-striped awnings mark the home of his apparel, gift, and fragrance collections. Open Monday to Friday 10am to 7pm, Saturday 10am to 6pm, and Sunday noon to 5pm.

VINTAGE CLOTHING

✪ Aardvark's Odd Ark

1516 Pacific Ave., Venice. ☎ **310/392-2996.**

This large storefront near the Venice Beach Walk is crammed with racks of antique and used clothes from the sixties, seventies, and eighties. They stock vintage everything, from suits and dresses to neckties, hats, handbags, and jewelry. And they manage to anticipate some of the hottest new street fashions. Open daily 11am to 7pm. There's another Aardvark's at 7579 Melrose Ave., ☎ 213/655-6769.

Wasteland

7428 Melrose Ave., Los Angeles. ☎ **213/653-3028.**

An enormous muraled facade fronts a large collection of vintage and contemporary clothes for men and women. Leathers, natural fibers, and dark colors predominate. Grandma's furniture is also for sale. Open Monday to Saturday 11:30am to 8:30pm and Sunday noon to 8pm.

FOOD

Grand Central Market

317 S. Broadway, downtown. ☎ **213/622-1763.**

This mostly Hispanic emporium is L.A's largest and oldest food hall (it's been here since 1917). Enter past a phalanx of shoe-shine boys into a big warehouse with sawdust floors, where the city's top chefs rub shoulders with those too poor to shop at Ralph's. Bakers, butchers, and fishermen sell morning-fresh bread, fresh-from-the-cow meats, and still-breathing fish alongside stands offering hot Chinese noodles and fresh Mexican tortillas. Any kind of chili you could want is here, along with seemingly endless varieties of fruits and vegetables. Open Monday to Saturday 9am to 6pm, Sunday 10am to 5pm.

Farmer's Market

6333 W. 3rd St. (near Fairfax Ave.), Los Angeles. ☎ **213/933-9211.**

The city's most famous food carnival is also one of Hollywood's top attractions. Dozens of stands sell fresh and prepared foods for consumption on or off the premises (see Chapter 7 for details). Open Monday through Saturday 9am to 6:30pm and Sunday 10am to 5pm.

GIFTS & NOVELTIES

Alamo Flags

1349A 3rd St., Santa Monica. ☎ **310/917-3344.**

In addition to country flags of all sizes, Alamo sells banners, ensigns, pennants, and standards emblazoned with all kinds of signs and sayings. Nautical and special-occasion flags are some of the shop's bestsellers. Open Sunday to Thursday 10am to 10pm, Friday and Saturday 10am to midnight.

Beverly Hills Baseball Card Shop

1137 S. Robertson Blvd., Beverly Hills. ☎ **310/278-4263.**

This warehouse of baseball history is home to literally millions of cards, from Ty Cobbs to Lou Gehrigs to Tom Seavers and Mookie Wilsons, plus rare rookie editions and other hard-to-find baseball collectibles. Open Tuesday to Friday 11am to 6pm, Saturday 11am to 5pm.

Condomania

7306 Melrose Ave., Los Angeles. ☎ **213/933-7865.**

A vast selection of condoms, lubricants, and kits creatively encourage safe sex. Glow-in-the-dark condoms, anyone? Open Sunday to Thursday noon to 8pm, and Friday and Saturday 11am to 10pm.

HOUSEWARES & INTERIOR DESIGN

Brian Jeffrey's Design Greenhouse

7556 Melrose Ave., Los Angeles. ☎ **213/651-2539.**

This is one of the most beautiful stores on Melrose. Brian Jeffrey's is a professional decorator's dream store for interior plants, baskets and containers, candleholders, and wind chimes. They have floating lotus flowers, pressed eucalyptus, and candles galore. A festival for the senses, the shop is cluttered with terrific visuals, sweet smells, and the sounds of music. Open Monday to Thursday 11am to 8pm, Friday and Saturday 11am to 9pm, and Sunday 11am to 7pm.

Details

8625$^1/_2$ Melrose Ave., Los Angeles. ☎ **310/659-1550.**

Appropriately located near West Hollywood's Pacific Design Center, Details offers a huge selection of hard-to-find home-decorating items, including imaginative cabinet and door pulls, hooks, knobs, towel bars, and kitchen and bath accessories from Europe and Japan. Open Monday to Friday 10am to 5pm.

Z Gallerie

2728 Main St., Santa Monica. ☎ **310/392-5879.**

This California-based chain offers a good selection of framed and unframed poster art, Crate and Barrel–style furnishings, stylish kitchenware, and unusual gift items. Open daily 10am to 6pm.

JEWELRY

Cartier

370 N. Rodeo Dr., Beverly Hills. ☎ **310/275-4272.**

Cartier, one of the most respected names in jewelry and luxury goods, has its Los Angeles outpost near Brighton Way. The boutique's setting is as elegant as the beautifully designed jewelry, watches, crystal, and accessories on display. Open Monday to Friday 10am to 5:30pm and Saturday 10am to 5pm.

King's Cross

13045 Ventura Blvd., Studio City. ☎ **818/905-3382.**

King's Cross specializes in crosses, crucifixes, and rosaries made of gold, ivory, and pearl, with an emphasis on Victoriana. Most are vintage models dating from the 1820s to the 1930s. Prices range from $200 to $2,000. Open Monday to Saturday 10am to 5pm.

Maya

7452 Melrose Ave., Los Angeles. ☎ **213/655-2708.**

This rather plain-looking store houses a huge—and fascinating—variety of silver and turquoise rings and earrings from South America, Nepal, Bali, and central Asia. The shop's walls are cluttered with Asian and South American ceremonial and ornamental masks. Open Monday to Thursday and Sunday 11am to 7pm, Friday and Saturday 11am to 9pm.

✪ Second Time Around Watch Co.

8840 Beverly Blvd., Los Angeles. ☎ **310/271-6615.**

The city's best selection of pre-1960s collectible timepieces includes dozens of classic Tiffanys, Cartiers, Piagets, and Rolexes. You might even find an 1850s Patek Philippe pocket watch. Open daily 11am to 5:30pm.

Tiffany & Co.

210 N. Rodeo Dr., Beverly Hills. ☎ **310/273-8880.**

Amid sporadic pieces of crystal and china, shoppers will find an exquisite collection of fine jewelry known the world over for classic styles. Top designers include Elsa Peretti and Paloma Picasso. Open Monday to Saturday 10am to 6pm, Sunday noon to 5pm.

Van Cleef & Arpels

300 N. Rodeo Dr., Beverly Hills. ☎ **310/276-1161.**

You'll find three rooms of breathtakingly beautiful gems and jewelry here. Pieces are expensive, but of the highest quality. Some creative designs highlight an otherwise conservative collection. Open Monday to Saturday 10am to 5:30pm.

MALLS & SHOPPING COMPLEXES

ARCO Plaza

505 S. Flower St., downtown. ☎ **213/486-3511.**

Located beneath the Atlantic Richfield/Bank of America's Twin Towers, ARCO Plaza is a honeycombed labyrinth of corridors with chain stores and boutiques on the second and third underground levels. You'll find the Greater Los Angeles Visitors and Convention Bureau here, as well. Most shops are open Monday to Friday 8am to 6pm, Saturday 10am to 7pm.

Beverly Center

8500 Beverly Blvd. (at La Cienega Blvd.), Los Angeles. ☎ **310/854-0070.**

When the Beverly Center opened on L.A.'s Westside, there was more than a bit of concern about the impending "mallification" of Los Angeles. Loved for its convenience and disdained for its penitentiary-style architecture, Beverly Center contains about 170 standard mall shops (leaning a bit toward the high end) anchored on either end by the Broadway and Bullock's department stores. Most shops are open Monday to Friday 10am to 9pm, Saturday 10am to 8pm, and Sunday 11am to 6pm. Most restaurants stay open later.

Century City Marketplace

10250 Santa Monica Blvd., Century City. ☎ 310/277-3898.

This open-air mall, anchored by Bullock's and the Broadway, is located on what was once a Twentieth-Century Fox back lot. Most of the dozens of smaller shops here are standard chain-store fare: among the offerings are the Pottery Barn, Ann Taylor, and Brentanos, as well as a giant Crate and Barrel and about a hundred (well, not quite) movie screens. Open Monday to Friday 10am to 9pm, Saturday 10am to 6pm, and Sunday 11am to 6pm.

Fisherman's Village

13763 Fiji Way, Marina del Rey. ☎ 310/823-5411.

Marina del Rey's waterfront village is one of the city's most pleasant strolling malls. International imports are available in shops lining the cobblestoned walks of this Old English whaling village–style shopping center. The stores and restaurants surround an authentic 60-foot-tall lighthouse. Open Sunday to Thursday 9am to 9pm and Friday and Saturday 9am to 10pm.

Glendale Galleria

Central Ave. (at Hawthorne Ave.), Glendale. ☎ 818/240-9481.

Located in the eastern San Fernando Valley, the Glendale Galleria is one of the largest malls in the nation, occupying two levels in two wings and housing about 250 retailers. Five department stores compete for business here, along with well-known name-brand shops like Benetton and ACA Joe. Open Monday to Friday 10am to 9pm, Saturday 10am to 8pm, and Sunday 11am to 7pm.

✪ Pacific Design Center

8687 Melrose Ave., West Hollywood, CA 90069. ☎ 310/657-0800. Fax 310/652-8576.

Something of an architectural and cultural landmark, the Pacific Design Center is the West Coast's largest facility for interior design goods and fine furnishings. It houses 200 showrooms filled with furniture, fabrics, flooring, wallcovering, kitchen and bath fixtures, lighting, and art and accessories for homes, offices, restaurants, and hotels. Although businesses here sell to the trade only, the public is welcome to browse. There's also an eclectic new Euro-Asian restaurant, Fusion (☎ 310/659-6012). The menu, which offers everything from borscht to pappardelle in rabbit sauce, is the creation of Bruce Marder, of Rebecca's and West Beach Cafe fame. Open Monday to Friday 9am to 5pm. (See "Architectural Highlights" in Chapter 7 for more information.)

Ports o' Call Village

Berth 77, Samson Way, (between 6th and 22nd sts.), San Pedro. ☎ 310/831-0287.

This collection of more than 80 specialty shops sells crafts and clothing from around the world. Look for hand-blown glass, Filipino jewelry, and Japanese gunpowder tea; several restaurants offer a myriad of cuisines. You can watch a steady stream of yachts, luxury liners, tankers, freighters, schooners, and sailboats cruise by as you browse along the village's winding cobblestone streets. To reach Ports o' Call, take the Harbor Freeway to the Harbor Boulevard off-ramp and turn right. Open Sunday to Thursday 10am to 7pm, Friday and Saturday 10am to 9pm.

Santa Monica Place

Colorado Ave. (at 2nd St.), Santa Monica. ☎ **310/394-5451**.

About 140 shops occupy three bright stories anchored by Robinson's/May and the Broadway department stores. The usual mall shops are augmented by more unusual finds like Frederick's of Hollywood and the KCET Public Television's Store of Knowledge. The mall's food pavilion sells an array of fast foods, including several health-oriented eateries. Open Monday to Saturday 10am to 9pm and Sunday 11am to 6pm.

Sherman Oaks Galleria

15301 Ventura Blvd. (at Sepulveda Blvd.), Sherman Oaks. ☎ **818/783-7100**.

This famous western San Fernando Valley mall is the hangout for dedicated valley girls. It was popularized in *Fast Times at Ridgemont High*. Trendy, mainstream fashions are in abundance. Open Monday to Friday 10am to 9pm, Saturday 10am to 6pm, and Sunday 11am to 6pm.

MEMORABILIA

Book City Collectibles

6631 Hollywood Blvd., Hollywood. ☎ **213/466-0120**.

More than 70,000 color prints of past and present stars are available, along with a good selection of autographs from the likes of Lucille Ball ($175), Anthony Hopkins ($35), and Grace Kelly ($750). Open Monday to Saturday 10am to 9pm, Sunday 10am to 6pm.

Cinema Collectors

1507 Wilcox Ave.(at Sunset Blvd.), Hollywood. ☎ **213/461-6516**.

Original movie posters, magazines, stills, head shots, and associated memorabilia are cross referenced on computer. Helpful employees will answer your questions and help you find your way around. Open daily 10am to 5:30pm.

Hollywood Book and Poster Company

6349 Hollywood Blvd., Hollywood. ☎ **213/465-8764**.

Owner Eric Caidin's excellent collection of movie posters (from about $20 each) is particularly strong in horror and exploitation flicks. Photocopies of about 5,000 movie and television scripts are also sold for $10 to $15 each. Open Monday to Thursday 11am to 6pm, Friday and Saturday 11am to 7pm, and Sunday noon to 5pm.

The Last Moving Picture Show

6307 Hollywood Blvd., Hollywood. ☎ **213/467-0838**.

Movie-related merchandise of all kinds is sold here, including stills from 1950s movies and authentic production notes from a variety of films. Open Monday to Saturday 11am to 6pm.

Mayhem

1411 3rd St., Santa Monica. ☎ **310/451-7600.**

This shop sells autographed guitars and other music memorabilia from U2, Nirvana, Springsteen, Bon Jovi, Pearl Jam, and other rockers to collectors, including the owners of the Hard Rock cafes. It's as much a museum as a store. Open Sunday to Thursday 10am to midnight and Friday and Saturday 10am to 2am.

MUSIC

Hear Music

1429 3rd St., Santa Monica. ☎ **310/319-9527.**

At the first L.A. branch of Boston's Hear Music chain, albums are grouped by genre, theme, and mood. Headphones are everywhere, so you can test a brand-new disk before you buy. Open Sunday to Thursday 11am to 11pm, Friday and Saturday 11am to 12:30am.

✪ Music & Memories

5057 Lankershim Blvd., North Hollywood. ☎ **818/761-9827.**

If you're looking for a copy of that Desi Arnaz mambo that you can't get out of your head, or an out-of-print Frank Sinatra record you've been scouring garage sales for, look no further; leave the modern world behind and head to this dusty but friendly mom-and-pop shop. Open Monday to Saturday 9:30am to 5pm.

Pyramid Music

1340 3rd St., Santa Monica. ☎ **310/393-5877.**

Seemingly endless bins of used cassette tapes and compact discs line the walls of this long, narrow shop on Santa Monica's 3rd Street Promenade. LPs, posters, cards, buttons, and accessories are also avalable. Open Monday to Thursday 11am to midnight, Friday and Saturday 11am to 1am, and Sunday noon to 11pm.

✪ Rhino Records

1720 Westwood Blvd., Westwood. ☎ **310/474-3786**

This is L.A.'s premier alternative shop, specializing in new artists and independent-label releases. In addition to new releases, there's a terrific used selection; this is where record industry types come to trade in the records they don't want for the records they do, so you'll be able to find never-played promotional copies of brand-new releases at half the retail price. You'll also find the definitive collection of records on the Rhino label here. Open daily 10am to 11pm.

Tower Records

8811 W. Sunset Blvd., Hollywood. ☎ **310/657-7300.**

Tower insists that it has L.A.'s largest selection of compact discs—over 125,000 titles—despite the Virgin Megastore's contrary claim. Even if Virgin has more, Tower's collection tends to be more interesting and browser friendly. And the enormous shop's blues, jazz, and classical selections are definitely greater than the competition's. Open Sunday to Thursday 9am to midnight, Friday and Saturday 9am to 1am— 365 days a year.

Virgin Megastore

8000 Sunset Blvd., Hollywood. ☎ **310/650-8666.**

Some 100 CD "listening posts" and an in-store "radio station" make this megastore a music lover's paradise. Virgin claims to stock 150,000 titles, including an extensive collection of hard-to-find artists. Open Sunday to Thursday 9am to 12:30am, Friday and Saturday 9am to 1am.

SPORTS EQUIPMENT

Golf Exchange

830 S. Olive St., downtown. ☎ **213/622-0403.**

L.A.'s golf megastore fills 10 rooms with clubs and accessories: An entire room is devoted to golf shoes, another to bags, another to used clubs, and so on. There's also an indoor driving range so you can try before you buy. Open Monday to Friday 9am to 5:30pm and Saturday 9am to 4:30pm.

Horizons West

2011 Main St., Santa Monica. ☎ **310/392-1122.**

Brand-name surfboards, wet suits, leashes, magazines, waxes, lotions, and everything else you need to catch the perfect wave are found here. Stop in and say "hi" to Randy, and pick up a free tide table. Open daily 10am to 7pm.

Rip City Sports

2709 Santa Monica Blvd., Santa Monica. ☎ **310/828-0388.**

Jim McDowell's top-rated designer skateboards are some of the world's most coveted. Many are handcrafted with the highest-quality wheels and bearings. Open Monday to Saturday 10:30am to 6pm and Sunday noon to 4pm.

TATTOOS

Bert Grimms Tattoo Studio

22 S. Chestnut Place, Long Beach. ☎ **310/432-9304.**

Open since 1927, Bert Grimms is one of the nation's oldest extant tattoo parlors. According to local legend, Bert tattooed gangsters Bonnie and Clyde and Pretty Boy Floyd. Open daily 10am to midnight.

Body Electric

7274½ Melrose Ave., Los Angeles. ☎ **213/954-0408.**

Popular with rock-star types, Body Electric specializes in large-size, Asian-style tattoos. The studio often hosts guest tattoo artists from Japan who are masters of hand shading. Open daily 11am to 8pm.

Sunset Strip Tattoo

8418 West Sunset Blvd., West Hollywood. ☎ **213/650-6530.**

Cher, Charlie Sheen, Lenny Kravitz, and members of the rock band Guns 'n' Roses all got inked at this celebrity-frequented spot. Open daily noon to midnight.

TEA

✪ Chado Tea House
8422 W. 3rd. St., Los Angeles. ☎ **213/655-4681.**

A temple for tea lovers, this cluttered shop has floor-to-ceiling shelves stacked with over 250 different varieties of tea from around the world. Among the choices are 15 kinds of Darjeeling, Indian teas blended with rose petals, and ceremonial Chinese and Japanese blends. They also serve tea meals here; call for details. Open Monday to Saturday 11:30am to 7pm, Sunday noon to 6pm.

TOYS

F.A.O. Schwarz
8500 Beverly Blvd. (in the Beverly Center), Los Angeles. ☎ **310/659-4547.**

One of the world's greatest toy stores for both children and adults is filled with every imaginable plaything, from hand-carved, custom-painted carousel rocking horses, dolls, and stuffed animals to gas-powered cars, train sets, and hobby supplies. The Barbie collection includes hundreds of models, from a three-foot-tall, fiber-optically lighted Barbie to a $200 doll dressed by designer Bob Mackie. The standard muscle-bound morphing toys and talking turtles are also available. Open Monday to Friday 10am to 9pm and Saturday 10am to 8pm, Sunday 10am to 6pm.

Puzzle Zoo
1413 3rd Street Promenade, Santa Monica. ☎ **310/393-9201.**

Puzzles have proved so popular that the Zoo recently expanded to better accommodate a large selection. You'll find the double-sided World's Most Difficult Puzzle, the Puzzle in a Bottle, and collector's serial-numbered Ravensburger series, among others. Open Sunday to Thursday 10am to 10pm, Friday and Saturday 10am to midnight.

Sadie
167 S. Crescent Heights Blvd., Los Angeles. ☎ **213/655-0689.**

A truly unique toy store for kids and adults, Sadie sells hard-to-find collectible reproductions of classic metal, windup, mechanical, and fashion toys from all over the world. Many are one of a kind. Open Monday to Saturday from 10am to 6pm, Sunday from 10:30am to 5pm.

TRAVEL GOODS

California Map and Travel Center
3211 Pico Blvd., Santa Monica. ☎ **310/829-6277.**

Like the name says, this store carries a good selection of domestic and international maps and travel accessories, including guides for hiking, biking, and touring. Globes and atlases are also sold. Open Monday to Fri-day 8:30am to 6pm, Saturday 9am to 5pm, and Sunday noon to 5pm.

WIGS

The Wig Factory

645 Pine Ave., Long Beach. ☎ **310/436-1888.**

Need to be a platinum blond to blend in with Hollywood's glam crowd? How about dreads, extensions, or a temporary bob? For over 25 years, the Wig Factory has been known for its huge selection of hundreds of wigs, stitched for every head. Open daily 10am to 5:30pm.

WINE

Bel-Air Wine Merchant

10421 Santa Monica Blvd., West Los Angeles. ☎ **310/474-9518.**

This is an exceedingly knowledgeable yet unpretentious shop with a nationwide clientele. They specialize in old and rare wines, at fair prices. Open Monday to Saturday 10:30am to 7pm.

L.A. Wine Co.

4935 McConnell Ave., West Los Angeles. ☎ **310/306-9463.**

Known for low mark-ups on recent releases, this is one of the best places to buy young wines by the case, with an eye on aging them in your own cellar. Open Monday to Saturday 10am to 6pm, Sunday noon to 5pm.

The Wine Merchant

9701 Santa Monica Blvd., Beverly Hills. ☎ **310/278-7322.**

"The Wine Merchant to the Stars" is more like it. Linger while looking for the right bottle and you may run into a famous local. Open Monday to Friday 9:30am to 6pm, Saturday 10am to 6pm.

10

Los Angeles After Dark

Nightlife in Los Angeles is a real mixed bag.

You'll find very good—but not world-class—performing arts here: The city's philharmonic and opera are excellent, but neither are America's best. There are over 100 active theaters in L.A., but you'll mostly find regional-quality theater—most of the city's actors would prefer to be in movies; wannabes head for New York if the stage is their thing. Sometimes, Broadway musicals (such as the 1995 Tony award–winning *Sunset Boulevard*) open in L.A. before they premiere in New York, and the top touring companies always put Los Angeles on the list. It might be worth catching a show to see your favorite film or TV star stretching his or her legs on the stage; but if it's top-notch original theater you're looking for, head to the Big Apple (or even Chicago) instead.

But, if you're like most travelers, you aren't heading to L.A. for ballet or Bach or Broadway. You're coming for the glamour and the glitter, to find out what's new before it's news, to see and hear today what—or who—everyone will be watching and listening to and doing and wearing tomorrow.

Well, you've come to the right place if that's what you're after. This is the cultural vanguard when it comes to popular music; dozens of competing clubs feature the world's best artists and bands every single night of the year. There may be more cutting-edge cities in the nation, but this is the final step before the head-first plunge into the mainstream.

The city's club scene is an exciting see-and-be-seen feast that's as vibrant and intoxicating as any in the world. A state-mandated post-2am ban on alcohol sales has never dampened L.A.'s enthusiasm; this creative city has borne some exciting alcohol-free alternatives—both before and after hours—that keep the party hopping.

Films make their debuts in L.A.—sometimes months ahead of their nationwide openings—so even a night at the movies can put you a step ahead of everybody back home (besides, you never know who'll be sitting next to you). If you're interested, you can catch a foreign or art-house film or two that might never make it to your home town. And, as you would expect in the center of the celluloid universe, there are several great movie houses here, including fabled Mann's Chinese and the Cineramadome, as well as a few smaller ones still dressed in all their deco finery.

For weekly updates on music, art, dance, theater, special events, and festivals, call the Cultural Affairs Hotline (☎ 213/688-ARTS), a 24-hour directory listing a wide variety of events, most of which are free. The "Calendar" section of the *Los Angeles Times* is also a good place to find out what's going on after dark. *L.A. Weekly,* a free weekly alternative tabloid available at sidewalk stands, shops, and restaurants is even better, especially for club happenings around town.

There are two major charge-by-phone ticket agencies in the city: Ticketmaster (☎ 213/480-3232) and Ticketron ☎ 213/642-4242). Both sell tickets to concerts, sporting events, plays, and special events.

Theater L.A. (☎ 213/688-ARTS) sells discounted, same-day tickets for such venues as the Mark Taper Forum, the Doolittle, Pantages, Pasadena Playhouse, and other, under-100-seat theaters. Tickets are usually about half price. Callers can either order tickets by phone or are referred to the theater box offices. Theater L.A. is open Tuesday through Saturday from noon to 5pm.

1 The Performing Arts

CLASSICAL MUSIC, OPERA & DANCE

Beyond the pop realms, music in Los Angeles generally falls short of that found in other cities. For the most part, Angelenos rely on visiting orchestras and companies to fulfill their classical music appetites; scan the papers to find out who's playing and dancing while you're in the city.

The **Los Angeles Philharmonic** (☎ 213/850-2000) is not just the city's top symphony; it's the only major classical music company in Los Angeles. Finnish-born music director Esa-Pekka Salonen concentrates on contemporary compositions; despite complaints from traditionalists, he does an excellent job attracting younger audiences. Tickets can be hard to come by when celebrity players like Itzak Perlman, Issac Stern, Emanuel Ax, and Yo-Yo Ma are in town. In addition to regular performances at the Music Center's Dorothy Chandler Pavilion, 135 N. Grand Ave., the Philharmonic also plays a popular summer season at the Hollywood Bowl. Tickets are as little as $6 or as much as $58; check prices for each performance.

Slowly but surely, the **L.A. Opera** (☎ 213/972-8001), is gaining both respect and popularity with inventive stagings of classic operas, usually with guest divas. The Opera also calls the Music Center "home"; tickets cost anywhere from $22 to $120.

The 120-voice **Los Angeles Master Chorale** (☎ 213/972-7211) sings a varied repertoire that includes classical and pops compositions. Concerts are usually held at the Music Center from October to June; tickets cost $7 to $48.

None of the world's best dance companies are headquartered in Los Angeles, but most—including the American Ballet Theater, the Joffrey Ballet, Martha Graham, and Paul Taylor—perform on an annual basis at one of the major concert halls listed below. Check the *L.A. Times* "Calendar" section or *Los Angeles* magazine for current performances.

THEATER
MAJOR THEATERS AND COMPANIES

The **Ahmanson Theater** and **Mark Taper Forum,** the city's top two playhouses, are both part of the all-purpose Music Center, 135 N. Grand Ave., downtown (☎ 213/972-0721). The Ahmanson reopened in 1995, after a $71 million renovation that improved acoustics and seating. This theater is active year round, either with shows produced by the in-house **Center Theater Group,** or with traveling Broadway productions. In-house shows are usually revivals of major Broadway plays, starring famous film and TV actors; I saw *Dangerous Liasions* with Lynn Redgrave and Frank Langella, and *The Little Shop Around the Corner* with Pam Dawber and Christopher Reeve a few years ago. Traveling shows are usually West Coast premieres of plays such as Neil Simon's *Broadway Bound* or Andrew Lloyd Webber's *Phantom of the Opera;* the renovated theater debuted with *Miss Saigon.* The Ahmanson is so huge that you'll want seats in the front third or half of the theater.

The Mark Taper Forum is a more intimate, circular theater staging contemporary works by international and local playwrights. Kenneth Branagh's Renaissance Theatre Company staged their only American productions of *King Lear* and *A Midsummer Night's Dream* at the Mark Taper, to give you an idea of the quality of the shows here. Productions are usually excellent, run with plenty of spirit and no shortage of controversy.

Tickets for the Ahmanson and Mark Taper range from $20 to $50; reductions are usually available on the day of performance for students and seniors.

Big-time traveling troupes and Broadway-bound musicals that don't go to the Ahmanson head instead for the **Shubert Theater** (in the ABC Entertainment Center, 2020 Ave. of the Stars, Century City; ☎ 800/447-7400). This plush playhouse presents major musicals on the scale of *Cats, Sunset Boulevard,* and *Les Misérables.* Tickets usually run $25 to $65.

Top-quality Broadway-caliber productions are also staged at the **James A. Doolittle Theater** (1615 N. Vine St. ☎ 213/462-6666 or 213/972-0700) in Hollywood. Tickets cost $20 to $42.

For current schedule at any of the above theaters, check the listings in *Los Angeles* magazine or the "Calendar" section of the Sunday *L.A. Times,* or call the box offices directly at the numbers listed above.

SMALLER PLAYHOUSES

Like New York's Off-Broadway or London's "Fringe," Los Angeles's small-scale theaters often outdo the slick, high-budget shows. Because this is Tinseltown, movie and TV stars sometimes headline, but more often than not, the talent is up and coming.

The **Colony Studio Theater** (1944 Riverside Dr., Silver Lake; ☎ 213/665-3011) has an excellent resident company that has played in this air-conditioned, 99-seat, converted silent-movie house for over 20 years. Recent productions include the musical *Candide* and the classic American comedy *The Front Page.*

Actors Circle Theater (7313 Santa Monica Blvd., West Hollywood; (☎ **213/882-8043**) is a 47-seater that is as acclaimed as it is tiny. Look for original contemporary works throughout the year.

The **Los Angeles Theater** (615 S. Broadway; ☎ **213/629-2939**) is worth a trip no matter what's on. Built in 1931 by cinema architect S. Charles Lee, this grand movie palace was designed in the ornate baroque style of 18th-century France. Live theater began to be staged here in 1995.

In addition to those listed above, there are about 100 other stages of varying quality throughout the city. Tickets for most plays usually cost from $10 to $25. Check newspaper listings for current offerings.

LANDMARK MULTI-USE VENUES

The theaters and concert halls listed below are so special that it's almost worth it to attend a performance here just to see the venue itself. Check the papers or call the venue direct to find out what's on while you're in town.

Dorothy Chandler Pavilion

In the Music Center, 135 N. Grand Ave., downtown. ☎ **213/972-7211**.

Home of the Los Angeles Philharmonic, Master Chorale, and the L.A. Opera, this 3,197-seat multipurpose theater hosts regular concerts, recitals, opera, and dance performances. You see this theater on TV every year; it hosts the annual Academy Awards.

Greek Theater

2700 N. Vermont Ave., Griffith Park. ☎ **213/665-1927**.

The entertainment here ranges from performances by the Dance Theater of Harlem to rock artists like Elvis Costello and the B-52s. This outdoor theater was designed in the style of the classical theaters of ancient Greece, complete with Doric columns. Performances are held from May to October.

✪ Hollywood Bowl

2301 N. Highland Ave. (at Odin St.), Hollywood. ☎ **213/850-2000**.

Any Tuesday or Thursday concerts, $1 on the lawn; Virtuoso concerts, $3 on the lawn, $5.50–$22.50 for bench seats, $39–$92 for box seats; other events vary in price. Parking $10 to $20, subject to availability and advance reservations; free in off-site lots, but $2.50 per-person shuttle charge to venue.

Built in the early 1920s, the Hollywood Bowl is an elegant, Greek-style natural outdoor amphitheater cradled in a small mountain canyon. This is the summer home of the Los Angeles Philharmonic Orchestra; internationally known conductors and soloists often sit in on Tuesday and Thursday nights. Friday and Saturday concerts are often "pops" shows that feature orchestrated contemporary music. The summer season also includes a jazz series; past performers have included Natalie Cole, Mel Tormé, Dionne Warwick, and Chick Corea. Other events, from Tom Petty concerts to an annual Mariachi Festival, are often on the season's schedule.

For many concertgoers, a visit to the Bowl is an excuse for a picnic under the stars, accompanied by music; gourmet picnics at the Bowl complete with a bottle of wine or two—are one of L.A.'s grandest traditions. You can prepare your own, or order a picnic basket with a choice of hot and cold dishes and a selection of wines and desserts from the theater's catering department (call 213/851-3588 the day before). Many local restaurants also make Bowl baskets. One of the best take-out dinners is offered at Joachim Splichal's Patina, 5955 Melrose Avenue (☎ 213/467-1108), where salmon with cold grilled fennel and cucumber salad, or roasted chicken with potato salad, will set you back anywhere from $22 to $40 per person.

John Anson Ford Amphitheater
2580 Cahuenga Blvd., Hollywood. ☎ **213/466-1767.**

This historic outdoor theater (a theatrical landmark since the 1930s) is nestled in a parklike setting with a hillside backdrop of palms and cypresses; crenelated towers frame the stage. With its intimate, natural setting, the Ford is one of the city's best outdoor venues, presenting a full program of "Summer Nights" concerts, opera, jazz, and children's shows.

Pantages Theater
6233 Hollywood Blvd., Hollywood. ☎ **213/468-1770.**

This luxurious Hollywood landmark dates from 1930. For 10 years it was the setting for the Academy Awards ceremony, including the first telecast. The theater has seen several incarnations, including one as a movie house. In 1977 the Pantages returned as a leading stage for live theater with a production of *Bubbling Brown Sugar*. Recent productions have included *Joseph and the Amazing Technicolor Dreamcoat* and concerts by Bob Dylan and the Gypsy Kings.

The Shrine Auditorium
665 W. Jefferson Blvd., Los Angeles. ☎ **213/748-5116.**

The unusual 1920s-era Shrine has a Middle Eastern flavor, and no wonder: It was once the Al Malaikah Temple. The 6,300-seat auditorium offers good sightlines for both local and international musical acts. This is where Michael Jackson was filming a Pepsi commercial when his hair caught fire.

Wiltern Theater
3790 Wilshire Blvd., Los Angeles. ☎ **213/380-5005.**

This glorious sea-green art deco–era theater is listed on the National Register of Historic Places. With its interior beautifully restored to its original glory, it's now one of the city's top concert halls and venues for live theater.

2 The Club & Music Scene

Angelenos are forever looking for the next wave—even if it's a retro one. Every kind of music is performed on the city's stages, from cutting edge to cabaret. L.A.'s club scene is one of the world's best for up-and-coming bands and pop styles. New talent from all over the globe gravitates here in hopes of landing a coveted recording contract.

Old names abound as well—where better to entirely reinvent yourself? Tom Jones would agree, I'm sure—L.A.'s the place.

Of course, the programs at the venues listed below change nightly. Check the papers or call the clubs direct to see what's on and for show times; clubs tend to keep erratic schedules. Because of the ban on alcohol sale after 2am, expect nightclubs to close at that hour, unless otherwise indicated. Also, because of the sale of alcohol on the premises, most clubs require you to be 21 in order to enter. However, some venues are more flexible, allowing those over 18—sometimes even all ages—in the doors; check the newspapers or call clubs direct to find out what their particular rules are.

NIGHTCLUBS & CABARET

The Cinegrill

7000 Hollywood Blvd. (in the Hollywood Roosevelt Hotel), Hollywood. ☎ **213/ 466-7000.** Cover varies, none–$5.

There's something going on every night of the week here, at one of L.A.'s most historic hotels. Some of the country's best cabaret singers pop up here regularly. On Thursdays, Mark Nadler takes the stage with his zany cabaret show, playing piano, singing, and telling bad jokes; he even tap dances on his piano or plays while standing on his head.

Luna Park

665 N. Robertson Blvd., West Hollywood. ☎ 310/652-0611. Cover varies, none–$10.

The city's most unusual mixed-use venue, Luna Park is a bi-level cabaret presenting an eclectic mix of music and comedy on two stages. The main room usually hosts an eclectic variety of world music groups—you might find salsa tonight, New Orleans blues tomorrow, and maybe Canadian folk the next. The cabaret room hosts more intimate musical performances as well as performance artists.

Queen Mary Show Lounge

12449 Ventura Blvd., Studio City. ☎ 818/506-5619. Cover varies, $5–$15.

The Queen Mary is a no-holds-barred, Vegas-style drag show, where you can laugh with "Joan Rivers," share makeup tips with "Diana Ross," or dance with "Tina Turner." But you'll have to make your way through the admiring throng of transvestites and drag queens first. Open Wednesday through Sunday.

COMEDY CLUBS

Each of the following venues claims—and justly so—to have launched the careers of the comics that are now household names. The funniest up-and-comers are playing all the clubs (except for the Groundlings, which is an improvisation group), so you're probably best off choosing a club for its location.

Comedy Store

8433 Sunset Blvd., West Hollywood. ☎ **213/656-6225.** Best Room, cover $6 Mon, $12–$14 Fri–Sat; Original Room, no cover Mon, $6 Tues–Fri and Sun, $8 Sat; Belly Room, cover varies, free–$3. Additional two-drink minimum in all rooms.

You can't go wrong here: New comics develop their material, and established ones work out the kinks from theirs, at owner Mitzi Shore's (Pauly's mom) landmark venue.

The Best of the Comedy Store Room, which seats 400, features professional stand-ups continuously on Friday and Saturday nights. Several comedians are always featured, each doing about a 15-minute stint. The talent here is always first rate, and includes comics who regularly appear on the *Tonight Show* and other shows.

The Original Room features a dozen or so comedians back-to-back nightly. Sunday night is amateur night: Anyone with enough guts can take the stage for three minutes, so who knows what you'll get?

The Belly Room alternates between comedy stage and piano bar, with Wednesday nights reserved for the "Gay and Lesbian Comedy Show."

Igby's Comedy Cabaret

11637 W. Pico Blvd., West Los Angeles. ☎ **310/477-3553.** Cover $10–$15, plus two-drink minimum.

Igby's is the best spot for comedy on the Westside. There's not a bad seat in the place. The comics are well "stacked," so the night usually becomes racier the later it gets. You can order from a full dinner menu during the show, as long as you don't mind eating right under the comedian's nose.

✪ Groundling Theater

7307 Melrose Ave.. Los Angeles. ☎ **213/934-9700.** Cover $8 Sun and Thurs, $10–$11 Fri–Sat. Additional two-drink minimum.

L.A.'s answer to Chicago's Second City has been around for over 20 years, yet remains the most innovative and funny group in town. Their collection of skits changes every year or so, but they take new improvisational twists every night, and the satire is often savage. In the current production, O. J. meets the Menendez brothers, and Universal CityWalk takes a hilarious beating. The Groundlings were the springboard to fame for Pee-Wee Herman, Elvira, and former *Saturday Night Live* stars Jon Lovitz, Phil Hartman, and Julia "It's Pat" Sweeney. Trust me—you haven't laughed this hard in ages. Phone for show times and reservations.

The Improvisation

8162 Melrose Ave., West Hollywood. ☎ **213/651-2583.** Cover $6–$11.

A showcase for top stand-ups since 1975, the Improv offers something different each night. The club's own television show, A&E's *Evening at the Improv* is now filmed at the Santa Monica location. Although there used to be a fairly active music schedule, the Improv is now mostly doing what it does best—showcasing comedy. Owner Bud Freedman's buddies—like Jay Leno, Billy Crystal, and Robin Williams—hone their skills here more often than you would expect. But even if the comedians on the bill the night you go are all unknowns, they won't be for long. Shows are at 8pm Sunday and Thursday, at 8:30 and 10:30pm Friday and Saturday.

ROCK

Canter's Kibitz Room

419 N. Fairfax Ave., Los Angeles. ☎ **213/651-2030**. No cover.

Canter's, one of the city's most established 24-hour Jewish delis, features Tuesday-night jams in the Kibitz Room. Members of Guns 'n' Roses, the Black Crowes, Pearl Jam, and other top names have been known to play here alongside lesser known rockers. The music begins just after 9pm, goes on till around 2am.

Club Lingerie

6507 Sunset Blvd., Los Angeles. ☎ **213/466-8557**. Cover $6–$15.

This was the epicenter of L.A.'s punk scene, the place bands like Black Flag and X called home. Well, the heyday of punk may be gone in Hollywood—even Henry Rollins has moved into the mainstream—but you'd never know it here. Home-grown bands—and, on occasion, emerging national acts—play almost every night at Hollywood's oldest continuously operating club. When the bands stop, DJs start spinning tunes. The club often sells out, so show up early.

Doug Weston's Troubador

9081 Santa Monica Blvd., West Hollywood. ☎ **310/276-6168**. Cover $5–$15.

The Troubador, a landmark club with a great sound system and more than 30 years under its belt, usually serves up local rock bands back to back by the half dozen. Everyone from Linda Ronstadt and the Stone Poneys to Beck paid their dues on this stage. An adventurous booking policy ensures a good mix, and the densely packed program usually means that there'll be at least one performer you'll like.

Hollywood Palladium

6215 Sunset Blvd., Hollywood. ☎ **213/962-7600**. Cover $15–$25.

Lawrence Welk used to do his famous New Year's Eve show from here. Today, the huge club is one of the best and most eclectic venues in town, featuring everything from rock to salsa.

The Roxy

9009 Sunset Blvd., West Hollywood. ☎ **310/276-2229**, or 310/276-2222 for a recording. Cover $5–$20.

This medium-size club is L.A.'s top showcase for national pop, rock, and jazz acts. This is where the record labels show off their hot new signings, as well as their smaller established bands; occasionally, even superstars such as David Bowie and Bon Jovi take the stage here. On other nights, the roster is usually packed with Los Angeles bands—three or four a night—you've never heard of, and probably never will.

Whiskey A-Go-Go

8901 Sunset Blvd., West Hollywood. ☎ **310/652-4205**. Cover $5–$15.

One of Hollywood's legendary clubs (among others, the Doors were quite at home here), the Whiskey packs 'em in with hard and alternative rock double and triple bills. Weekends still turn up more than their fair share of tight leather and teased hair.

FOLK & ACOUSTIC

Crooked Bar
8121 Sunset Blvd., Hollywood. ☎ **213/654-4887**. Cover varies, none–$7.

In-the-know locals love this intimate all-acoustic club, located under the Coconut Teaszer bar. Five or six acts are featured every night.

Genghis Cohen Cantina
740 N. Fairfax Ave., Los Angeles. ☎ **213/653-0640**. Cover $5.

Live acoustic music and good Chinese food commingle at this smart hangout. The kitchen is open 5 to 10:30pm Sunday to Thursday and until 11:30pm on Friday and Saturday. Music usually starts around 9pm. Phone for reservations and to see what's on.

✪ McCabe's
3101 Pico Blvd., Santa Monica. ☎ **310/828-4403** or 310/828-4497. Cover $13–$20.

One of the most unusual—and most respected—music venues in the city, McCabe's is actually a guitar store that features live performances in its small, guitar-lined, 150-seat theater on weekends. Top-level performers include both new and established local and national artists; Bruce Springsteen and R.E.M. have even been known to grab a guitar and take the stage. The atmosphere is as intimate and down to earth as you're likely to find in L.A., making this one of the finest venues in the area. There's a camaraderie among audience members, as well as between the artist and the audience, that's seldom seen at live music shows—everybody here knows that they're a part of something special. No alcohol is sold, but coffee, tea, juices, and cookies are available. McCabe's usually sells out quickly, so buy your tickets in advance.

JAZZ & BLUES

B.B. King's Blues Club
1000 Universal Center Dr., Universal CityWalk. ☎ **818/6-BBKING**. Cover $5–10.

Despite its location on the touristy Universal CityWalk, B.B. King's Blues Club is everything a down-home southern venue should be. It's big and has great acoustics, but feels intimate enough so that there's not a bad seat in the house. Best of all, the acts are really hot. The food's pretty good, too.

Harvelle's
1432 4th St., Santa Monica. ☎ **310/395-1676**. Cover $3–$7.

The Westside's oldest blues club is a Chicago-style room catering to a casually dressed group of mixed ages and backgrounds. The quality of the nightly live music is consistently high, and the always-reasonable cover charge won't ever give you the blues.

✪ House of Blues
8430 Sunset Blvd., West Hollywood. ☎ **213/650-0247**. Cover varies, none–$30.

Looking very much like a Disney-inspired shanty shack, this new blues joint—owned in part by Harvard University, actors Dan Aykroyd and Jim Belushi, and members of the rock band Aerosmith—features live blues performances and surprisingly good southern-style cooking daily; bands usually start around 9pm. The club is the third in a series of successful blues houses; founder Isaac Tigrett (Ringo Starr's ex-wife Maureen's husband until her death last year—how's that for a Beatles connection?) also helped found the mega-chain of Hard Rock Cafes.

The Mint

6010 W. Pico Blvd., Los Angeles. ☎ **213/937-9630.** Cover $5–$10.

A tiny and dark jazz room, The Mint feels like a speakeasy or an old-time Harlem jazz club. This intimate blues lounge presents top session players and hot up-and-comers nightly.

The Baked Potato

3787 Cahuenga Blvd. West, North Hollywood. ☎ **818/980-1615.** Cover $7–$15.

A Los Angeles mainstay, the Baked Potato is one of the oldest jazz venues in the city. It's a tiny place that jams every night of the week.

5th Street Dick's Company

3347$^1/_2$ West 43rd Pl., Los Angeles. ☎ **213/296-3970.** Cover $5.

This coffeehouse offers nightly jazz and after-hours jam sessions. 5th Street Dick's is the place where up-and-coming talents come to play after their paying gigs let out. Acts scheduled almost every night; sets can start as late as 1am.

LATIN

El Floridita

1253 North Vine St., Hollywood. ☎ **213/871-8612.** Cover $5–$20.

El Floridita is as Cubano as L.A. gets. The music is hot and the clientele is almost entirely Latino. There's probably never been a night here that didn't end with a packed dance floor.

La Masia

9077 Santa Monica Blvd., West Hollywood. ☎ **310/273-7066.** Cover $10 Fri–Sat, no cover Tues–Thurs.

The city's only Spanish supper club, Le Masia serves some of the best northeastern Spanish food in the city, along with hot salsa and Latin jazz. The atmosphere is *muy* upscale, but the patrons come here to shake it.

REGGAE

Kingston 12

814 Broadway, Santa Monica. ☎ **310/451-4423.** Cover $5–$15.

Kingston 12 features sounds from all over the islands—ska, dancehall, reggae, you name it. Local talent is often spotlighted, along with an occasional international star. Authentically good Jamaican food and drink is also served. Open Thursday to Sunday.

DANCE CLUBS & DISCOS

The down-and-dirty Sunset Strip is the epicenter of L.A.'s dance club scene. The very nature of the club circuit demands new blood and fresh faces, thus making recommendations outdated before the ink can even dry on the page. Most of the venues below are promoted as different

---

Caffeine Nation: The Other Bar Scene

Java isn't just for breakfast anymore. Coffeehouses have become the bars of the nineties; they're trendy hangouts with atmospheres—and clienteles—as cosmopolitan as the hottest nightclubs. But, despite their highbrow hipness, coffeehouses are fundamentally democratic institutions—at about $1.50 per cup, coffee is, after all, the drink of the masses.

L.A.'s best coffeehouses—besides having colorful, comfortable settings and great social scenes—make their brew nice and strong. And why not? If I owned a legal drug shop, I'd pump up the volume and hook as many users as possible, too.

Anastasia's Asylum (1028 Wilshire Blvd., near 11th St., Santa Monica; ☎ 310/394-7113) has an upscale beatnik ambience, created by a hip, eclectic crowd that comes for both good coffee and conversation. There's a terrific upstairs stage where musicians and poets sometimes show their stuff. Anastasia's is open Sunday to Thursday 7am to 2am, Friday to Saturday 7am to 3am.

Betelgeuse (7160 Melrose Ave., Los Angeles; ☎ 213/243-8229) is as close as L.A. comes to Parisian cafe society. Pronounced like the title of the Tim Burton movie, Betelgeuse serves great espresso drinks, as well as the best crepes outside of the 1st arrondissement. Betelgeuse is open Tuesday to Thursday 8am to 1am, Friday to Saturday 8am to 2am, Sunday 8am to 11pm.

Congo Square (1238 3rd St., Santa Monica; ☎ 310/395-5606), located on the pedestrians-only 3rd Street Promenade, is a modern,

---

clubs on various nights of the week; each has its own look, sound, and style. Call to see what's on, and to confirm that the club you're interested in is open the night you want to go; schedules tend to be erratic. The *L.A. Weekly* contains the most comprehensive published listings of dance clubs around town, but it's not complete; discount passes and club announcements are often available at the trendy clothing stores along Melrose. Many of the rock clubs listed above are also dedicated to dance music on various nights of the week; call to check.

Glam Slam

333 S. Boylston St., downtown. ☎ 213/482-6626. Cover $10–$15.

A dodgy location gives this downtown L.A. offshoot of the Artist formerly known as Prince's Minneapolis pleasure palace an authentically dangerous atmosphere. There's a huge dance floor where you can groove to funk, retro, and hip-hop sounds. The crowd is stylish and sexy, and the mood is definitely seductive.

Love Lounge

657 N. Robertson Blvd., West Hollywood. ☎ 310/659-0472. Cover $10 Fri; no cover Wed, Thurs, and Sat.

brick-walled cafe with outside tables that are great for people watching. There's a spacious indoor seating area, too. Congo heats up at night with live music, poetry, open mike nights, and damn good cappuccino. It's open Sunday to Thursday 8am to 1am, Friday and Saturday 8am to 2am.

Grounds Zero (124 North San Fernando Blvd., Burbank; ☎ **818/ 567-4257**) should be your destination if you ever find yourself stuck in the cultural vortex that is Burbank. This bohemian getaway has comfortable couches, great board games, and plenty of suburban youth. It's open daily 11am to 2am.

Hollywood's **Highland Grounds** (742 N. Highland Ave., a half-block north of Melrose Ave.; ☎ **213/466-1507**) serves excellent coffee drinks and hosts occasional poetry readings, but it's best known for its strong lineup of folky-poppy musical acts that play to a young crowd almost every night of the week. There's sometimes a cover charge at night, but it's rarely more than $3. Highland Grounds is open Monday to Saturday 9am to midnight, Sunday 10am to midnight.

Kiosk Coffee House (8851 Sunset Blvd., West Hollywood; ☎ **310/652-6613**) always has something going on. Local musicians and poets take the stage on Monday, open mike night. Wednesday, unplugged night, features local "acousticats." A light menu and pastries are always available. Kiosk is open Monday to Thursday 7am to midnight, Friday 7am to 3am, Saturday 10am to 3am, and Sunday 10am to midnight.

This flamboyant, loud, and anti-pretty dance hall is not for the meek. The sounds range from seventies rock to nineties alternative, and the top male and female hip-swingers dance on elevated platforms. Projections of sixties cult films and trippy psychodelia round out the ambiance.

Roxbury

8225 Sunset Blvd., Hollywood. ☎ **213/656-1750.** Cover $10.

This labyrinthine dance club attracts a trendy crowd that dresses to impress. The tri-level funhouse is usually a good spot for stargazing; in fact, it was in front of this hot spot that Shannen Dougherty hauled off and belted a wannabe she wasn't too keen on. There are four full bars and a DJ spinning tunes.

3 The Bar Scene

The Hotel Bel-Air Bar

701 Stone Canyon Rd., Bel Air. ☎ **213/472-1211.**

One of the mellower places for a quiet, romantic evening, the ritzy Bel Air bar offers good piano music in an upscale setting.

The Brasserie Bar
In the Wyndham Bel Age Hotel, 1020 N. San Vicente Blvd., West Hollywood.
☎ **310/854-1111.**

One of the classiest and prettiest bars in the city, this place regularly features top-notch jazz performers.

The Grand Avenue Bar
In the Biltmore Hotel, 506 S. Grand Ave., downtown. ☎ **213/624-1011.**

This is a popular showcase of top-name jazz performers.

Lava Lounge
1533 La Brea Ave. (at Sunset Blvd.), Hollywood. ☎ **213/876-6612.**

This retro dive bar, owned by a former set decorator, is a one-of-a-kind Polynesian paradise that panders to the city's faddies. Great jazz, often trios, plays in a room with a sordid tiki-hut decor. Weekdays can be hit or miss, but weekends are always crowded.

The Lobby Club Bar
In the Peninsula Beverly Hills, 9882 Santa Monica Blvd., Beverly Hills. ☎ **310/551-2888.**

Beverly Hills's best-looking crowd comes here nightly to see and be seen, drink overpriced drinks, and hear pianist George Bugatti tickle the ivories of his Kimball baby grand. Sinatra's even stopped in and stayed after hours to croon.

✪ Viper Room
8852 Sunset Blvd., West Hollywood. ☎ **310/358-1880.** Cover $5–$10.

The Viper Room, partly owned by Johnny Depp, is home to Hollywood's hippest crowd. The famous drop in sometimes to perform, other times to just hang out. River Phoenix's untimely death here has made this club world famous, but it's gotten past those unpleasant times and still exudes good vibes.

The Whiskey
In the Sunset Marquis Hotel, 1200 N. Alta Loma Rd., West Hollywood. ☎ **310/657-1333.**

The Whiskey is one of the most exclusive rooms in Hollywood. Rockers like Mick Jagger, Axl Rose, and Robert Plant cavort with model/actresses, Eurotrash, rubber-clad bimbettes, and well-sculpted guys with pony tails and tank tops under their Armani jackets. If you're not staying at the hotel or you don't know somebody, it's best to head somewhere else; that may be your best bet anyway.

4 The Gay & Lesbian Scene

West Hollywood is the center of gay and lesbian life in Los Angeles, but not all the nightlife spots catering to the community are located there. For the latest on the scene, pick up a copy of *Nightlife,* a local weekly with comprehensive gay-oriented entertainment listings, complete with maps; it's available at most newsstands citywide.

Check the papers or call the clubs direct to see what's on and for open days and hours; clubs tend to keep erratic schedules. Because of the ban on alcohol sale after 2am, expect nightclubs to close at that hour, unless otherwise indicated. Also, because of the sale of alcohol on the premises, most clubs require you to be 21 in order to enter. However, some venues are more flexible, allowing those over 18—sometimes even all ages—in the doors; check the news-papers or call clubs direct to find out what their particular rules are.

Catch One

4067 W. Pico Blvd., Hollywood. ☎ **213/734-8849.** Cover $4.

This is one of the best dance clubs in the city for gays and lesbians. The good sound system attracts big crowds. There are four bars on two floors. Theme nights vary; call to see what's on. In addition to its regular hours, the club is open late, until 4am, Thursday to Saturday.

Circus Disco

6655 Santa Monica Blvd., Hollywood. ☎ **213/462-1291.** Cover $8–$12.

It's not always gay night, but when it is, the club is packed with a predominantly young, Latino crowd. Hip-hop and house music are the preferred sounds.

Club 7969

7969 Santa Monica Blvd., West Hollywood. ☎ **213/654-0280.** Cover $10–$12.

Anything goes in this exotic world—guys spanking guys, girls pulling on other girls' G-strings. It's a wonderfully strange gay/straight mix that could only come together in a city like this one.

Micky's

8857 Santa Monica Blvd., West Hollywood. ☎ **310/657-1176.** Cover varies, none–$7.

Both a dance club and a restaurant, Micky's has a high-energy atmosphere that's popular with a youngish crowd. The good-looking club occupies two levels and serves full meals.

The Mother Lode

8944 Santa Monica Blvd., West Hollywood. ☎ **310/659-9700.** No cover.

This collegiate-looking bar is frequented by a young, upwardly mobile crowd; there's often a line to get in.

The Palms

8527 Santa Monica Blvd., West Hollywood. ☎ **310/652-6188.** No cover.

Reputedly the oldest lesbian bar in the city, this busy hangout is becoming more popular with gay men as well.

Spike

7746 Santa Monica Blvd., West Hollywood. ☎ **213/656-9343.** Cover varies, none–$7.

A pool- and pinball-playing Levi's-and-leather crowd likes the bar's techno, house, and rock sounds. The club is open until 4am on Friday and Saturdays.

5 More After-Dark Activities

MOVIES

There are hundreds of movie screens in Los Angeles; many show the same first-run Hollywood films that play across America, but there are a few terrific theaters that show offbeat films, or are just worth a trip because they're so spectacular. L.A.'s most special movie houses are listed below.

IMAX Theater

In the California Museum of Science and Industry, Exposition Park, 700 State Dr., Los Angeles. ☎ **213/744-2014.**

Awesome 40-minute adventure reels are projected onto a 5-story, 70-foot-a-side screen, accompanied by dynamic surround sound. Usually three different films are shown daily, from about 10am to 9pm.

New Beverly Cinema

7165 Beverly Blvd., Los Angeles. ☎ **213/938-4038.**

This is one of the city's best revival houses. The New Beverly usually screens themed double features of older films—you might see a *Thin Man* double feature or *A Hard Day's Night* paired with the Monkees' *Head*—as well as newer flicks on their second run. Programs change every few days, and there are usually midnight showings on weekends.

The Nuart

11272 Santa Monica Blvd., West Los Angeles. ☎ **310/478-6379.**

L.A.'s premier arthouse screens the best offbeat films throughout the day, and *The Rocky Horror Picture Show* every night at midnight. The theater is now very comfortable, thanks to brand-new seating, but it's small, so arrive early.

Pacific Cineramadome

6360 Sunset Blvd., Hollywood. ☎ **213/466-3401.**

This unique moviehouse—a giant geodesic dome—shows first-run films on a gigantic screen that wraps around your field of vision. It's best for epics and films made by great cinematographers. If the new release you want to see is playing here, don't miss it.

Silent Movie

611 North Fairfax Ave., Los Angeles. ☎ **213/653-2389.**

This pocket-size theater screens the best shorts and features to live organ accompaniment. Programs from the golden age of silents are usually devoted to a particular star or director, and are preceded by a fantastic cartoon (usually *Felix the Cat*).

POOL HALLS

✪ Gotham Hall

1431 3rd St., Santa Monica. ☎ **310/394-8865.**

Grape- and mustard-hued walls, cut-steel railings, and ultramodern furniture and textiles make this futuristic place one of the most interesting pool halls in L.A.—and beyond, for that matter. A balcony bar overlooks seventeen regulation-size tables. Pool prices are $7 to $14 per hour. Open Monday through Friday 4pm to 2am, and Saturday and Sunday noon to 2am.

Yankee Doodles

1410 3rd St., Santa Monica. ☎ **310/394-4632.**

Grimier, if not noisier, than Gotham Hall, this sports bar cum pool hall features 32 pool tables on two levels, battling satellite TVs, and lousy food. Pool costs $6 to $12 per hour. Open daily from 11am to 2am.

Hollywood Athletic Club

6525 Sunset Blvd., Hollywood. ☎ **213/962-6600.**

The art deco decor and Generation X crowd make for quite an interesting contrast; the upscale interior attracts celebrities and good-lookng wannabes, rather than pool sharks and serious contenders. There are a whopping 42 tables, and decent food and cocktails are served. It's open daily from noon to 2am.

6 Midnight Snacks

L.A. is no 24-hour town. Surprisingly, the city has only about a dozen bona fide restaurants that are open after 2am; even fewer serve all night. Most of these late-nighters get busy when the bars close, filling up with bleary-eyed, black-clothed hipsters who look out of place in brightly lit coffee shops and all-night delis. There are, of course, some people who actually work late—film editors and foreign correspondents are chief among them; they, too, can be found chowing down while the rest of the city is sleeping. If you want a serious meal after 2am, head for the **Pacific Dining Car,** the **Original Pantry Cafe,** or **Jerry's Famous Deli,** all of which are open 24 hours (see Chapter 6 for details). Or you can try the following:

Ben Frank's

8585 Sunset Blvd. (east of La Cienega Blvd.), West Hollywood. ☎ **310/652-8808.** Main courses $7–13; lunch $5–$7; breakfast $4–$8. AE, CB, DC, DISC, MC, V. Daily 24 hours. AMERICAN.

Although it's open all day, the most colorful time to go to this Sunset Strip joint is late at night, when it's jam-packed with long-haired rockers and their attendant pierced and tattoed babes. The food, however, is far more traditional than the crowd. They serve up surprisingly great coffee-shop fare here: French toast, eggs Benedict, hamburgers, meatloaf, and many more American favorites. Shakes and malts are served alongside beer and wine.

✪ Canter's Fairfax Restaurant, Delicatessen & Bakery

419 N. Fairfax Ave., Los Angeles. ☎ **213/651-2030.** Main courses $6–$12. MC, V. Daily 24 hours. JEWISH.

Canter's has been a hit with late-nighters since it opened over 65 years ago. If you show up after the clubs close, you're sure to spot a bleary-eyed celebrity or two alongside the rest of the after-hours crowd, chowing down on a giant pastrami sandwich, matzoh-ball soup, potato pancakes, or another deli favorite. Try a potato knish with a side of brown gravy—trust me, you'll love it. There's often live music in the restaurant's Kibitz Room (see "Rock," above).

Denny's

7373 W. Sunset Blvd., West Hollywood. ☎ **213/876-6660.** Main courses $4–$7. AE, MC, V. Daily 24 hours. AMERICAN.

When people say "Let's go to Rock-and-Roll Denny's," they don't mean just *any* Denny's; they're referring to this convenient location, near many of L.A.'s notorious hard-rock clubs. Expect to wait a half-hour for a seat if you arrive between 2 and 4am on a weekend. You can get the same food at a dozen other Denny's citywide, but the colorful crowd makes dining at this one worth the wait.

Larry Parker's 24-Hour Diner

206 S. Beverly Dr., Beverly Hills. ☎ **310/274-5655.** Main courses $4–$8. AE, MC, V. Daily 24 hours. AMERICAN.

This is the most popular of the after-bar eateries. It blasts high-decibel hip-hop, sports a spinning disco ball, and attracts a flashy crowd. Don't be surprised to find a 45-minute wait at 4am on a Saturday or Sunday morning. Just like they did at their favorite club hours before, patrons line up behind a doorman-guarded velvet rope in order to satisfy the after-hour munchies.

Easy Excursions from Los Angeles

The area within a 100-mile radius of Los Angeles is one of the most diverse regions in the world. There are arid deserts, rugged mountains, industrial cities, historic towns, alpine lakes, rolling hillsides, and sophisticated seaside resorts. You'll also find an offshore island that's been transformed into the ultimate city-dweller's hideaway, not to mention the happiest place on earth—Disneyland, of course. Below are some of our favorite L.A. escapes. For coverage of other vacation destinations within reach of Los Angeles, see *Frommer's California '96* (Macmillan). Or, if you're seeing Southern California with children, pick up a copy of *Frommer's California with Kids,* 4th edition (Macmillan).

1 Pasadena & the San Gabriel Valley

11 miles NE of Los Angeles

Pasadena is considered to be part of Los Angeles, but this community is so far removed from the rest of the city, both physically and in spirit, that we think of it as an excursion. Pasadena is an exceptional community offering excellent dining, an outstanding array of arts and entertainment, some beautiful examples of 20th-century architecture, and great shopping in the historic downtown. In addition to all of this, it's the site of the Tournament of Roses Parade, the world's most famous New Year's Day event. Its beauty, particularly that of its mansions, makes it a favorite location of feature films and television programs. This rose of a town wilts slightly in summer, when heat and smog can be positively oppressive.

ESSENTIALS

America's first freeway, the 6-mile Arroyo Seco Parkway, opened in 1940, linking Hollywood and Pasadena. It later connected to greater L.A.'s planned 1,500-mile freeway system as the **Pasadena Freeway (I-210).** Narrower and curvier than modern freeways, the Pasadena Freeway, with its lush, overgrown landscaping, now seems like a quaint relic of an earlier era. Though bumper-to-bumper during rush hours, it's refreshingly traffic-free in the late morning, and a lot of fun to drive.

If you are flying to L.A., and are planning to make Pasadena or another San Gabriel Valley town your base, see if you can land at the quiet, convenient Burbank Airport (2627 N. Hollywood Way, Burbank; ☎ 818/840-8840).

For a free destination guide and information, contact or stop by the **Pasadena Convention and Visitors Bureau,** 171 S. Los Robles Ave., Pasadena, CA 91101 (☎ **818/795-9311;** fax 818/795-9656). The office is open Monday to Friday 8am to 5pm, and Saturday 10am to 4pm. The Bureau also has an information hotline (☎ 818/795-9311) that operates when the office is closed for holidays.

WHAT TO SEE & DO

One of the best activities Pasadena has to offer is merely strolling through pretty **Old Pasadena.** Along Colorado Boulevard between Pasadena and Los Robles Avenue, you'll find popular clothing shops like Armani Exchange, Victoria's Secret, and Banana Republic, all of which are open late on weekends to accommodate the crowds. Browse through Penny Lane, a great used-record store. When you're ready to sit down, Cleo & Cucci or any one of the other coffeehouses at hand can make you a great cappucino.

Free **Pasadena ARTS Buses** (☎ **818/405-4055**), each painted with original murals, travel through Old Pasadena along Colorado Boulevard, Green Street, and South Lake Avenue. Buses run every 12 minutes, Monday to Thursday from 11am to 8pm, Friday 11am to 9pm, and Saturday noon to 8pm.

Descanso Gardens

1418 Descanso Dr., La Cañada. ☎ **818/952-4402** or 818/952-4401. Admission $5 adults, $3 students and seniors (over 62), $1 children 5–12, kids under 5 free. Daily 9am–4:30pm.

Camellias—evergreen flowering shrubs from China and Japan—were the passion of ameteur gardener E. Manchester Boddy, who began planting them here in 1941. Today his Descanso Gardens, Spanish for "ranch of rest," contains more than 100,000 camellias in over 600 varieties, blooming under a 30-acre canopy of California oak trees. The shrubs now share the limelight with a 5-acre Rose Garden, home to hundreds of varieties.

It's really a magical place, with paths and streams that wind through the towering forest, bordering a lake and bird sanctuary. Each season features different plants: daffodils, azaleas, tulips, and lilacs in the spring; chrysanthemums in the fall; and so on. Monthly art exhibits are held in the garden's hospitality house.

There's also a beautifully landscaped Japanese-style teahouse. Tea and cookies are served on Saturday and Sunday from 11am to 4pm. Free docent-guided walking tours are offered every Sunday at 1pm; guided tram tours, which cost $1.50, run Tuesday through Friday at 1, 2, and 3pm, and on Saturday and Sunday at 11am, 1pm, 2pm, and 3pm. Picnicking is allowed in specified areas.

✪ Gamble House

4 Westmoreland Place, Pasadena. ☎ **818/793-3334.** Admission $4 adults, $3 seniors, $2 students, children under 12 free. Open Thurs–Sun noon–3pm.

Pasadena

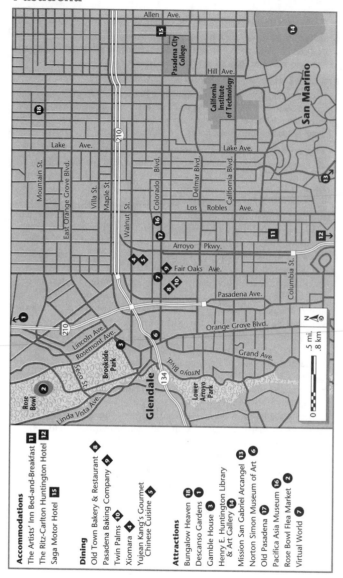

Allen Ave.
15
14
Pasadena City College
Hill Ave.
California Institute of Technology
San Marino
18
Lake Ave.
Lake Ave.
Mountain St.
East Orange Grove Blvd.
Villa St.
Maple St.
Walnut St.
Colorado Blvd.
Delmar Blvd.
California Blvd.
Los Robles Ave.
16
13
17
11
12
Arroyo Pkwy.
4 5
9
Fair Oaks Ave.
7
8 10
Columbia St.
Pasadena Ave.
1
Lincoln Ave.
Rosemont Ave.
210
Orange Grove Blvd.
6
Seco St.
3
Brookside Park
Grand Ave.
N
.5 mi.
.8 km
2
Rose Bowl
Glendale
134
Arroyo Blvd.
Lower Arroyo Park
Linda Vista Ave.
0

The huge two-story Gamble House, built in 1908 as a California vacation home for the wealthy family of Procter and Gamble fame, is a sublime example of arts and crafts architecture. Designed by the famous Pasadena-based Greene and Greene architectural team, the interior abounds with hand craftsmanship, including intricately carved teak cornices, custom-designed furnishings, elaborate carpets, and a fantastic Tiffany glass door. No detail was overlooked. Every oak wedge, downspout, air vent, and switchplate contributes to the unified design. Admission is for one-hour guided tour only; tours depart every 15 minutes. No reservations are necessary.

✪ Henry E. Huntington Library & Art Gallery

1151 Oxford Rd., San Marino. ☎ **818/405-2100** or 818/405-2141. Admission suggested donation $7.50 adults, $6 seniors ages 65 and above, $4 students and children over 12; free for children under 12. Tues–Fri 1–4:30pm, Sat–Sun 10:30am–4:30pm. Closed major holidays.

The Huntington Library is the jewel in Pasadena's crown. The 207-acre hilltop estate was once home to railroad magnate Henry E. Huntington (1850–1927), an industrialist who bought books on the same massive scale that he acquired businesses. The continually expanding collection includes 12 folios and 37 quartos of Shakespeare's; the original handwritten manuscript of Benjamin Franklin's autobiography; the library of William Caxton, England's first printer; a large assemblage of manuscripts by Abraham Lincoln and George Washington; a Gutenberg Bible from the 1450s; and the earliest known manuscript of Chaucer's *Canterbury Tales*.

Huntington also put together a terrific 18th-century English art collection. His most celebrated paintings are Gainsborough's *The Blue Boy* and *Pinkie*, a companion piece by Sir Thomas Lawrence depicting the youthful aunt of Elizabeth Barrett Browning.

It's worth a trip just to tour the mansion's spectacular gardens. The Japanese Garden showcases traditional Northeast Asian plants and stone ornaments, and encompasses a Kyoto-style rock garden. The Desert Garden is home to one of the world's largest collections of mature cacti and other drought-resistant plants. Other gardens include scores of varieties of camellias, a rose garden featuring over 1,000 varieties displayed in the chronological order of their breeding, and a Shakespeare Garden—designed in traditional English style, of course.

The Huntington is one of Southern California's greatest attractions—if you know how to approach this vast complex. First-timers should begin by viewing a 12-minute slide show that offers an overview of the galleries. Even better, attend one of the regularly scheduled 15-minute introductory talks, or the more in-depth 1-hour garden tour, scheduled daily. Phone for tour times.

A terrific à la carte high tea is served in a delightful tearoom overlooking the Rose Garden Wednesday through Sunday, from 1:30 to 3:30pm. Phone **818/683-8131** for reservations.

Mission San Gabriel Arcangel

537 W. Mission Dr., San Gabriel. ☎ **818/457-3035.** Admission $3 adults, $1 children 6–12 years, kids under 6 free. Daily 9:30am–4:30pm. Closed Easter, half day on Good Friday, Thanksgiving, Christmas.

Founded in 1771, Mission San Gabriel Arcangel still retains its original facade, notable for its high oblong windows and large capped buttresses that are said to have been influenced by the cathedral in Cordova, Spain. The mission's self-contained compound encompasses an aqueduct, a cemetery, a tannery, and a working winery. Within the church stands a copper font with the dubious distinction of being the first one used to baptize a native Californian. The most notable contents of the mission's museum are Native American paintings depicting the Stations of the Cross, painted on sailcloth, with colors made from crushed petals of desert flowers.

✪ Norton Simon Museum of Art

411 Colorado Blvd., Pasadena. ☎ **818/449-6840.** Admission $4 adults, $2 students and seniors, children under 12 free. Thurs–Sun noon–6pm; bookshop, Thurs–Sun noon–5:30pm.

Named for a food-packing king who reorganized the failing Pasadena Museum of Modern Art, the Norton Simon Museum has become one of California's most important museums. Comprehensive collections of masterpieces by Degas, Picasso, Rembrandt, and Goya are augmented by sculptures by Henry Moore and Auguste Rodin, including *Burghers of Calais,* which greets you at the gates. The "Blue Four" collection of works by Kandinsky, Jawlensky, Klee, and Feininger is particularly impressive, as is a superb collection of Southeast Asian sculpture. *Still Life with Lemons, Oranges, and a Rose* (1633), an oil by Francisco de Zurbáran, is one of the museum's most important holdings. One of the most popular pieces is Mexican artist Diego Rivera's *The Flower Vendor/Girl with Lilies.*

Pacific Asia Museum

46 North Los Robles Ave., Pasadena. ☎ **818/449-2742.** Admission $3 adults, children under 12 free. Free for everyone on the third Saturday of each month. Open Wed–Sun noon–5pm.

The most striking aspect of this museum is the building itself. Designed in the 1920s in Chinese Imperial Palace style, it's rivaled in flamboyance only by Mann's Chinese Theatre. Rotating exhibits of Asian art span the centuries, from 100 B.C. to the current day. This manageably sized museum is usually worth a peek.

✪ Rose Bowl Flea Market

At the Rose Bowl, 991 Rosemont Ave., Pasadena. ☎ **818/577-3100.** Admission $5. Second Sunday of every month, 6am–5pm.

Built in 1922, the horseshoe-shaped Rose Bowl is one of the world's most famous stadiums. Home to UCLA's football Bruins and the annual Rose Bowl Game, the stadium is also the site of one of California's largest bimonthly swap meets. Look for everything from used surfboards and car stereos to antique restaurant furniture, secondhand clothing, and one-of-a-kind lawn statuary.

Virtual World

In the One Colorado Mall, 35 Hugus Alley, Pasadena. ☎ **818/577-9896.** $7 Mon–Fri before 5pm, $8 after; $9 Sat–Sun. Mon–Fri 10am–9pm, Sat–Sun 10am–8pm.

This is the ultimate "easy excursion" from Los Angeles. Several different adventures are offered at the world's first virtual reality play center, including a run through the mining tunnels of Mars in the year 2053 and a jousting tournament on the fictitious desert planet Solaris VII. The experience begins in a turn-of-the-century, alcohol-free club room, fitted with faux French high-back easy chairs and a polished wooden

Yesteryear Revisited, Arts & Crafts Style: Bungalow Heaven

Long adored by "bungalowners" and nostalgic architecture buffs, Pasadena's Bungalow Heaven is now a formally preserved slice of Southern California history. This charming neighborhood's nickname became its official designation in 1989, when determined homeowners and preservationists succeeded in having a Landmark District created to encompass the approximately 900 pre-Depression-era bungalows here.

Ironically, the bungalow, inexpensive to construct and often sold in kits, was never intended to be a lasting part of the landscape. Easterners had been drawn to the unspoiled beauty, abundant fruits, and hospitable climate of Pasadena (a Chippewa word meaning "crown of the valley") since Victorian times. In the first few decades of the 20th century, Midwesterners, looking for a warm, economically friendly place to settle down, work, and raise families, came in droves—hence the prevalence of street names like Michigan, Madison, Peoria, and Wabash. Their desire for affordable housing, coupled with the growing Arts and Crafts movement in design, proved fertile ground for the growth of bungalow neighborhoods.

Around the turn of the century, many artists, designers, and architects were beginning to reject the stifling ornateness of Victorian style and to stress simplicity, organic motifs, and natural materials in their work. The philosophy of this new Arts and Crafts movement grew to emphasize lifestyle, inspiring a greater appreciation of and interaction with nature. The distinctive elements of the bungalow illustrate this trend: Abundant windows, expansive porches, and limited indoor space all extend the living area to include the outdoors. The widespread use of raw natural materials, such as exposed beams,

bar. It's a startling contrast to the post-modern gunmetal games room, containing seven player "pods" surrounded by exposed ducts and a plethora of pipes.

Many of the virtual worlds are set up like intergalactic war games, where you don heavy helmets and try to "neutralize" your friends. After the VR adventure, you can review your game from various angles on videotape.

PASADENA AFTER DARK

Ambassador Auditorium

300 W. Green St. ☎ **818/304-6161.**

Home to the Los Angeles Chamber Orchestra, the Ambassador is celebrated for its particularly fine acoustics. It's especially worth attending an event here when a world-renowned classical or pop artist is on the bill. Call for program schedule.

rough-hewn boulders, and simple clay tiles, reflects a respect for nature shaped by Southern California's Spanish, Mexican, and Japanese heritage. And bungalow design spoke directly to the climate: There were overhanging eaves for daylight shading and lots of windows for cross-ventilation—summertime necessities prior to air-conditioning. The interiors were outfitted along the same lines; the furniture style was often called "mission" because it resembled the stark simplicity of the nearby Spanish missions.

North Mentor Avenue defines the western border of Bungalow Heaven and boasts the oldest home in the neighborhood, number 714. Built in 1883, this eerie ramshackle Victorian still awaits the attention of a restorer. At 775 North Mentor, don't miss a striking 1913 example of an "airplane bungalow," whose wide lower gables resemble the spreading wings of a plane, topped with the second-story "cockpit." Over on North Michigan Avenue, notice the unusual entrance to number 875, a Craftsman bungalow from 1909, whose front door passes right through the wide, lopsided brick chimney. Stroll these blocks and choose your own favorites.

Bungalow Heaven, easily reached from the Calif. 134 and I-210 freeways, is centered around McDonald Park, between Lake and Hill avenues north of Orange Grove Boulevard. The Bungalow Heaven Neighborhood Association conducts a house tour each April, with detailed histories of each of the homes open to visitors during the tour. But feel free to check out the neighborhood whenever you're in Pasadena—without bothering the residents, of course. For more information, call the BHNA at (818)585-2172.

—Stephanie Avnet

Espresso Bar

34 S. Raymond St. (south of Colorado Blvd.). ☎ **818/356-9095.** Coffee and cakes $1–$4. No credit cards. Mon–Tues noon–1am, Wed–Thurs and Sun 9am–1am, Fri–Sat 9am–2am.

This simply named coffeehouse, hidden down a hard-to-find alleyway, has been around so long that it almost seems as though Pasadena grew up around it. It's popular with punk poets, who come here to emote before one of the area's most eclectic audiences.

Gordon Biersch Brewery & Restaurant

41 Hugus Alley. ☎ **818/449-0052** or 818/449-0067. Main courses $8–$15. AE, MC, V. Sun–Wed 11am–midnight, Thurs–Sat 11am–1pm.

The Pasadena branch of the northern California chain is one of the most successful brewpubs in Southern California. The wood-and-brick interior is large and noisy, and the food woefully uneven, but the golden lager is great and the atmosphere upbeat. Go for drinks and an appetizer, then head to a real restaurant for dinner.

The Ice House

24 N. Mentor Ave. ☎ **818/577-1894.**

Pasadena's best-known comedy and music club since 1960, the Ice House claims to have launched the careers of such world-famous comedians as Robin Williams, Steve Martin, David Letterman, and Lily Tomlin. There are usually three acts nightly, with two shows on Friday and three shows on Saturday. The adjacent Ice House Annex presents blues, improvisational theater, and intimate performance art shows. Phone for the latest.

Pasadena Playhouse

35 S. El Molino Ave. (at Colorado Blvd.). ☎ **818/356-7529.**

One of the most highly acclaimed professional theaters in L.A., Pasadena Playhouse was founded in 1917 and has served as the training ground for many theatrical, film, and television stars. Productions are staged both in the main theater and in a smaller one on the second floor. Call to find out what's on.

WHERE TO STAY
EXPENSIVE

✪ The Ritz-Carlton Huntington Hotel

1401 S. Oak Knoll Ave. (west of Elliott), Pasadena, CA 91109. ☎ **818/568-3900** or 800/241-3333. Fax 818/568-3700. 383 rms, 21 suites. A/C MINIBAR TV TEL. $160–$275 double; suites from $350. AE, DC, MC, V. Parking $12.

Built in 1906, the Huntington is one of America's grandest hotels. The large Spanish-Mediterranean hotel gained popularity early on among celebrated writers, entertainers, political and business leaders, even royalty. Set on 23 meticulously landscaped acres, it seems a world apart from downtown Los Angeles, though it's only about 20 minutes away. Closed for six years after a particularly destructive earthquake, the hotel reopened in 1991 under the Ritz-Carlton banner, but the unique charm and elegant aura of yesteryear are intact. Each oversize guest room is dressed in conservatively elegant Ritz-Carlton style, with marble baths, thick carpets, terry robes, and the like. Behind the hotel is a bucolic Japanese garden that's great for strolling.

Dining/Entertainment: Older locals love to celebrate in the Georgian Room, where continental meals are prepared by a classically trained French chef. The less formal Grill serves traditional fare in a comfortable, clublike setting. The Café serves all day, either indoors or out; it's best on Sundays, for champagne brunch. High tea is served daily in the Lobby Lounge.

Services: Concierge, 24-hour room service, nightly turndown, babysitting.

Facilities: Olympic-size outdoor heated pool, small exercise room, outdoor Jacuzzi, sundeck, three lighted tennis courts, car rental desk, mountain bike rental, pro shop, gift shop.

MODERATE

The Artists' Inn Bed-and-Breakfast

1038 Magnolia St., South Pasadena, CA 91030. ☎ and fax **818/799-5668**. 4 rms. A/C. $100–$110 double. Rates include full breakfast. AC, MC, V. Free Parking.

This Victorian-style inn was built in 1895 as a farmhouse. Each of the four rooms is thematically decorated to reflect the style of a particular artist or period. The English Room, fitted with good-quality antique furnishings and cheerful rose-patterned wallpaper, is the best room in the house; it's also the only one with a king-size bed. The Impressionist and Fauve rooms both have a queen-size bed and a bathroom with a claw-foot tub and separate shower. The Van Gogh Room has a double bed and a bathroom with shower only. The unpretentious yellow-shingled home, pleasantly furnished throughout with wicker, is on a quiet residential street.

INEXPENSIVE

Saga Motor Hotel

1633 E. Colorado Blvd. (between Allan and Sierra Bonita aves.), Pasadena, CA 91106. ☎ **818/795-0431**. 69 rms. A/C TV TEL $57 double; $59 double with king bed and refrigerator; $75 suite. All rates include continental breakfast. AE, CB, DC, MC, V. Free parking.

This motel has some of the most attractive accommodations in its price range. The rooms are pleasantly decorated with brass beds and tile baths. Guest rooms are split between two buildings: The first is a single-story structure wrapped around a pool; the other is a small three-story building between the pool and a quiet street at the rear of the building. The best rooms face the pool. The hotel is about a mile from the Huntington Library and within easy distance of the Rose Bowl.

WHERE TO DINE
EXPENSIVE

✪ Xiomara

69 N. Raymond Ave. (at Walnut St). ☎ **818/796-2520**. Main courses $18–$23; lunch $12–$19. Nightly $25 fixed-price menu. AE, MC, V. Mon–Fri 11:30am–2:30pm and 5:30–10:30pm; Sat–Sun 5:30–10:30pm. FRENCH COUNTRY.

By any other name, Xiomara (SEE-o-ma-ra) would still be one of the top restaurants in Los Angeles, despite the fact that it has never made Zagat's "top-rated" list. Chef Patrick Healy's best dishes are rustic country concoctions like sausage-laden cassoulet and veal shanks braised so long the meat practically falls off the bone. Chicken is simmered for an eternity in a sealed cast-iron pot with artichokes and carrots. The nightly fixed-price meal is a good value. The three-course menu is determined by the chef's mood and the fresh ingredients at hand. A long list of obscure country wines complements the menu. The dining room is as soothing as the food, fitted with comfortable armchairs and presided over by the enthusiastic Xiomara herself.

In 1995 the restaurant added an oyster and clam bar featuring oyster shooters, ceviche, and a large selection of raw oysters and clams on the half shell.

MODERATE

Twin Palms

101 W. Green St. (at De Lacey Ave.). ☎ **818/577-2567.** Main courses $10–$14. AE, DC, CB, MC, V. Mon–Thurs 11am–10pm, Fri–Sat 11am–11pm, Sun noon–10pm. MEDITERRANEAN/AMERICAN.

Twin Palms is big. The 400-seat restaurant, under two palm trees and a tent, is also busy; it's a hit with recession-weary Angelenos, who come here for some of the best-value meals in the entire city. The simple entrance leads to an open-air, canvas-topped town square–size dining room set with dozens of generous round tables. The festival atmosphere is augmented by a nightly reggae band, two lively bars, and meats turning on an open spit over hardwood logs. Chef Michael Roberts is well known for his daring combinations and fine flavorings; his reputation is solidified here, with excellently prepared peasant grills and roasts. Everyone talks about the salt cod mashed potatoes, a delicious appetizer that's big enough to serve four—and, at $3, it's cheaper than the valet parking. The best main courses come off the grill and spit; they include juicy roasted sage-infused pork and honey-glazed, coriander-scented duck. Sautéed dishes and salads are not as successful. A number of exciting wines are priced well, under $20.

Yujean Kang's Gourmet Chinese Cuisine

67 N. Raymond Ave. (between Walnut St. and Colorado Blvd.). ☎ **818/585-0855.** Main courses $14–$21. AE, MC, V. Daily 11am–10pm. CHINESE CONTEMPORARY.

Many Chinese restaurants put the word "gourmet" in their name, but few really mean—or deserve—it. Not so at Yujean Kang, where Chinese cuisine is taken to an entirely new level. A master of "fusion" cuisine, the eponymous chef/owner snatches bits of techniques and flavors from both China and the West, commingling them in an entirely fresh way. Signature dishes include lobster with caviar and fava beans, Chilean sea bass in passion-fruit sauce, and pork loin with mustard greens and chilies. The serious wine list is also unusual for an Asian restaurant. Where else can you pair a German Spätlese with tea-smoked duck? The red-wrapped dining room is less subtle, but just as elegant, as the food.

INEXPENSIVE

Old Town Bakery & Restaurant

166 W. Colorado Blvd. (between Pasadena and Miller sts.). ☎ **818/792-7943.** Reservations not accepted. Main courses $5–$11; breakfast $3–$7. DISC, MC, V. Sun–Thurs 7:30am–10pm, Fri–Sat 7:30am–midnight. CONTINENTAL.

Set back from the street in a quaint courtyard, this cheery bakery is an especially popular place to read the morning paper over cappuccino and a croissant. The display counters are packed with cakes, muffins, scones, and other confections, all baked expressly for this shop. Meals include eggs, pastas, salads, sandwiches, and nouveau-style pan pizzas.

Pasadena Baking Company

29 E. Colorado Blvd. (east of Fair Oaks Ave.), Old Pasadena. ☎ **818/796-9966.**
Reservations not accepted. Baked goods 50¢–$3; breakfast $3–$6; lunch $2–$8.
AE, MC, V. Mon–Thurs 7am–11pm, Fri 7am–midnight, Sat 8am–midnight, Sun 8am–
11pm. CONTINENTAL.

This little bakery holds just a handful of small tables, which spill out
onto the sidewalk during nice weather. Their particularly large—and
sweet-smelling—selection of fresh pastries, tarts, truffles, cakes, and
candies are all proudly displayed. There's also an assortment of fresh
breads and a fresh fruit stand. Breakfast foods include homemade croissants and muffins as well as omelets. The generous sandwiches are
lunch favorites, as are salads and "vegestronni," a pie prepared with
fresh seasonal vegetables.

2 Santa Barbara

96 miles N of Los Angeles

This sun-blessed town between the Santa Ynez Mountains and the
Pacific is one of the world's most perfect places. Charming, spoiled
Santa Barbara is coddled by wooded mountains, caressed by baby
breakers, and sheltered from tempestuous seas by rocky offshore islands.
And it's just far enough from Los Angeles to make the Big City seem
at once remote and accessible. There are few employment opportunities and real estate is expensive, so demographics have favored college
students and rich retirees, thought of by the locals as the "almost wed
and almost dead."

Downtown Santa Barbara is distinctive for its Spanish-Mediterranean
architecture; all the structures sport matching red-tile roofs. But it
wasn't always this way; Santa Barbara had a thriving Native American
Chumash population for hundreds, if not thousands, of years. The
European era began in the late 18th century, around a presidio (fort)
that's been reconstructed in its original spot. The earliest architectural
hodgepodge was destroyed in 1925 by a powerful earthquake that
leveled the business district. Out of the rubble rose the Spanish-
Mediterranean town of today, a stylish planned community that
continues to rigidly enforce its strict building codes.

ESSENTIALS
GETTING THERE

By Plane   The Santa Barbara Municipal Airport (☎ **805/967-7111**)
is located in Goleta, about 10 minutes north of downtown Santa Barbara. Airlines serving Santa Barbara include American Eagle (☎ **800/
433-7300**), Skywest/Delta (☎ **800/453-9417**), United (☎ **800/
241-6522**), and USAir Express (☎ **800/428-4322**).

Yellow Cab (☎ **805/231-2222**) and other metered taxis line up
outside the terminal; the fare is about $20 to downtown.

By Rail   Amtrak (☎ **800/USA-RAIL**) offers daily service from Los
Angeles. Trains arrive and depart from the Santa Barbara Rail Station
at 209 State Street (☎ **805/963-1015**); fares can be as low as $20
from Los Angeles.

By Bus   Greyhound/Trailways (☎ 800/231-2222) maintains a daily schedule from Los Angeles. The central bus station is located downtown at Carillo and Chapala streets.

By Car   U.S. 101 runs right through Santa Barbara; it's the fastest, and most direct, route from Los Angeles.

ORIENTATION

State Street, the city's primary commercial thoroughfare, is the geographic center of town. It ends at Stearns Wharf and Cabrillo Street; the latter runs along the ocean and separates the city's beaches from touristy hotels and restaurants.

The **Santa Barbara Visitor Information Center** (1 Santa Barbara St., Santa Barbara, CA 93101; ☎ **805/965-3021**) is on the ocean, at the corner of Cabrillo Street. The center distributes maps, literature, an events calendar, and excellent advice. Be sure to ask for the handy guide to places of interest and public parking. The office is open Monday through Saturday from 9am to 5pm and Sunday from 10am to 5pm; it closes one hour earlier in winter and one hour later in July and August. A second center, open Monday through Friday from 9am to 5pm, is located at 504 State Street, in the heart of downtown. Pick up a free copy of *Things to See and Do* at one of the offices.

Be sure to pick up a copy of *The Independent,* an excellent free weekly paper with a comprehensive listing of events. It's available in shops and from sidewalk racks around town.

WHAT TO SEE & DO

County Courthouse
1100 Anacapa St. ☎ **805/962-6464.** Admission free. Daily 8:30am–5pm.

Moreton Bay Fig Tree
Chapala and Montecito sts.

Santa Barbara's best-known tree has a branch spread that would cover half a football field, and its roots run under more than an acre of ground. It has been estimated that well over 10,000 people could stand in the tree's shade. Planted in 1877, it's a native of Moreton Bay in eastern Australia. The tree is related to both the fig and rubber tree, but produces neither figs nor rubber. It is, hands down, the largest of its kind in the world. Once in danger of being leveled (for a proposed gas station) and later threatened by excavation for nearby U.S. 101, the revered tree is now the unofficial home of Santa Barbara's homeless community.

✪ Santa Barbara Mission
Laguna and Mission Sts. ☎ **805/682-4173** or 805/682-4175. Admission $3 adults, free for children under 16. Daily 9am–5pm.

Called the "Queen of the Missions" for its twin bell towers and graceful beauty, this hilltop mission overlooks the town and the Channel Islands beyond. Santa Barbara Mission was established by Franciscan friars in 1786, and is still used by a local parish. Inside you'll find 18th- and 19th-century furnishings, Mexican paintings and statuary, and period

Downtown Santa Barbara

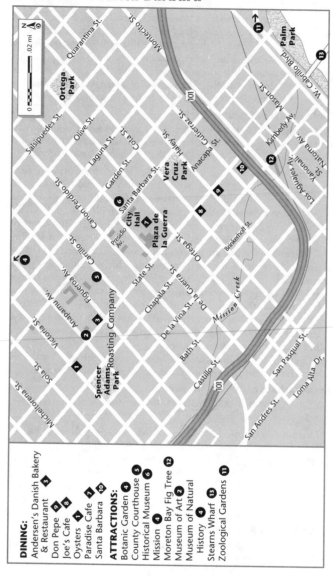

DINING:
Andersen's Danish Bakery & Restaurant ❸
Don Pepe ❾
Joe's Cafe ❽
Oysters ❶
Paradise Cafe ❼
Santa Barbara ❿

ATTRACTIONS:
Botanic Garden ❹
County Courthouse ❺
Historical Museum ❻
Mission ❹
Moreton Bay Fig Tree ⓬
Museum of Art ❷
Museum of Natural History ❹
Stearns Wharf ⓭
Zoological Gardens ⓫

kitchen utensils. The museum also displays Native American tools, crafts, and artifacts.

Santa Barbara Museum of Natural History

2559 Puesta del Sol Rd. ☎ **805/682-4711.** Admission $5 adults, $4 seniors and teens, $3 children. Mon–Sat 9am–5pm, Sun and holidays 10am–5pm.

This museum, located about two blocks uphill from Santa Barbara Mission, focuses on the display, study, and interpretation of Pacific Coast natural history. Native American history is emphasized in the exhibits, which include basketry, textiles, and a full-size replica of a Chumash canoe. Other displays encompass everything from fossil ferns to live insects and the complete skeleton of a blue whale. An adjacent planetarium projects sky shows every Saturday and Sunday.

Santa Barbara Museum of Art

1130 State St. ☎ 805/963-4364. Admission $4 adults, $3 seniors (over 65), $1.50 children 6–16, children under 6 free. Free for everyone Thurs and the first Sun of each month. Tues–Wed and Fri–Sat 11am–5pm, Thurs 11am–9pm, Sun noon–5pm.

A trip to this museum feels like an exclusive visit to the private galleries of a wealthy art collector. Works by Monet and mid-quality oils by Dali, Picasso, Matisse, Chagall, and Rousseau are displayed on a rotating basis in rooms that, for the most part, are ample, airy, and well lit. Quantitatively, the museum's strengths lie in early 20th-century Western American paintings and 19th- and 20th-century Asian art. Qualitatively, the best are the antiquities and Chinese ceramics collections. Many pieces are often on loan to other museums, but good temporary shows are indicative of a high degree of reciprocity. Some awkward arrangements don't always make sense, and lighting could be improved on the explanatory plaques. For the most part, though, SBMA is a jewel of a museum that's wonderfully compact and a terrific visual counterpoint to the monotonous Spanish-Mediterranean architectural theme outside.

Free docent-led tours are scheduled Tuesday through Sunday at 1pm. Focus tours are held on Wednesday and Saturday at noon.

Santa Barbara Historical Museum

136 E. de la Guerra St. ☎ 805/966-1601. Admission free, but donation requested. Tues–Sat 10am–5pm, Sun noon–5pm.

Local-lore exhibits include late-19th-century paintings of the California missions by Edwin Deakin; a 16th-century carved Spanish coffer from Majorca, home of Junipero Serra; and objects from the Chinese community that once flourished here, including a magnificent carved shrine from the turn of the century. A knowledgeable docent leads a most interesting free tour every Wednesday, Saturday, and Sunday at 1:30pm.

Santa Barbara Botanic Garden

1212 Mission Canyon Rd. ☎ 805/682-4726. Admission $3 adults, $2 children 13–19 and seniors (over 64), $1 children 5–12, children under 5 free. Nov–Feb, Mon–Fri 9am–4pm, Sat–Sun 9am–5pm; Mar–Oct, Mon–Fri 9am–5pm, Sat–Sun 9am–6pm.

The gardens, about 1½ miles north of the mission, encompass 65 acres of native trees, shrubs, cacti, and wildflowers, and more than five miles of trails. They're at their aromatic peak just after spring showers. Docent tours are offered daily at 2pm, with additional tours on Thursday, Saturday, and Sunday at 10:30am.

Stearns Wharf

At the end of State St. ☎ 805/963-2633.

In addition to a small collection of second-rate shops, attractions, and restaurants, the city's 1872-vintage pier offers terrific views of the city and good drop-line fishing. The Dolphin Fountain at the foot of the wharf was created by local artist Bud Bottoms for the city's 1982 bicentennial.

Santa Barbara Zoological Gardens

500 Ninos Dr. ☎ **805/962-5339** or 805/962-6310 for a recording. Admission $5 adults, $3 seniors and children 2–12, children under 2 free. Daily 10am–5pm; last admission is one hour prior to closing. Closed Thanksgiving, Christmas.

When you're driving around the bend on Cabrillo Beach Boulevard, look up—you might spot the head of a giraffe poking up through the palms. This is a thoroughly charming, pint-size place, where all 700 animals can be seen in about 30 minutes. Most of the animals live in naturalistic, open settings. The zoo has a children's Discovery Area, a miniature train ride, and a small carousel. The picnic areas (complete with barbecue pits) are underutilized and especially recommendable.

OUTDOOR ACTIVITIES

BICYCLING

A relatively flat, palm-lined two-mile coastal pathway runs along the beach and is perfect for biking. More adventurous riders can pedal through town, up to the mission, or to Montecito, the next town over. The best mountain bike trail begins at the end of Tunnel Road and climbs up along a paved fire road before turning into a dirt trail to the mountaintop.

Beach Rentals (22 State St.; ☎ **805/966-6733**) rents well-maintained 1- and 10-speeds. They also have tandem bikes and surrey cycles that can hold as many as four adults and two children. Rates vary depending on equipment. Bring an ID (driver's license or passport) to expedite your rental. They're open daily from 8am to dusk.

GOLF

At the **Santa Barbara Golf Club** (3500 McCaw Ave., at Las Positas Road ☎ **805/687-7087**), there's a great 6,009 yard, 18-hole course and driving range. Unlike many municipal courses, the Santa Barbara Golf Course is well maintained and was designed to present a moderate challenge for the average golfer. Greens fees are $18 Monday to Friday ($13 for seniors) and $20 on Saturday and Sunday ($17 for seniors). Optional carts rent for $20.

The 18-hole, 7,000-yard course **Sandpiper,** at 7925 Hollister Avenue (☎ **805/968-1541**), a pretty oceanside course, has a pro shop and driving range, plus a coffee shop. Greens fees are $60 Monday to Friday and $80 on Saturday and Sunday. Carts cost $24.

HIKING

The hills and mountains surrounding Santa Barbara have excellent hiking trails. One of my favorites begins at the end of Tunnel Road. Take Mission Canyon Road past the mission, turn right onto Foothill Road, and take the first left onto Mission Canyon Drive. Bear left onto Tunnel Road and park at the end (where all the other cars are). You can buy a trail map at the Santa Barbara Visitor Information Center.

HORSEBACK RIDING

Several area stables rent horses, including **Circle Bar B Ranch** (1800 Refugio Rd.; ☎ **805/968-3901**) and **Rancho Oso** (Paradise Road, off Hwy. 154; ☎ **805/964-8985**).

POWER BOATING & SAILING

The **Sailing Center of Santa Barbara,** at the Santa Barbara Breakwater (☎ **805/962-2826** or 800/350-9090), rents sailboats from 13 to 50 feet, 40-horsepower boats, and jet skis. Both crewed and bare-boat charters are available by the day or hour. Sailing instruction for all levels of experience is also available.

SKATING

The paved beach path that runs along Santa Barbara's waterfront is perfect for skating. **Beach Rentals** (22 State St.; ☎ **805/966-6733**), located nearby, rents both in-line and conventional roller skates. The $5 per hour fee includes wrist and knee pads.

SPORT FISHING, DIVE CRUISES & WHALE WATCHING

Sea Landing, at the foot of Bath Street and Cabrillo Boulevard (☎ **805/963-3564**), makes regular sport fishing runs from specialized boats. They also offer a wide variety of other fishing and diving cruises. Food and drink are served on board, and rental rods and tackle are available. Rates vary according to excursion; call for reservations.

Whale-watching cruises are offered from February through April, when the California gray whale makes its migratory journey from Baja, Mexico, to Alaska. Tours are $24 for adults and $14 for children; sightings of large marine mammals are guaranteed.

SHOPPING

State Street from the beach to Victoria Street is the city's main thoroughfare, and has the largest concentration of shops. Many specialize in T-shirts and postcards, but there are a number of boutiques as well. If you get tired of strolling, hop on one of the electric shuttle buses (25¢) that run up and down State Street at regular intervals.

Also check out **Brinkerhoff Avenue** (off Cota St., between Chapala and De La Vina sts.), Santa Barbara's "antique alley;" most shops are open Tuesday to Sunday 11am to 5pm. **El Paseo** (814 State St.) is a picturesque shopping arcade reminiscent of an old Spanish street. Built around an 1827 adobe home, the mall is lined with charming shops and art galleries that are worth a look.

SANTA BARBARA AFTER DARK

THEATERS

To find out what's going on while you're in town, check the free weekly *The Independent,* or call the following venues direct: the **Center Stage Theater,** upstairs at the Paseo Nuevo Shopping Center, Chapala and De La Guerra streets (☎ **805/963-0408**); the **Lobero Theater,** at 33 E. Canon Perdido Street (☎ **805/963-0761**); the

Arlington Theater, at 1317 State Street(☎ **805/963-4408**); and the **Earl Warren Showgrounds,** at Las Positas Road and U.S. 101. (☎ **805/687-0766**).

BARS & CLUBS

Backstage
18 E. Ortega St. ☎ **805/730-7383.** Cover free–$7.

Santa Barbara's most alternative nightclub enjoys a Los Angeles—style warehouse setting and a mixed gay/straight crowd. Under high ceilings are two bars, a pool table, an indoor fountain, and the largest dance floor in town. Regular theme nights are interspersed with occasional live local bands. Open Sunday, Monday, and Wednesday to Friday from 9pm to 2am and Saturday from 7:30pm to 2am.

Beach Shack
500 Anacapa St. ☎ **805/966-1634.** Cover free–$5.

Live local bands attract a good-looking college crowd. Tiki hut–themed bars are located both inside and out, away from the busy dance floor. Open Tuesday through Sunday from 7pm to 2am.

Joe's
536 State St. ☎ **805/966-4638.** No cover.

Joe's is known for its particularly powerful drinks and good-looking beachy/college crowd. Food is served at tables and booths until 11pm, but mingling at the adjacent bar is best. Open Monday to Saturday from 11am to 11pm and Sunday from noon to 9pm.

Mel's
6 W. De La Guerra St., in the Paseo Nuevo Mall. ☎ **805/963-2211.** No cover.

This is a divey old drinking room in the heart of downtown. The compact bar attracts a good cross-section of regulars. Open daily from 7am to 2am.

The Wildcat Lounge
15 W. Ortega St. ☎ **805/962-7970.** No cover.

This is easily the most happening place in town. The excellent CD jukebox and kitschy decor attract local 20- and 30-somethings to what otherwise amounts to little more than an interestingly lit bar with a pool table. Open daily from 4pm to 2am.

WHERE TO STAY

Hot Spots Accommodations (36 State St., Santa Barbara, CA 93101; ☎ **805/564-1637**), a one-stop shop for hotel and bed-and-breakfast rooms, keeps an updated list of what's available in all price categories. There's no charge for their services. Significantly discounted rates are often available at the last minute, when hotels need to fill their rooms. All hotels provide free parking unless otherwise noted.

VERY EXPENSIVE

✪ Four Seasons Biltmore
1260 Channel Dr. (at the end of Olive Mill Road), Santa Barbara, CA 93108. ☎ **805/ 969-2261** or 800/332-3442; fax 805/969-4682. 234 rms, 24 suites. A/C MINIBAR

TV TEL. $199–475 double; suites from $650. Special midweek and package rates available. AE, DC, MC, V. Parking $10.

The most elegant hotel in town is also one of the most prestigious in the state, excelling in service since opening its doors in 1927. The award-winning Spanish Revival architecture is a graceful blend of arcades, winding staircases, patios, and walkways, with lovely hand-painted Mexican tiles and grillwork throughout. That beauty is further enhanced by imposing views of the Pacific, the Santa Ynez Mountains, and the hotel's own palm-studded formal gardens. The deluxe accommodations feature plush Iberian-style furnishings; many have romantic Spanish balconies and/or fireplaces, and some have private patios. All have ceiling fans, climate controls, terry robes, and hairdryers.

Dining/Entertainment: Elegant La Marina offers a select list of California-inspired specialties. The Patio, a glass-enclosed atrium, is more casual, serving three meals daily and Santa Barbara's best Sunday brunch. La Sala is a terrifically comfortable lounge serving afternoon tea and evening cocktails. There's live jazz on Wednesday and Friday nights.

Services: Concierge, 24-hour room service, overnight shoe shine, laundry services, nightly turndown, in-room movies.

Facilities: Two outdoor heated pools, three lighted tennis courts, two health clubs, putting green, shuffleboard and croquet courts, beachfront cabanas, sundeck, complimentary bicycle rental, special children's programs, beauty salon, and gift shop.

○ San Ysidro Ranch

900 San Ysidro Lane (off U.S. 101), Montecito, CA 93108. ☎ **805/969-5046** or 800/368-6788. Fax 805/565-1995. 45 cottages, 26 suites. MINIBAR TV TEL. $235–$385 double; $485–$560 cottage room; suites from $660. AE, MC, V.

Since 1940, when Vivien Leigh and Laurence Olivier were married here, San Ysidro Ranch has won raves as one of Southern California's most distinguished hotels. Over the years, guests from Groucho Marx to Winston Churchill signed the register at this quiet, beautifully landscaped 540-acre retreat; in 1953 John and Jacqueline Kennedy honeymooned here.

The hundred-year-old hotel is comprised of about a dozen free-standing cottages nestled near the base of their own private mountain. Rooms are decorated with charming country inn–style antiques. All have working fireplaces, most have private decks or patios, and some have outdoor hot tubs. Weddings are held most weekends in truly magnificent jasmine- and honeysuckle-edged gardens, which explode year-round with color.

Dining/Entertainment: The Stonehouse is a charming candlelit restaurant, which has stumbled through some recent chef changes but is still one of Santa Barbara's best. The Plow and Angel bar is a good place for drinks; there's live music on weekends.

Services: Concierge, room service.

Facilities: Outdoor heated pool, two tennis courts, badminton, croquet, hiking trails.

EXPENSIVE

The Upham

1404 De La Vina St. (at Sola St.), Santa Barbara, CA 93101. ☎ **805/962-0058** or 800/727-0876. Fax 805/963-2825. 49 rms, 3 suites. TV TEL. $120–$185 double; suites from $250. All rates include breakfast. AE, CB, DC, DISC, MC, V.

Located right in the heart of town, this is one of the oldest and most charming hotels in Santa Barbara. The two-story clapboard structure, reminicent of an old-fashioned New England boardinghouse, has wide eaves, a glassed-in cupola, a widow's walk facing the sea. Rooms are outfitted with antique armoires, brass or four-poster beds, and pretty textiles; many have private porches and fireplaces. Complimentary wine, cheese, and crackers are served in the lobby and garden each afternoon. Louie's at the Upham, a cozy restaurant, is open for lunch and dinner.

MODERATE

Bath Street Inn

1720 Bath St. (north of Valerio St.), Santa Barbara, CA 93101. ☎ **805/682-9680** or 800/341-BATH; 800/549-BATH in California. 12 rms. $95–$175 double. All rates include breakfast. AE, MC, V.

This handsome Victorian inn has two unusual features—a semicircular "eyelid" balcony and a hipped roof, unique even for Santa Barbara. Century-old trees, a flower-filled patio with white wicker furniture, a brick courtyard, and the graciousness of the innkeepers are all part of the inn's charm. The living room is the comfortable and inviting hearth of the home. Each individually decorated room has its own special charm: One features a queen-size pencil post bed; from another, you can enjoy superb sunsets from a private balcony. Guests enjoy complimentary evening wine and cheese and afternoon tea. No smoking is allowed in the house.

Best Western Encina Lodge & Suites

2220 Bath St. (at Los Olivos St.), Santa Barbara, CA 93105. ☎ **805/682-7277** or 800/526-2262. Fax 805/563-9319. 121 rms, 38 suites. A/C TV TEL. $118–$128 double; suites from $126. AE, CB, DC, DISC, MC, V. Free parking.

Set in a quiet residential area, this hotel is a short walk from the mission and a five-minute drive from the beach. All rooms are immaculate and tastefully decorated. Furnishings, bedspreads, rugs all look spanking new. Second-floor rooms in the old building, outfitted with beamed raw-pine ceilings, are best. All rooms come with coffeemakers, hairdryers, fresh fruit, candies, and cookies. Old-wing rooms have showers only; the rest have tub/shower combinations and dressing rooms. Facilities include a pool, whirlpool, sauna, lobby shop, beauty parlor, and barbershop. There's also complimentary airport and Amtrak pickup.

Miramar Hotel-Resort

1555 S. Jameson Lane (San Ysidro exit off U.S. 101), (P.O. Box 429), Montecito, CA 93102. ☎ **805/969-2203.** Fax 805/969-3163. 160 rms, 40 suites. A/C TV TEL. $75–$145 double; cottage suites from $130. AE, MC, V.

The Miramar's blue-roofed cottages have long been a famous area landmark. The modern Miramar is set on 14 garden acres overlooking the Pacific Ocean. Guest rooms are nondescript but comfortable; the best ones are oceanfront on the second floor, though train tracks are just steps away. Some of the attractive, homey cottages have fully equipped kitchens. Facilities include two pools, four tennis courts, a paddle-tennis court, 500 feet of private sandy beach, saunas, exercise rooms, bike rental, and table tennis. Golf and horseback riding are nearby. There's a dated restaurant, a coffee shop, and live music Thursday through Saturday nights in the Santa Fe–Amtrak Railcar Diner.

Tropicana Inn and Suites

223 Castillo St. (between Montecito and Yanonali sts.), Santa Barbara, CA 93101. ☎ **805/966-2219** or 800/468-1988. Fax 805/962-9428. 31 rms, 16 suites. TV TEL. $90–$122 double; suites $122–$199. Additional person $5 extra. All rates include continental breakfast. AE, DISC, MC, V.

This recently renovated pink-stucco structure is just a short walk from the beach. The rooms are homey, attractive, and equipped with refrigerators. The suites, which have a large bedroom, a living room, and a large, fully equipped eat-in kitchen, accommodate up to eight adults. Facilities include a heated pool and Jacuzzi, both of which are away from the street and very private. No smoking is allowed in the rooms.

INEXPENSIVE

⑤ Franciscan Inn

109 Bath St. (near Mason St.), Santa Barbara, CA 93101. ☎ **805/963-8845.** Fax 805/564-3295. 53 rms, 25 suites. TV TEL $65–$95 double; suites from $100. Additional person $8 extra. All rates include breakfast. AE, CB, DC, MC, V. Free parking.

This excellent choice is just off Cabrillo Boulevard, one short block from the marina and beach. Each individually decorated room is airy, comfortable, and spacious; most have ceiling fans. Bathrooms come stocked with thick, fluffy towels. Several rooms have fully equipped kitchenettes. Suites are split-level, complete with a living room, a separate kitchen, and sleeping quarters for up to four adults; one has a fireplace. Breakfast is served in the comfortable lobby. There's a heated pool, Jacuzzi, and coin-operated laundry; complimentary newspapers are distributed every morning. Reservations should be made well in advance, especially for May through September.

Motel 6

443 Corona del Mar (east of Milpas St.), Santa Barbara, CA 93103. ☎ **805/564-1392.** 52 rms. TV TEL. $52 double. AE, DISC, MC, V. Free parking.

If you're looking for clean, inexpensive accommodations near the beach, this basic motel fits the bill. There's a small heated pool. Reserve far in advance, as this place books up quickly.

Mountain View Inn

3055 De La Vina St. (at State St.), Santa Barbara, CA 93105. ☎ **805/687-6636.** 34 rms. TV TEL. Late Sept–May, $60–$75 double. June–early Sept, $75–$87 double. Two-night minimum on weekends. Rates include continental breakfast. AE, DISC, MC, V.

Although it's on a busy street corner, this well-priced inn maintains a hometown bed-and-breakfast atmosphere. Each individually decorated room is bright and cheery, outfitted both with niceties (fresh flowers) and necessities (small refrigerators). The inn surrounds a large heated pool, and is adjacent to a small park with a children's playground. Coffee, tea, juice, and croissants are served each morning in the lobby.

❺ Sandpiper Lodge

3525 State St. (west of Las Positas), Santa Barbara, CA 93105. ☎ **805/687-5326.** Fax 805/687-2271. 75 rms. TV TEL. Nov–Apr, $49–$59 double, $59–$69 triple; May–Oct, $69–$79 double, $79–$99 triple. Weekly rates available. AE, CB, DC, MC, V. Free parking.

Modest accommodations at low rates make this small hotel one of Santa Barbara's best buys. Nothing's fancy here, but the rooms are clean and tastefully (if sparsely) decorated; some have small refrigerators. Coffee and tea are available all day. There's also a pool. You'll have to drive to the beach and downtown shopping areas, but both are just 10 minutes away.

WHERE TO DINE
MODERATE

❻ Brophy Bros. Clam Bar & Restaurant

Yacht basin and marina at Harbor Way. ☎ **805/966-4418.** Reservations not accepted. Main courses $9–$16. AE, MC, V. Sun–Thurs 11am–10pm, Fri–Sat 11am–11pm. SEAFOOD.

I'm reluctant to spill the beans on one of my favorite restaurants in Santa Barbara. First-class seafood is served in beautiful surroundings that overlook the city's lovely marina. Dress is casual, service is excellent, and it's hard to beat the view. The restaurant is a convivial mix of locals and tourists almost every night of the week. Portions are huge, and everything on the menu is good. Favorites include New England clam chowder, cioppino (California fish stew), and any one of an assortment of seafood salads. The scampi is consistently good, as is all the fresh fish. A nice assortment of beers and wines is available. But be forewarned: The wait at this small place can be up to two hours on a weekend night.

Joe's Cafe

536 State St. (at Cota St.). ☎ **805/966-4638.** Reservations not accepted on Sat. Main courses $9–$17. AE, MC, V. Mon–Thurs 11am–11:30pm, Fri–Sat 11am–12:30am, Sun noon–9pm. AMERICAN.

Joe's food is not great, but there's something about this down-home eatery that's very alluring. Maybe it's the strong mixed drinks? One of downtown's longest-lived institutions, Joe's has been offering home cooking since 1928: southern-style fried chicken, hefty 12-ounce charcoal-broiled steaks, and pan-fried rainbow trout are menu staples. And every Wednesday seems like Thanksgiving as the kitchen turns out plate after plate of turkey, mashed potatoes, cranberry sauce, and stuffing. More modern offerings include a chicken caesar and a garden burger.

Oysters

Victoria Court, 9 W. Victoria St. (at State St.). ☎ **805/962-9888.** Reservations recommended on weekends. Main courses $11–$17; lunch $5–$7. AE, DC, DISC,

MC, V. Tues–Sat 11:30am–2:30pm; Tues–Thurs, and Sun 5–9pm, Fri–Sat 5–10pm. CALIFORNIAN.

Hidden behind lush bushes near State Street, Oysters' small, oddly shaped, window-wrapped dining room serves some of the best food in the city. Despite its name, this isn't a shellfish bar; California cuisine is offered by Jerry and Laurie Wilson, a brother-and-sister team. Still, oyster appetizers are on the menu: grilled with cilantro butter, chopped into corn fritters, and stewed with spinach and shallots. The best main courses are usually the daily fresh market specials, like pumpernickel-crusted sea bass with asparagus cream; and Spanish rice with clams, mussels, chicken sausage, shrimp, and scallops. For dessert, even the richest chocolate torte should be passed up for the restaurant's home-churned ice cream.

✪ Pan e Vino

1482 E. Valley Rd., Montecito. ☎ **805/969-9274.** Reservations required. Pastas $8–$10; meat and fish dishes $11–$18. AE, MC, V. Mon–Sat 11:30am–9:30pm, Sun 5–9:30pm. ITALIAN.

Allow me to wax philosophical about my favorite restaurant in Santa Barbara: It's the perfect Italian trattoria, with food as good as you'd find in Rome, and surroundings that are far better. The simplest dish, spaghetti topped with basil-tomato sauce, is so delicious it's hard to understand why diners would want to occupy their tastebuds with more complicated concoctions. But this kitchen is capable of most anything. A whole artichoke appetizer, steamed, chilled, and filled with breading and marinated tomatoes, is absolutely fantastic. Pasta puttanesca, with tomatoes, anchovies, black olives, and capers, is always tops. Pan e Vino gets high marks for its terrific food, attentive service, and authentic and casual atmosphere. Although many diners prefer to eat outside on the intimate patio, my favorite tables are in the cluttered, charm-filled dining room.

Paradise Cafe

702 Anacapa St. (one block east of State St. at Ortega). ☎ **805/962-4416.** Reservations accepted only for parties of five or more. Main courses $8–$18; breakfast $5–$9; lunch $7–$11. AE, MC, V. Mon–Sat 11am–11pm, Sun 8:30am–11pm. AMERICAN.

The relaxed elegance here is quintessential Santa Barbara. The most coveted seats are on the open brick patio. Excellent salmon, swordfish, half-pound burgers, and 22-ounce T-bone steaks are prepared on an open oak grill. Meals here are consistently fresh and simple. Paradise Pie, an extremely decadent chocolate dessert, is an absolute must.

Your Place

22A N. Milpas St. (at Mason St.). ☎ **805/966-5151.** Reservations recommended on weekends. Main courses $7–$13. AE, DC, MC, V. Tues–Thurs and Sun 11am–10pm, Fri–Sat 11am–11pm. THAI.

There are an unusually large number of Thai restaurants in Santa Barbara, but when locals argue about which one is best, Your Place invariably ranks high on the list. Traditional dishes are prepared with the freshest ingredients and represent a wide cross-section of Thai cuisine. It's best to begin with tom kah kai, a hot-and-sour chicken soup with coconut milk and mushrooms, ladled out of a hotpot tableside, enough for two or more. Siamese duckling, a top main dish, is prepared with sautéed vegetables, mushrooms, and ginger sauce. Like other dishes, it can be made mild, medium, hot, or very hot. There's wine, sake, beer, and a variety of nonalcoholic drinks, including hot ginger tea.

INEXPENSIVE

Andersen's Danish Bakery and Restaurant

1106 State St. (near Figueroa St.). ☎ **805/962-5085.** Reservations recommended on weekends. Breakfast $4–$9; lunch $5–$10. No credit cards. Wed–Mon 8am–6pm. DANISH.

Only tourists eat here, but this small place is eminently suited to people watching or reading the day's paper. You'll spot it by the red-and-white Amstel umbrellas over wrought-iron garden tables and chairs. The food is both good and well presented. Portions are substantial, and the coffee is outstanding. And if you yearn for smorgasbord, Andersen's is a first-rate choice. Wine is available by the bottle or glass; beer is also served.

✪ Cuca's

315 Meigs Rd. ☎ **805/966-5951.** Reservations not accepted. Tacos $3–$4; burritos $3–$5. No credit cards. Daily 10am–10pm. MEXICAN.

Around lunchtime, it's hard to find a single seat at any of the half-dozen outdoor tables. Cuca's extra-large, brick-weight burritos are packed solid with chicken or beef, rice, beans, and avocado. The excellent vegetarian version, made with stir-fried vegetables, suggests a giant egg roll and would be heralded as "genius" if it showed up on one of Wolfgang Puck's menus.

Cuca's is atop an elevated area known as "The Mesa." There's a second Cuca's at 626 W. Micheltorena (☎ **805/962-4028**).

Don Pepe

617 State St. ☎ **805/962-4495.** Reservations not accepted. Main courses $5–$8; tacos and burritos $2–$4; breakfast $3–$5. MC, V. Sun–Thurs 8am–11pm, Fri–Sat 8am–2am. MEXICAN.

This full-service restaurant serves traditional Mexican dishes to Mexican and American workers and a few adventurous tourists. Every meal starts with freshly made tortilla chips; most come with rice, beans, and salad. Main dishes include whole fish cooked in garlic butter and grilled shrimp with wine and olives; there are also meat or fish burritos. My favorite dish, chicken mole, isn't on the menu, but it's always available.

La Super-Rica Taqueria

622 N. Milpas St. (between Cota and Ortega sts.). ☎ **805/963-4940.** Reservations not accepted. Main courses $3–$6. No credit cards. Sun–Thurs 11am–9:30pm, Fri–Sat 11am–10pm. MEXICAN.

Following celebrity chef Julia Child's lead, aficionados have deemed this place the state's best Mexican eatery. Excellent soft tacos are the restaurant's real forte; filled with any combination of chicken, beef, cheese, cilantro, and spices, they make a good meal. My primary complaint about the place is that the portions are quite small; you have to order two or three items in order to satisfy average hunger. There's nothing grand about La Super-Rica except the food; you might want to get your food to go and take it to the beach.

Santa Barbara Roasting Company

321 Motor Way. ☎ **805/962-0320.** Coffee $1.25; pastries $1–$2.50. AE, DISC, MC, V. Daily 7am–midnight. CAFE.

The RoCo is a morning ritual for what seems like half of Santa Barbara—and for good reason. The strongly brewed beans are freshly roasted on the premises, and your choice of regular or unleaded is served bottomless. This is the coffee I dream of when I'm away; I can't say the same for their baked goods, which used to be better.

3 Santa Catalina Island

22 miles W of mainland Los Angeles

Catalina is a small, cove-fringed island famous for its laid-back inns, largely unspoiled landscape, and crystal-clear waters. Because of its relative isolation, tourists tend to stay away; but those who do show up have plenty of elbow room to boat, fish, swim, scuba, and snorkel. There are miles of hiking and biking trails, and golf, tennis, and horseback-riding facilities abound.

Catalina is so different from the mainland that it almost seems like a different country, remote and unspoiled. In 1915 the island was purchased by William Wrigley, Jr., the chewing gum manufacturer, in order to develop a fashionable pleasure resort. To publicize the new vacationland, Wrigley brought big-name bands to the Avalon Ballroom and moved the Chicago Cubs, which he owned, to the island for spring training. His marketing efforts succeeded, and this charming and tranquil retreat became—and still is—a favorite vacation resort for mainlanders.

ESSENTIALS

GETTING THERE

By Plane   Valley Executive Charter (☎ 310/982-1575) flies from the Long Beach Municipal Airport (4100 Donald Douglas Dr., Long Beach; ☎ 310/421-8293) to Catalina's Airport in the Sky (☎ 310/510-1403). Tickets are $300 per person. Taxis and buses meet each flight in Catalina.

By Helicopter   Island Express Helicopter Service (900 Queens Way Dr., Long Beach; ☎ 310/510-2525; fax 310/510-9671) flies from Long Beach to Catalina in about 15 minutes. They fly on demand, charging $60 each way.

By Boat   This is the most common way to get to and from Catalina. The **Catalina Express** (☎ 310/519-1212) operates up to 20 daily departures year-round to Catalina from San Pedro and Long Beach. The trip takes about an hour. One-way fares from San Pedro are $17.75 for adults, $16 for seniors, $13 for children 2 to 11, and $1 for infants. Long Beach fares are about $2 higher for all except infants, who are still charged $1. The trip is an additional $1.80 if you travel to Two Harbors. The *Catalina Express* departs from the Sea/Air Terminal at Berth 95, Port of L.A. in San Pedro; the *Catalina Express* port at the *Queen Mary* in Long Beach; and from the *Catalina Express* port at 161 N. Harbor Drive in Redondo Beach. Call for information and reservations.

Note: There are specific baggage restrictions on the *Catalina Express.* Luggage is limited to 50 pounds per person; reservations are necessary for bicycles, surfboards, and dive tanks; and there are restrictions on transporting domestic pets. Call for information.

ORIENTATION

The picturesque town of Avalon is the island's only city. Named for a passage in Tennyson's *Idylls of the King,* Avalon is also the port of entry for the island. From the ferry dock you can wander along Crescent Avenue, the main road along the beachfront, and easily explore adjacent side streets.

Visitors are not allowed to drive cars on the island. There are only a limited number of autos on the island; most residents motor around in golf carts (many of the homes only have golf cart–sized driveways). But don't worry—you'll be able to get everywhere you want to go. About 86% of the island remains undeveloped. It's owned by the Santa Catalina Island Conservancy, which endeavors to preserve the island's natural resources.

The **Catalina Island Chamber of Commerce and Visitor's Bureau** (P.O. Box 217, Avalon, CA 90704; ☎ **310/510-1520;** fax 310/ 510-7606), located on the Green Pleasure Pier, distributes brochures and information on island activities, including sightseeing tours, camping, hiking, fishing, and boating. It also offers information on hotels and boat and helicopter transport. Write for an extremely useful free 100-page visitor's guide.

The Santa Catalina Island Company–run **Visitor's Information Center,** which is just across from the chamber of commerce, on Crescent Avenue (☎ **310/510-2000**), handles hotel reservations, sightseeing tours, and other island activities.

WHAT TO SEE & DO

Avalon Casino and Catalina Island Museum

At the end of Crescent Ave. ☎ **310/510-2414.** Admission $1 adults, children under 12 free. Daily 10:30am–4pm.

The Avalon Casino is the most famous structure on the island, and one of its oldest. Built in 1929 as a vacation resort, its massive circular rotunda, topped with a red-tiled roof, is the building's most famous feature. The Avalon Casino is widely known for its beautiful art deco ballroom, which once hosted such top bands as the Tommy Dorsey and Glen Miller orchestras. You can see the inside of the building by attending a ballroom event or a film (the Casino is Avalon's primary movie theater). Otherwise, admission is by guided tour only, operated daily by the Santa Catalina Island Company (see "Organized Tours," below).

The **Catalina Island Museum,** located on the ground floor of the Casino, features exhibits on island history, archeology, and natural history. The small museum also has an excellent relief map that details the island's interior.

Avalon Pleasure Pier

Crescent Ave. and Catalina St., Avalon.

Jutting out into Crescent Cove, the wood-plank pier offers excellent views of the town and surrounding mountains. Food stands and bait-and-tackle shops line the pier, selling fish to eat and cast.

Lover's Cove

At the end of Crescent Ave., Avalon.

One of Catalina's top draws is its crystal-clear waters and abundant sea life. Lover's Cove is filled with colorful fish and rich kelp beds. Several Avalon companies rent scuba and snorkeling equipment. **Santa Catalina Island Company,** Avalon Harbor Pier (☎ **800/626-7489**), offers glass-bottom-boat tours every hour daily from 11am to 4pm. The trip takes about 40 minutes and costs $7.50 for adults and $3.75 for children. The company also offers tours of the underworld in their new semisubmersible submarine. This 60-foot, 50-ton vessel allows visitors to see panoramic underwater views. The trip costs $18 for adults and $12 for children. Call for times.

ORGANIZED TOURS

The **Santa Catalina Island Company's Discovery Tours** (Avalon Harbor Pier; ☎ **800/626-7489**) operates several motorcoach excursions that depart from the tour plaza in the center of town on Sumner Avenue.

The Skyline Drive tour basically follows the perimeter of the island and takes about 1³/₄ hours. Trips leave several times a day from 11am to 3pm and cost $18 for adults, $16 for seniors, and $10 for children 3 to 11.

The Inland Motor Tour is more comprehensive; it includes some of the 66 square miles of preserve owned by the Santa Catalina Island Conservancy. You'll see El Rancho Escondido, and probably have a chance to view buffalo, deer, goats, and boars. Tours, which take about 3³/₄ hours, leave at 9am; from June to October, they leave at other times. Tours are $27.50 for adults, $24.50 for seniors, and $14.50 for children 3 to 11; free for children under 3.

Other excursions offered by the company include the 40-minute Casino Tour, which explores Catalina's most famous landmark; the 50-minute Avalon Scenic Tour, a nine-mile introductory tour of the town; and the one-hour Flying Fish Boat Trip, during which an occasional flying fish lands right on the boat.

Check with the Catalina Island Company for other tour offerings, as well as for information on various dining cruises.

WHERE TO STAY

Catalina's 30 or so independent hotels are beautifully situated and maintain an almost affected unpretentiousness—they seem to go out of their way not to be quaint or charming. But don't worry; there's nary an eyesore on the entire island. If you do plan to stay overnight, be sure to reserve a room in advance; hotels regularly reach 100% occupancy, especially on weekends.

EXPENSIVE

✪ The Inn on Mt. Ada

398 Wrigley Rd., P.O. Box 2560, Avalon, CA 90704. ☎ **310/510-2030.** 6 rms, 2 suites. Weekends and June–Oct, $320–$490 double, $490–$590 suite. Mon–Thurs and Nov–May, $230–$370 double, $370–$470 suite. All rates include three meals. MC, V.

When William Wrigley, Jr., purchased Catalina Island in 1921, he built this remarkably ornate Georgian Colonial mansion as his summer vacation home. In 1985 several local residents signed a 30-year lease for the estate and lovingly transformed it into one of the finest small hotels in California. The opulent inn has several ground-floor salons, a fireplaced club room, a deep-seated formal library, and a wickered sun room where tea, cookies, and fruit are always available. The best guest room is the Grand Suite—once the master bedroom—fitted with a fireplace and a large private patio. Room 2 has a queen-size four-poster bed, a fireplace, and a sitting lounge with wingback chairs. Amenities include bathrobes; TVs are available on request. There are no telephones in the rooms. Rates include a hearty full breakfast, a light deli-style lunch, and a beautiful multicourse dinner complemented by a limited wine selection.

MODERATE

Catalina Canyon Hotel

888 Country Club Dr. (north of Tremont St.), Avalon, CA 90704. ☎ **310/510-0325** or 800/253-9361. Fax 310/510-0900. 80 rms. A/C TV TEL. $75–$135 double. AE, MC, V.

This hotel is set on beautifully landscaped grounds in the foothills of Avalon. The guest rooms are tastefully decorated and comfortably furnished; all have balconies overlooking the outdoor pool and Jacuzzi. No-smoking rooms are available. The Canyon Restaurant serves continental breakfast, lunch, and dinner. Room service is available. Cocktails may be enjoyed in the lounge or on the outdoor terrace overlooking the pool. The hotel is adjacent to a golf course and tennis courts. A courtesy van meets guests at the air and sea terminals.

Catalina Island Inn

125 Metropole (north of Crescent Ave.), P.O. Box 467, Avalon, CA 90704. ☎ **310/510-1623.** Fax 310/510-7218. 35 rms, 1 minisuite. TV TEL. May–Sept, holidays, and weekends year-round, $89–$179 double; $189 minisuite. Oct–Apr except holidays and weekends, $45–$99 double; $155 minisuite. All rates include continental breakfast. AE, DISC, MC, V.

Innkeepers Martin and Bernadine Curtin have created some of the most attractive accommodations in town. Shuttered windows and ceiling fans add further charm.

Hotel Macrae

409 Crescent Ave. (north of the Avalon Pleasure Pier), P.O. Box 1517, Avalon, CA 90704. ☎ **310/510-0246** or 800/698-2266. 23 rms. TEL. Summer, $90–$170 double. Winter, $50–$110 double. All rates include continental breakfast. MC, V.

This pleasant two-story hostelry is right across from the beach. Rooms are individually equipped with heaters for chilly nights. In the center of the bright, cheerful hotel is a large, open courtyard, perfect for lounging or sunning.

Zane Grey Pueblo Hotel

Off Chimes Tower Rd. (north of Hill St.), P.O. Box 216, Avalon, CA 90704. ☎ **310/510-0966** or 800/378-3256. 17 rms. June–Sept, $75–$125 double. Nov–Mar, $55 double. Rest of the year, $65–$85 double. Slightly higher on weekends and holidays. All rates include continental breakfast. AE, MC, V.

You'll have the most superb views on the island from here. This Shangri-la mountain retreat is the former home of novelist Zane Grey, who spent his last 20 years in Avalon. He wrote many books here, including *Tales of Swordfish and Tuna*, which tells of his fishing adventures off Catalina Island.

The hotel has teak beams that the novelist brought from Tahiti on one of his fishing trips. Most of the rooms also have large windows and ocean or mountain views. They have all been renovated with new furniture, carpeting, and ceiling fans. An outdoor patio has an excellent view. The original living room has a grand piano, a fireplace, and a TV. The hotel also has a pool and sundeck, with chairs overlooking Avalon and the ocean. Coffee is served all day, and there's a courtesy bus to town.

WHERE TO DINE
MODERATE

The Busy Bee

306 Crescent Ave. (north of Pleasure Pier), Avalon. ☎ **310/510-1983**. Reservations not accepted. Main courses $7–$15. AE, CB, DC, DISC, MC, V. Summer, daily 8am–10pm. Winter, daily 8am–8pm. AMERICAN.

The Busy Bee, an Avalon institution since 1923, is located right on the beach. The fare is light–deli style. The extensive menu offers breakfast, lunch, and dinner at all times. The restaurant grinds its own beef and cuts its own potatoes for french fries; salad dressings are also made on the premises. Even if you're not hungry, come here for a drink; it's Avalon's only waterfront bar.

El Galleon

411 Crescent Ave., Avalon. ☎ **310/510-1188**. Reservations recommended on weekends. Main courses $7–$18 at lunch, $11–$37 at dinner. AE, DISC, MC, V. Daily 11am–2:30pm and 5–10pm. Bar: daily 10am–1:30am. AMERICAN.

El Galleon is large, warm, and woody, complete with portholes, rigging, anchors, wrought-iron chandeliers, oversize leather booths, and tables with red-leather captain's chairs. There's additional balcony seating, plus outdoor cafe tables overlooking the ocean harbor. Lunch and dinner feature seafood. Favorite dinner dishes include fresh swordfish steak and broiled Catalina lobster tails in drawn butter. "Turf" main dishes range from country-fried chicken to broiled rack of lamb with mint jelly.

INEXPENSIVE
Sand Trap

Avalon Canyon Rd. (north of Tremont St.), Avalon. ☎ **310/510-1349.** Reservations not accepted. Main courses $4–$12. No credit cards. Daily 7:30am–3:30pm. CALIFORNIA/MEXICAN.

This local favorite is a great place to escape from the bayfront crowds. Enjoy breakfast, lunch, or snacks while overlooking the golf course. Specialties of the house include delectable omelets served until noon, and soft tacos served all day. Either can be made with any number of fillings. Burgers, sandwiches, salads, and chili are also served. Beer and wine are available.

---

4   Disneyland & Other Anaheim Area Attractions

27 miles SE of downtown Los Angeles

Disneyland is family entertainment at its best. But you don't have to be a kid to enjoy yourself here; whether you're wowed by Disney animation come alive, thrilled by the roller-coaster rides, or interested in the history and hidden secrets of this American icon, you won't walk away disappointed.

The sleepy Orange County town of Anaheim grew up around the West's most famous theme park. Now, Anaheim and its neighboring communities are kid central. Otherwise unspectacular, sprawling suburbs have become a playground of family-oriented hotels, restaurants, and unabashedly tourist-oriented attractions beyond the Happiest Place on Earth. Among the nearby draws are Knott's Berry Farm, another family-oriented theme park, in nearby Buena Park; at the other end of the scale is the Richard Nixon Library and Birthplace, a surprisingly compelling presidential library and museum, just seven miles from Disneyland in Yorba Linda.

ESSENTIALS
GETTING THERE

Los Angeles International Airport (LAX) is located about 30 minutes from Anaheim. If you're heading directly to Anaheim and want to avoid Los Angeles altogether, try to land at John Wayne International Airport (☎ **714/252-5200**) in Irvine, Orange County's largest airport. It's about 15 miles from Disneyland. The airport is served by Alaska, American, Continental, Delta, Northwest, TWA, and United airlines. Once you've landed, you'll have to rent a car to get to Disneyland.

AREA INFORMATION

The **Anaheim/Orange County Visitor and Convention Bureau** (800 W. Katella Ave., P.O. Box 4270, Anaheim, CA 92803; ☎ **714/ 999-8999**) can fill you in on area activities, beaches, and attractions, including Disneyland. The **Buena Park Convention and Visitors Office** (6280 Manchester Blvd., Suite 103; ☎ **714/562-3560** or 800/541-3953), will provide specialized information on their area, including Knott's Berry Farm.

DISNEYLAND

Disney was the originator of the mega–theme park. Opened in 1955, Disneyland remains unsurpassed. Despite constant threats from pretenders to the crown, Disneyland (and its sister park, Walt Disney World in Orlando, Florida) remains the King of the Theme Parks. At no other park is fantasy elevated to an art form. Nowhere else is as fresh and fantastic every time you walk through the gates, whether you're 6 or 60—and no matter how many times you've done it before. There's nothing else like Disney Magic.

The park stays on the cutting edge by continually updating and expanding, while still maintaining the hallmarks that make it the world's top amusement park (a term coined by Walt Disney himself). Look for the most recent Disney additions during your visit: Toontown, a new land added in 1993, and last year's Indiana Jones Adventure, a high-tech thrill that's not to be missed—no matter how long you have to wait in line. Also look for new shows, introduced last summer, based on Disney's most recent animated features, *The Lion King* and *Pocahontas.*

GETTING TO THE PARK

Disneyland is located at 1313 Harbor Boulevard in Anaheim. It's about an hour's drive from downtown Los Angeles. Take I-5 south to the well-marked Harbor Boulevard exit.

ADMISSION, HOURS & INFORMATION

Admission to the park, including unlimited rides and all festivities and entertainment, is $33 for adults and children over 12, $25 for seniors and children 3 to 11; children under 3 are free. Parking is $5.

Disneyland is open Monday to Friday 9am to 6pm and Saturday and Sunday from 9am to midnight from mid-September to May; and daily from 8am to 1am from June to mid-September, plus Thanksgiving, Christmas, and Easter.

For information, call **714/999-4565** or 213/626-8605, ext. 4565. If you've never been to Disneyland before and would like to get a copy of their *Souvenir Guide* to orient yourself to the park before you go, write to Disneyland Guest Relations, P.O. Box 3232, Anaheim, CA 92803. Or, pick up a copy of *The Unofficial Guide to Disneyland* (Macmillan) at your local bookstore.

TOURING THE PARK

The Disneyland complex is divided into several themed "lands," each of which has a number of rides and attractions that are, more or less, related to that land's theme.

Main Street U.S.A., at the park's entrance, is a cinematic version of turn-of-the-century small-town America. This whitewashed Rockwellian fantasy is lined with gift shops, candy stores, a soda fountain, and a silent theater that continuously runs early Mickey Mouse films. You'll find the practical things you might need here, too, such as stroller rentals and storage lockers. Because there are no rides here, it's best to tour Main Street during the middle of the afternoon, when lines for rides are longest, and in the evening, when you can rest your

Anaheim Area Attractions

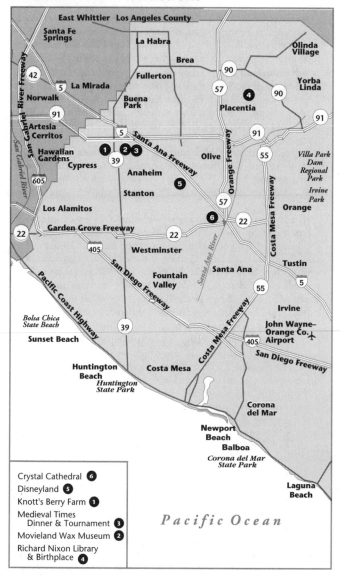

Crystal Cathedral **6**
Disneyland **5**
Knott's Berry Farm **1**
Medieval Times
  Dinner & Tournament **3**
Movieland Wax Museum **2**
Richard Nixon Library
  & Birthplace **4**

feet in the theater that features "Great Moments with Mr. Lincoln," a patriotic look at America's 16th president. There's always something happening on Main Street; stop in at the information booth to the left of the main entrance for a schedule of the day's events. The Main Street Electrical Parade is a spectacular mobile light show that takes place here daily just after sunset in summer months, followed by a short fireworks show.

You might start your day by circumnavigating the park by train. An authentic 19th-century steam engine pulls open-air cars around the park's perimeter. Board at the Main Street Depot and take a complete turn around the park, or disembark at any one of the lands.

Adventureland is inspired by most of the exotic regions of Asia, Africa, India, and the South Pacific. There are several popular rides here. This is where you'll find the Swiss Family Treehouse. On the Jungle Cruise, passengers board a large authentic-looking Mississippi River paddleboat and float along an Amazon-like river. En route, the boat is threatened by "animatronic" wild animals and hostile natives, while a tour guide entertains with a running patter. A spear's throw away is The Enchanted Tiki Room, one of the most sedate attractions in Adventureland. Inside, you can sit-down and watch a 20-minute musical comedy featuring electronically animated tropical birds, flowers, and "tiki gods."

The Indiana Jones Adventure is Adventureland's newest ride. Based on the Steven Spielberg series of films, this ride takes adventurers into the Temple of the Forbidden Eye, in the center of which lies a powerful Indian deity, "Mara." Getting to the middle is not so easy, however, as there is dense smoke, bubbling lava pits, crumbling ceilings, horrible bugs and snakes, and other booby traps along the way. Of course, there's also the gigantic rolling ball. One of the most high-tech rides ever built, its designers promise a different experience with each visit. And don't forget—you'd better not look into Mara's eyes.

New Orleans Square, a large, grassy, gaslamp-dotted green, is home to the Haunted Mansion, the most high-tech ghost house I've ever seen. The spookiness has been toned down so kids won't get nightmares anymore, so the events inside are as funny as they are scary. Even more fanciful is Pirates of the Caribbean, one of Disneyland's most popular rides. Here, visitors float on boats through mock underground caves, entering an enchanting world of wine, women, and song. Even in the middle of the afternoon you can dine by the cool moonlight and to the sound of crickets in the Blue Bayou Restaurant, the best eatery in the land.

Critter Country is supposed to be an ode to the backwoods—a sort of Frontierland without those pesky settlers. Little kids like to sing along with the animatronic critters in the musical Country Bear Jamboree show. Older kids and grown-ups head straight for Splash Mountain, one of the largest water flume rides in the world. Loosely based on the Disney movie *Song of the South*, the ride is lined with about 100 characters who won't stop singing "Zip-A-Dee-Doo-Dah." Be prepared to get wet, especially if someone sizable is in the front seat of your log-shaped boat.

Frontierland gets its inspiration from 19th-century America. It's full of dense "forests" and broad "rivers" inhabited by hearty looking (but, luckily, not smelling) "pioneers." You can take a raft to Tom Sawyer's Island, a do-it-yourself play island with balancing rocks, caves, and a rope bridge, and board the Big Thunder Mountain Railroad, a runaway roller coaster that races through a deserted 1870s gold mine. You'll also find a petting zoo and an Abe Lincoln–style log cabin here; both are great for exploring with the little ones.

Disney Dossier

Believe it or not, the Happiest Place on Earth holds more than a few skeletons—as well as some just plain interesting facts—in its closet. Did you know that:

- Disneyland was carved out of orange groves; original plans called for carefully chosen individual trees to be left standing and included in the park's landscaping. On groundbreaking day, July 21, 1954, each tree in the orchard was marked with a ribbon—red to be cut and green to be spared. But the bulldozer operator went through and mowed down *every* tree indiscriminately . . . no one had foreseen his color-blindness.

- Disneyland designers utilized forced perspective in the construction of many of the park's structures to give the illusion of height and dramatic proportions while keeping the park a manageable size. The buildings on **Main Street U.S.A.,** for example, are actually 90% scale on the first floor, 80% on the second, and so forth. The stones on **Sleeping Beauty Castle** are carved in diminishing scale from the bottom to the top, giving it the illusion of towering height.

- The faces of the **Pirates Of the Caribbean** were modeled after some of the early staff of Walt Disney Imagineering, who also lent their names to the second-floor "businesses" along **Main Street U.S.A.**

- Walt Disney maintained two apartments inside Disneyland. His private apartment above the Town Square Fire Station has been kept just as it was when he lived there.

- The elaborately carved horses on Fantasyland's **King Arthur Carousel** are between 100 and 120 years old; Walt Disney found them lying neglected in storage at Coney Island, and brought them home to be carefully cleaned and restored.

- **It's A Small World** was touted at its opening as "mingling the waters of the oceans and seas around the world with Small World's Seven Seaways." This was more than a publicity hoax—records from that time show such charges as $21.86 for a shipment of seawater from the Caribbean.

- The peaceful demeanor of Disneyland was broken during the summer of 1970 by a group of radical Vietnam protesters who invaded the park. They seized **Tom Sawyer Island** and raised the Viet Cong flag over the fort before being expelled by riot specialists.

- **Indiana Jones: Temple Of The Forbidden Eye,** Disneyland's newest attraction, won't be experienced the same way by any two groups of riders. Like a sophisticated computer game, the course is programmed with so many variables in the action that there are 160,000 possible combinations of events.

—*Stephanie Avnet*

Disneyland

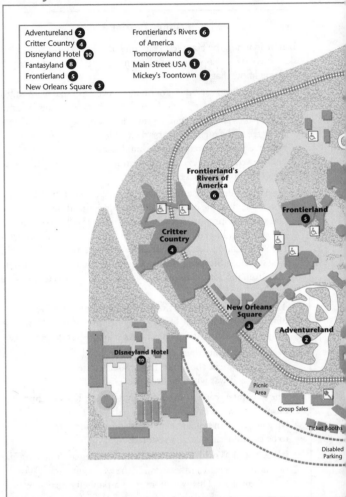

Adventureland ②	Frontierland's Rivers ⑥
Critter Country ④	of America
Disneyland Hotel ⑩	Tomorrowland ⑨
Fantasyland ⑧	Main Street USA ①
Frontierland ⑤	Mickey's Toontown ⑦
New Orleans Square ③	

Frontierland's Rivers of America ⑥

Frontierland ⑤

Critter Country ④

New Orleans Square ③

Adventureland ②

Disneyland Hotel ⑩

Picnic Area

Group Sales

Ticket Booths

Disabled Parking

On Saturdays, Sundays, holidays, and vacation periods, head to Frontierland's Rivers of America after dark to see the FANTASMIC! show—a mix of magic, music, live performers, and sensational special effects. Just as he did in *Sorcerer's Apprentice*, Mickey Mouse appears and uses his magical powers to create giant water fountains, enormous flowers, and fantasy creatures. There's plenty of pyrotechnics, lasers, and fog, as well as a 45-foot-tall dragon that breaths fire and sets the water of the Rivers of America aflame. Cool.

Mickey's Toontown, opened in 1993, is a colorful, wacky, whimsical world inspired by the *Roger Rabbit* films. This is a gag-filled land

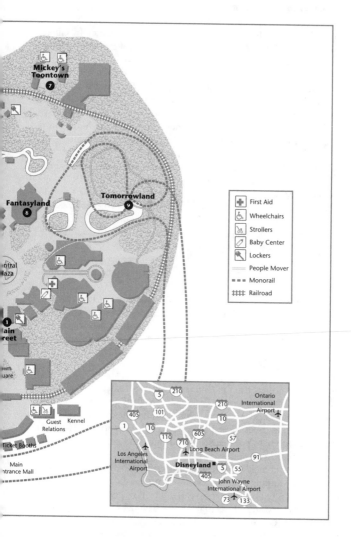

Mickey's Toontown
❼

Fantasyland
❽

Tomorrowland
❾

➕	First Aid
♿	Wheelchairs
👶	Strollers
✏	Baby Center
🔍	Lockers
‒‒‒	People Mover
▪▪▪	Monorail
┼┼┼	Railroad

Central Plaza

❶
Main Street

own quare

Guest Relations Kennel

Ticket Booths

Main ntrance Mall

Los Angeles International Airport

Long Beach Airport

Disneyland ■

John Wayne International Airport

Ontario International Airport

populated by toons. There are several rides here, including Roger Rabbit's CarToonSpin, but these take a backseat to Toontown itself— a trippy, smile-inducing world without a straight line or right angle in sight. This is a great place to talk with Mickey, Minnie, Goofy, Roger Rabbit, and the rest of your favorite toons. You can even visit their "houses" here. Mickey's red-shingled house and movie barn is filled with props from some of his greatest cartoons.

Fantasyland has a storybook theme and is the catch-all "land" for all the stuff that doesn't quite seem to fit anywhere else. Most of the rides here are geared to the under-six set, including the King Arthur

Carousel, Dumbo the Flying Elephant ride, and the Casey Jr. Circus Train, but some, like Mr. Toad's Wild Ride and Peter Pan's Flight, grown-ups have an irrational attachment to as well. You'll also find Alice in Wonderland, Snow White's Scary Adventures, Pinocchio's Daring Journey, and more in Fantasyland. The most lauded attraction is It's a Small World, a slow-moving indoor river ride through a saccharine nightmare of all the world's children singing the song everybody loves to hate. For a different kind of thrill, try the Matterhorn Bobsleds, a zippy roller coaster through chilled caverns and drifting fog banks. It's one of the park's most popular rides.

Tomorrowland may now seem a bit dated, but it still offers some of the park's best attractions. Space Mountain, a pitch-black indoor roller coaster, is one of Disneyland's best rides. Captain EO, a 3-D motion picture musical, is a space adventure starring Michael Jackson. Star Tours, the original Disney/George Lucas joint venture, is a 40-passenger StarSpeeder that encounters a spaceload of misadventures on the way to the Moon of Endor; the line can last an hour or more, but it's worth the wait. In addition to all this, you can take a dive in a submarine and soar in a rocket jet in Tomorrowland; there's also a huge video arcade.

The "lands" themselves are only half the adventure. Other joys include roaming Disney characters, penny arcades, restaurants and snack bars galore, summer fireworks, mariachi and ragtime bands, parades, shops, marching bands, and much more. Oh yeah—there's also the storybook Sleeping Beauty Castle.

DISNEY TIPS

Disneyland is busiest from mid-June to mid-September, and on weekends and holidays year-round. Peak hours are from noon to 5pm; plan on seeing the most popular rides before and after these hours and you'll cut your waiting times substantially. If you plan on arriving during a busy time, purchase your tickets in advance and get a jump on the crowds at the ticket counters.

Many visitors tackle Disneyland systematically, beginning at the entrance and working their way clockwise around the park. But a better plan of attack is to arrive early and run to the most popular rides first— the Indiana Jones Adventure, Star Tours, Space Mountain, Big Thunder Mountain Railroad, Splash Mountain, the Haunted Mansion, and Pirates of the Caribbean. Lines for these rides can last an hour or more in the middle of the day.

KNOTT'S BERRY FARM

Cynics say that Knott's Berry Farm is for people who aren't smart enough to find Disneyland. Well, there's no doubt that visitors should tour Disney first, but it's worth staying in a hotel nearby so you can tour Knott's the following day.

Like Disneyland, Knott's Berry Farm is not without its historical merit. Rudolph Boysen crossed a loganberry with a raspberry, calling the resulting hybrid the "boysenberry." In 1933 Buena Park farmer Walter Knott planted the boysenberry, thus launching Knott's Berry farm on 10 acres of leased land. When things got tough during the

Great Depression, Mrs. Knott set up a roadside stand, selling pies, preserves, and home-cooked chicken dinners. Within a year, she was selling 90 meals a day. Lines became so long that Walter decided to create an Old West Ghost Town as a diversion for waiting customers.

The Knott family now owns the farm that surrounds the world-famous Chicken Dinner Restaurant, an eatery serving over a million fried meals a year. And Knott's Berry Farm is the nation's third-best-attended family entertainment complex (after the two Disney parks, of course).

GETTING TO THE PARK

Knott's Berry Farm is located at 8039 Beach Boulevard in Buena Park. It's about an hour's drive from downtown Los Angeles, and about a five-minute ride north on I-5 from Disneyland. From I-5 or Calif. 91, exit south onto Beach Boulevard. The park is located about half a mile south of Calif. 91.

ADMISSION, HOURS & INFORMATION

Admission to the park, including unlimited access to all rides, shows, and attractions, is $28.50 for adults and children over 12, $18.50 for seniors over 60 and children ages 3 to 11, free for children under 3. Admission is $14.25 for everyone after 4pm. Knott's Berry Farm is open during the summer Monday through Thursday from 9am to 11pm, and Friday through Sunday from 9am to midnight. The rest of the year, the park is open from Monday through Thursday from 10am to 6pm, and Friday through Sunday from 10am to 10pm.

For information, call 714/827-1776, or 714/220-5200 for a recording. Closing times may vary from those listed above, so inquire when you call.

TOURING THE PARK

Knott's Berry Farm still maintains its original Old West motif. It's divided into five "Old Time Adventures" areas.

Old West Ghost Town, the original attraction, is a collection of refurbished 19th-century buildings that have been relocated from actual deserted Old West towns. Here, you can pan for gold, ride aboard an authentic stagecoach, ride rickety train cars through the Calico Mine, get held up aboard the Denver and Rio Grande Calico Railroad, and hiss at the villain during a melodrama in the Birdcage Theater.

Fiesta Village has a south-of-the-border theme that means festive markets, strolling mariachis, and wild rides like Montezooma's Revenge and Jaguar!, a huge new rollercoaster that includes two heart-in-the-mouth drops and a loop that turns you upside down. The ride's swerving route covers much of the park, careening within inches of the Timber Mountain Log Ride. In deference to its namesake, Jaguar! is meant to give riders the feeling of a cat stalking its prey as the trains speed up and slow down—simulating the sensation of a jungle hunt.

The Roaring '20s Amusement Area contains Sky Tower, one of the park's most thrilling rides. A parachute jump drops riders into a 20-story free fall. Other white-knuckle rides include XK-1, an excellent flight simulator "piloted" by the riders; and Boomerang, a state-of-the-art roller coaster that turns riders upside down six times in less than a minute. Kingdom of the Dinosaurs features extremely re-alistic Jurassic Park–like creatures. It's quite a thrill, but it may scare the little kids. For some lighthearted relief, there's a huge arcade right outside the entrance to the Kingdom.

Wild Water Wilderness is a $10-million, $3^{1}/_{2}$-acre attraction styled like a turn-of-the-century California wilderness park. The top ride here is a white-water adventure called Bigfoot Rapids, featuring a long stretch of artificial rapids; it's the longest ride of its kind in the world.

Camp Snoopy will probably be the little ones' favorite area. It's meant to re-create a wilderness camp in the picturesque High Sierra. Its six rustic acres are the playing grounds of Charles Schulz's beloved beagle and his pals, Charlie Brown and Lucy, who greet guests and pose for pictures. The rides here, including Beary Tales Playhouse, are tailor made for the six-and-under set.

Thunder Falls, Knott's newest area, contains Mystery Lodge, a truly amazing high-tech, trick-of-the-eye attraction based on the legends of local Native Americans. Don't miss this wonderful theater piece.

Stage shows and special activities are scheduled throughout the day. Pick up a schedule at the ticket booth.

WHAT TO SEE & DO BEYOND THE THEME PARKS

Crystal Cathedral

12141 Lewis St., Garden Grove. ☎ **714/971-4013.**

This angular, mirror-sheathed church, otherwise known as the Garden Grove Community Church, is a shocking architectural oddity, with nine-story-high doors, and a vast, open interior that's shaped like a four-pointed star. Opened in 1980, it's the pulpit for televangelist Robert Schuller. The Crystal Cathedral broadcasts hymns of praise on radio and television to an international audience of millions. Each Sunday the church attracts an overflow crowd that listens to the church service from the parking lot, where it blares over loudspeakers. Annual Christmas and Easter pageants feature live animals, floating "angels," and other theatrics. A $5 million stainless-steel carillon, which began ringing in 1991, has prompted some of the Cathedral's neighbors to complain that they want less joyful noise and more peace on earth.

Medieval Times Dinner & Tournament

7662 Beach Blvd., Buena Park. ☎ **714/521-4740** or 800/899-6600. Admission Sun–Fri $33–$36 adults, $23 children 12 and under. Shows Mon–Thurs at 7pm, Fri at 6:30 and 8:45pm, Sat at 6 and 8:15pm, Sun at 2 and 5pm. Times can vary, so call for the latest information.

Basically, Medieval Times is a dinner show for those of us who were unlucky enough (or lucky enough, depending on your point of view) not to have been born into a royal family in 11th-century Europe (though many Californians claim to have been—in a former life). Guests crowd around long wooden tables and enjoy a four-course ban-quet of roast chicken, ribs, herbed potatoes, and pastries—all eaten with your hands, of course. More than 1,100 people can fit into the castle, where sword fights, jousting tournaments, and various feats of skill are performed by colorfully costumed actors, including fake knights on real horseback. It's kind of ridiculous, but kids love it; Medieval Times is extremely popular year-round.

Movieland Wax Museum

7711 Beach Blvd. (Calif. 39), Buena Park. ☎ **714/522-1155.** Admission $12.95 adults, $10.55 seniors, $6.95 children 4–11, free for children under 4. Daily 9am–7pm. Free parking.

In this goofy museum, located one block north of Knott's Berry Farm in Buena Park, you can see wax-molded figures of all your favorite film stars, from Leslie Nielsen in the *Naked Gun* movies to Bela Lugosi as *Dracula* and Marilyn Monroe in *Gentlemen Prefer Blondes.* "America's Sweetheart," Mary Pickford, dedicated the museum on May 4, 1962; it has risen steadily in popularity ever since, with new stars added yearly, taking their place next to the time-tested favorites. The museum was created by film addict Allen Parkinson, who saw to it that some of the most memorable scenes in motion pictures were re-created in exacting detail in wax. In the seemingly unrelated Chamber of Horrors, you almost expect the torture victims to scream "tourist trap!"

Richard Nixon Library and Birthplace

18001 Yorba Linda Blvd., Yorba Linda. ☎ **714/993-5075.** Fax 714/528-0544. Admission $5.95 adults, $3.95 seniors, $2 children 8–11; children under 8 free. Mon–Sat 10am–5pm, Sun 11am–5pm.

There's always been a warm place in the hearts of Orange County locals for Richard Nixon, the most vilified U.S. president in modern history. This presidential library, located in Nixon's boyhood town, celebrates the roots, life, and legacy of America's 37th president. The nine-acre site contains the actual modest farmhouse where Nixon was born, manicured flower gardens, a modern museum containing presidential archives, and the final resting place of the 37th president and his wife.

Displays include videos of the famous Nixon-Kennedy TV debates, an impressive life-size statuary summit of world leaders, gifts of state (including a gun from Elvis Presley), and exhibits on China and Russia. There's also an exhibit of the late Pat Nixon's sparkling First Lady gowns. There's a 12-foot-high grafitti-covered chunk of the Berlin Wall, symbolizing the defeat of Communism, but hardly a mention of Nixon's leading role in the anti-Communist McCarthy "witch hunts" of the fifties. There are exhibits on Vietnam, yet no mention of Nixon's illegal expansion of that war into neighboring Cambodia. Only the Watergate Gallery is relatively forthright, where visitors can listen to actual White House tapes and view a montage of the President's last day in the White House. Rotating exhibits include never-before-displayed photographs and Nixonalia that illuminate this controversial President's private and public life.

The excellent gift shop sells an array of presidential and White House souvenir items, from historic campaign buttons to presidential dessert plates. In addition to lots of other collectibles, you can also pick yourself up a birdhouse shaped like Nixon's boyhood home or a T-shirt bearing the famous Oval Office photo of Nixon and Elvis.

WHERE TO STAY
VERY EXPENSIVE

✪ Disneyland Hotel

1150 W. Cerritos Ave. (west of the Disneyland parking lot), Anaheim, CA 92802. ☎ **714/778-6600.** Fax 714/965-6597. 1,131 rms, 62 suites. A/C MINIBAR TV TEL. $150–$240 double; suites from $425. AE, MC, V. Parking $10.

The "Official Hotel of the Magic Kingdom," attached to Disneyland via a monorail system that runs right through the hotel, is the perfect place to stay if you're doing the park. You'll be able to return to your room anytime you need to during the day, whether it's to take a much-needed nap or to change your soaked shorts after your Splash Mountain Adventure.

The theme hotel is a wild attraction unto itself. The rooms aren't fancy, but they're comfortably and attractively furnished like a good-quality business hotel. Many rooms feature framed reproductions of rare Disney conceptual art. The beautifully landscaped hotel is an all-inclusive resort, offering 6 restaurants, 5 cocktail lounges, 20 shops and boutiques, every kind of service desk imaginable, a "wharfside" bazaar, a walk-under waterfall, 3 pools, and 10 night-lit tennis courts. There's even an artificial white-sand beach.

When you're planning your trip, inquire with the hotel about the packages they offer, including multiday packages that allow you to take on the park at your own pace.

Dining/Entertainment: The best restaurant is Stromboli's, an Italian/American eatery that serves all the pasta staples. Kids love Goofy's Kitchen, where the family can enjoy breakfast and dinner with the Disney characters.

Services: Concierge, room service, overnight shoe shine, laundry services, nightly turndown, large selection of in-room movies.

Facilities: Three large outdoor heated pools, ten lighted tennis courts, complete health club, putting green, shuffleboard and croquet courts, sundeck, special children's programs, beauty salon, and gift shop.

Sheraton-Anaheim Hotel

1015 W. Ball Rd., Anaheim, CA 92802. ☎ **714/778-1700** or 800/325-3535. Fax 714/535-3889. 500 rms, 31 suites. A/C MINIBAR TV TEL. $110–$155 double; suites from $245. AE, CB, DC, MC, V. Free parking.

This hotel rises to the festive theme-park occasion, with an unusual architectural design—it looks like an English Tudor castle—and unique public facilities that include a 24-hour restaurant. Rooms are modern but not distinctive. All have separate dressing areas; some have refrigerators. The hotel is perfectly acceptable, but guests are really paying for a great location, just blocks from Disneyland.

Dining/Entertainment: There's a 24-hour California-style delicatessen and a lobby lounge.

Services: Concierge, room service, overnight shoe shine, laundry services, nightly turndown, large selection of in-room movies, free shuttle service to and from Disneyland and the airport.

Facilities: Outdoor heated pool, health club, sundeck, gift shop.

MODERATE

Anaheim Desert Palm Inn & Suites

631 W Katella Ave., Anaheim, CA 92802. ☎ **714/535-1133** or 800/635-5423. Fax 714/491-7409. 103 rooms and suites. A/C TV TEL. $69–$139 double, extra person $4 and children under 18 stay free. AE, DISC, DC, MC, V. Free parking.

This is a perfectly nice hotel whose main advantage is its location, close to all the Anaheim attractions. Some units have terraces and/or Jacuzzis. Facilities include a pool, fitness center, game room, sauna, and whirlpool. Free transportation is provided to Disneyland and LAX.

Best Western Stardust Inn

1057 W Ball Rd., Anaheim, CA 92802. ☎ **714/774-7600** or 800/222-3639. Fax 714/535-6953. 103 rooms. A/C TV TEL. $54–$100 double, extra person $6 and children under 17 stay free. AE, DISC, DC, MC, V. Free parking.

Ideally located on the back side of Disneyland, this older hotel offers large, clean, perfectly adequate rooms. Some units have terraces and minibars. There's a pool, sauna, whirlpool, restaurant, and bar on the premises.

Candy Cane Inn

1747 S Harbor Blvd., Anaheim, CA 92802. ☎ **714/774-5284** or 800/345-7057. Fax 714/772-5462. 172 rooms. A/C TV TEL. $70–$84 double. Children under 17 stay free. All rates include breakfast. AE, DISC, DC, MC, V. Free parking.

Really a motel, the Candy Cane Inn is located within walking distance of the Magic Kingdom and close to a dozen more attractions. The rooms are decorated in bright floral motifs with comfortable furnishings, including queen-size beds and a separate dressing and vanity area. Complimentary breakfast is served in the courtyard. Shuttle service is provided to Disneyland.

Hampton Inn

300 E Katella Way, Anaheim, CA 92802. ☎ **714/772-8713** or 800/426-7866. Fax 714/778-1235. 136 rms. A/C TV TEL. $65–$69 double. Rates include continental breakfast. AE, DISC, DC, MC, V. Free parking.

This five-story inn is located about a mile from Disneyland. The average-size rooms are very clean and fresh-looking. No-smoking rooms are available. Coffee and tea are available 24 hours a day, and a continental breakfast is served in the lobby. Additional services include free transportation to Disneyland and the airport, and baby-sitting services.

☉ Howard Johnson Motor Lodge

1380 S. Harbor Blvd., Anaheim, CA 92802. ☎ **714/776-6120** or 800/654-2000. Fax 714/533-3578. 319 rms. A/C TV TEL. $60–$85 double. AE, CB, DC, DISC, MC, V. Free parking.

This elegant building, set on six parklike acres, was designed in an award-winning postmodern style. Something of a resort unto itself, the hotel occupies an enviable location, directly opposite Disneyland. Roofed balconies open onto a central garden with two heated pools for adults and one for children. Garden paths lead under eucalyptus and olive trees to a splashing circular fountain. During the summer, you can see the nightly fireworks display at Disneyland from the upper balconies. Some of the modestly decorated rooms offer Disney views. Services and facilities include a game room, a car rental desk, room service, self-service laundry facilities, and baby-sitting for $8 per hour (four-hour minimum). There's a Howard Johnson's restaurant on the premises, open 24 hours.

Peacock Suites

1745 S Haster St., Anaheim, CA 92802. ☎ **714/535-8255** or 800/522-6401. Fax 714/535-8914. 140 suites. A/C TV TEL. $99–$179 suite. Children under 16 stay free. AE, DISC, DC, MC, V. Free parking.

These attractive new suites offer shuttles to nearby Disneyland, baby-sitting services, and transportation to and from the airport. Some suites have Jacuzzis. No-smoking rooms are available. To occupy the few minutes of your stay that you're not at the theme parks, there's a game room, pool, whirlpool, and fitness center on the premises.

Travelodge Maingate

1717 S Harbor Blvd., Anaheim, CA 92802. ☎ **800/826-1616.** Fax 714/635-1502. 254 rooms and suites. A/C TV TEL. $65–$85 double. Children under 18 stay free. AE, DISC, DC, MC, V. Free parking.

This 10-story motel is located within walking distance from Disneyland. Family suites and oversize rooms are available. The front desk will help arrange tours and shopping shuttles. Facilities include a sauna, pool, children's wading pool, whirlpool, and restaurant.

INEXPENSIVE

⑤ Farm de Ville

7800 and 7878 Crescent Ave. (west of Beach Blvd.), Buena Park, CA 90620. ☎ **714/527-2201.** Fax 714/826-3826. 130 rms. A/C TV TEL. $40 double; units for four to six $80. AE, MC, V. Free parking.

Although it's just a motel, the Farm de Ville has a lot to offer. It's located close to Knott's Berry Farm's south entrance and is convenient to all the nearby attractions, including Disneyland (just 10 minutes away). Rooms are spacious and comfortably outfitted with conservatively styled furnishings. There are two pools, two wading pools for kids, two saunas, and a coin-op laundry on the premises.

Motel 6

921 S. Beach Blvd. (about five miles south of I-5), Anaheim, CA 92804. ☎ **714/220-2866.** 55 rms. A/C TV TEL. $35 per room (up to four adults). AE, MC, V. Free parking.

The best feature of this popularly priced chain motel is its location, close to both Disneyland and Knott's Berry Farm. The motel is modest, clean, and thoroughly recommendable. There's a small swimming pool.

WHERE TO DINE

Neither Anaheim nor Buena Park is famous for its restaurants. If you're visiting the area just for the day, you'll probably eat inside the theme parks; there are plenty of restaurants to choose from at both Disneyland and Knott's Berry Farm. At Disneyland, the Creole-themed **Blue Bayou,** where you can sit under the stars inside the Pirates of the Caribbean ride—no matter what time of day it is. At Knott's, try the fried chicken dinners and boysenberry pies at Mrs. Knott's historic **Chicken Dinner Restaurant.** For the most unusual dinner you've ever had with the kids, see **Medieval Times** (see "What to See & Do Beyond the Theme Parks," above).

EXPENSIVE

Chanteclair

18912 MacArthur Blvd. (between Campus and Douglas drs.), Irvine. ☎ **714/ 752-8001.** Reservations required. Main courses $15–$24. AE, CB, DC, MC, V. Mon–Fri 11:30am–2:30pm; nightly 5–10pm. CONTINENTAL.

Chanteclair is expensive and a little difficult to reach, but it's worth seeking out. The excellent restaurant is designed in the style of a provincial French inn. The rambling stucco structure, built around a central garden court, houses several dining and drinking areas, all with their own unique ambiances. The antique-furnished restaurant has five fireplaces. At lunch you might order grilled lamb chops with herb-and-garlic sauce, chicken and mushroom crepes, or Cajun-charred ahi. Dinner is a worthwhile splurge that might begin with a lobster bisque with brandy or Beluga caviar with blinis. For a main dish, I recommend the rack of lamb with thyme sauce and roasted garlic. A considerable wine selection is always available.

MODERATE

Mr. Stox

1105 E. Katella Ave. (east of Harbor Blvd.), Anaheim. ☎ **714/634-2994.** Reservations recommended on weekends. Main courses $12–$23. AE, DC, MC, V. Mon–Fri 11am–2:30pm; daily 5:30–10pm, Sun 5–9pm. AMERICAN.

Hearty steaks and fresh seafood are served in an early California setting here at Mr. Stox. Specialties include roast prime rib and mesquite-broiled fish, veal, and lamb; sandwiches and salads are also available. Homemade desserts, such as chocolate mousse cake, are unexpectedly good. Mr. Stox has an enormous wine cellar, and there's live entertainment every night.

Peppers Restaurant

12361 Chapman Ave. (east of Harbor Blvd.), Garden Grove. ☎ **714/740-1333.** Reservations recommended on weekends. Main courses $9–$14. AE, CB, DC, DISC, MC, V. Mon–Fri 11am–3pm; daily 5:30–10pm; Sun 10am–3pm. CALIFORNIA/MEXICAN.

This colorful California/Mexican–themed restaurant just south of Disneyland features mesquite-broiled dishes and fresh seafood daily. Mexican specialties include lots of variations of tacos and burritos, but the grilled meats and fish are best. Dancing is available nightly to Top 40 hits, starting at 8pm. There's a free shuttle to and from the area hotels.

Index

Now Save Money on All Your Travels by Joining

Frommer's

TRAVEL BOOK CLUB

The Advantages of Membership:

1. Your choice of any **TWO FREE BOOKS.**

2. Your own subscription to the **TRIPS & TRAVEL** quarterly newsletter, where you'll discover the best buys in travel, the hottest vacation spots, the latest travel trends, world-class events and festivals, and much more.

3. A **30% DISCOUNT** on any additional books you order through the club.

4. **DOMESTIC TRIP-ROUTING KITS** (available for a small additional fee). We'll send you a detailed map highlighting the most direct or scenic route to your destination, anywhere in North America.

Here's all you have to do to join:

Send in your annual membership fee of $25.00 ($35.00 Canada/Foreign) with your name, address, and selections on the form below. Or call 815/734-1104 to use your credit card.

Send all orders to:

FROMMER'S TRAVEL BOOK CLUB

P.O. Box 473 • Mt. Morris, IL 61054-0473 • ☎ 815/734-1104

YES! I want to take advantage of this opportunity to join Frommer's Travel Book Club.

[ ] My check for $25.00 ($35.00 for Canadian or foreign orders) is enclosed.
      All orders must be prepaid in U.S. funds only. Please make checks payable to Frommer's Travel Book Club.

[ ] Please charge my credit card: [ ] Visa or [ ] Mastercard

   Credit card number: _____

   Expiration date: ___ / ___ / ___

   Signature: _____

   Or call 815/734-1104 to use your credit card by phone.

Name: _____

Address: _____

City: _____ State: _____ Zip code: _____

Phone number (in case we have a question regarding your order): _____

Please indicate your choices for TWO FREE books (*see following pages*):

   Book 1 - Code: _____ Title: _____

   Book 2 - Code: _____ Title: _____

For information on ordering additional titles, see your first issue of the *Trips & Travel* newsletter.

Allow 4–6 weeks for delivery for all items. Prices of books, membership fee, and publication dates are subject to change without notice. All orders are subject to acceptance and availability.   AC1

The following Frommer's guides are available from your favorite bookstore, or you can use the order form on the preceding page to request them as part of your membership in Frommer's Travel Book Club.

FROMMER'S COMPLETE TRAVEL GUIDES

(Comprehensive guides to sightseeing, dining and accommodations, with selections in all price ranges—from deluxe to budget)

FROMMER'S $-A-DAY GUIDES

(Dream Vacations at Down-to-Earth Prices)

FROMMER'S SPECIAL-INTEREST TITLES

Arthur Frommer's Branson!	P107	Frommer's Where to	
Arthur Frommer's New World		Stay U.S.A., 11th Ed.	P102
of Travel (avail. 11/95)	P112	National Park Guide, 29th Ed.	P106
Frommer's Caribbean		USA Today Golf	
Hideaways (avail. 9/95)	P110	Tournament Guide	P113
Frommer's America's 100		USA Today Minor League	
Best-Loved State Parks	P109	Baseball Book	P111

FROMMER'S BEST BEACH VACATIONS

(The top places to sun, stroll, shop, stay, play, party, and swim—with each beach rated for beauty, swimming, sand, and amenities)

California (avail. 10/95)	G100	Hawaii (avail. 10/95)	G102
Florida (avail. 10/95)	G101		

FROMMER'S BED & BREAKFAST GUIDES

(Selective guides with four-color photos and full descriptions of the best inns in each region)

California	B100	Hawaii	B105
Caribbean	B101	Pacific Northwest	B106
East Coast	B102	Rockies	B107
Eastern United States	B103	Southwest	B108
Great American Cities	B104		

FROMMER'S IRREVERENT GUIDES

(Wickedly honest guides for sophisticated travelers and those who want to be)

Chicago (avail. 11/95)	I100	New Orleans (avail. 11/95)	I103
London (avail. 11/95)	I101	San Francisco (avail. 11/95)	I104
Manhattan (avail. 11/95)	I102	Virgin Islands (avail. 11/95)	I105

FROMMER'S DRIVING TOURS

(Four-color photos and detailed maps outlining spectacular scenic driving routes)

Australia	Y100	Italy	Y108
Austria	Y101	Mexico	Y109
Britain	Y102	Scandinavia	Y110
Canada	Y103	Scotland	Y111
Florida	Y104	Spain	Y112
France	Y105	Switzerland	Y113
Germany	Y106	U.S.A.	Y114
Ireland	Y107		

FROMMER'S BORN TO SHOP

(The ultimate travel guides for discriminating shoppers—from cut-rate to couture)

Hong Kong (avail. 11/95)	Z100	London (avail. 11/95)	Z101

FROMMER'S COMPLETE CITY GUIDES

(Comprehensive guides to sightseeing, dining, and accommodations in all price ranges)

Amsterdam, 8th Ed.	S176	Miami '95-'96	S149
Athens, 10th Ed.	S174	Minneapolis/St. Paul, 4th Ed.	S159
Atlanta & the Summer Olympic		Montréal/Québec City '95	S166
Games '96 (avail. 11/95)	S181	Nashville/Memphis, 1st Ed.	S141
Atlantic City/Cape May,		New Orleans '96 (avail. 10/95)	S182
5th Ed.	S130	New York City '96 (avail. 11/95)	S183
Bangkok, 2nd Ed.	S147	Paris '96 (avail. 9/95)	S180
Barcelona '93-'94	S115	Philadelphia, 8th Ed.	S167
Berlin, 3rd Ed.	S162	Prague, 1st Ed.	S143
Boston '95	S160	Rome, 10th Ed.	S168
Budapest, 1st Ed.	S139	St. Louis/Kansas City, 2nd Ed.	S127
Chicago '95	S169	San Antonio/Austin, 1st Ed.	S177
Denver/Boulder/		San Diego '95	S158
Colorado Springs, 3rd Ed.	S154	San Francisco '96 (avail. 10/95)	S184
Disney World/Orlando '96		Santa Fe/Taos/	
(avail. 9/95)	S178	Albuquerque '95	S172
Dublin, 2nd Ed.	S157	Seattle/Portland '94-'95	S137
Hong Kong '94-'95	S140	Sydney, 4th Ed.	S171
Las Vegas '95	S163	Tampa/St. Petersburg, 3rd Ed.	S146
London '96 (avail. 9/95)	S179	Tokyo '94-'95	S144
Los Angeles '95	S164	Toronto, 3rd Ed.	S173
Madrid/Costa del Sol, 2nd Ed.	S165	Vancouver/Victoria '94-'95	S142
Mexico City, 1st Ed.	S175	Washington, D.C. '95	S153

FROMMER'S FAMILY GUIDES

(Guides to family-friendly hotels, restaurants, activities, and attractions)

California with Kids	F105	San Francisco with Kids	F104
Los Angeles with Kids	F103	Washington, D.C. with Kids	F10
New York City with Kids	F101		

FROMMER'S WALKING TOURS

(Memorable strolls through colorful and historic neighborhoods, accompanied by detailed directions and maps)

Berlin	W100	San Francisco, 2nd Ed.	
Chicago	W107	Spain's Favorite Cities	
England's Favorite Cities	W108	(avail. 9/95)	
London, 2nd Ed.	W111	Tokyo	
Montréal/Québec City	W106	Venice	
New York, 2nd Ed.	W113	Washington, D.C., 2nd Ed.	
Paris, 2nd Ed.	W112		

FROMMER'S AMERICA ON WHEELS

(Guides for travelers who are exploring the U.S.A. by car, feat brand-new rating system for accommodations and full-color ro

Arizona/New Mexico	A100	Florida	
California/Nevada	A101	Mid-Atlantic	